WORDS OF WISDOM

Words *of* Wisdom

A PHILOSOPHICAL DICTIONARY
FOR THE PERENNIAL TRADITION

John W. Carlson

UNIVERSITY OF NOTRE DAME PRESS
NOTRE DAME, INDIANA

Notre Dame, Indiana 46556
www.undpress.nd.edu

Manufactured in the United States of America

Library of Congress Cataloging-in-Publication Data

Carlson, John W.
Words of wisdom : a philosophical dictionary for the perennial tradition / John W. Carlson.
p. cm.
Includes bibliographical references and index.
ISBN-13: 978-0-268-02370-6 (pbk. : alk. paper)
ISBN-10: 0-268-02370-0 (pbk. : alk. paper)
E-ISBN: 978-0-268-07693-1
1. Philosophy—Dictionaries. 2. Catholic Church and philosophy—Dictionaries. I. Title.
B41.C37 2012
103—dc23

2011041939

∞*The paper in this book meets the guidelines for permanence and durability of the Committee on Production Guidelines for Book Longevity of the Council on Library Resources.*

To Chris Carlson

and

To the memory of Mo Carlson

Happy is the husband of a good wife;
the number of his days will be doubled.

(Ecclesiasticus/Sirach 26:1)

I believe that those philosophers who wish to respond today to the demands which the word of God makes on human thinking should develop their thought . . . in organic continuity with the great tradition which, beginning with the ancients, passes through the Fathers of the Church and the masters of Scholasticism and includes the fundamental achievements of modern and contemporary thought.

A particular place in this long development belongs to St. Thomas. . . . In an age when Christian thinkers were rediscovering the treasures of ancient philosophy, and more particularly of Aristotle, Thomas had the great merit of giving pride of place to the harmony which exists between faith and reason.

I appeal also to *philosophers,* and to all *teachers of philosophy,* asking them to have the courage to recover, in the flow of an enduringly valid philosophical tradition, the range of authentic wisdom and truth.

—John Paul II, *Fides et ratio*

CONTENTS

ACKNOWLEDGMENTS

The idea for this philosophical dictionary grew out of efforts, over a period of years, to give my students accurate and nuanced accounts of the terminology of the perennial tradition. Thus, many young people contributed to the project—more so than most of them realized—through their prodding and their insistence on clarity.

At an early stage, *Words of Wisdom* was presented at a 2005 conference sponsored by the Center for Ethics and Culture at the University of Notre Dame. I appreciate the support of the Center's Director, W. David Solomon, as well as that of the participants who attended my session and offered their insights and encouragement.

The following scholars graciously read, in whole or in large part, versions of this dictionary, and they made many valuable suggestions: John Trapani, V. Bradley Lewis, John C. Cahalan, and David R. Foster. Two readers for the University of Notre Dame Press reviewed the penultimate manuscript; their comments also led to significant improvements.

Deficiencies that remain in *Words of Wisdom* are, of course, the author's responsibility.

Special mention should be made of the editorial, production, and marketing staff at the University of Notre Dame Press. In particular, I wish to thank Senior Acquiring Editor Charles Van Hof, who quickly recognized the potential significance of my project and guided it through the approval process; and Assistant Editor Elizabeth Sain, whose careful attention to textual details helped produce what we all hope will be a useful volume.

This work is dedicated to two extraordinary women who have shared key portions of my adult life: Mo Donovan Carlson and Chris Heaston Carlson. The former shared the early years, was the mother of my dear children, and—even in the midst of devastating illness—was an unfailing source of inspiration and good cheer. The latter shares my mature years, during which time the present project has been conceived and (due in no small part to her patience and support) carried out. She too, for all who know her, inspires and brings good cheer. To a man thus twice blessed, the words of Ecclesiasticus/Sirach take on special meaning: my days, and my happiness, indeed have been doubled.

Omaha, Nebraska
May 2011

WORDS OF WISDOM

INTRODUCTION

The Nature of This Dictionary

The present volume offers students and other interested readers a dictionary of philosophical terms. Its distinctiveness lies, in part, in its being shaped by the understanding of rational reflection—and of wisdom—expressed in John Paul II's *Fides et ratio.*[1] This dictionary focuses on terms central to what the encyclical called the "enduringly valid philosophical tradition" (*Fides et ratio,* #106). Although he was careful to note that the Catholic Church does not tie itself to any particular "school" of philosophy, it is clear—both from his own philosophical writings and from remarks in the encyclical itself—that John Paul II (as well as his predecessors throughout the late 19th and 20th centuries) accorded a special place to the thought of St. Thomas Aquinas.[2]

Aquinas's thought itself of course stood within a broader tradition—one that John Paul II sometimes called simply the "great tradition" (see, e.g., *Fides et ratio,* #85). The latter might be characterized more fully, following an expression of Cardinal Avery Dulles, S.J., as the tradition of "integral Christian wisdom." This approach to wisdom, wrote Cardinal Dulles, "draws on the full resources of reason and revelation alike."[3]

Where John Paul II spoke of a philosophical tradition that is "enduringly valid," many Thomists (i.e., thinkers who adopt the central concepts and principles of St. Thomas) have spoken of one that is "perennial." Jacques Maritain, for example, described the latter as a tradition which, although rooted in ancient and medieval sources, nonetheless "is eternally young and always inventive, and involves a fundamental need, inherent in its very being, to grow and renew itself" in every age.[4]

There are many signs that a renewal of this perennial tradition now in fact is under way.[5] If the full fruits of this movement are to be reaped—especially as these fruits were contemplated by John Paul II—two points need to be borne in mind. First, throughout most of its history, this tradition has drawn from and contributed to a wider body of Christian reflection. And so it often does today. In discussing what he calls a contemporary "Thomistic renaissance," Aidan Nichols, O.P., notes that a "distinguishing feature of the new movement" is its "desire to integrate the philosophy more thoroughly within an essentially theological vision."[6] Second, in addition to being true to its sources, a revitalization of this enduringly valid philosophy requires engagement with various elements of contemporary intellectual culture. This includes awareness of movements of thought that are fundamentally incompatible with the perennial tradition; it also includes efforts to incorporate into the tradition recent philosophical themes and approaches of genuine value. (As is well known, John Paul II, under his given name Karol Wojtyla, himself was especially interested in incorporating insights of the 20th-century movements called phenomenology and personalism.)

Putting these various lines of reflection together, John Paul II remarked in a key passage in *Fides et ratio* that "philosophers who wish to respond today to the demands which the word of God [i.e., Christian revelation] makes on human thinking should develop their thought . . . in organic continuity with the great tradition which, beginning with the ancients, passes through the Fathers of the Church and the masters of Scholasticism and includes the fundamental achievements of modern and contemporary thought" (#85). He also noted that, within this "great tradition," the work of Aquinas occupies a special place (although not a point of final completion): "In an age when Christian thinkers were rediscovering the treasures of ancient philosophy, and more particularly of Aristotle, Thomas had the great merit of giving pride of place to the harmony which exists between faith and reason"—and to ways in which reason, when properly attuned to reality, can make substantive contributions to this harmony. Thus "the Church has been justified in consistently proposing St. Thomas" as a "master" of Christian wisdom and a "model" for other thinkers to follow (#43).

In accordance with the above, this dictionary seeks—through the exposition, discussion, and noting of relations among terms—to contribute to the ongoing renewal of the perennial philosophy,[7] as well as the broader tradition of integral Christian wisdom in which it has flourished; as a structured wordbook, it seeks especially to help make an understanding of the terminology of this tradition available to students.

In order to specify this project further, let us situate it within the overall genre of the specialized dictionary.

Among materials developed to facilitate student learning, as well as scholarly activity, specialized dictionaries have come to occupy an important place. This perhaps is most obvious in relation to disciplines of the natural sciences, along with associated areas of technology and biomedical practice. In these areas, positive knowledge and the language used to express it make regular and commonly agreed upon advances—advances that need to be accessible in an organized fashion to students, practitioners, and others. For somewhat similar reasons, one also finds dictionaries of technical terms related to law and other areas of professional practice.

What should be said in this regard about specialized wordbooks related to philosophy? Here well-crafted dictionaries also can play an important role—although in somewhat different ways and for somewhat different reasons.

As its etymology suggests, philosophy (the "love of wisdom") is best understood as a disciplined search for, and attempt to articulate, answers to most basic questions—in particular, questions about how things ultimately are (the subject matter of "speculative" philosophy), as well as questions about the good to be done or about how human persons, both as individuals and as societies, should act (the subject matters of "practical" and especially moral philosophy). Philosophy does not—except in an incidental way (i.e., via the history of its theories and systems)—result in a body of positive, factual knowledge. Moreover, given the intrinsic difficulty of philosophical topics, along with a variety of cultural factors, this enterprise, while disciplined, only rarely produces commonly agreed-upon advances. (This is not to say that philosophy cannot result in profound truths; for proponents of the perennial tradition, it certainly can. But such truths are seen to be of a different "order" than ones developed in the empirical or positive sciences.)

In light of all this, a dictionary of philosophy will have other purposes, and will gain its importance in other ways, than a dictionary of science or technology or of professional practice. At one level, of course, a philosophical dictionary (like other specialized wordbooks) presents and defines terms; but its deeper purpose is to serve as a resource for those who wish to master—and perhaps to participate in—a comprehensive tradition (or traditions) of thought.[8]

In their efforts to address ultimate questions, philosophers often have used everyday words in extended or novel ways. In addition, new forms of language are regularly developed to express a philosopher's or a tradition's insights. The result is a profuse outgrowth of conflicting terminologies (or of conflicting interpretations of terms used in common). This in turn makes it difficult for the student—and even, at times, for the academic specialist—to follow philosophical discussions with confidence.

In part to address the need for clarity and understanding, a number of philosophical dictionaries have appeared in English in recent years. Those in print at the time of this writing include the following: *Adler's Philosophical Dictionary,* by Mortimer J. Adler, ed. Betsy Radin (New York: Touchstone, 1996); *Blackwell Dictionary of Western Philosophy,* by Nicholas Bunnin and Jiyuan Yu (New York: Blackwell, 2004); *The Cambridge Dictionary of Philosophy,* rev. ed., general ed. Robert Audi (New York: Cambridge University Press, 1999); *A Dictionary of Common Philosophical Terms,* by Gregory Pence (New York: McGraw-Hill, 2000); *A Dictionary of Continental Philosophy,* ed. John Protevi (New Haven and London: Yale University Press, 2006); *A Dictionary of Philosophy,* ed. Antony Flew and Stephen Priest (London: Pan Books Limited, 2002); *The Dictionary of Philosophy,* ed. Dagobert D. Runes (New York: Citadel Press Reprint, 2001); *Dictionary of Philosophy and Religion: Eastern and Western Thought,* expanded ed., by William L. Reese (New York: Humanity Books, 1998); *The HarperCollins Dictionary of Philosophy,* 2nd ed., by Peter A. Angeles (New York: HarperCollins, 1992); *The Oxford Companion to Philosophy,* new ed., ed. Ted Honderich (New York: Oxford University Press, 2005); *The Oxford Dictionary of Philosophy,* rev. ed., by Simon Blackburn (Oxford: Oxford University Press, 2007); *The Penguin Dictionary of Philosophy,* 2nd ed., by Thomas Mautner (London: Penguin Books, 2005); *Philosophical Dictionary,* enlarged ed., by Mario Bunge (Amherst, N.Y.: Prometheus Books, 2003); *The Philosopher's Dictionary,* 3rd ed., by Robert M. Martin (Peterborough, Ontario: Broadview Press, 2003); *The Routledge Dictionary of Philosophy,* 4th ed. (formerly *A Dictionary of Philosophy*), by Michael Proudfoot and A. R. Lacey (New York: Taylor and Francis, 2010); and *A World of Ideas: A Dictionary of Important Theories, Concepts, Beliefs, and Thinkers,* by Chris Rohmann (New York: Ballantine Books, 2000).

More focused dictionaries have also been produced that are devoted to the specialized terminologies of individual historical figures, as well as glossaries appended to introductory textbooks in philosophical subject areas and to volumes of selected writings.[9]

The dictionaries of philosophy listed above manifest great diversity in both style and content. Some of them (e.g., *The Cambridge Dictionary of Philosophy* and *The Oxford Companion to Philosophy*) might more accurately be characterized as one-volume encyclopedias.[10] These works incorporate articles (some of them quite lengthy) by scholars representing various schools and areas of interest. The articles themselves are generally self-contained and only minimally connected with one another. Moreover, while these volumes certainly undertake some explanation of philosophical terms, their focus is rather on the topics, approaches, and thinkers being surveyed.

Other recent philosophical dictionaries focus more directly on terms and their meanings. However, in general they make little effort to give a systematically ordered presentation—let alone one that coheres with integral Christian wisdom. Indeed, a search of these volumes' entries for terms of special importance to the perennial tradition (e.g., **act**, **being**, **conscience**, **end**, **existence**, **good**, **intellect**, **moral precept**, **natural**, **perfection**, **subsistence**, **transcendental**, **voluntary**, and **wisdom**) reveals that, although they contain useful information, they are only marginally helpful for the reader whose aim is to master the type of philosophy for which Aquinas serves as a source and model.[11]

Moreover, while glossaries of terms are welcome additions to recent philosophical texts, they are neither sufficiently broad nor sufficiently detailed for present purposes; even the most accurate of them do not facilitate a grasp of the present tradition in its comprehensiveness and depth, or in the complexity of relations among its key concepts.

Another genre of scholarly dictionary merits attention: that of the linguist or literary scholar. Such a work contains very detailed accounts of all words (sometimes including an exhaustive list of their actual occurrences) that appear in the original writings of a historical figure or movement. An excellent example of such a literary dictionary—and one relevant to our own subject matter—is the magisterial *A Lexicon of Saint Thomas Aquinas*, prepared by Roy J. Deferrari et al., originally published by The Catholic University of America Press in 1948–49, and recently reprinted by Loretto Publications.[12] For all its value, however, a dictionary such as this is not designed to elucidate matters of philosophical significance and complexity, such as is needed for a renewal of the perennial tradition. It also will prove forbidding to typical students, especially undergraduates and others who are new to philosophical studies.

In situating the present volume within the above context, the following points may be highlighted. First, this dictionary is less universal in scope than the philosophical encyclopedias and even some (although not all) of the other genuine dictionaries.[13] At the same time, however, it is more systematically organized than current instances of either type of volume. For example, while many of the other dictionaries offer accounts of key philosophical terms, none of them note the terms' respective parts of speech—or the significant differences in meaning that can attend a single word when it is used as different parts of speech. As indicated below, the present dictionary takes care to do these things. Moreover, regarding the tradition on which it focuses, this wordbook in fact is significantly more comprehensive than any other philosophical dictionary in print. It also, of course, is both more comprehensive and more systematic than the topical or historical glossaries. And, while it is less exhaustive in its treatment of linguistic items than the work of a literary scholar, this is due to its being grounded in a distinctive set of intellectual concerns and its being aimed at a distinctive set of audiences. These last points call for elaboration.

As a comprehensive dictionary, this volume seeks to present a relatively complete account of the (sometimes multiple) uses of philosophical terms regularly employed within the perennial tradition, with attention to their interrelations as well as their theoretical contexts. Further, the present volume seeks to equip readers to compare and contrast these philosophical ideas with those of other traditions—especially ones with which it competes in our day. It also treats a number of recently developed concepts that show promise of contributing to the perennial philosophy. In all of this, the book proceeds in a systematic manner and from a consistent point of view.

Such features are perhaps especially appropriate in a work that seeks to contribute to a renewal of the tradition shaped by St. Thomas Aquinas. As Yves R. Simon remarked, for Thomists there can be no substitute for "clarity in the statement of questions and principles, firmness in inference, appropriateness in predication, integral preservation of past developments, lucid order, and the unique defense against error that rational forms alone can provide."[14]

As far as the present writer can determine, the last attempt to produce a comprehensive dictionary of terms for this tradition was undertaken over a half-century ago by Bernard Wuellner, S.J., in his *Dictionary of Scholastic Philosophy.*[15] Wuellner's volume, while still useful, has long been out of print. Moreover, given certain dramatic changes in Western intellectual culture, as well as developments within the "great tradition" itself, a new effort along this line seems eminently warranted.

As already noted, one key development within the perennial tradition during recent decades has been a renewed recognition of the historical importance of situating philosophy within the broader stream of integral Christian wisdom.[16] Such a recognition coheres fully with John Paul II's understanding of relations between reason and faith. In *Fides et ratio,* he referred to certain "requirements of the word of God" for philosophers who wish their work to contribute to Christian reflection—for example, that they seek to develop a philosophy of "genuinely metaphysical range" (see ##80–84). He also referred to certain "demands of philosophical reason" regarding the work of theology—for example, that theological concepts be formulated in a critical and universally communicable way (##64–67). Significantly, in an extended discussion of this encyclical, Cardinal Joseph Ratzinger—later to become Pope Benedict XVI—stressed these very points; he also remarked that, given Christianity's universal claims and universal destiny, "it must stand in dialogue with philosophy."[17]

Commenting on John Paul II's vision, Cardinal Dulles suggested that—due to inhospitable features within the contemporary intellectual climate—"philosophers and theologians who wish to implement [this vision] must resolutely struggle against mighty odds;" but he also proposed that "a measure of success is attainable, especially in universities that stand within the Christian and Catholic tradition." He added that "a revitalized Christian philosophy could reinvigorate our nation and our culture."[18]

Regarding the intended audience, or audiences, for this dictionary, first mention goes to students of philosophy (and also of theology) who wish to participate in—or at least grasp more clearly—the historically central philosophical strand of integral Christian wisdom. It seems likely that, as Cardinal Dulles suggested, such students, and their teachers, will be found primarily at institutions that maintain a Catholic identity. Second, the volume may be of interest to other philosophers and students of philosophy—whether favorably or unfavorably disposed toward Thomism, or toward classical philosophy more generally—insofar as it offers (by contrast with other recent philosophical dictionaries) a full and accurate presentation of terms typically used in the perennial tradition. A third audience for the dictionary consists of broadly educated readers with some knowledge of this approach to philosophy (e.g., through basic undergraduate courses, or through adult religious education programs) who wish to appreciate it in greater comprehensiveness and depth. Finally, but importantly, the author hopes that Catholic seminaries and institutes of theological formation—as well as their graduates in the ministerial priesthood—will find the volume a useful resource.

Regarding the last-mentioned audience, the Catholic hierarchy regularly has commended the pursuit of integral Christian wisdom in the training of priests. The fathers of the Second Vatican Council wrote, "Philosophical subjects should be taught in such a way that students are first of all gradually led to a solid and coherent account of human nature, the world and God, guided by the philosophical tradition of lasting value [i.e., at least as the present writer would interpret the text, the perennial tradition]" (*Optatam totius*, #15). In accord with this statement, John Paul II frequently called for the philosophy principally associated with the great tradition—suitably open to newer forms of reflection—to be an important part of priestly formation. Near the end of *Fides et ratio*, he spoke of the "grave responsibility to provide for the appropriate training of those charged with teaching philosophy both in seminaries and ecclesiastical faculties;" he added that "teaching in this field [viz., philosophy] necessarily entails . . . a systematic presentation of the great heritage of the Christian tradition and due discernment in the light of the current needs of the Church and the world" (#105).[19] Also worthy of note is the revised Program of Priestly Formation adopted by the American Catholic Bishops in June of 2005. In addition to retaining philosophy requirements in the college seminary curriculum, the bishops called for the completion of a minimum thirty credits in philosophy as part of a two-year pre-theology program for candidates who enter the seminary after completing undergraduate studies.[20]

Selection and Internal Structure of Entries

The present volume contains 1,173 distinct entries, not counting those that simply refer the reader to other entries. Each entry is a term—that is, a word or phrase, together with its philosophical use(s)—judged to be significant in light of the intellectual concerns articulated above. Terms of the following general types have been selected for inclusion in this dictionary.

First, the great majority of entries are ones that have specific meanings for philosophers who continue the intellectual tradition of St. Thomas Aquinas. Where no other indication is given, the reader may assume that the term in question, together with its definition or definitions, represents standard usage within this tradition. Regarding certain terms, and the issues that incorporate them, there has been development, and even dispute, among proponents of perennial thought. Indeed, development took place through the course of Aquinas's own writings.[21] In formulating entries for this dictionary, the present author occasionally has alluded to points of these sorts. In general, however, the *Summa Theologiae* has been taken as expressing Aquinas's mature philosophical (as well as theological) perspective; and, where interpretive choices have been necessary, the writings of Jacques Maritain and Yves R. Simon[22]—as well as more recent scholars who maintain and develop themes of these 20th-century Thomists—have been relied upon for authentic understandings of Aquinas's terminology. Of course, a number of philosophical terms (e.g., basic terms of logic such as **deduction**, **premise**, and **validity**) are shared by diverse intellectual traditions. Thus there is nothing peculiarly Thomist—or Catholic or Christian—about them.

Second, a number of terms are included that are related to other major figures and movements in Western philosophy, especially ones with which the Christian tradition has had significant interaction. Among these terms are adjectival forms of the names of key historical figures (e.g., **Cartesian**, **Humean**, and **Kantian**), as well as standard designations for certain doctrines associated with them (e.g., **rationalism**, **empiricism**, and **deontology**). As explicitly noted in many entries, the latter doctrines usually present significant contrasts with positions developed within the perennial philosophy.

Third, there are various terms representing what John Paul II called "the fundamental achievements of modern and contemporary thought." He urged that these achievements be incorporated as fully as possible within the ongoing tradition. Examples from this category would be the names of certain recent philosophical movements (e.g., **phenomenology**, **personalism**, and **analytic philosophy**), together with technical concepts developed within these movements but now commonly used by thinkers of the perennial tradition as well (e.g., **self-transcendence**, **being vs. having**, and **necessary and sufficient conditions**).

Fourth, terms are included that represent significant contemporary challenges to a philosophy (and also, therefore, a theology) rooted in the ancient and medieval authors. As it happens, a number of these challenges are mentioned in passing in *Fides et ratio* itself (see especially ## 86–91)—for example, **eclecticism**, **historicism**, **scientism**, **postmodernism**, and **nihilism**. Contemporary students of the perennial philosophy should have access to the meanings of these contrary views, as well as to their intellectual backgrounds.

Fifth, in light of this dictionary's setting within Christian and specifically Catholic intellectual life, there are certain terms that have arisen in theological and doctrinal contexts—for example, **gifts of integrity and grace** (including the technical concept "natural"), **Incarnation** (including the technical concept "hypostatic union"), and **Real Presence** (including the technical concept "transubstantiation").[23] In all such cases, the author's judgment has been that the terms merit inclusion because they represent significant and still pertinent encounters between the perennial philosophy and Christian faith.

Four additional sets of remarks should be made at this point.

1) It frequently happens that a single root word gives rise to more than one term of philosophical significance. In such cases, if the meanings of the terms in question differ importantly from one another, each is given its own entry in the present volume (e.g., **act**, **action**, **active**, and **actual**). Similarly, in cases where a single word is used as more than one part of speech, and the meaning in the second instance is not simply derivative from that in the first, each part of speech is given its own entry—for example, **abstract** (adj.) and **abstract** (v.). On the other hand, in cases where root-related words are such that one of them can be regarded as primary, and the meanings of the others can readily be construed by reference to it, the latter words (and/or parts of speech)—unless explicitly referred to in other dictionary entries—are simply gathered together at the end of the single entry. In such cases, the identification of the "primary" word has been made in part by way of an assessment of the frequency of the words' respective occurrences, and in part by way of an assessment of the structures of and relations among the words' respective meanings.[24] Judgments of these sorts are, of course, fallible—and even, in some cases, arbitrary. The author's

chief concern in dealing with such matters has been to ensure that all relevant words (and parts of speech) are somehow represented, and that their respective meanings are rendered intelligible, without thereby producing any unnecessary multiplication of entries.

2) This dictionary is intended to serve as an adjunct to—not a substitute for—a careful reading of actual texts of Aquinas and others in the "great tradition." Of course, the intelligent apprehension of these very texts sometimes will involve identifying which of the various meanings identified in this volume best fits particular occurrences of key terms.

3) The present volume does not contain entries for words of interest used in non-Western philosophies or in other world religions (e.g., "Atman," "Brahman," "karma," "moksha," "samsara," "Tao"). This is not because of disdain for these other traditions; indeed, the reverse is the case. (As John Paul II himself frequently noted, proponents of the perennial philosophy and of integral Christian wisdom more generally must increasingly come to engage in fruitful contact with these other traditions.) Rather, the absence of terms such as those listed above is due to their treatment in other dictionaries and glossaries—for example, specialized volumes devoted to Eastern philosophies and religions, as well as comprehensive volumes such as Reese's *Dictionary of Philosophy and Religion: Eastern and Western Thought.*[25] Such works serve quite adequately the need for resources to facilitate comparison and contrast with the tradition of integral Christian wisdom.

4) Finally, many words of significance for philosophy do not appear in this—or in any—philosophical dictionary. These are words that form the common heritage of educated persons. In fact, it seems likely that, at least for many readers, a full understanding of the accounts offered in this volume will require occasional consultation with another, more general, wordbook. Thus the adept student of philosophy (like the adept student of most other disciplines) will have access to a good standard dictionary of the English language.

❧ The entries in this volume are constructed according to a common pattern. Each includes some or all of the following elements, arranged in the order indicated.

1) The term is introduced in **bold** type, with its (primary) part(s) of speech indicated in parentheses. In keeping with typical scholarly practice, terms from languages other than English are printed in italics. Standard

abbreviations for parts of speech are used: "adj." for "adjective," "n." for "noun," "v." for "verb," and "adv." for "adverb." (A number of entries here treated as linguistic units are, from the standpoint of grammar, compound terms or phrases rather than individual words and parts of speech.) After this basic information, there sometimes follows an etymological note. Given historical factors related to the Christian tradition, many philosophical terms that have been selected for the dictionary are of Greek or Latin origin. Where Greek origins are noted, the words in question are transliterated and anglicized according to the usual custom; readers interested in the Greek orthography should consult a dictionary of Ancient Greek or a Greek/English lexicon.[26]

2) An account of the term's meaning follows. Where a term has more than one meaning of philosophical significance, these are introduced separately by Arabic numerals: for example, "**absolutely** (adv.): (1) . . . (2) . . ." and "**natural** (adj.): (1) . . . (2) . . . (3) . . . (4). . . ." Within each account, any English word placed in *italics* has an entry of its own, to which the interested reader may refer. This system of internal cross-referencing, it is hoped, will be an especially helpful feature of the present dictionary. Of course, not all possible cross-references are explicitly indicated—if they were, many terms would have definitions expressed almost entirely in italics! Rather, terms selected for cross-referencing were judged to have special importance and/or to be ones whose connections might otherwise be overlooked. In cases where an italicized term has two or more distinct and numerically separated meanings, the one in question is indicated by a subscript numeral in parentheses: for example, "*being* $_{(2)}$" or "*matter* $_{(3)}$."

3) An explanation of meaning may be followed by a phrase or phrases that illustrate the term in actual use. Such phrases are marked by diamond-shaped brackets (i.e., "<. . . .>"). (For example, under **absolute** (adj.) the reader finds "<One's absolute duty in a concrete situation. God's existence as absolute.>")

4) In some cases the entry includes further elaboration and discussion. Where such discussion serves primarily to clarify the meaning of the term by way of historical or other information, it is placed in parentheses: that is, "(. . . .)." Where such discussion involves critical comments from the standpoint of Thomist philosophy, or the tradition of integral Christian wisdom more generally, it is placed in square brackets: that is, "[. . . .]." (Thus under **being of reason** a note about the distinction between concepts of "first" and "second" intention is set off by parentheses; whereas

under **compatibilism** a comment that this view, as well as its opposite—**incompatibilism**—are regarded by followers of St. Thomas as missing a key insight is marked by square brackets.)

5) After the explanation of the meaning(s) and the additional discussion(s), if any, there sometimes occur indications of synonyms (preceded by "Syn:") or antonyms (preceded by "Ant:"), as well as other entries of special relevance (preceded by "Compare," "Contrast," or "See"). All such entries are printed in **bold** and placed in parentheses.

6) Finally, words of philosophical interest that are formed from the same root, but do not receive distinct entries because their meanings are derivative and readily construed in light of the meaning(s) already given, are listed together, along with their parts of speech, as follows: "Also:."

Following the dictionary proper is a comprehensive bibliography. It is divided into three parts: first, writings by St. Thomas Aquinas available in English; second, resources of recent vintage that represent expressions of or commentaries upon the perennial tradition; and third, works of other individuals and movements of thought that either may be contrasted with this tradition or show promise of contributing to its ongoing development. All authors mentioned in individual dictionary entries have appropriate items listed in the bibliography.

Notes

1. John Paul II, *Fides et ratio* (On the Relationship between Faith and Reason), Vatican Translation (Boston: Pauline Books and Media, 1998).

2. For example, in "The Human Person and Natural Law," reprinted in *Person and Community,* trans. Theresa Sandok, O. S. M. (New York: Peter Lang, 1993), 181–82, the future pope, Karol Wojtyla, wrote, "We in the Thomistic school, the school of 'perennial philosophy,' are accustomed [to stress] . . . nature in the metaphysical sense, which is more or less equivalent to the essence of a thing taken as the basis of all the actualization of the thing." And in other essays in that volume (e.g., "Thomistic Personalism"), he was explicitly concerned with articulating Thomist views in ways that benefit from engagement with phenomenological and personalist thought. Moreover, in the preface to *The Acting Person,* ed. Anna-Teresa Tymieniecka, trans. Andrzej Potocki (Dordrecht and Boston: D. Reidel, 1979), John Paul II mentioned the philosophical anthropology of St. Thomas Aquinas as one of the two main sources of his enterprise (the other, of course, being the phenomenological method he had adapted from Edmund Husserl and his followers). Regarding *Fides et ratio* itself, it is significant that John Paul II devoted two full sections

(##43–44) to Aquinas's achievements, and that his emphasis throughout was on the need for a revitalization of a metaphysics of realism and a theory of knowledge according to which the human mind can reach to "the very being of the object which is known" (##82–83). He also called for an "ethics [and thus a moral theology] which looks to the truth of the good"—which in turn "presupposes a philosophical anthropology and a metaphysics of the good" (#98). (In his 1993 encyclical on fundamental moral theology, *Veritatis splendor,* he also drew heavily on Thomist themes.) Finally, John Paul II expressed the Church's understanding of revealed truth as a "splendor emanating from subsistent Being itself" (#79).

3. Avery Dulles, S.J., "Can Philosophy Be Christian?" in *The Two Wings of Catholic Thought: Essays on Fides et ratio,* ed. David Ruel Foster & Joseph W. Koterski, S.J. (Washington, D.C.: The Catholic University of American Press, 2003), 20.

4. Jacques Maritain, *A Preface to Metaphysics* (London: Sheed & Ward, 1945), 2. See also the discussion by Ralph McInerny ("RM") in the article "*Philosophia perennis,*" in *The Cambridge Dictionary of Philosophy,* general ed. Robert Audi (New York: Cambridge University Press, 1995), 580. Note as well Karol Wojtyla's own use of "perennial philosophy" in the essay quoted in note 2, above; and note the heading he gives his discussion of Aquinas's work in *Fides et ratio,* ##43–44: "*Perennis sancti Thomae Aquinatis sententiarum novitas*"—with the Latin *perennis* expressing the enduring character of this tradition and *novitas* expressing its openness to new insights. Unfortunately, during the past century the phrase "perennial philosophy" has come to be equivocal in its use, insofar as it also is applied to a range of esoteric and syncretistic religious movements—the latter use stimulated in part by Aldous Huxley's 1946 book with the very title *The Perennial Philosophy.* For the distinction between and a discussion of the phrase's two diverse senses, see James S. Custinger, "Christianity and the Perennial Philosophy," in *Christianity: The Complete Guide,* ed. John Bowden (New York: Continuum Press, 2007), 912–14.

5. Among such signs are the following:

First, as can be gathered from section II of this dictionary's bibliography (Recent Commentaries and Elaborations on Perennial Themes), a large number of titles recently published in English are devoted to the range of Aquinas's philosophical work and to its revitalization and relevance for theology.

Second, works of key figures from the previous generation of Thomist scholars have been maintained in print or reissued. Examples here include Jacques Maritain (the full corpus of his writings is being published in 20 volumes by The Jacques Maritain Center at the University of Notre Dame), Yves R. Simon, and Josef Pieper. Moreover, the past two decades have seen the translation and publication of works by Polish Thomists, under the general title "Catholic Thought from Lublin." Authors here include M. A. Krapiec, O.P., Stefan Swiezawski, and, of course, Karol Wojtyla. Also worthy of note are the reprints of classical textbooks by 20th-century Jesuit teacher-scholars (e.g., Austin Fagothey and George P. Klubertanz).

A third sign involves new initiatives to make the writings of St. Thomas even more widely accessible in English. Two important examples are Aquinas translation projects being undertaken by The Catholic University of America Press and by Hackett Publishing Co. Another example is the reissue by Dumb Ox Books, in conjunction with St. Augustine's Press, of English translations of Aquinas's commentaries on Aristotle's basic works. These and other print editions of Aquinas's writings now are supplemented by online versions, notably the full text of the *Summa Theologiae* (trans. Fathers of the English Dominican Province) at http://www.newadvent.org/summa/ and an annotated, slightly abridged text of the *Summa Contra Gentiles* (trans. Joseph Rickaby, S.J.), at http://www2.nd.edu/Departments/Maritain/etext/gc.htm. Also noteworthy are other internet translation projects, as well as English-language websites devoted to the perennial tradition. See, for example, the websites of Thomas International Center at http://www.ticenter.net; the Society for Aristotelian Studies at http://www.aristotle-aquinas.org; the Jacques Maritain Center, University of Notre Dame, at http://www2.nd.edu/Departments/Maritain; Joseph M. Magee's website, Thomistic Philosophy, at http://www.aquinasonline.com; Mark Johnson's website at http://thomistica.net; Francisco Romero Carrasquillo's *Ite ad Thomam,* at http://iteadthomam.blogspot.com; the philosophy section of James Arraj's Inner Explorations at http://www.innerexplorations.com; and John C. Cahalan's Resources for Modern Aristotelians, at http://www.foraristotelians.info/.

Finally, the author would note a renewed vitality in professional societies that focus on the perennial philosophy—notably the American Catholic Philosophical Association and the American Maritain Association (both of which maintain websites and publish annual proceedings)—and smaller groups such as the Gilson Society and the Society for Thomistic Natural Philosophy. Additionally, a large number of pertinent articles regularly appear in such journals as *The Thomist, American Catholic Philosophical Quarterly, The Modern Schoolman,* and the English edition of *Nova et Vetera.*

6. Aidan Nichols, O.P., *Discovering Aquinas* (Grand Rapids, Mich.: Eerdmans Publishing Co., 2002), 142.

7. It is not possible to set precise boundaries around the concept "perennial"—or, for that matter, the concept "Thomist." To be a Thomist is to adopt the essential concepts, principles, and philosophical positions that informed Aquinas's work. But sometimes it is a complex matter to distinguish what is essential from what is inessential. Clearly, Aquinas's (along with his contemporaries') acceptance of the ancient theory of the "four elements"—earth, air, fire, and water—is *not* essential to his philosophical or theological themes. Clearly, too, his teaching that terms designating "transcendentals" (being, goodness, intelligibility, etc.) are analogous in their instantiations *is* an essential feature of his framework. But other topics are more difficult to place—for example, the view that physical reality manifests what have been called "essentially subordinated" series of causality. This general view forms part of the background of Aquinas's first and second ways of reasoning to God, and thus is clearly significant; but can one be a Thomist while holding that, in light of contemporary science, there in fact is only one such series, and indeed

that this series is comprised of only two members—the whole, complex network of natural causes and effects, and God as ontologically First Cause? (For a discussion of this topic, see John W. Carlson, *Understanding Our Being: Introduction to Speculative Philosophy in the Perennial Tradition* [Washington, D.C.: The Catholic University of America Press, 2008], 197–98.) Similarly, according to some usages the term "perennial" is more or less equivalent to "Thomist" (recall the first quotation from Karol Wojtyla in note 2, above). But according to others it has a wider extension—although how much wider is not readily agreed upon or easily specified. For purposes of the present dictionary, the following convention will be adopted: concepts, principles, and philosophical positions will be identified as part of the perennial tradition either if they arguably have been central to the work of Aquinas and his close followers or if, although arising within other—especially recent—schools of thought, they arguably express themes that are consistent with this tradition and have shown promise for enriching its contemporary renewal and exposition (whether or not the result is formally termed "Thomist").

8. As we shall see just below, the word "dictionary" is sometimes applied to volumes that in effect are encyclopedias; in the case of the latter works, the aims are somewhat different from those articulated here.

9. Regarding historical figures, see the Blackwell Philosopher Dictionaries Series, which currently includes volumes on the specialized terminologies of Descartes, Rousseau, Hobbes, Hegel, and Wittgenstein. (Significantly, there are no such works devoted to Aquinas or other Scholastics.) For glossaries appended to introductory texts, see, for example, the ones by Louis P. Pojman in *Ethical Theory: Classical and Contemporary Readings,* 4th ed. (Belmont, Calif.: Wadsworth/Thomson, 2002); and by the present author in *Understanding Our Being.* For glossaries in editions of selected writings, see in particular that by Peter Kreeft in *A Summa of the Summa* [i.e., the *Summa Theologiae* of St. Thomas Aquinas] (San Francisco: Ignatius Press, 1990); and those by Richard J. Regan, S.J., in *Thomas Aquinas: On Law, Morality, and Politics,* 2nd ed., and in *Thomas Aquinas: A Summary of Philosophy* (Indianapolis: Hackett, 2002 and 2003, respectively). See as well the glossaries appended to the sixty volumes of the mid-20th-century Blackfriars edition of the entire *Summa Theologiae,* by the Dominicans of the English Province and their associates, general ed. Thomas Gilby, O.P. (London: Blackfriars, 1963 et seq.). (A difficulty sometimes arises in relation to the last-mentioned set: since each volume's explanation of terms was prepared by the individual translator of the text in question, when one reads across the respective glossaries one sometimes discovers that a single term is given rather different accounts.)

10. For more formally encyclopedic works, see *The Shorter Routledge Encyclopedia of Philosophy,* ed. Edward Craig (New York: Routledge/Taylor and Francis, 2005), as well as the older, but still useful, eight volumes of *The Encyclopedia of Philosophy,* editor in chief Paul Edwards (New York: Macmillan, 1967). Also to be noted are the online sources *The Internet Encyclopedia of Philosophy,* at http://www.iep.utm.edu, and *The Stanford Encyclopedia of Philosophy,* at http://plato.stanford.edu.

11. To take just one range of examples—but a crucial one. The present dictionary develops complex accounts of **be** (v.), **become** (v.), **being** (n.), **essence** (n.), **exist** (v.), and **existence** (n.). It also has separate entries on **act** or **actuality** (n.), **reality** (n.), and **subsistence** (n.), as well as on **time** (n.) and **eternity** (n.) as modes of existence (or, more strictly, of duration). Regarding "being" in particular, five different uses are distinguished: 1) as a term that corresponds to "that which is;" 2) as a term that refers to the first of the transcendental perfections; 3) as a term that names the formal subject matter of metaphysics; 4) as a term that indicates the very act through which a thing exists; and, in the context of logic, 5) as a term that expresses the uniting of a predicate with a subject. Now, some of the dictionaries mentioned earlier (e.g., Runes's *The Dictionary of Philosophy,* and Reese's *Dictionary of Philosophy and Religion*), although not marking all of these distinctions, provide helpful discussions of historical approaches to the topic of being, including those of Aristotle and Aquinas and other medieval Scholastics. Other dictionaries, however, are from the present perspective truly disappointing. For example, the *Penguin Dictionary of Philosophy* offers no account of either "be" or "being," and its entry for "existence" simply identifies this concept as "the main subject matter of metaphysics" (186). Again, in *The Oxford Dictionary of Philosophy,* Blackburn opens his discussion of "being" with the following statements: "Everything real and nothing unreal belongs to the domain of Being. But there is little useful that can be said about everything that is real, especially from within the philosopher's study, so it is not apparent that there can be such a subject as Being by itself." And he adds, "A central mistake in the area is to treat Being as a noun that identifies a particularly deep subject matter" (1996 ed., 40). From the standpoint of the perennial philosophy, such remarks themselves reveal a deep misunderstanding. Finally, in the entry for "existence" in his *Philosophical Dictionary,* Bunge distinguishes "conceptual" from "material" existence, then offers the opinion that "an object exists materially (or *really*) iff [short for 'if and only if'] it is changeable" (97, emphasis added)—and thus he rules out by definition the very type of existence (namely, unchanging and eternal) that Aquinas and his tradition have identified as supremely real and the source of all other existence!

12. Roy J. Deferrari, Sr. M. Inviolata Berry, C. D. P., and Ignatius McGuiness, O.P., *A Lexicon of Saint Thomas Aquinas* (Fitzwilliam, N.H. and Boonville, N.Y.: Loretto Publications and Preserving Christian Publications, 2004). See also the abridged version, first published in 1960: Roy J. Deferrari, *A Latin-English Dictionary of St. Thomas Aquinas,* St. Paul Editions reprint (Boston: Daughters of St. Paul, 1986).

13. In particular, the present dictionary treats considerably more terms than those of either Adler or Pence, mentioned above. (This of course is not to deny the value of those volumes. Adler, in particular, gives well-crafted and engaging discussions of 125 key terms in his dictionary.)

14. Yves R. Simon, from the foreword to *The Material Logic of John of St. Thomas,* trans. Simon et al. (Chicago: University of Chicago Press, 1955), xxiii.

15. Bernard Wuellner, S.J., *Dictionary of Scholastic Philosophy* (Milwaukee: Bruce Publishing Co., 1956). One might note as well two books published during the succeeding decades. The first, called *Thomas Aquinas Dictionary,* ed. Morris Stockhammer (New York: Philosophical Library, 1965), consisted entirely of quotations from Aquinas's works—without any comment or elaboration—related to an alphabetized list of words from "Abstinence" to "Zeal." The second, called *Philosophical Dictionary,* was an encyclopedic volume originally published in German by Walter Brugger, S.J., and translated and adapted for American readers by Kenneth Baker, S.J. (Spokane, Wash.: Gonzaga University Press, 1972). Like Wuellner's dictionary, these volumes have been out of print for several decades.

16. See again Aidan Nichols, O.P., *Discovering Aquinas,* especially Chapters 9 and 10.

17. See Cardinal Joseph Ratzinger, "Culture and Truth: Some Reflections on the Encyclical Letter, *Fides et Ratio,*" given as a lecture at St. Patrick's Seminary, Menlo Park, Calif., and published in the seminary quarterly *The Patrician* (Winter, 1999). Compare his treatment of these issues in *Truth and Tolerance,* trans. Henry Taylor (San Francisco: Ignatius Press, 2004), 183–209. Finally, note this admirable passage in Cardinal Ratzinger's *Principles of Catholic Theology,* trans. Sister Mary Frances McCarthy, S. N. D. (San Francisco: Ignatius Press, 1987): "The Christian mission [from the earliest period] sought to persuade men to abandon false religions and turn to the true one. . . . In the struggle for the human soul it regarded, not the existing religions, but rational philosophy as its partner, and, in the constant disputes among the various groups, it aligned itself with philosophy" (327).

18. Avery Dulles, S.J., "Can Philosophy Be Christian?" 20–21.

19. See also similar remarks in John Paul II's *Sapientia Christiana* (1979), *Ex corde ecclesiae* (1990), and *Pastores dabo vobis* (1992).

20. *Program of Priestly Formation,* 5th ed. (Washington, D.C.: United States Conference of Catholic Bishops, 2006). In 2010, Mount St. Mary's Seminary in Maryland hosted a conference on the role of philosophy in seminary education. The keynote speaker, Msgr. Robert Sokolowski (mentioned in certain dictionary entries as well as the bibliography), emphasized the central role of the perennial tradition in the philosophical training of future priests.

21. For an overview of Aquinas's work, including some discussion of internal developments, see Jean-Pierre Torrell, O.P., *St. Thomas Aquinas.* Vol. 1, *The Person and His Work,* rev. ed., trans. Robert Royal (Washington, D.C.: The Catholic University of America Press, 2005).

22. See the many works by these authors listed in the comprehensive bibliography appended to this volume. In *Fides et ratio,* #74, John Paul II mentions Maritain (along with other 20th-century figures such as Etienne Gilson and St. Edith Stein) as a principal example of a thinker rooted in the perennial tradition but at the same time fully engaged with contemporary intellectual culture.

23. As sources for these matters, the author has relied on the *Catechism of the Catholic Church,* 2nd ed. (Vatican: Libreria Editrice Vaticana, 1997); and *Our Sun-*

day Visitor's Encyclopedia of Catholic Doctrine, ed. Russell Shaw (Huntington, Ind.: Our Sunday Visitor, Inc., 1997).

24. In many cases this has resulted in taking a noun form as primary in relation to an adjectival form—for example, "abundance" in relation to "abundant," and "agnosticism" in relation to "agnostic" (but see "alienable" in relation to "alienability"). Similarly, in many cases this has resulted in listing a shorter word form as primary in relation to a longer word form—for example, "act" in relation to "active," and "accidental" in relation to "accidentally" (but see "aversion" in relation to "averse [to]").

25. Regarding specialized treatments of non-Western terms, see a number of volumes in the series "Historical Dictionaries of Religions, Philosophies, and Movements" published by Rowman and Littlefield Publishers, Inc. Among the more general reference works, see the revised second edition of *The Cambridge Dictionary of Philosophy* (1999), which includes a number of articles related to non-Western movements and topics.

26. Standard examples of such volumes are S. C. Woodhouse, *English-Greek Dictionary: A Vocabulary of the Attic Language* (London and New York: Taylor and Francis, 1972); and H. G. Liddell and R. Scott, *A Greek-English Lexicon,* 9th ed., with a revised supplement (Oxford and New York: Oxford University Press, 1996). Although less distinctive, features of Latin orthography also are missing from typical anglicized versions. For details of the Latin, see, for example, Roy J. Deferrari et al., *A Lexicon of Saint Thomas Aquinas,* cited in note 12.

ab*, *esse (Latin phrase): See ***esse-ab.***

abduction (n.): Form of inference identified by Charles S. Peirce (1839–1914) and held by some to constitute a third type of reasoning between *deduction* and *induction.* Such reasoning involves the following type of schema: "*F* is a fact that at present is surprising. If general theory *T* should be true, *F* would be explainable by means of it. Therefore, there is (to this extent) reason to accept *T.*" [Although abduction has been studied primarily in relation to the natural *sciences* $_{(2)}$, Peirce also suggested that *teleological* $_{(2)}$ arguments for God's existence, such as the fifth of Aquinas's *Five Ways,* are best understood as involving this form of inference—rather than, as held by Thomists, being rooted in genuine insight into *final causes* adequate to support a *demonstration.*] (Compare **dialectical** $_{(3)}$, as well as **illative sense.**) Also: "abductive" (adj.), "abductively" (adv.).

abnormal (adj.): (1) In the modern natural sciences, a phenomenon that deviates from a statistical norm. <Abnormal behaviors such as excessive hand-washing, as studied in psychology.> (Ant: **normal** $_{(1)}$.) (2) For some writers in the perennial tradition, a human act that goes against a *natural* $_{(3)}$ tendency or end and thus, to the extent it is freely chosen, is morally bad. <Politically free people voting to become ruled by a dictator as abnormal.> (Ant: **normal** $_{(3)}$.) Also: "abnormalcy" or "abnormality" (n.), "abnormally" (adv.).

abortion (n.): The forced expulsion of a fetus from the mother's uterus, especially in cases where the death of the fetus is the *object*$_{(3)}$ of the act, or the subjective *end*$_{(2)}$ of the act, and is willed as such. (According to traditional usage—which sometimes generates confusion—abortions can be "direct" or "indirect." The former term applies to cases in which the death of the fetus is willed either as a means or as an end; the latter term applies to cases involving, for example, the removal of a life-threatening cancerous uterus, where the death of the fetus is a foreseen consequence but is neither the object of the act nor part of the agent's intention (see ***praeter intentionem***).) As a willed human act, abortion is to be distinguished from the *natural*$_{(1)}$ event of *miscarriage,* even though the latter is sometimes termed "spontaneous abortion."

absolute (adj.): Free from potentiality, limitation, dependency, or qualification; unconditioned. <One's absolute duty in a concrete situation. God's existence as absolute.> Also: "absoluteness" (n.).

absolute (n.): Point of origin of being, knowledge, or action. <Objects of sense as absolutes in the genesis of knowledge about nature. God as the Absolute in the order of existence.>

absolutely (adv.): (1) (Corresponding to Latin *simpliciter,* for "simply.") Taken in itself or in its essential *formal* character. <Animality taken absolutely—i.e., just as an essence or general type of living being, apart from a consideration of particular animal species (canine, feline, etc.)> (2) Holding or applying in an *absolute* manner. <According to traditional moral teaching, certain negative precepts hold absolutely.>

absolutism (n.): In ethics, the view that at least some moral principles (or rules, precepts, etc.) are *absolute*—i.e., that they hold without exception. (Note: On this account, the perennial moral philosophy as well as the Catholic *magisterium* can be regarded as holding a form of absolutism. But the matter is complex, as can be seen from this dictionary's discussion of the parallel issue of *exceptionless moral rules.*) (Compare **universalism**.) Also: "absolutist" (adj. or n.).

abstract (adj.): (1) Of or pertaining to an *essence*$_{(1)}$—i.e., to a nature or type of *substance, quality, relation,* etc.—considered apart from existing subjects that instantiate or share that essence. <The abstract nature of humanness, redness, being greater than, etc.> (2) Characteristic of disciplines that take as their subject matters formal entities of a high *degree* or *order of abstraction.* <Abstract mathematics

or metaphysics.> (Ant: **concrete**.) Also: "abstractly" (adv.), "abstractness" (n.).

abstract (v.): (1) To consider a particular feature or characteristic apart from others to be found in the individual in question. <To abstract the color of a rose from its size, shape, etc.> (Compare **prescind**.) (2) To engage in the "first" act of human *intellect;* that is, to develop an intelligible *species* $_{(2)}$. <To abstract the essence of rose insofar as it is knowable.> (See **apprehension** or **intellection** (**simple**).) Also: "abstractable" (adj.).

abstraction (n.): (1) The act or process by which one abstracts (in either sense). (2) A concept of, or verbal formula expressing, an *essence* $_{(2)}$—or, less strictly, any matter of generality. (3) The condition of intellectual knowledge that involves the *objective* $_{(2)}$ presence of what is known. This condition involves two aspects, the terminology for which has varied among Thomistic commentators. However, the following accounts are typical: a) "Total abstraction" (Latin *abstractio totalis*), or "extensive abstraction," or "abstraction of a whole," is that aspect according to which the object of knowledge does not include features that individuate it in actual *existence* $_{(1)}$ (e.g., humanness apart from its particular features in Mary, Peter, and John); and b) "Formal abstraction" (Latin *abstractio formalis*), or "intensive abstraction," or "typological abstraction," is that aspect according to which the object of knowledge does not include features that are only contingently related to it as an essence (e.g., triangularity apart from its being divisible into equilateral, isosceles, and scalene). (Regarding sense (3), see **degrees** or **orders of abstraction**.)

abundance, sometimes **superabundance** (n.): Condition of fullness, sufficiency, or *plenitude* in the possession of a quality or perfection. (Strictly, the term "superabundance" is used only of God.) (Ant: **poverty** $_{(2)}$.) Also: "abundant" (adj.), "abundantly" (adv.).

accident (n., from Latin *accidit,* for "it happens to"): (1) A reality that exists as an attribute, characteristic, feature, or property of another or others (e.g., the color or shape of a rose), rather than one that exercises existence on its own (e.g., the rose itself). Following remarks by Aristotle—although he himself did not use the term "accident"—Scholastics typically divided such features into nine categories: quantity, quality, relation, place, time, posture, state, action, and passion. (Accidents are sometimes divided into "proper" and "common." The former derive from a particular *nature*$_{(2)}$. <The power of free choice, which flows from rationality, as a proper accident in human persons.> The latter do not derive from a specific nature, but are shared among beings of diverse types. <The color red as a common accident found in roses, apples, tomatoes, etc.>) (Contrast **substance**.) (2) An event or occurrence that is a result of *chance* and, if it involves a human act, one that is not foreseeable by the agent(s).

accidental (adj.): (1) Of or pertaining to an *accident*$_{(1)}$, rather than a *substance*. <Growth in size (quantity), or the production of a blossom (action), as accidental changes in a plant.> (Contrast **substantial**.) (2) Incidental; not related to the *essence*$_{(1)}$ of the thing. <Being of a particular ethnicity or height as accidental to a human person.> (Ant: **essential**.) (3) Merely associated with, rather than formally or causally related to. <An accidental connection between a visit with one's family and the onset of an illness.> (Syn. in senses (2) and (3): **contingent**.) Also: "accidentally" (adv.).

acedia, sometimes ***acidia*** (Latin n., from Greek *akedeia*, for "indifference"): See **sloth**.

acquired (adj.): Received or achieved, or dependent upon circumstance, rather than belonging to an individual by nature. <One's acquired rights, e.g., to vote in federal elections.> (Contrast **innate**.)

act (v.): To exercise real being—either to exist (Latin verb *esse*) or to exercise some other mode of being (Latin verb *agere*)—e.g., to sense, to make, etc. (Note: *Personalist* philosophers use this term especially to refer to freely chosen undertakings of human beings.) (Contrast **undergo** or **suffer**.)

act or **actuality** (n.): Any mode or perfection of real being; sometimes divided into "first" act (*existence*$_{(2)}$) and "second" act (*activity* or other feature that characterizes the being(s) in question). <Sensation as an instance of second act in animals.> (Ant: **potency** or **potentiality**.)

action (n.): (1) One of the nine categories of *accident*$_{(1)}$ identified by Scholastics; a doing or bringing about. (Ant: **passion**$_{(1)}$.) (2) A *change* considered from the standpoint of the initiator of the change. (Ant: **passion**$_{(2)}$.)

active (adj.): Pertaining to *act* or to an *action* or an *activity*. (Contrast **passive**.) Also: "actively" (adv.).

activity (n.): The exercise of a *power*$_{(1)}$ or *faculty*; a "second" *act* or *actuality* of a real being. Sometimes divided into "immanent" and "transient" (see **immanence**$_{(1)}$, and **transience** or **transitivity**).

act of a man (Latin *actio* or *actus hominis*): See the discussion under **human act**.

act of being (sometimes **act of existence**; in either form, sometimes hyphenated): See **being** $_{(4)}$ and **existence** $_{(2)}$.

actual (adj.): Having real *existence* or some other *perfection*. (Ant: **potential**. Contrast as well being merely **possible** $_{(1)}$.) Also: "actually" (adv.).

actualization (n.): The process of coming to be real as regards a thing's *being* $_{(1)}$, *power* $_{(1)}$, or *perfection*. <The actualization of the power of speech in a developing child.>

actualize or **actuate** (v.): To bring about the reality or actual being of something. <To actuate the process of healing in a patient.> Also: "actuation" (n.).

ad, esse (Latin phrase): See the discussion under ***esse-ab***.

adequate (adj.): Sufficient for the reality of the thing in question. Also: "adequately" (adv.).

adequate (v.): To render one thing in a relation of correspondence or proportion to another. <To adequate one's mind to the essence being studied; to adequate one's will to the authentic good.> (Regarding the first example, see **correspondence theory of truth**.) Also: "adequation" (n.).

aesthetic or **aesthetical** (adj., from Greek *aisthesis*, for "experience"): (1) Of or pertaining to *beauty* or *art*, or to the discipline of *aesthetics*. (2) Having a form that is pleasing to well-tutored awareness. Also: "aesthetically" (adv.).

aesthetics (n.): Discipline that studies *beauty*, as well as the principles of *art*. (The noun "aesthetic" [singular] sometimes designates a particular principle or theory of art.)

aeviternity (n.): Mode of being such that, once a creature exists, there is no natural process by which it might perish—and indeed there is no physical change at all, although there may be a succession of purely spiritual acts. <The pure spirits called angels as beings that enjoy aeviternity.> (See the discussion under **duration**.) Also: "aeviternal" (adj.).

affection (n.): (1) Any movement of *affectivity*. (2) More narrowly, an *emotion*, *feeling*, or *passion* $_{(4)}$, especially a positive one. <One's spouse as the primary object of one's affection.>

affective (adj.): Of or pertaining to *affectivity* or to an *affection*, in either sense of the latter term. (Contrast **cognitive**.) Also: "affectively" (adv.).

affective key: As adapted from phenomenological and existentialist sources by certain Thomist writers (e.g., Pierre-Marie Emonet), a term designating a generalized attitude toward the world—for example, *hope* or, by contrast, *despair.* (See **emotion**.)

affective knowledge: Term used by 20th-century Thomist Jacques Maritain to emphasize the role of rightly ordered *affectivity* in correct judgments about *values,* whether abstract or concrete. (At the level of the individual case, genuine affective knowledge can attain a comparable or even higher degree of *certitude* than is available through related processes of practical *reasoning.*) <A business person's affective knowledge that a particular financial proposal is morally suspect.>

affectivity (n.): Set of powers and operations of the *soul* (and of the living being as a whole) involving *desire* and *aversion,* and thus giving rise to movements toward objects that promise benefit and away from objects that threaten harm. <Affectivity, stirred by the words of Jesus, as a key dimension of a life of Christian faith.> (Compare **appetite**. Contrast **cognition** or **cognitivity**.)

affirm (v.): To *judge* that something is the case. (Ant: **deny** or **negate**.)

affirmation (n.): See **judgment** $_{(1)}$. (Ant: **denial** or **negation**.) Also: "affirmative" (adj.), "affirmatively" (adv.).

a fortiori (Latin phrase, for "by way of the stronger case"): Term of logic, applied to a proposition that holds with greater objective force than another that is mentioned—e.g., because it is logically presupposed by the other. <If it is true of a particular being that it thinks, then *a fortiori* it is true that the being is alive.>

agape (Greek n., equivalent to Latin *caritas*): As understood within Christianity, unconditioned and self-sacrificing *love* $_{(3)}$ for the sake of the other—a love that, in us, is a *participation* in God's love, as perfectly modeled by Christ. This type of love is said to exceed purely human love, whether in the form of sensual attraction (Greek *eros*) or in the form of friendship (Greek *philia*); its consistent practice is said to require the theological virtue called "charity." (Note: As a religious ideal, *agape* constitutes the first principle of a specifically Christian ethic [see John 13]; and it challenges the *de facto* normative adequacy of any purely philosophical ethic. This does not mean, however, that philosophy can make no genuine and independent contributions to moral knowledge.) (See **charity** $_{(3)}$ and **love** $_{(3)}$.)

agent (n.): A being that acts or that undertakes an operation; in particular, an *efficient cause.* <An agent of change within society.> Also: "agency" (n.).

agent intellect (Latin *intellectus agens*): The human intellect in its function of illuminating reality, by working on objects of sense (external and/or internal) and thereby eliciting an intelligible *species* $_{(2)}$. Insofar as the activity of illumination is successful, a *form* of reality thereby comes to have concrete, *intentional* $_{(1)}$ existence. (See **apprehension** or **intellection** (**simple**), and ***species impressa.*** Contrast **possible intellect.**)

aggression (n.): In the language of traditional *just war theory,* an unjustified act of violence by one sovereign entity (especially a *nation* or a *state* $_{(2)}$) against another; such an act is said to constitute a "just cause" for the second sovereign entity's going to war. Also: "aggressor" (n.).

aggressive (adj.): (1) Of or having to do with *aggressiveness.* <Aggressive drives, tendencies, etc.> (2) Having something of the character of an act of *aggression.* <An aggressive reaction to a perceived foreign threat.> Also, in both senses: "aggressively" (adv.).

aggressiveness, sometimes **aggressivity** (n.): In the *philosophical psychology* of the Scholastics, a basic mode of *affectivity* involving instinctive responses to perceived prospects of good and harm, especially in the context of challenging circumstances. Aggressiveness is said to give rise to the *irascible* passions (e.g., *courage* $_{(1)}$ and *fear*).

agnosticism (n., from Greek *agnostos,* for "unknown" or "unknowable"): Position holding that we cannot know anything (either positive or negative) about God—even whether a God exists; and sometimes holding more generally that we cannot know anything about possible realms of being that transcend *nature* $_{(1)}$. (Compare **positivism.** Contrast both **atheism** and **theism.**) Also: "agnostic" (adj. or n.).

akrasia (Greek n.): Moral weakness; practical inability to act in accord with what one recognizes to be the concrete good. (For Aristotle, the pervasiveness of this condition counted decisively against the view that moral virtue is equivalent to or is a necessary accompaniment of moral knowledge, as proposed by the Platonic school.)

alien (adj. or n.): Foreign or different, or a being that is or seems to be so. <Alien ideas; being treated

as an alien in one's own society.> (Compare **otherness** and **xeno-**.)

alienable (adj.): Separable; able to be lost, forfeited, or taken away. <Alienable rights—e.g., the right to drive a car or to own a gun.> (Ant: **inalienable.**) Also: "alienability" (n.).

alienate (v.): (1) To separate, especially where a condition of unity is *natural* $_{(3)}$ or appropriate. (2) To make a person feel *alien* or separated.

alienation (n.): (1) As understood by 19th-century social theorist Karl Marx and his followers, the condition of laboring men and women in *capitalist* economic systems: since they are unable to directly enjoy the fruits of their labor, they in effect become—and come to regard themselves as—mere "cogs in the machinery" of the system. (2) For recent *personalist* thinkers, including Karol Wojtyla, a condition in which human beings are unable to recognize and fulfill themselves as persons because of some *disorder* or combination of disorders—economic, political, legal, etc.—in the social system. (Contrast **participation** $_{(2)}$.) (3) In some theological writings, the fundamental human condition of separation from God brought about by *Original Sin.*

Allah (Arabic n.) God, as designated in Islam.

Alpha point: See **Teilhardian**.

altruism (n., from Latin *alter,* for "other"): (1) Attitude disposing a person to seek the good of others. (Ant: **egoism** $_{(1)}$.) (2) Normative theory commending such an attitude, as well as associated behavior. (Ant: **egoism** $_{(2)}$.) Also: "altruist" (adj. or n.), "altruistic" (adj.), "altruistically" (adv.).

amoral (adj.): Not concerned with morality. <An amoral society—one in which, for example, convenience or efficiency alone dictate human choices.> (Contrast **moral** $_{(1)}$, as well as **immoral.**) Also: "amorally" (adv.).

amorality (n.): Condition or attitude of not being concerned with morality. (Contrast **morality** $_{(1)}$, as well as **immorality**.)

amplitude (n.): (1) Broadness of range in being or operation. <The amplitude of the human intellect, insofar as it in principle is proportioned to knowing the natures of all physical beings.> (2) Analogously, broadness of range in the application of a concept or term. <The amplitude of the term "goodness," insofar as it designates a transcendental perfection.>

anabatic (adj., from Greek *anabainein,* for "to rise" or "go up"): Term initially used by certain Greek Fathers of the Church to characterize knowledge about God that can be pursued in a *philosophical* manner—i.e., by "rising" from what in created being can be affirmed as shared by uncreated being, namely the *transcendental* (1) and *pure perfections.* <Anabatic corollaries of Aquinas's "Five Ways"—e.g., that God is One.> (Catholic tradition consistently has sought a synthesis of the anabatic approach, which is undertaken by natural reason, and its opposite—the *katabatic* approach—which requires divine revelation. A 20th-century revival of this theme is to be found in the work of Swiss theologian Hans Urs von Balthasar, who spoke of "ana-logic" and "cata-logic.")

analogate or **analogue** (n.): One member of a set of terms, all of which are unified by, or ordered to one another by, *analogy.* (Thomists sometimes distinguish—either from the standpoint of our knowledge and use of language, or from the standpoint of the realities themselves—"primary" and "secondary" analogates. Thus, in the instances "John is wise" and "God is wise," the primary analogate from the standpoint of our use of language is the former, whereas the primary analogate from the standpoint of reality is the latter.)

analogical or **analogous** (adj.): Of or pertaining to *analogy.* <The concept of goodness as genuinely analogical in character.> (Compare and contrast **metaphorical.** Contrast as well **univocal** and **equivocal.**) Also: "analogically" or "analogously" (adv.).

analogy (n.): Condition of a *term* in use when the "formal objects" (i.e., *object* (2)) in question are partially the same and partially different, or different but systematically related—for example, the term "healthy" when used to describe a human person and that person's exercise program, with the latter instance involving an activity that is conducive to health. (In a derivative way, "analogy" and its cognates are sometimes applied to the beings which, by way of causality and/or by way of their internal structures, provide the basis in reality for the associated relationships among meanings—for example, the goodness of a meal in relation to the nature and function of meals as standing in *proportion* to the goodness of a lecture in relation to the nature and function of lectures.) (Regarding principal types of analogy, see **attribution, analogy of**; and **proportionality, analogy of.** Compare and contrast **metaphor.** Contrast as well **univocity** and **equivocity.**) Also: "analogicity" or "analogousness" (n.).

analysis (n.): (1) For Scholastic philosophy, the process by which the mind traces effects and consequences to proper *causes* and *principles*—e.g., the presence of rain to specific atmospheric conditions. (2) Also for Scholastic philosophy, the process by which the mind goes from a concrete multiplicity of notions to a single *abstract* and *simple* notion, the latter being applicable to each instance of the multiplicity—e.g., from notions of many kinds of beings to the notion of being itself. (Contrast **synthesis** $_{(2)}$.) (3) In the modern natural and, especially, physical sciences, explanation via decomposition of a whole into its constituent material parts. Also: "analyze" (v.).

analytic (adj.): (1) Of or pertaining to some sense of or type of *analysis*—e.g., the tracing of an effect to its cause, or the breaking down of a whole into its constituent parts. (2) According to usage popularized by the German philosopher Immanuel Kant, the character of a statement that can be known to be true by virtue of the meanings of its terms, for example, a statement of the form "S is P" in which the meaning of the *predicate* ("P") is contained in the meaning of the *subject* ("S"). <"Bachelors are unmarried" as analytic.> (Compare **evident** or **self-evident**. Contrast **synthetic**. See also ***per se nota***.) Also: "analytically" (adv.) and, related to sense (2), "analyticity" (n.).

analytic philosophy: An approach or set of approaches to philosophy, prevalent in the English-speaking world during the 20th and now 21st centuries and associated with such figures as Bertrand Russell, Ludwig Wittgenstein, J. L. Austin, W. V. O. Quine, Donald Davidson, and others. Analytic philosophers—sometimes also called "linguistic philosophers"—emphasize the careful analysis of language as a key to philosophical progress. Early proponents, influenced by developments in modern formal logic, tended to be reductive in their approaches; that is, they sought to elucidate the contents of propositions via their most "elementary" components. Later analytic philosophers, especially in Great Britain, tended to focus on the actual use of words—noting, in Wittgenstein's phrase, that the meanings of a term (especially a term of philosophical significance such as "being" or "good") often "form a family" with overlapping "resemblances," rather than the term designating a single, simple type of reality. Currently, analytic philosophy itself comprises a family of approaches. [Note: John Paul II had little direct acquaintance with this movement of thought. In *Fides et ratio*, #84, he remarked (correctly) that "the analysis of language . . .

tend[s] to stop short at the question of how reality is understood and expressed, without going further to see whether reason can discover its essence." Nonetheless, because certain key traits of analytic philosophy were shared by Aristotle and the Scholastics, possibilities of mutual enrichment between the two traditions are significant. See the next entry, **analytic Thomism.**]

analytic Thomism: Somewhat loosely organized school of philosophy that combines the methodology of recent *analytic philosophy* with themes of Aquinas and traditional *Thomism*. Prominent figures among this group of scholars include Elizabeth Anscombe, Peter Geach, John Haldane, and Eleonore Stump.

ananoetic (adj.): According to the terminology of Jacques Maritain, the character of knowledge (Greek *noesis*) that is gained through intellection via *analogy*—for example, the knowledge that goodness and other transcendental and pure perfections inhere in God in an absolute way. (Contrast **perinoetic** and **dianoetic**.) Also: "ananoetically" (adv.).

angel (n.): A purely *spiritual* being, yet one that is *finite* and dependent on God for its existence. Such a being might enjoy a kind of succession of acts, but would not be subject to any processes of literal, physical change—including natural generation or corruption. (In biblical and theological literature, angels are presented as "messengers of God"—a role that obviously falls outside the scope of philosophy to articulate or assess. However, Aquinas believed that natural reason prompts us to suppose that purely spiritual but dependent beings exist, given the order and hierarchy within finite being, and given our human nature as physical yet spiritual.) (See **aeviternity**.)

angelic (adj.): (1) Of or pertaining to angels. <Angelic knowledge (i.e., angels' special mode of knowledge by intellectual *intuition*).> (2) (Metaphor.) Associated with or like the angels in some way. <"The Angelic Doctor [of the Church]"—a title given to St. Thomas Aquinas.>

anger (n.): (1) In traditional philosophical psychology, regarding both animals and human persons, a *passion* (3) or *emotion* arising in the context either of a perceived good that cannot be achieved (or cannot be achieved without what is felt to be inordinate difficulty) or has been taken away; or of a perceived harm that has occurred or is threatening to occur. (2) In human persons, a state in which the above passion rises to a fixed pattern of desire for vindication of perceived goods lost or perceived harms suffered. (Anger in this latter sense is listed among the *capital vices.*)

animal (n., from Latin *anima,* for "soul"): (1) In the philosophy of nature, a living being with powers of *sensation* (and associated powers of self-movement due to attraction or aversion). (2) In modern scientific biology, one of two ultimate categories (or "kingdoms")—the other comprising plant life. The animal kingdom is further divided according to *empiriological* characteristics into, for example, "families," "genera," and "species." Also: "animal" (as an adj. [e.g., in the phrase "animal appetites"]).

animate (adj., from Latin *anima,* for "soul"): Of or pertaining to beings of nature that are living, or that manifest activity of *soul.* (Sometimes the application of this term is restricted to animals and human beings, although technically it can be used of plant life as well.) <The emergence of animate nature as posing both a scientific question and a mystery.> (Ant: **inanimate**.)

animism (n.): Religious belief, or range of religious beliefs, attributing powers of mind and will to all beings. Those who hold such beliefs, called "animists," often regard certain aspects of physical reality as having superhuman powers—and accordingly develop rituals to please or appease them. (Compare **panpsychism**; see as well **vitalism**.) Also: "animistic" (adj.).

annihilate (v., from Latin *nihil,* for "nothing"): (1) Strictly, to remove something from the exercise of *existence* (2). <To annihilate a spiritual soul (an act that would be possible only for the Creator).> (2) More loosely and perhaps metaphorically, to destroy a unity; to break into pieces. <To annihilate a nation's infrastructure.> Also: "annihilation" (n.).

antecedent (adj. or n.): See **conditional**. (Contrast **consequent**.)

anthropic principle: A recently proposed—and controversial—principle of scientific *cosmology* (sometimes operating under the influence of philosophical and/or religious beliefs), according to which the universe is deemed to have had from the beginning properties that made the emergence of intelligent life (or of *man* (1), corresponding to Greek *anthropos*) inevitable, or at least a matter of very high probability.

anthropology (n., from Greek *anthropos,* for "man" (1)): The study, or the family of studies, of humankind or human nature. (1) The *philosophical* discipline of anthropology (also called philosophy of the human person or of human nature) proceeds primarily from the common experience of our lives and pursues *ontological* questions—that is, questions concerning generic and specific features of our being as rational animals (e.g., whether we are capable of genuine free choice). (2) The *positive science* of anthropology proceeds in light of *empiriological* questions and methods, and develops comparisons, contrasts, and generalizations about human populations (e.g., their marital and child-rearing practices). (3) *Theological* anthropology often includes elements of the first two, but is also rooted in religious experience and texts taken as *revelation* by the believing community. Also: "anthropological" (adj.), "anthropologist" (n.).

anthropomorphism (n.): Treating other types of being as if they shared with human reality (Greek *anthropos*) the same type of form (Greek *morphe*). <The problem of anthropomorphism in attempts to characterize God.> Also "anthropomorphic" (adj.), "anthropomorphically" (adv.).

antinomian (adj. or n.): Of or pertaining to, or a person who embraces, *antinomianism.* (Contrast **deontological.**)

antinomianism (n.): Ethical theory holding that there are no general moral rules (Greek *nomoi*)—or that such rules do not have the strict directive force often attributed to them. This theory is sometimes associated with *existentialism* $_{(1)}$. (Compare **situation ethics**. Contrast **deontology**.)

antinomy (n.): As discussed by 18th-century philosopher Immanuel Kant and now taken into philosophy generally, a pair of thoughts or propositions, both of which seem to be necessary conclusions of sound reasoning, but which nonetheless seem to be incompatible with one another. <The antinomy of time as being both constantly in motion and made up of a series of static instants.> Also: "antinomous" (adj.).

anti-perfectionism (n.): Position in political philosophy opposed to *perfectionism,* as this has been developed in the perennial as well as other traditions. (John Rawls and political philosophers who follow him are well-known for holding "anti-perfectionist" views.)

antirealism (n.): Position, or family of positions, challenging claims of metaphysical and/or epistemological *realism*—i.e., claims that the mind can make contact with real features of being and to some extent can come to know and name them. Principal types of antirealism include *nominalism* (which holds that our general concepts or "names" have no counterpart in extra-mental reality); *positivism* (which holds that what can be known is restricted to what can be verified by the senses); and *phenomenalism* (which holds that what can be known is restricted to sensory data). Also: "antirealist" (adj. or n.).

apodictic (adj.): Alternative term for knowledge that is *demonstrative;* especially used in cases in which the premises themselves do not rely on prior arguments, but are true *evidently* or *self-evidently.* <"No cube is also a sphere" as an apodictic judgment involving application of the principle of identity.> (Contrast **dialectical** $_{(2)}$.) Also: "apodictically" (adv.).

apophatic (adj., from Greek *apo,* for "separate" or "detached" + *phanein,* for "to say"): Without words, silent in the face of inexpressible reality. The term is especially used to characterize *mystical* experience of God—e.g., that received by St. John of the Cross and other Christian mystics. (Contrast **kataphatic**, sometimes **cataphatic.**

a posteriori (Latin phrase, for "from what comes after or depends upon"): (1) For Scholastic thought, the type of reasoning—common in everyday life and the natural sciences, as well as in philosophy—that proceeds from propositions about accepted *facts* (ultimately facts of experience) to propositions about the *causes* or *principles* on which these facts depend and in which they find their proper explanation. <Reasoning *a posteriori* from the activities or powers of a living being to propositions about the type of form (in this case, the type of soul) that animates it.> (2) Characteristic of knowledge resulting from such reasoning. (Contrast ***a priori***; and see that entry for discussion of the rather different understandings of both *a posteriori* and *a priori* that have arisen within modern philosophy.)

appearance (n.): What appears; especially as a matter of sensory awareness. (In the philosophy of Plato and certain others, this is specifically contrasted with "reality," a knowledge of which can only be purely intellectual. However, for Aristotle and the perennial tradition, sensory appearances can provide the matter for *abstraction* and thus for genuine knowledge of *form* $_{(1)}$.)

appetite (n., Latin *appetitus*): An inclination or tendency toward some good or suitable object, or away from some bad or unsuitable object. (Appetites are differentiated according to the *natures* $_{(2)}$ of the things that have them. Among living beings, three types of appetite are recognized by perennial philosophy—a) the *vegetative* [e.g., tendency toward growth]; b) the *sensible* $_{(2)}$ [e.g., tendency toward a perceived object of pleasure]; and c) the *rational* [e.g., tendency toward truth]. Among animals and human persons, appetites are sometimes further distinguished into "natural" and "elicited;" the former are innate, while the latter arise in response to the awareness—sensory or intellectual—of a particular good or a particular threat of harm.) (Compare **affectivity**.) Also: "appetitive" (adj.), "appetitively" (adv.).

applied ethics: Moral reflection focused on one or more of a range of *practical* topics, or topic areas, rather than on *ethical theory* itself. Prominent areas of applied ethics today include biomedical ethics, business ethics, environmental ethics, legal ethics, marital and sexual ethics, social ethics, and the ethics of war and peace.

apprehension or **intellection** (**simple**) (n.): The basic or, formally speaking, "first" act of human *intellect*—namely, the grasping a *nature* $_{(2)}$ or *essence* $_{(2)}$ (i.e., an answer to the question, "What type of thing is this?") via a process in which the mind, ideally, *abstracts* $_{(2)}$ the *intelligible* features of things. The results of apprehension are expressed in universal *concepts*. (See **agent intellect** and **possible intellect**.)

a priori (Latin phrase, for "from what is prior to or comes before"): (1) For Scholastic thought, the type of reasoning that proceeds from propositions about *principles* $_{(2)}$ (ultimately first principles) to propositions that demonstrably follow from and are explained by them. <Reasoning *a priori* from the rational nature of the human soul to our souls' immateriality.> (2) Characteristic of knowledge resulting from such reasoning. [Note: Modern philosophy, dominated by disputes among rationalists and empiricists, produced rather different and competing understandings of *a priori* (as well as *a posteriori*)—understandings that continue to be widely held. According to these latter understandings, the two phrases apply primarily to the content of statements and to the way such content can be justified. Thus an *a priori* statement is one that would be *analytic* $_{(2)}$, for its justification would come from an analysis of the meanings of the terms that comprise the statement; whereas an *a posteriori* statement would be *synthetic* (2), for its justification would come from direct experience. Complicating matters further is the view of Immanuel Kant, who held that there also can be knowledge that is *a priori* yet synthetic, since it reflects the necessary forms of sensory intuition and categories of understanding that characterize the human mind itself—for example, according to Kant, all concrete objects of knowledge are spatiotemporal in character.] (Contrast ***a posteriori***.)

archetype (n.): (1) In philosophy and theology, a form or model (said to be present to the eternal mind of God) of things of the natural world. (2) In the theory of 20th-century Swiss psychoanalyst Carl Jung, a very general notion (e.g., the "hero") rooted in the common experience of humankind, and thus present in and affecting the *unconscious* of each individual. Also: "archetypical" (adj.).

arete (Greek n.): (1) Excellence. According to the Aristotelian understanding, *arete* is manifested not only in human persons, but throughout nature, insofar as things of various sorts can be recognized as fulfilled instances of the types of beings they are. <A plant's flowering as a manifestation of *arete*.> (2) (Translated as "virtue.") Our specifically human types of excellence—ones involving stable dispositions to pursue and enjoy the true and the good. <Wisdom as an element of human *arete*.> (See ***habitus*** and **virtue**.)

areteology (n., from Greek *arete*, for "excellence" or "virtue"): Disciplined study of the virtues, or the types of excellence achievable in human life. Also: "areteological" (adj.), "areteologist" (n.).

argument (n.): Process of *reasoning* whereby a conclusion is proved or rendered probable on the basis of better known propositions. Modern logicians generally divide arguments into *deductive* and *inductive* types. In addition, arguments are said to be either "formal" or "informal." (Regarding the evaluation of formal deductive arguments, see **validity** and **soundness**. For what sometimes is regarded as a third form of argument, see **abduction**.)

argumentation (n.): Presentation of a position by way of *argument*, in oral or written form. <Argumentation concerning the existence of God.>

aristocracy (n.): (1) For Aristotle, organization of political society so that it is led by the "best," that is, most virtuous citizens (Greek *aristoi*). (2) More commonly, in modern and contemporary political thought, organization of society so that it is led by persons of inherited wealth, or property, or some comparable social marker. (Regarding the second sense, compare **oligarchy**. In either sense, contrast **democracy**.) Also: "aristocrat" (n.), "aristocratic" (adj.).

Aristotelian (adj. or n.): Of or pertaining to, or a person who embraces, ideas and themes of the Greek philosopher Aristotle (384–322 BC). Modifying the thought of his teacher, Plato, Aristotle emphasized, in speculative philosophy, that the *forms* of things are internal principles of activity and knowability (rather than being other-worldly models), and that they can become available to the human mind by the process of *abstraction* (1). (His Greek term for this, *epagoge,* sometimes is translated as "induction;" but see the discussion in the entry for the latter.) Aristotle developed an account of natural substance in terms of what is called *hylemorphism;* this account extended to living beings, including human persons, in which substantial form is *psuche* or soul. In practical philosophy, Aristotle emphasized that it is concretely possible—in limited measure, and supposing certain internal and external conditions are fulfilled—to achieve the human good, which is knowable in general terms via reflection on *teleology* (1), or the *ends* (1) of human action. Among the internal conditions for achieving the good is possession of moral *virtue.* In addition to his contributions to speculative and practical philosophy, Aristotle was the first Western thinker to formalize principles of logic, in particular the valid forms of *syllogism.*

Aristotelianism (n.): The historical tradition or movement that takes inspiration from concepts and themes of Aristotle, especially those noted above within speculative and practical philosophy. This tradition has survived various vicissitudes. Many key works of the Aristotelian corpus were lost to the Christian West for a number of centuries. When they were recovered by way of Islamic and Byzantine Greek sources and translated into Latin, they had an enormous impact on Christian (as well as other Western) thinkers, especially during the 13th century and beyond. (A token of this is the fact that Aquinas often referred to Aristotle simply as "the Philosopher.") The philosophical challenges posed by the development of empirical and mathematized approaches to nature were not adequately addressed by Aristotelians of the early modern period. During the 20th century, further progress in the natural sciences, together with reflection by classically-oriented thinkers on relations between philosophy and the sciences of nature (e.g., Mortimer J. Adler, Jacques Maritain, and Yves Simon, as well as the Dominican scholars James Weisheipl and William Wallace), did much to rehabilitate Aristotelianism as a viable philosophy of nature—and thus as a basis for associated elements of other philosophical disciplines, including ethics.

art (n.): (1) An activity whose *end*$_{(1)}$ is "production"—by contrast with ethics and politics (in which the end is "action"), as well as with speculative studies, for example, mathematics, natural science apart from its technological applications, and metaphysics (in which the end is "contemplation"). (2) A *habitus* of the practical intellect, the ability to bring about objects with appropriate or pleasing forms—sometimes by contrast with a mere skill (Greek *techne*), since agents who possesses the latter need know nothing of the relevant ends of the activities in which they are engaged. (3) The actual bringing about of beautiful objects (in painting, music, etc.). Also: "artist" (n.), "artistic" (adj.).

artificial (adj.): Resulting from art or other human intervention, rather than from an internal principle of a thing's operation, or from what occurs in *nature*$_{(1)}$ itself, apart from our choices and acts. <The use of artificial pacemakers in the treatment of heart patients.> [Note: To be artificial is thus to be *unnatural*$_{(1)}$; but this does not entail being *unnatural*$_{(3)}$—i.e., "unnatural" in the sense relevant to ethics. If it did, the whole field of medical practice, for example, would be morally suspect. Failure to recognize this point has been the source of confusion in discussions of *natural* (*moral*) *law.* Moreover, something—e.g., a city—can itself be the result of artifice, while having a basis in human nature (in this case, our orientation toward rationally ordered community).] (Contrast **natural**$_{(1)}$.) Also: "artificially" (adv.).

aseity (n.): Property of having *existence* simply in and of oneself (Latin *a se*), that is, having literally no cause. According to perennial philosophy, this property is attributable uniquely to God. (See the discussion under **sufficient reason, principle of.**)

assemblism (n.): View among certain recent philosophers of nature and of science (e.g., Peter Atkins and Richard Dawkins) according to which unified physical beings, of whatever degree of complexity (including human persons), in principle could be built up out of their constituent parts—and thus, in effect, do not manifest new and higher types of *formal cause.* (Compare **reductionism.**) Also: "assemblist" (adj. or n.).

assent (n.): Agreement to a proposition or acceptance of an idea, ordinarily as formally expressed. <The believer's assent to doctrine formulated by religious authorities.>

assent (v.): To formally agree to or accept.

atheism (n.): (1) Belief or affirmation that there is no God. (2) (Sometimes called "practical atheism.") Lifestyles and patterns of choice that suppose or imply that there is no God. (Contrast both **theism** and **agnosticism.**) Also: "atheist" (adj. or n.), "atheistic" (adj.).

attribution, **analogy of**: Type of *analogy* according to which a term has a diverse set of meanings, but the respective meanings have a tendency toward unity, since they are bound together by similar relations to a primary member of the set. (Thus, in the case of "healthy," the primary member of the set is the term's application to proper functioning in an organism, say a human person; secondary members would include the term's application to an exercise regimen and a blood test result, which can be, respectively, a cause and a sign of health in the organism.)

audacity (n.): See **foolhardiness.**

Augustinian (adj. or n.): Of or pertaining to, or a person who embraces, ideas and teachings of St. Augustine (354–430), Bishop of Hippo in North Africa, a "Father of the Church," and enormously influential on later Western Christian thought. Augustine came of age in the flux of Hellenistic philosophy—an era represented by Stoics, Epicureans, Skeptics, and Neo-Platonists. From the last group he took the theory of the "emanation" of forms, adapting it to Christian teaching on Creation by noting that such emanation is under the direction of God. Other generally Platonic elements are to be found in Augustine's account of human knowledge in terms of divine illumination. Concerned throughout his life with the nature and origin of *evil,* Augustine originally was a follower of the Manicheans (who held that there was a fundamental principle of evil, as well as one of good); after his conversion to orthodox Christianity, he sought to account for evil in terms of the absence of good, as well as in terms of inferior choices made by finite wills. Augustine stressed the gulf between existing human cultures (the "City of Man") and the way of living intended and made possible by God (the "City of God"); and he proposed as the primary task of Christians in the world the transformation of the earthly city into an image—however inadequate—of the heavenly city. (In his historical survey of the Christian faith's encounters with reason, John Paul II noted that Augustine "succeeded in producing the first great synthesis of philosophy and theology" [*Fides et ratio*, #40].)

Augustinianism (n.): Historical tradition of thought that has sought to develop *Augustinian* themes, sometimes by conscious contrast with Aristotelian ones. During the medieval period, the Franciscan order, through the work of St. Bonaventure, became associated with Augustinianism; whereas the Dominican order, through the work of St. Albert the Great, became associated with the revival of Aristotelianism. (Aquinas, however, drew from both traditions.) Since the time of the Reformation, Augustinianism has flourished especially among Protestant thinkers, although the work of Augustine continues to be highly regarded in Catholic theological circles as well. In particular, the writings of Cardinal Joseph Ratzinger, later Benedict XVI, often display a strong Augustinian character.

authenticity (n.): Congruence between a person's thoughts, choices, and actions, and his or her stated (or implied) moral principles and ideals, and ultimately his or her true psychological *self.* (Accounts of authenticity by *personalist* philosophers, as well as other modern students of *subjectivity* $_{(1)}$, e.g., the Canadian Charles Taylor, offer important contributions to the development of the perennial tradition.)

authority (n.): (1) Directive function within a *community,* by which the latter is able to pursue its *common good* concretely and effectively (thus this notion is to be contrasted with that of sheer *power* $_{(2)}$). (2) The person or persons to whom a community's directive function is assigned. (According to the perennial tradition, authority itself is *natural* $_{(3)}$, but the specific structures of authority are not. Thus, forms of government legitimately vary from one society to another—although a recognition of the rational and social nature of human persons favors structures by means of which all members have a voice in matters of common concern. [See **democracy**.]) (3) Regarding *knowledge,* and especially the communication of knowledge, a person who is generally recognized to be an expert or reliable source regarding the matters in question. Also: "authoritative" (adj.), "authoritatively" (adv.).

autonomy (n., from Greek *autos,* for "self" + *nomos,* for "rule"): (1) Independence—e.g., of an adult child from his or her parents, or of philosophy from other disciplines and extrinsic cultural forces. (2) In ethics, especially since Immanuel Kant, the property of the will whereby a person determines for himself or herself the principles by which the moral worth of actions is to be judged. [Note: Recent Christian thinkers sensitive to Kantian ideas (including John Paul II) have affirmed human autonomy but have regarded it as ultimately consisting in a "participated *theonomy.*"] (Ant: **heteronomy**.) Also: "autonomous" (adj.), "autonomously" (adv.).

avarice or **greed** (n.): The habitual tendency or state—one of the seven *capital vices*—by which a person is disposed to inordinate desires for wealth or material possessions (thus, in this respect, a contrary of *temperance*). Also: "avaricious" or "greedy" (adj.)

aversion (n.): (1) In traditional philosophical psychology, a movement of *concupiscible* appetite away from a *sensible* $_{(2)}$ evil. <Animal sensitivity as involving an aversion to pain.> (2) More generally, any movement of *affectivity,* sensory or intellectual, away from an object that is perceived or judged to be bad or harmful. <The will's natural aversion to things recognized as evil.> (In both senses, contrast **desire**.) Also: "averse [to]" (adj.).

axiology (n., from Greek *axios,* for "worthy"): On some accounts, a part of the discipline of *ethics* that studies the nature and norms of *value.* Also: "axiological" (adj.), axiologist" (n.).

axiom (n.): (1) In *mathematics,* a statement taken as a starting point of the discipline, and thus not itself subject to proof. (In general, especially since the development of non-Euclidean geometries, mathematical axioms are not regarded as necessarily corresponding to features of physical reality.) (2) In *philosophy,* another designation for a "first *principle* $_{(2)}$" of knowledge, whether in the *speculative* or the *practical* order. <The fundamental axioms known as the principle of identity and the principle of *synderesis.*> Also: "axiomatic" (adj.), "axiomatically" (adv.).

awe (n.): State of *wonder,* especially in the face of natural or supernatural *mystery.* <Awe at the intellect's power to know real being.> Also: "awesome" (adj.).

B

~

bad (adj.): Opposite of *good* in any of its three senses. (But see the remark in parentheses under **badness.**) (Compare "evil" [as an adj.]; see **evil.**) Also: "badly" (adv.).

badness (n.): Opposite of *goodness* in any of its three senses. (However, by contrast with absolute Goodness [i.e., God], there can be no actually existing *absolute* badness; for, if a thing exists at all it is, to that extent, good. Thus "badness," unlike "goodness," does not express a truly *transcendental* property.) (Compare **evil.**)

basic goods: (1) In traditional Thomistic accounts, objects fulfilling human needs that correspond to our ordered *natural inclinations.* Taken together, basic goods in effect form a hierarchical system—one whose achievement is sometimes referred to as "integral human good." Regarding the structure of goods, Thomists hold that certain of them (in particular, the good of life itself) are the most "fundamental," in that they are presupposed by all the others; while others (e.g., coming to know and embrace the truth about God) are the "highest," in that they are most important in the overall scheme of human *teleology* $_{(1)}$. (2) According to a variation on the above account propounded by contemporary American Catholic philosopher and theologian Germain Grisez, a set of eight identifiable goods—four that are referred to as "substantive" (life, speculative knowledge, aesthetic experience, and play), and four that are referred to as "reflexive or "relational" (self-integration, practical reasonableness, friendship, and religion). In recent years, marriage has been added to some versions of the list. For Grisez and those who follow him in this matter (e.g., John Finnis), these basic goods are all underivable objects of human will; and, while they are interrelated in various ways, they cannot be measured against one another because all are equally "basic." Thus these thinkers eschew the traditional notion of hierarchically ordered natural finalities noted above. (For more on this approach, see **incommensurability thesis**, as well as **new natural law theory**.)

basic needs or **basic human needs**: As referred to in perennial accounts of *distributive justice* (as well as official Catholic social teaching), human needs whose status as fundamental morally requires that they be satisfied (at least in a minimal way) for all of a society's members before other criteria for the distribution of goods—e.g., individual merit or level of societal contribution—are justifiably introduced into the economic system. <Humanity's basic needs for food, shelter, health care, etc.>

be (v., Latin *esse*): To exist, whether in an *entitative* or *intentional* manner, whether *substantial* or *accidental;* etc. (See the various divisions introduced under **being** $_{(1)}$.)

beatitude (n., Latin *beatitudo*): Happiness, blessedness, ultimate human fulfillment. Extensively discussed by ancient philosophers under the heading of "happiness" (Greek *eudaimonia*), this state is taken by Catholic tradition to be found in its completeness only in the life to come—when human persons, elevated by *grace,* share fully in the life of the Triune God. (A theological distinction is often made, therefore, between *natural* $_{(4)}$ beatitude, which is to some degree knowable and available in this life and through human means, and *supernatural* beatitude, which is knowable and available only through God's saving acts in Jesus Christ.)

Beatitudes, the (n.): Collective name given to *ideals* and *norms* enunciated by Jesus in the Sermon on the Mount, as expressed in the Gospels of Matthew and Luke. Each beatitude begins with "Blessed [or "Happy"—Latin *Beati*] are those who . . . [are poor in spirit, hunger and thirst for justice, etc.];" and each concludes with a clause such as "for theirs is the kingdom of heaven." (As norms for perfection, and as leading to the "kingdom of heaven," the Beatitudes go beyond dictates of *natural (moral) law.* There is controversy within Catholic thought about whether, and the extent to which, these prescriptions are strongly *normative*, rather than [merely] expressive of ideals. John Paul II tended to regard them as the former.)

beauty (n.): Property due to which a *being*$_{(1)}$ awakens *delight* when it is beheld or understood. According to many (although not all) philosophers of the perennial tradition, this is a *transcendental* property, characteristic of being as being. Also: "beautiful" (adj.).

become (v., Latin *fieri*): To pass from *potency* to *act;* to take on a new *form* or forms, whether as a *substance* or as an *accident*$_{(1)}$. (Compare **coming to be**.) Also: "becoming" (n.).

begin (v.): To originate; to start to be or to do. <To begin life as a married couple. To begin production of a new type of electronic device.>

beginning (n.): Origin, especially in a temporal sense. <Scientific estimates as to the time that has elapsed since the beginning of our physical universe.>

being (n.): (Corresponding to Latin *ens.*) (1) A singular thing; that which is, either in *actuality* or in *potentiality*—although being in act has both ontological and logical priority. (Divisions of types of being in this general sense include *real* or *entitative* vs. *intentional; substantial* vs. *accidental; material, physical,* and *sensible* vs. *immaterial, spiritual,* and *supersensible; finite* vs. *infinite;* and *contingent* [or "possible"] vs. *necessary.*) (2) The *transcendental* property according to which each thing, in its respective way, participates in reality or existence. (3) The formal subject matter of *metaphysics,* that is, being as being (Latin *ens qua ens* or *ens inquantum est ens*), or being in common (Latin *ens commune*), considered in its generic or proportionately shared intelligible features. (4) (Corresponding to Latin *esse,* used as a substantive, or to *actus essendi.*) The act of being, or act of existence—i.e., the ontologically primary *act* or *perfection* through which any reality (as well as its features) actually is. (See **existence**$_{(2)}$.) (5) (In the context of logic.) The *intentional*$_{(1)}$ being expressed in propositions, especially those in which a *predicate* is united to a *subject* (i.e., propositions of the form "S is P"); sometimes called the "is" (or "being") of the "copula." (Note: The above is a summary of the uses of "being" in the Thomist tradition. For other, partially competing Scholastic accounts, see the discussions under **Ockhamist**, **Scotist**, and **Suarezian**; see also, regarding modern developments, the discussions under **existentialism** and **x** (logical symbol).)

being of reason (Latin *ens rationis*): A being that depends for its existence on some activity of the mind; an *intentional* $_{(1)}$ being, such as a concept. In the initial and most prevalent type of case, a being of reason expresses a form of reality (e.g., human being or triangle, insofar as these are understood); in other cases, a being of reason expresses something purely logical (e.g., to be a *subject* $_{(1)}$ or a *predicate*). (The former type of being of reason is sometimes called a concept of "first" *intention* $_{(1)}$, the latter a concept of "second" *intention* $_{(1)}$.)

being vs. having: A contrast drawn by Christian *existentialist* and *personalist* philosopher Gabriel Marcel (1889–1973), who emphasized the importance of human existence itself over the accumulation of goods, however valuable the latter may be. (This theme was taken up and used in the Vatican II document *Gaudium et spes*, #35, thus exemplifying a fruitful encounter between Catholic tradition and 20th-century philosophical developments.)

being-with-nothingness: Phrase adapted from 20th-century existentialism by certain recent Thomist philosophers (e.g., Jacques Maritain and Pierre-Marie Emonet, O.P.). It expresses the radical *contingency* of all *natural* $_{(1)}$ beings and thus, ultimately, the dependence of such beings upon a Being without contingency (or "without nothingness")—i.e., God. (Note: This notion plays a crucial role in the third of Aquinas's *Five Ways*.)

Biblicism (n.): An approach to religious questions, associated with *fundamentalist* Christian bodies (but not unknown within Catholicism), according to which "the reading and exegesis of Sacred Scripture [becomes] the sole criterion of truth" (John Paul II, *Fides et ratio*, #55). This approach pays little attention to either the philosophical presuppositions of or the need for critical clarifications of the biblical texts. Also: "Biblicist" (adj. or n.).

biologism (n.): A term applied by certain critics of Aquinas's ethics, as well as certain critics of moral teachings by the Catholic *magisterium*—especially regarding marital and sexual ethics. According to such critics, the traditional explanations of morality are inordinately centered on biological or physical features of human acts (thus the term "physicalism" is also sometimes used in the present sense); moreover, the traditional explanations are said to ignore (what to these critics are) the morally more important features of personal context and meaning. [Note: While "biologism" as thus described in fact may have affected certain presentations of traditional sexual ethics, Thomistic philosophy does not stress biological features as such, but rather the proper *use* of human powers, in light of the *teleology* $_{(1)}$ or end-directed character of our acts. Recent formulations of magisterial teaching—especially during the pontificate of John Paul II—have supplemented traditional accounts with reflection on people's experience of the intrinsically given, personal *meanings* $_{(3)}$ of the types of acts being discussed.] Also: "biologistic" (adj.), "biologistically" (adv.).

birth regulation or **control**: The spacing of pregnancy and childbirth in keeping with a couple's circumstances as prudently judged. [It is sometimes supposed—incorrectly—that traditional Catholic teaching, with support from perennial philosophy, is opposed to the regulation of births. What the Church's *magisterium* opposes are acts that directly frustrate what are judged—in light of *revelation* and *natural (moral) law*—to be intrinsic *ends* $_{(1)}$ or *meanings* $_{(3)}$ of personal sexual union (in this case, the end of *procreation*). Hence Catholic teaching rejects *contraception,* properly and narrowly understood. But birth or fertility management itself, so far from being prohibited, can be in light of circumstances a duty of a married couple. Today, Catholic teachers point to the experience of many couples who have discovered that such a duty can be met in highly effective and personally fulfilling ways by the means called *natural family planning*—means which, since they do not directly frustrate the procreative end of sexual acts, are morally acceptable on traditional accounts.]

body (n.): A unified, individual physical being (i.e., an instance of formed *matter* $_{(3)}$). <A molecule of water as a body in the philosophical sense.> [Note: In everyday speech regarding human beings, "body" is sometimes contrasted with "soul." Although innocent in itself, this use of words can lead the unwary (including unwary philosophers) into mistakes—e.g., a radical *dualism* in the understanding of the human person. See the discussions under **matter** and **soul.**]

bonum honestum (Latin phrase, literally "honest" or "fitting" or "suitable good"): A good that fulfills a type of being, power, or appetite, because of the natures of the things in question. (The term *bonum honestum* is contrasted with Latin *bonum utile* ["useful good"] and *bonum delectabile* ["pleasant" or "pleasurable good"]. <The virtue of justice as a *bonum honestum* for human persons.> (Note: This account in no way suggests that useful and pleasant goods are not genuinely good. Moreover, while the term "honest" [good] continues to appear in expositions of perennial ethics, "intrinsic" [good] is sometimes substituted.)

capacity (n.): Range of a *potency* or *power.* <The human intellect as in principle having a capacity to know all natural being (in Latin: *intellectus capax omnium*).>

capital (adj., from Latin *caput,* for "head"): First in importance, highest, chief; also the source of others. <The capital vices.>

capital (n.): In economic systems, those goods, including both material and financial resources, that are needed for production. <Sufficient capital to undertake a particular venture.> (This term also has been used, sometimes with an uppercase "C," to designate collectively the holders of such goods.) (Contrast **labor** $_{(2)}$.)

capitalism (n.): Modern economic system that features private ownership and control of goods and services, large-scale production, freedom of enterprise, profit accepted as a primary motive of human activity, and strict limits on governmental oversight. Also called a "market economy"—although the latter phrase sometimes signals an openness to greater public oversight. [Note: Although capitalism can lead to significant goods—for example, a generally high standard of living—it also, given normal human tendencies (exacerbated by the effects of sin as understood by Christian tradition), gives rise to serious ethical concerns: the danger of overemphasis on profits and the prerogatives of owners, and the neglect of *social justice* and the *natural rights* of laboring people. Both the potential benefits of capitalism and the ethical concerns that surround it are magnified by the movement toward economic globalization.] (Contrast **socialism**. See as well **distributism** and **third way**.) Also: "capitalist" (adj. or n.).

capital punishment: See **death penalty**.

capital vices: See **vices, capital**.

cardinal virtues: See **virtues, cardinal**.

caritas (Latin n., for "charity" or "love"): See the discussions under ***agape***, **charity** $_{(3)}$, and **love** $_{(3)}$.

Cartesian (adj. or n.): Of or pertaining to, or a person who holds, the philosophical ideas of French philosopher René Descartes (1596–1650). Although Descartes was taught a version of Scholastic philosophy, early in his career he determined to make a fresh start (thus he is sometimes called the "father" of modern philosophy). In methodology, he introduced an extreme version of *rationalism.* In natural philosophy, he introduced (by contrast with the project of identifying *natures* $_{(2)}$, as pursued by Aristotle and the Scholastics) a purely quantitative and spatial approach to physical being. In metaphysics, he introduced a radical *dualism* of "extended being" (Latin *res extensa*) and "thinking being" (Latin *res cogitans*)—a dualism that contrasts with perennial philosophical accounts of the *hylemorphic* unity of *form* (in living beings, *soul*) and *matter* $_{(3)}$. Also: "Cartesianism" (n.).

casuistry (n.): In ethics, including moral theology, a method of *reasoning* that focuses on concrete cases (Latin *casus* plural), rather than on principles, in an effort to shed light on new moral situations by comparison and contrast with others that are thought to be well-settled in their ethical analysis. (Contrast **principlism**—although some attention to casuistry is compatible with a recognition of the significance of moral principles. In this regard, see as well **prudentialism**.) Also: "casuist" (adj. or n.).

categorial (adj.): Belonging to or otherwise associated with *categories.* <The categorial distinction between substance and quantity.>

categorical (adj.): Characteristic of a judgment that is *absolute* (i.e., made without qualifications). <A categorical denial of what one's opponent asserts.> Also: "categorically" (adv.).

categorical imperative: See the discussion under **Kantian**.

category (n.): A basic class, by contrast with others similarly basic, into which items may fall. For followers of Aristotle, the term is used especially of the ten ultimate genera of being—i.e., *substance* and nine types of *accident* $_{(1)}$. (By extension, this word also applies to corresponding basic classes of terms, although, strictly speaking, the proper word for the latter is "predicament.")

catharsis (n.): In *aesthetic* theory, the purification of *emotions* or the release of emotional tension that can accompany the experience of a dramatic performance. (In his book *Poetics,* Aristotle emphasized in this regard the emotions of pity and fear.) <Catharsis at the resolution of a drama.> Also: "cathartic" (adj.).

catholic (adj., Greek *katholikos*): (1) (Lowercase "c.") Universal. (2) (Uppercase "C.") Of or pertaining to *Catholicism.*

Catholicism (n., from Greek adj. *katholikos,* for "universal"): The communion of *Christian* churches—with their traditions of belief, sacraments, practices, and prayer—that are in union with the pope (the bishop of Rome), who for Catholics is the successor of St. Peter and a visible sign of the Church unity for which Christ prayed (see John 17). (Notes: The Orthodox Churches not in communion with Rome also typically identify themselves as "Catholic" because of their common origin in the apostolic period and their profession of the universal doctrines of the first Christian millennium. Moreover, certain schismatic bodies such as the Slavic Old Catholic churches—Polish, Croat, and Yugoslav—continue to use the term "Catholic" in their names. Finally, while the term "Roman Catholicism" most properly applies to churches of the Western or Latin Rite, it is sometimes used to refer to all churches and rites [including the Coptic, Maronite, Melchite, etc.] that are in union with Rome.)

Catholic tradition: (1) Tradition (or set of traditions) of belief, sacraments, practices, and prayer associated with *Catholicism.* (2) More specifically, and as often used in this dictionary, the intellectual tradition (encompassing both theology and philosophy, as well as other disciplines that contribute to Christian reflection) that began in conjunction with classical Greek and Latin sources, flourished in the Scholasticism of the High Middle Ages, and continues in a coherent form to the present day—responding all the while both to new intellectual developments and to the guidance of the Catholic *magisterium.*

causality (n.): In the broadest sense, a relationship in which one being (the "cause") is in some *real* way responsible for a feature (the "effect") in another—the latter's *existence,* its *essence* or substantial nature, or one of its *accidents.* Aristotle developed a system of four causes (Greek *aitiai*), or modes of explanation of a thing's being or coming into being. (See **material cause**, **formal cause**, **efficient cause**, and **final cause**.) Scholastic philosophers developed additional distinctions, which can operate within each of the four orders—e.g., between *first* or *primary* vs. *secondary* causes, *principal* vs. *subordinate* or *instrumental* causes, and *proper* or *essential* vs. *accidental* causes. (In this traditional philosophical account, "causality" expresses a notion broader than that employed in the empirical sciences; the latter tend to focus on factors of the material and efficient [or "agent"] types.) (Compare and contrast **condition**.) Also: "causal" (adj.), "causally" (adv.), "causation" (n.).

causality, principle of: A first principle in the philosophy of nature, namely, "Every natural being or event has a cause." (Compare and contrast **sufficient reason, principle of**.)

cause (n. or v.): See the discussion under **causality**.

caution (n.): A component of the cardinal virtue *prudence,* by which a person is able to exercise appropriate care in decision-making, rather than acting impulsively. Also: "cautious" (adj.).

central sense: See **common sense** $_{(1)}$.

certain (adj.): Objectively enjoying, or subjectively experiencing, *certainty* or *certitude.* <A clear and certain proposition. A person certain of the rightness of his or her cause.> (Ant: **uncertain**. Contrast **doubtable** or **dubitable**, as well as **doubtful**.) Also: "certainly" (adv.).

certain conscience: Condition of an individual *conscience* according to which, after full and appropriate reflection on the matter at hand, there is no doubt in the agent's mind as to whether a particular action would be, for example, morally good, morally required, or morally prohibited. (According to Catholic tradition, a person must seek to follow the dictates of a certain conscience, if it meets the conditions here specified.) (Contrast **doubtful conscience** and **perplexed conscience**.)

certainty or **certitude** (n.): (1) Personal state in which one makes a judgment without fear of error. (Ant: **uncertainty**. Contrast as well **doubt** $_{(1)}$.) (2) Objective feature of a judgment such that it can be made without fear of error. (Note: Some authors distinguish "certainty" and "certitude," identifying the former with sense (1) and the latter with sense (2).) Different types and bases of certitude can be distinguished: "metaphysical" (where a contradictory judgment is excluded by the fact that the proposition in question is reducible to the *principle of identity*); "physical" (where a contradictory judgment is excluded—barring the occurrence of a *miracle*—by seeing that the predicted event is necessitated by known laws of nature); "moral" (where a contradictory judgment is excluded by seeing that the moral proposition in question is contained in or reducible to precepts of either *natural* (*moral*) *law* or *divine law*); and "practical" (where a contradictory judgment is excluded—sufficiently at least for purposes of confident action—by appeal to common experience or individual knowledge). (Contrast "doubtability" or "dubitability," mentioned under **doubtable** or **dubitable.**)

chance (adj.): Pertaining to or occurring by *chance* (n.). <A chance coincidence of two individuals' subjective goals.>

chance (n.): (1) In traditional natural philosophy, the result of the intersection of two or more lines of natural *causality,* whereby the outcome is not the necessary result of any type of force or act. Therefore, the outcome has "accidental" causes but no "proper" or "essential" cause. (2) In contemporary natural science, especially quantum physics, an event whose features cannot be predicted due to the impossibility of a complete and simultaneous understanding of the relevant antecedent conditions. (In spite of their differences, events of sorts (1) and (2) are both sometimes called "random.") (3) According to certain recent philosophical speculations, the supposed condition of a being or event of *nature* $_{(1)}$—or even of the whole physical universe—according to which it simply is without cause. [Such speculations are rejected by the perennial tradition as being incompatible with a proper grasp of the *principle of causality.*]

change (n.): Alteration; process by which some type of *matter* goes from a state of *privation* of a particular *form* to actual possession of that form. (In the *Physics,* Aristotle said change is "the actualization of a being in potency insofar as it is in potency"—that is, as long as the change is still taking place, the being with the new form is not yet fully actual.) A principal division among types of change is *accidental* vs. *substantial.* <Suffering an injury as undergoing accidental change; death as the occurrence of substantial change.> Further, change can be either real (i.e., *entitative* $_{(1)}$), or related to the mind's consideration of its objects (i.e., *intentional*$_{(1)}$). <A species of animal's becoming more plentiful as involving an entitative change; its becoming better understood by biological science as involving an intentional change.> (Ant: **permanence**.)

change (v.): (1) (Intransitive.) To pass from a state of *potentiality* to one of *actuality;* to become or take on such-and-such a form of being. <A larva changing into a butterfly.> Also: "changeable" (adj.). (2) (Transitive.) To bring about a *change* (n.), either in another or in oneself. <Wind changing the flight of an arrow.>

change of matter (Latin *mutatio materiae*) or **change of species**: In moral philosophy, a shift in the "matter" or *object*$_{(3)}$ of a human act, or in the act's *moral*$_{(1)}$ species. Thus, for example, telling lies is always wrong. But in a stage production a person may say what is false without being guilty of a lie: rather, his or her act is to be understood as expressing the lines of a player in the drama. Again, genuine theft is always morally wrong. But, at least for most writers in the perennial tradition, in a genuine life-threatening emergency for which the agent is in no way responsible, what otherwise would be an act of theft (e.g., taking a modest amount of food without paying) can become, by change of matter or species, an instance of a different type of moral act (e.g., providing for one's family in the only available manner—which is permitted in light of the *universal destination of goods*). (Note: Contrary to what is sometimes supposed, in such a case there is not a "justified violation" of the moral precept against theft; rather, there is, morally speaking, no act of theft.) (See **exceptionless moral rules** and **necessity**$_{(2)}$.)

character (n.): The concrete set of inclinations and dispositions of *temperament,* together with the *habits* and *virtues* (or lack thereof), that affect an individual's *moral*$_{(1)}$ choices. <A person of exemplary character.>

charity (n.): (1) The desire to contribute to the good of other persons for their own sakes, in ways that go beyond the demands of strict *justice.* (2) An act or acts flowing from this desire, especially in cases that from the standpoint of moral philosophy would be regarded as ones of *supererogation.* (3) The *theological virtue* (also called "love") whereby, through *grace,* one participates in God's Love (Greek *agape,* Latin *caritas*), and thus is able to choose and act in accordance with Gospel mandates in relation to God, neighbor, and oneself. (In Christian accounts of the moral life, charity is chief among the virtues; it binds together and animates all the others. For an exposition, see Pope Benedict XVI's first encyclical, *Deus Caritas est.*) Also: "charitable" (adj.).

chastity (n.): An aspect of the cardinal virtue of *temperance,* by which one regulates one's sexual desires and acts in a manner appropriate to one's *marital* state, and also exercises care in related matters of dress and bodily demeanor. Also: "chaste" (adj.), "chastely" (adv.).

choice (n., Latin *electio*): (1) Act of the *will,* also called "decision," by which a rational agent selects a particular act as a *means* to a desired *end* $_{(2)}$. Choice is the result of *deliberation* and is formally specified by a *command* (Latin *imperium*)—i.e., a self-recognized directive of the form "Such-and-such is to be done." (See **volition.**) (2) An option, or a selection from among alternatives. Also: "choose" (v.).

Christian (adj. or n., from Greek *Christos,* for "anointed"): Of or pertaining to Jesus Christ or to *Christianity;* or a person who embraces the associated religious faith. <Christian influences in art and literature.>

Christian ethics: See **ethics, Christian.**

Christianity (n.): The religion—or the presently diverse family of religious bodies, with their respective beliefs and practices—that, insofar as these bodies are *orthodox,* accept Jesus as Christ, Lord, and Son of God.

Christian philosophy: Philosophy, speculative or practical, undertaken in the context of, or in some way conditioned by, Christian *faith* $_{(3)}$. Throughout the history of the Christian West, there has been controversy regarding the ways in which, and the degrees to which, matters of faith can directly influence philosophy, or philosophy can consider questions of faith. (In the United States, a present-day "Society of Christian Philosophers"—primarily Protestant and Evangelical, but including some Catholics—is aggressive in pursuing these possibilities.) In *Fides et ratio,* #76, John Paul II proposed that Christian philosophy is indeed genuinely philosophical in character. That is, it is a use of reason that formally relies on naturally knowable *principles* and common *experience* rather than on data of *revelation;* but it nonetheless can be aided by faith—both subjectively (e.g., by purifying the thinker's mind and heart) and objectively (e.g., by suggesting philosophical topics to be pursued). (The Vatican II document *Gaudium et spes* is, according to John Paul II, a "virtual compendium of biblical anthropology from which philosophy too can draw inspiration"[Ibid., #60].) At the same time, Christian philosophy can contribute to the development of sacred theology by introducing categories and modes of thought in terms of which the intellectual content of faith might be articulated. Finally, philosophical reason in its highest plane of activity actually joins with religious faith, so that together they function "like two wings on which the spirit rises to the contemplation of truth"(Ibid., Salutation).

circumstances (n.): Features of a *human act,* beyond its moral *object* $_{(3)}$ and its subjective *end* $_{(2)}$ or *motive* or purpose, that affect its moral *rightness* or *wrongness.* Types of circumstances would include existential conditions and relationships (e.g., physical abilities/disabilities; marriage) of the persons involved, foreseeable consequences of the act, external pressures on the agent(s), etc. <A morally good act made even better by the difficult circumstances in which it was accomplished.>

citizen (n.): One who participates (or has the right to participate) in a *political* society—especially a *state* $_{(2)}$.

civic or **civil society**: Organized political society, including the means of *authority* it incorporates. Ideally and by nature, a civil society is aimed at the *common good* of its citizens. Such a society will include specific *governmental* structures, but also subsidiary forms of *community*—which are necessary in light of both the complexity and the personal character of the human good. Typically, a society also will have other types of organized entities (sometimes called "mediating institutions") developed for particular purposes. The prime example of a subsidiary community would be the *family;* examples of other types of organized entities would be educational institutions, service organizations, cultural societies, and religious groups.

civil law: Set of concrete ordinances regulating behavior and relationships that are duly developed and promulgated by those in authority within a political society; there are a range of *sanctions* associated with such ordinances for those who violate them. (Compare **human law** and **positive law**.)

civil rights: Specific rights that all citizens have simply by virtue of their membership in a particular *political* society. (Compare and contrast **natural rights**.)

clarification (n.): The analysis of *concepts* and/or of *experience.* (All philosophy has involved elements of clarification; among 20th- and 21st-century movements, *analytic philosophy* has focused on analysis of concepts, while *phenomenology* has focused on analysis of experience.)

classical (adj., sometimes capitalized): As understood in Western philosophy and theology, modes or traditions of thought rooted in ancient Greek and Roman authors—Plato, Aristotle, Cicero, etc.; also used as a general label for these authors themselves.

cogitative power (Latin *vis cogitativa*): Psychic power in human persons (and, apparently, in other sign-using animals) by which sensible objects are recognized and named—e.g., "ball," "red," "four-cornered," or "rectangular." In human persons, this power mediates between sensory awareness and *concepts*—i.e., the results of intellectual *abstraction* $_{(2)}$. Such mediation occurs because we not only recognize and give things names but come to know, at least to some extent, the essences signified by these names.

cognition or **cognitivity** (n.): In animals and human persons, the set of powers and activities related to *knowledge,* by contrast with those related to *appetite;* also the movement or exercise of such powers and activities. (Specifically human cognition goes beyond the sensory level to include intellectual knowledge.) <Sensory cognition of the presence of another animal.> (Contrast **affection** and **affectivity**.) Also: "cognitive," (adj.), "cognitively" (adv.).

cognitive (adj.): Of or pertaining to **cognition** or **cognitivity**. (Contrast **affective**.) Also: "cognitively" (adv.).

coherence (n.): The ability of diverse parts or aspects to stand together, or to make a consistent whole. <Coherence of one's normative theory with one's judgments concerning concrete moral issues.> (Ant: **incoherence**. Contrast as well **eclecticism**.) Also: "coherent" (adj.), "coherently" (adv.).

coherence theory of truth (sometimes **coherentism**): Epistemological position holding that truth is primarily a matter of the coherence or internal consistency of the propositions within a system of knowledge. Such a theory avoids complex issues about the representational character of propositions, which must be addressed by a *correspondence theory of truth;* and it may deny such representational character altogether. [For their part, correspondence theorists, including followers of Aristotle and St. Thomas Aquinas, typically argue that while coherence is a necessary condition, it is not a sufficient condition for the truth of a set of propositions.] Also: "coherentist" (adj. or n.).

collectivism (n.): See **statism**.

coming to be (sometimes hyphenated): Origination of a being, especially *generation* $_{(1)}$ in the case of natural *substance*. (Compare **become**.)

command (n., Latin *imperium*): In philosophical psychology and ethics, the conclusion of a *practical syllogism* insofar as it is proposed to the will of the person(s) involved—for example, a statement or directive of the form "Therefore, this is what I (or we) must do (or not do)." (See **ultimate practical judgment**.)

commensurable (adj., from Latin *mensura,* for "standard of measure"): As said of two or more things, able to be measured according to a common rule or standard because of sharing a common nature, and/or common conditions or circumstances. <Levels of achievement on an examination by individuals with comparable backgrounds as commensurable with one another.> (Ant: **incommensurable**.) Also: "commensurability" (n.), "commensurably" (adv.).

common (adj.): Shared by a number of individuals, as in the case of a *nature* $_{(2)}$.

common good: For the perennial tradition, a good of a whole rather than simply of a part; or a good of a *community*—e.g., a *family* or a *civic society*—rather than simply of a particular individual. The good in question is "common" both in the sense that, insofar as it is concretely achieved, it is equally enjoyed by all members of the community; and in the sense that its actual achievement requires that it be pursued or at least accepted as a goal by all (or the vast majority). <The common good of mutual support in a family. The common good of justice in a society's distribution of responsibilities and rewards.> (Note: This term applies in *analogous* ways to all forms of community. The Vatican II document *Gaudium et spes,* #26 et al., extended the treatment of "common good" to include, in principle, global society; accordingly, it discussed the conditions that are necessary for peoples of the world to enjoy authentic community and achieve authentic goods.)

common matter: Sensible feature shared by all instances of a specific kind of physical reality, as indicated in its definition (e.g., for animals, having living tissues)—by contrast with "individual" matter, which pertains to a singular thing (e.g., for this animal, having these particular tissues, with these particular characteristics, etc.). (In terms of perennial philosophy's account of *abstraction,* physical concepts abstract from individual or particular matter, while mathematical concepts [e.g., number or triangularity] abstract from common matter as well. See **degrees** or **orders of abstraction**.)

common sense: (1) (Latin *sensus communis;* sometimes also called the "central" or "unifying" sense.) An "internal" *sense* identified by Aristotle and taken over by Scholastics; a power of synthesis by means of which *sensible* $_{(1)}$ objects are constituted as wholes (types of plant or animal, for example) from the discrete data of the "external" senses. (2) Assemblage of widely shared opinions and modes of thought, sometimes including a comprehensive if vague picture of the world, along with a rudimentary *ontology.* <A common sense understanding of physical objects.> (3) For some members of the perennial tradition (e.g., Mortimer Adler), the deliverances of common human experience—a touchstone for philosophical reflection.

communicable (adj.): Able to be shared by more than one. (1) Metaphysically, where what is shared is an *essence* $_{(1)}$ or *transcendental* perfection. <Being as communicable to all reality.> (Contrast **individuating**.) (2) Logically, where what is shared is a concept or *intention* $_{(1)}$. <The concept of being as communicable to students of philosophy.> (In both senses, Ant: **incommunicable**.) Also: "communicability" (n.).

communicate (v.): To share, or to engage in *communication.*

communication (n.): (1) In metaphysics, the sharing of an essence or transcendental perfection with other existing beings. <God's communication of goodness to all beings.> (2) In logic and the philosophy of the human person, the sharing of a *judgment*—as well as, analogously, the undertaking of other forms of *cognitive* and *affective* interaction. <Difficulties in the communication of one's deepest longings.>

communion of persons (Latin *communio personarum*): A *community*—with the Latin phrase (which occurs in Vatican II's *Gaudium et spes,* #23) emphasizing that, in the fullest and deepest sense, a communal form of reality can be found only in a relationship among personal *subjects* $_{(2)}$.

communitarian (adj. or n.): Of or pertaining to, or a person who embraces, *communitarianism.* <Communitarian theories of the just distribution of goods.> (Ant: **libertarian**. Contrast as well **liberal** $_{(1)}$.)

communitarianism (n.): Theory in social and political philosophy holding that genuine goods of the community (or "common goods") in principle take precedence over—but at the same time contribute to—the good of individual members or citizens. (Much Catholic social teaching can be said to involve a form, or forms, of communitarianism.) (Ant: **libertarianism**. Contrast **individualism** (1). Also, since communitarianism holds that authentic goods of the whole are ordered to the good of the person, contrast **statism** and **totalitarianism**.)

community (n.): A natural or freely chosen group, defined by a *common good* or set of such goods. *Families* and *civil societies* are *natural* (3) communities (although subject in the concrete to certain types and degrees of *choice*); labor unions and universities are communities of *free* human devising (although having a basis in *nature* (3)). (Strictly speaking, a community is to be contrasted with a "partnership;" while the latter may involve certain common activities, each member pursues his or her private good, rather than a common good.) Also: "communal" (adj.), "communally" (adv.).

community, moral: As understood by certain recent ethical theorists (e.g., Mary Anne Warren and Michael Tooley), a community, membership in which is a *necessary and sufficient condition* for having full *moral status*. (Usually, such theorists hold that membership in this community requires a being to actually possess characteristics of *personhood* (2), such as self-awareness and the ability to communicate. Thus, for them—by contrast with thinkers of the perennial tradition—human embryos, fetuses, and newborns, as well as those who are permanently comatose or otherwise unable actually to exercise specifically human faculties, are not genuine members of the moral community.) (See the discussion under **person**.)

commutative justice: Type of *justice* (2) that regulates relations and exchanges between parties that are equal in relation to the proposed transaction—e.g., one citizen or institution and another (as in commercial transactions, or in determining compensation for individual damages); or one sovereign state and another (as in trade agreements among nations). Principles of commutative justice may be specified in concrete systems of *legal justice*.

compatibilism (n.): As understood in much recent philosophy, the view that—when both are properly understood—a belief in *freedom* (or *free choice*) is compatible with a belief in *determinism*$_{(1)}$, and indeed that both beliefs are true. Proponents of compatibilism have included the American psychologist and philosopher William James (1842–1910), who spoke correspondingly of "soft determinism." [Note: From the perspective of the school of St. Thomas, both compatibilism and its opposite miss a crucial point: namely, that freedom itself is a form of *causality*—although one that should be attributed to a personal whole, rather than to physical necessity or the interaction of constituent parts.] (Ant: **incompatibilism.**) Also: "compatibilist" (adj. or n.).

compatible (adj.): Able to go together, as said of sets of qualities or traits. (Ant: **incompatible.**) Also: "compatibility" (n.), "compatibly" (adv.).

complementarity (n.): (1) In philosophical and theological anthropology, the relationship between male and female persons such that, while sharing equally in human *nature*$_{(2)}$ and personal *dignity,* they also differ from, and are ordered to, one another in significant ways: ways that include biological, psychological, and social factors. (Medieval Scholastics, including St. Thomas Aquinas, did not adequately articulate the significance of this relationship; however, it has been a prominent theme of John Paul II, St. Edith Stein, and other Christian *personalists*—both male and female—who continue the perennial tradition.) (2) More generally, any type of dual, ordered relationship—e.g., between *matter* and *form, essence* and *existence,* or *philosophy* and *theology.*

complementary (adj.): Of or related to *complementarity,* in either the specifically anthropological or the more general sense.

complete (adj.): Full; integral; whole and entire. <A complete human act (i.e., one that is a product of genuine deliberation and choice).>

complete or **perfect society**: A *community* that enjoys within itself all things necessary for its fulfillment, both corporately and in its individual members. (In Catholic theological tradition, the Church, with Christ as its head, is said to be such a society. Among natural societies, it is doubtful—and perhaps increasingly doubtful, given economic *globalization*—that any individual civil society can qualify as "complete" in this sense.)

complete return (Latin *reditio completa*): Act by which the *intellect* is able to reflect upon itself, and thus to become "aware of its awareness." As far as is known, among natural beings this act and this ability are *properties* (2) of human persons.

components of a right: See **rights, structure of.**

composite (adj. or n.): Composed of parts or principles (e.g., *matter* (3) and substantial *form*), or an individual thing that is so composed. <Philosophically considered, a physical substance as a composite.>

composition and division: See **judgment** (1).

comprehensive good: See the discussion under **good** (n.).

compulsion (n.): (1) State in which one is forced or coerced to act by another. (2) An internal psychic tendency that has the effect of force or coercion. (In either sense, compulsion diminishes and can even eliminate personal *responsibility* (2) for an act.) <A sexual compulsion; a compulsion to lie.> Also: "compulsive" (adj.), "compulsively" (adv.).

concept (n.): Philosophically, a product of activity by *agent intellect* (i.e., a *species* (2)) by means of which a human person is able to know, at least to some extent, a *nature* or *essence*. Since, for purposes of communication, a concept is expressed by a *term* (1), it also is called a "mental word" (Latin *verbum mentis*). [Note: In everyday language, and even in modern empirical psychology, the term "concept" often is used more loosely: namely, as signifying in effect a retained image or set of images, or an ability to respond to verbal commands—rather than a result of intellectual activity, properly speaking. This fact can lead to confusion in comparing works of perennial philosophy with those of modern scientific research. Moreover, it has implications for the consideration of whether animals other than human beings can form concepts.] (See **abstraction** and **apprehension** or **intellection** (**simple**), as well as **intelligible** and **idea**.) Also: "conceptual" (adj.).

conceptualism (n.): According to some philosophical typologies, a view about knowledge and reality that is midway between *realism* (1) as developed by Plato, and *nominalism* as held by William of Ockham and others, including many thinkers today. (The Thomist tradition can be regarded as holding a form of conceptualism in this sense, although some prefer the term "moderate realism"; that is, it maintains that *essences,* as universals, exist only in the mind as concepts, but that they nevertheless have a real basis in the shared features of individual existing things). (See **universals, problem of.**) Also: "conceptualist" (adj. or n.).

conclusion (n.): In formal logic, a statement claimed to be true because it follows necessarily from others (called *premises*), which themselves are true. (See **validity** and **soundness.**) Less formally, a statement taken to be true on whatever relevant grounds.

concrete (adj.): Existing either as an ontological *subject* $_{(3)}$ or in such a subject (i.e., as one of its *accidents*). <This concrete rose; its concrete redness.> (Ant: **abstract.**) Also: "concretely" (adv.), "concretize" (v.).

concupiscence (n.): In the philosophical psychology of the traditional schools, a basic mode of *sensory appetite*—one that inclines us toward objects promising pleasure and away from objects threatening pain. This general affective drive is said to give rise to the *concupiscible* passions, that is, *sensory desires* and *aversions* including, but not limited to, the sexual. (Contrary to what is sometimes supposed, "concupiscence" in this technical sense is a morally neutral term—i.e., it does not in itself carry any negative connotations. For Christian tradition, however, the actual state of human concupiscence is significantly compromised by *sin.*)

concupiscible (adj.): Of or related to the *passions* of sense appetite arising from *concupiscence.* (Contrast **irascible.**)

condition (n.): (1) A thing's *state* $_{(1)}$, by contrast with its *nature* $_{(2)}$. (2) As sometimes spoken of within perennial philosophy, a *cause* or a *real* factor in a thing's being or coming-to-be, either absolutely or in relation to a particular characteristic. <Necessary conditions for a just war.> (3) In the *empiriological* sciences, an event or circumstance regularly associated with another, whether or not real *causality* is attributed or has been established. <Economic conditions associated with student achievement.> Also: "conditional" (adj.), "conditionally" (adv.).

conditional (n.): In logic, a compound statement of the form "If *p*, then *q*"—with *p* called the "antecedent" and *q* called the "consequent."

conflict of rights and duties: Type of situation arising in concrete moral decision-making when rights and duties—as considered in the abstract—appear to conflict with one another. (From the standpoint of perennial ethics, in the concrete any such conflict in principle can be resolved, since whichever is the stronger right or duty in the situation prevails, and the other simply ceases to be a genuine right or duty. However, judgments about which right or duty in fact is the stronger can be difficult. Certain writers—e.g., Austin Fagothey, S.J.—have developed guidelines for such cases related to the four components of a right [see **rights, structure of**].)

conjugal (adj.): See **marital** (sometimes **conjugal**).

connaturality (n.): Mutual suitability of a *power* or *appetite* and its natural *end* or *good.* (The phrase "knowledge by connaturality" was used by Jacques Maritain to refer to ways in which the exercise of specifically human modes of *affectivity*—e.g., love and a desire for truth—enables the practical intellect to penetrate questions of *value* more deeply and with greater certainty than it can by discursive reasoning.) Also: "connatural" (adj.), "connaturally" (adv.).

connotation (n.): Meaning as *sense* or *intension.* (Ant: **denotation**.)

conscience (n.): The power and the activity of *judging* what concretely to do, or avoid doing, through reflection on a concrete situation in light of relevant *moral precepts.* (See **certain conscience**, **doubtful conscience**, and **perplexed conscience**.) [Note: According to some philosophers, as well as much popular opinion, the term "conscience" also applies to the selection of *precepts* or *norms* themselves. However, for the perennial tradition, the apprehension of moral precepts is a matter of practical *knowledge* (2). Such norms—at least in the case of *primary precepts of natural* (*moral*) *law*—hold objectively for all human persons, and in principle they are equally knowable by all. (See **synderesis.**)] Also: "conscientious" (adj.), "conscientiously" (adv.).

conscience formation: The process by which one develops the ability to judge well in concrete moral matters. This process involves acquiring *integral virtue,* as well as practical *knowledge* (2) of relevant precepts and norms.

conscious (adj.): Of or pertaining to a living being, or a psychic state, that manifests *consciousness.* (Sometimes, although rarely today, this term also is used as a noun—i.e., as short for "consciousness.") (Ant: **nonconscious**. Contrast as well **preconscious** or **precognitive**, **unconscious**, and **subconscious**.) Also: "consciously" (adv.).

consciousness (n.): Psychic state of explicit awareness, by contrast with nonconscious or subconscious levels of appetite or experience. (This term is sometimes confused with "conscience," but the meanings of the two are distinct: the latter term refers to, or includes, *moral* (1) consciousness.) [Note: Although Edmund Husserl and his close followers took consciousness to be the basic and irreducible starting point of philosophical reflection, philosophers of the perennial tradition (including those influenced by *phenomenology,* such as Karol Wojtyla) offer an account of it as a *natural* (2) property of specifically *cognitive* beings in a developed state of actuality—i.e., beings that can perform operations of sense and/or intellectual knowledge, as well as related operations of affectivity.] (Regarding specifically *personal* consciousness, see **ego** (1) and **self**.)

consent (n.): Personal affirmation or agreement, especially with regard to undertaking moral responsibilities, or acting and/or being acted upon in certain ways. <Patient consent to a medical procedure.> (See **voluntary**.) Also: "consent" (as a v.), "consensual" (adj.), "consensually" (adv.).

consequence (n.): A result, especially a foreseeable result, of a human act. (For normative ethics in the perennial tradition, consequences, both positive and negative, typically fall under the heading of *circumstances*—one of the three *determinants* or *sources of morality.*) Also: "consequential" (adj.).

consequent (adj. or n.): See **conditional**. (Ant: **antecedent**.)

consequentialism (n.): In the history of ethics, any of a family of *normative* theories holding that the *moral* (1) quality of human acts is wholly determined by their good and bad *consequences.* (Often such theories are classified as *teleological* (3) approaches to ethics, by contrast with *deontological* approaches.) (Compare **utilitarianism**, as well as **proportionalism**.) Also: "consequentialist" (adj. or n.).

conservation (n.): (1) (Sometimes capitalized.) In philosophical theology, the act by which God maintains all *finite* and *dependent* beings in existence (thus sometimes contrasted, in terms of human concepts of God, with *creation* (1)). (2) In applied ethics, a society's effort to preserve and/or renew physical resources, with a view to serving the *common good* across generations. Also, in relation to sense (2): "conservationism" (n.), "conservationist" (adj. or n.).

conservatism (n.): In social and political (and sometimes religious) thought, the view that an organized community is well served by maintaining its traditions of belief and practice, and that novel ideas and proposals—especially insofar as they appear to be promoted primarily because of their novelty—are to be regarded with caution. (Ant: **liberalism** $_{(2)}$ and **progressivism** $_{(2)}$.) Also: "conservative" (adj. or n.), "conservatively" (adv.).

consistent (adj.): As said of a set of propositions or beliefs, able to be affirmed or to be true at the same time. (Ant: **inconsistent**.) Also: "consistency" (n.), "consistently" (adv.).

constitution (n.): Within a society, especially one claiming at least relative sovereignty, a founding document that specifies principles of governance, the rights and duties of members, etc. (As Aristotle notes in the *Politics,* a constitution gives *form* to political life.)

constitutive (adj.): Forming part of the *essence* or *substance* of a thing. <Soul and matter (i.e., *matter* $_{(3)}$) as constitutive principles of a living being.> Also: "constitutively" (adv.).

construct (n.): As understood by contemporary philosophical methodologists, a term, image, or diagram, etc., that is developed as an aid to understanding—usually with the implication that it is not to be taken strictly as expressing a formal *object* $_{(2)}$ of knowledge. <The Freudian notions of "id," "ego," and "superego" as psychological constructs.>

consubstantial (adj.): One in being or one in substance. (See the discussion under ***homoousios***.) Also: "consubstantiality" (n.), "consubstantially" (adv.).

consumerism (n.): (1) A tendency of *capitalist* economic systems, according to which—for the sake of the expansion of the system itself—consumers come to be conditioned to purchase more and more goods, whether or not these meet *objective* $_{(1)}$ human needs. (2) The generalized attitude of members of a society who in fact are conditioned in this way. Also: "consumerist" (adj.).

contemplation (n.): The ultimate goal of the human desire to know—a pure activity of understanding, without any extrinsic end or purpose. (As a philosophically available goal for humans, *natural* contemplation—by contrast with *theological* and *mystical* contemplation—takes as its focus *being* $_{(2)}$ in its analogical amplitude, with each finite reality *participating* proportionately in this perfection, which belongs first and properly to Subsistent Being Itself [Latin *Ipsum Esse Subsistens*], that is, to God.) (Compare **wisdom**.) Also: "contemplative" (adj. or n.).

contingency (n.): (1) Regarding a being, its state of possibly but not necessarily existing, and thus its depending for actual *existence* $_{(2)}$ on causes. (2) Regarding a proposition, its state of being possibly *true,* or true under certain conditions, but not necessarily true. (3) Regarding a feature or characteristic of a thing, its state of being *accidentally* rather than *essentially* related to the nature of the thing in question. (Ant: **necessity**.)

contingent (adj.). Of or pertaining to *contingency,* in any of the senses indicated. Also: "contingently" (adv.).

continuum (n.): In the category of *quantity,* a whole whose parts are adjacent to one another, with their limits coinciding; such a whole is, in potentiality, infinitely divisible. <A surface as a type of continuum.> Also: "continuous" (adj.), "continuously" (adv.).

contraception (n.): In what otherwise is a *normal* $_{(2)}$ use of the human sexual function—i.e., in the ideal case, an instance of *marital* or *conjugal* intercourse—an intervention which alters either the practice itself (e.g., through the use of condoms) or the physiology of one of the partners (e.g., through the use of anovulant pills or through surgical sterilization) so as to prevent the possibility of conception. (See the discussion under **birth regulation** or **control**.) Also: "contraceptive" (adj. or n.), "contraceptively" (adv.).

contract (n.): An agreement freely made that binds two or more *persons* to an exchange of rights or goods. In light of genuine interests of the larger society, certain types of contract (e.g., marriage) often are governed by *civil law.* (See as well **social contract**.) Also: "contractual" (adj.), "contractually" (adv.).

contradiction (n.): Complex proposition that cannot be true because its constituent propositions are incompatible with one another. <A contradiction of the form "*p* and not-*p*."> Also, a state in which two incompatible propositions are affirmed.

contradictoriness (n.): Relation between two *propositions* such that if one of them is true, the other is false; and vice-versa. For example, "This rose is red" and "This rose is not red."

contradictory (adj.): Of or pertaining to propositions that display *contradictoriness.* (In the case of propositions of the form "S is P" and "S is not-P," the word "contradictory," along with its plural form, "contradictories," is also used substantively of the terms in question—e.g., in the above case, "red" and "not red.")

contrariety or **contrariness** (n.): Relation between two *propositions* such that at most one of them can be true. For example, "This rose is red" and "This rose is white."

contrary (adj.): Of or pertaining to two propositions that display *contrariety.* (The word "contrary," along with its plural form, "contraries," also is used substantively of the terms in question—e.g., in the above case, "red" and "white.")

convention (n.): Human decision or agreement determining concrete matters—e.g., specific types of punishment within a system of criminal justice, or specific societal regulations regarding marriage—by contrast with what is taken to be inherent in the very *nature* $_{(2)}$ and *end* $_{(1)}$ of the realities in question. Also: "conventional" (adj.), "conventionally" (adv.).

conventionalism (n.): The philosophical position that morality is reducible to the merely conventional or customary, as found, for example, in a particular society, culture, or subculture. (Compare **relativism.**)

conversion to phantasms (Latin *conversio ad phantasmata*): According to Thomist epistemology, the means by which the intellect arrives at judgments about particulars—i.e., via the "conversion" (or the "re-relating") of universal concepts to sense images and data of experience.

cooperation (n.): The joint human pursuit of *ends* $_{(2)}$, either in a "partnership" (where the ends are goods of the individuals as such), or in a *community* (where the ends are *common goods*). Also: "cooperative" (adj.), "cooperatively (adv.).

cooperation in evil, principles governing: Principles used in judging whether one can rightly do something that furthers another's undertaking of moral *evil.* (Although a matter of general philosophical interest, this topic has been discussed most fully by Catholic moral theologians. A distinction is made between "formal" and "material" cooperation, and, within the latter category, between "immediate" and "mediate" cooperation. Formal cooperation in evil involves embracing the other's bad moral *object* $_{(3)}$—e.g., directly and willingly assisting in the performance of an abortion. Material cooperation involves facilitating the other's act in some concrete way, without sharing the moral object or the *intention* $_{(2)}$, and, in the case of mediate cooperation, without being a *proximate* factor in the act. For example, if a hospital rents space to abortion providers it would be engaging in immediate material cooperation; but if a hospital participates financially in a large, diverse system of health care providers, other members of which practice abortion, it would be engaging in mediate material cooperation. The traditional Catholic position allows only mediate, material cooperation in moral evil.)

co-principles (n.): Two *principles* that are always found together in the constitution of real beings—e.g., *matter/form* (throughout the realm of natural being), and *potentiality/actuality* (throughout the realm of finite being).

correspondence theory of truth: Account of truth—standard in the perennial tradition and shared by other *realist* approaches to knowledge—according to which it is achieved in acts of *judgment*, in particular, ones in which the intellect conforms to how things are in actual existence. Questions arise for correspondence theorists concerning the representational character of judgments (or the propositions that express them) and concerning the precise meaning of conformity. (Contrast **coherence theory of truth**, as well as **pragmatism**. See **direct realism**.)

corruption (n.): (1) Dissolution, disintegration, or going out of being—one of the two types of *substantial change* in beings of nature. (Ant: **generation** $_{(1)}$.) (2) (Metaphorical use.) Dissolution of *virtue* (or the very possibility of virtue) that comes from the practice of moral evil.

cosmogony (n., from Greek *kosmos* + *gonos*, for "offspring"): Theory of the origin and development of the *cosmos*. Also: "cosmogenic" (adj.).

cosmological (adj.): (1) Pertaining to *cosmology*. (2) In *philosophical theology*, pertaining to types of argument for the existence of God (e.g., the first three of Aquinas's *Five Ways*) that are rooted in considerations of the physical universe as such.

cosmology (n., from Greek *kosmos* + *logos*, for "account"): Study of the physical universe as an ordered whole: philosophically, through the methods of the natural sciences, or both.

cosmos (n., Greek *kosmos*): All of physical reality, or the universe, considered as an ordered whole.

country (n.): See **nation** or **country**.

courage (n.): (1) An *irascible* passion or emotion—sometimes called "natural" courage to distinguish it from the moral virtue of the same name. (See sense (2), below). Courage in this sense can arise with the awareness of threatened evils or threatened losses of goods; when it does arise, it enables a person or an animal to confront a difficult situation with a degree of steadiness. (Ant: **fear**.) (2) The moral virtue also known as *fortitude*. (Ant: **cowardice**.) Also: "courageous" (adj.), "courageously" (adv.).

cowardice (n.): State of deficiency in the ability to confront difficult situations. (See the discussion under **fortitude**.) Also: "coward" (n.), "cowardly" (adj.).

create (v.): (1) (Strictly and philosophically.) To bring into existence from nothingness. <God as creating finite reality.> (2) (Metaphorically and in common usage.) To serve as an *efficient* or agent cause of the coming to be of a new reality from pre-existing materials. <Technicians creating a human embryo in a petri dish via in vitro fertilization.> Also: "creative" (adj.), "creator" (n.).

creation (n.): (1) (Strictly and philosophically, and sometimes written with a capital "C.") God's act of giving existence to all finite being. ("Creation" in this sense often is taken to signify a *temporal* beginning of natural being, perhaps identifiable with the "Big Bang" postulated by modern scientific *cosmology*. For the school of Aquinas, such a notion can only be accepted as a matter of faith, since neither scientific nor philosophical reason can establish whether there was an *absolute* temporal beginning of created being. Moreover—and contrary to some recent accounts—the philosophical concept of creation does not have any implications, positive or negative, for the evaluation of *scientific* (2) theories regarding the evolution of species; nor do such theories, properly formulated and understood, affect the correctness of this philosophical concept.) (2) (Metaphorically and in common usage.) The bringing about of a new being, or new type of being, through the application of art or technology. <The creation of a new, more powerful microchip.>

creationism (n.): (1) A position that rejects, or at least questions, the general biological theory of the *evolution* of species and argues that the best *positive* account of the history of the world involves an appeal to an intelligent Creator. (This view is not to be confused with the specifically *philosophical* position outlined in the preceding entry and argued for in, e.g., the third and fifth of Aquinas's *Five Ways*. Moreover, it seems doubtful whether creationism, as here described, can be regarded as a genuinely *scientific* (2) theory, since it is unclear how it generates *hypotheses* that can be confirmed or disconfirmed.) (Compare **intelligent design theory**. See as well **teleology** (2).) (2) The position—argued for by Thomist philosophers and proposed for belief by the ordinary Catholic *magisterium*—that the rational *soul* of each human being, since it is *immaterial* in nature yet ordered to the individual and personal whole, is directly created by God and received at the moment the human being begins to exist in bodily nature. Also: "creationist" (adj. or n.).

creative fidelity: Term introduced in the writings of 20th-century Christian existentialist Gabriel Marcel and expressive of the various ways in which persons (or, in Marcel's language, "personal presences") can be faithful to one another, whatever the concrete conditions or circumstances.

criminal justice: That aspect of *legal justice* having to do with violations of positive law, as well as the ascertainment and punishment of such violations.

criteriology (n., from Greek *kriterion* + *logos*, for "account"): As used especially by European contributors to the perennial tradition, a synonym for *epistemology*—or for that part of epistemology that studies and formulates rules ("criteria") for making justified *judgments*. Also: "criteriological" (adj.), "criteriologist" (n.).

criterion (n., Greek *kriterion;* the plural form, which follows the Greek, is "criteria"): A rule or principle governing a type of *judgment*—and thus appealed to in justifying such a judgment—whether factual, mathematical, value-related, or of some other sort. <The need for appropriate criteria in assessing the suitability of candidates.>

critical realism: The *epistemological* position according to which the human senses and intellect are powers making *objective*$_{(1)}$ contact with reality, and (in the case of intellect) capable of *understanding*$_{(2)}$ that reality—albeit progressively, self-correctingly, and, in the end, incompletely. (The school of Aquinas, as represented in the 20th century by Etienne Gilson, Jacques Maritain, and others, has developed one significant form of this position.) (Compare **realism**$_{(2)}$ and **direct realism**.)

critical turn (also sometimes called "turn to the subject"): Feature of modern thought, begun by Descartes and renewed by Kant, which focuses philosophical attention on the *subject*$_{(2)}$ and his or her possibilities and limitations as a knower—rather than, as had been the case in prior eras, on reality itself (often taken by "critical" thinkers to have been naively understood).

culpability (n.): Liability for a moral evil, or the state in which there is evil done through one's fault (Latin *culpa*); thus blameworthiness—by contrast with cases in which an objective evil is undertaken in ignorance or under *compulsion* (external or internal), and thus is *involuntary* $_{(1)}$, and cases in which one's participation in an evil act does not rise to the level of either "formal" or "immediate material" *cooperation*. (Ant: **inculpability**. Contrast as well **innocence**.) Also: "culpable" (adj.), "culpably" (adv.).

cultural relativism: See the discussion under **ethical relativism**.

culture (n.): The set of institutions, traditions, and customs, along with intellectual orientations and practical attitudes, that characterize and shape a nation, people, or subgroup. (From the standpoint of the perennial tradition, relations between culture and *philosophy* are complex. On one hand, any particular expression of philosophy arises in the context of some culture; on the other hand, philosophy, through its application of critical reason, can and should positively influence the development of culture.) Also: "cultural" (adj.), "culturally" (adv.).

culture of death/culture of life: Contrasting expressions made prominent by John Paul II's encyclical *Evangelium vitae* (1995), where "culture" in each case refers primarily to a network of pervasive societal attitudes and practices. As noted by John Paul II, the most prominent and most certain morally unacceptable elements of the "culture of death" (because they relate to *intrinsic* evils) are the widespread acceptance of abortion and, more recently, of euthanasia and assisted suicide, as well as the destruction of human embryos for purposes of research on stem cells. (A number of Christian philosophers and theologians hold that other practices—e.g., capital punishment and warfare—deserve to be grouped with these. These thinkers argue that even if the practices in question can be justified in certain circumstances, an overall respect for the *sanctity* of human life demands that, if at all possible, nonlethal solutions be sought for even the gravest problems of social order.)

custom: Socially maintained and sanctioned practice that is not codified in civil law. (For Aquinas, however, custom is part of *human law*, broadly interpreted.)

Dasein (German n.): See the discussion under **existentialism.**

data of sense, also **sense** or **sensory data**: The individual deliverances of the "external" senses (colors, sounds, tactile impressions, etc.). According to the Aristotelian philosophical tradition, in principle and absent a specific reason for a contrary judgment (e.g., diseased sense organs), such data, as objects of awareness, are to be regarded as identical in *form* with real features of the object sensed while having an *intentional* $_{(1)}$, rather than *entitative* $_{(1)}$, mode of existence. (See **direct realism** and **species** $_{(2)}$.)

death (n.): Cessation of *life*. For perennial philosophy of nature and philosophical anthropology, the point at which a *substantial change* occurs; that is, the point at which a being's substantial form (in the case of a living being, its *soul*) no longer animates that being as a vital and organized physical whole.

death, determination of: The ascertainment, through the application of accepted physiological standards and concrete tests, that a living organism (in particular, a human being) has died. Such a determination has implications for a range of issues in *applied ethics* and *positive law*—e.g., the transfer of property and, in certain cases, judgments of homicide. Regarding general physiological standards, a consensus has emerged in the United States—and has been enshrined in respective state laws—that a human being has died if either or both of the following occur: a) there is an irreversible cessation of all cardiovascular function; b) there is an irreversible cessation of all brain function, including that of the brain stem. (The term "function" here refers to activity of organs and organ systems, not to residual activity that for a time may continue in individual cells after the organism as a whole has died.) Concrete tests related to the above standards are subject to change and development in light of progress in the biomedical sciences.

death penalty: The state-administered killing of capital offenders as a punishment determined through judicial proceeding. Among states that retain the practice (also called "capital punishment"), this constitutes the ultimate *sanction* within their systems of *criminal justice.* (See discussions under **culture of death/culture of life** and **punishment**.)

debt (n., Latin *debitum*): What is due; in ethics, and especially in traditional moral theology, a synonym for *duty* or *obligation.* (In common English usage, the word "debt" is usually restricted to financial obligations; however, in the technical ethical sense it has been applied across the range of human interaction. Thus, in the past theologians spoke of *conjugal* intercourse as the "marital debt" between husband and wife.)

decide (v.): To make a *choice* between two or more alternatives.

decision (n.): See **choice**.

deconstructionism (n.): A contemporary intellectual movement, represented by the French philosopher Jacques Derrida and other proponents of *postmodernism,* which seeks to clarify (and sometimes to show the incoherence of) various arguments and positions in light of meanings and/or assumptions implicit in the positions themselves; the arguments and positions in question are said thereby to be "deconstructed." [Although its explicit targets usually are modern *rationalist* views, deconstructionism challenges the perennial tradition as well, since it argues against the idea of a language or form of thought that can express *definitions* $_{(2)}$—i.e., ones that accord with the very nature of things and our knowledge of them. Similarly, while the perennial tradition can learn from the techniques of deconstruction, it cannot embrace what is typically the movement's fundamental perspective.] Also: "deconstruction" (n.), "deconstructionist" (adj. or n.).

deduce (v.): To reach a conclusion by way of *deduction.*

deduction (n.): Mode of *reasoning* or *argument* according to which, certain propositions (the *premises*) having been stated, a *conclusion* is said to follow of logical necessity. If such an argument is correct in its essential features (i.e., if it has true premises and valid reasoning), it is said to be *sound* and the conclusion is thereby known to be true. (Contrast **induction**.) Also: "deductive" (adj.), "deductively" (adv.).

de facto (Latin phrase): In fact, or as a matter of fact, by contrast with being formally established by law or principle. <The *de facto* status of political liberty within a particular society.> (Contrast ***de jure***.)

definition (n.): (1) An expression of the *meaning* $_{(1)}$ or the *sense* of a word—sometimes called a "verbal" or "nominal" (from the Latin *nomen,* for "name") definition. (Recent philosophers of language have come to identify various types of definition of this sort. For example, "ostensive definition," which expresses the meaning by directly showing the type of thing to which a term refers [e.g., "red"]; "recursive definition," which gives a rule for identifying the range of a term [e.g., "ancestor"]; and "stipulative definition," which gives a particular meaning to a term for the purposes of disciplined study or discussion [e.g., "line" in geometry].) (2) An expression of the *essence* of the type of reality to which a word refers—sometimes called a "real" definition. (Ideally, for Aristotelian *science* $_{(1)}$, such definitions are to be given in terms of the proximate *genus* $_{(1)}$ and "specific difference" within that genus. While real definitions continue to be highly prized by the perennial tradition, they have proved exceedingly difficult to attain in the natural order; and they do not ordinarily form a goal of the modern *sciences* $_{(2)}$, whose methods encourage the study of nature in other ways. Moreover, within philosophy many key terms are *analogical;* thus the corresponding realities can be expressed only in terms of analogous sets representing specific types of *attribution* or *proportionality.*) (3) An account of a sensible nature via *necessary and sufficient conditions,* whereby its presence can be determined by methods appropriate to a particular *empiriological* discipline.

degrees or **orders of abstraction**: A threefold scheme for distinguishing and classifying types of *concepts* (and the types of *intelligibilities* they mediate, and accordingly the types of disciplines concerned with them) in terms of the intensiveness of their "formal" *abstraction* $_{(3)}$, or the degree of their "remotion from matter"—i.e., in terms of the extent to which their definitions do not include conditions of materiality. Thus: a) Natural science in the broadest sense (both empirical and philosophical) abstracts from, or does not include, "individual" sensible matter—i.e., it focuses on physical kinds or natures, rather than on peculiar features of the individuals that share them. b) Mathematics ignores even "common" sensible matter—i.e., it focuses on quantitative elements and relations as such, rather than on physical realities of which quantity is a feature. c) Lastly, metaphysics abstracts from or ignores all matter (even the purely "intelligible" matter of mathematics)—i.e., it focuses on being just as being, or *being* $_{(3)}$ in its proportionate character, as well as being's principles and properties. (Note: Some Thomistic writers—e.g., Yves R. Simon—distinguish "degrees" from "orders" of abstraction, especially in relation to category a). That is, they say the empirical sciences of nature and natural philosophy share the first "order" of abstraction, with natural philosophy having a higher or more intensive "degree" of abstraction within that order.)

deism (n.): In philosophical theology and related intellectual endeavors, a view that accepts a Creator, but denies that this Creator (or God, Latin *Deus*) is present to or active in the world, or is in any way provident over the lives of human persons. <Certain founders of the American republic (e.g., Thomas Jefferson) as adherents of deism.> Also: "deist" (adj. or n.).

de jure (Latin phrase): As a matter of principle, or in light of the application of some form of *law*. <*De jure,* all persons within a society should have some voice in matters of governance.> (Contrast ***de facto***.)

deliberate (adj.): Pertaining to a *choice* or a *human act* that is the result of *deliberation*. <The deliberate taking of innocent life.>

deliberate (v.): To undertake a process of *deliberation*. Also: "deliberately" (adv.), "deliberative" (adj.).

deliberation (n.): Activity of *practical* reason or intellect directed toward choosing a *means* to a desired and intended *end* $_{(2)}$. <Congress's deliberation over revisions in federal tax policy.>

delight (n.): In traditional philosophical psychology, a movement of *concupiscible* appetite arising in the presence of an object of sensory desire. By extension, the term also applies to positive movements of affectivity in the context of *rational* or *spiritual* goods—e.g., the delight that accompanies knowledge that one has acted virtuously in a difficult situation. (Syn: **joy**. Contrast **sorrow**.) Also: "delightful" (adj.).

democracy (n.): Form of government or civil *polity* according to which the people play a direct role in the selection of leaders and, either directly or through the latter, in the formulation of law and public policy. Democracies are sometimes divided into "pure" and "representative" types. In the former, all issues are decided by immediate vote of the whole people. In the latter, most issues are decided by a group of leaders and representatives elected by the people for this purpose. Contrasted with these are forms of polity such as kingship, in which there is a single, sovereign ruler; and oligarchy, in which a small, nonelected group of people make law and policy for all. (Note: Although St. Thomas Aquinas, writing in the 13th century, favored a polity of enlightened kingship, and Catholic hierarchy in the past often did so as well, such a tendency in no way is an essential feature of the perennial tradition. Recent Thomist philosophers such as Jacques Maritain and Yves R. Simon, as well as theologians such as John Courtney Murray, S.J., have developed powerful accounts of the foundations of democracy that are entirely in keeping with, and indeed that flow from, ideas central to Aquinas's thought.) Also: "democrat" (adj. or n.), "democratic" (adj.), "democratically" (adv.).

demonstrate (v.): For the Aristotelian tradition, to prove a proposition by *sound* deductive reasoning on the basis of premises known by the person(s) in question to be true.

demonstration (n., Latin *demonstratio*): For philosophy—and, according to the Aristotelian ideal, for all strict science—*sound* deductive reasoning that brings to light either a) the existence of or a feature of a reality, but without specifying its *reason* $_{(2)}$ or *cause;* or b) the reason or cause of the reality, in addition to the fact itself. (According to their Latin designations, demonstrations of the former sort are said to be *quia;* demonstrations of the latter sort are said to be *propter quid*. Aquinas's *Five Ways* of establishing the existence of God are presented as demonstrations *quia*.) (Compare **proof** $_{(1)}$. Contrast **dialectical** $_{(3)}$ arguments.) Also: "demonstrative" (adj.), "demonstratively" (adv.).

denial or **negation** (n.): See the discussion under **judgment** $_{(1)}$. (Ant: **affirmation**.)

denotation (n.) Meaning as *reference* or *extension*. (Contrast **connotation**.)

deny or **negate** (v.): To *judge* that something is not the case. (Ant: **affirm**.)

deontological (adj.): Of or pertaining to *deontology*. Also: "deontologically" (adv.).

deontology (n., from Greek *deon*, for "duty"): In *normative* ethics, a theory, or family of theories, that emphasize the following of moral rules and/or respect for moral duty. A primary historical instance of such a theory involves Immanuel Kant's idea of the "categorical imperative" (see the discussion under **Kantian**). (Contrast **antinomianism** and **teleology** $_{(3)}$.) Also: "deontologist" (n.).

dependence or **dependency** (n.): Condition of not being self-sufficient with regard to a particular act or property, but rather needing another (or others) to provide or secure that act or property. (Compare **contingency** $_{(1)}$.) Also: "dependent" (adj.), "dependently" (adv.).

depersonalization (n.): A diminishment or loss of personal *dignity* and/or personal integration through degrading practices and conditions. <Slavery, prostitution, and forced (or virtually forced) labor in subhuman working conditions as leading to depersonalization.> (See **alienation** $_{(2)}$.)

depersonalize (v.): As said of human *agents*, and of practices and conditions either fostered or allowed to exist by human agents, to degrade or bring about a loss of personal *dignity* and/or personal integration in another human being or group.

descriptive (adj.): Type of judgment or statement expressing how things are (often in direct empirical language), by contrast with ones that are *normative* or *prescriptive*. (Contrast as well "evaluative;" see **evaluate**.)

desirable (adj.): (1) Pertaining to what can be desired, as a matter of fact. (2) Pertaining to what ought to be or is worthy of being desired, in light of a being's final *end* $_{(1)}$ or *good*. [Note: In his articulation of *utilitarianism*, John Stuart Mill offered a proof of his "greatest happiness principle" which—in the opinion of Thomists as well as other critics—trades on the ambiguity between these two senses. Mill claimed that, just as the proof of a thing's being visible is that people actually see it, the proof of a thing's being desirable is that people actually desire it.] Also: "desirability" (n.).

desire (n.): (1) In traditional philosophical psychology, a movement of *concupiscible* appetite, responding to a sensible good (an object offering pleasure) that is not presently enjoyed by the subject. (2) More generally, any movement of *affectivity,* sensory or intellectual, toward an object perceived or judged to be good. (In both senses, contrast **aversion**. In sense (2), also contrast **hate** [as a n.].)

desire (v.): (1) To respond positively to and seek a measure of fulfillment via an object offering some sensible good or pleasure. (2) More generally, to experience a positive movement of *affectivity,* whether conscious or unconscious, and whether at the sensory or the intellectual level. (Syn: **love** $_{(1)}$. Ant: **hate** [as a v.].)

despair (n.): (1) In traditional philosophical psychology, an *irascible* passion arising from the awareness of goods that are deemed impossible to attain, or harms that are deemed impossible to avoid. (Compare **fear**, which may arise in the context of goods that seem difficult to attain, or harms that seem difficult to avoid.) (2) As discussed by certain existentialist philosophers, a generalized attitude according to which nothing good, but instead only evil, is to be anticipated (see the discussion of "affective key" under **emotion**). (3) In Christian theology, a state in which one is unable or unwilling to accept God's promise of ultimate fulfillment—sometimes referred to as the "sin against the Holy Spirit." (Contrast **hope** [as a n.].)

despair (v.): To experience or engage in *despair,* in any of the senses indicated above. (Contrast **hope** [as a v.].)

destiny, human: Final state of human beings, as individuals and/or as a totality. The question of our destiny has been a principal object of philosophical speculation throughout the ages and across world cultures. (For Aquinas, some answers to the question of human destiny—e.g., certain implications of the soul's spiritual nature—can be given at the *natural* $_{(4)}$ level, and by philosophical *reason;* however, he held along with the Christian tradition more generally that a full articulation of this matter—expressed in terms of sharing in the life of the Triune God—requires religious *faith* $_{(4)}$ and the embracing of *supernatural* mysteries.) (See **beatitude**. Compare **meaning of life**.)

determinants or **sources** (Latin *fontes*) **of morality**: Features of a *human act* that are sources of its *goodness* $_{(3)}$ or *badness,* and thus are factors that must be considered in its moral evaluation. These factors are traditionally listed as three: a) the act's moral *object* $_{(3)}$—i.e., what the act accomplishes by its very *nature* or *species* (rationally described and evaluated in terms of its promoting or detracting from integral human good); b) the agent's subjective *end* (2), or *motive* or purpose; and c) relevant *circumstances*—e.g., concrete existential relations among the persons involved, as well as certain of the act's conditions and consequences. (For the perennial philosophical and theological traditions, feature a) is logically independent of features b) and c). That is, one can and should ask whether an act, just insofar as it has a certain object or involves a certain choice, can be a morally appropriate *means* of achieving an end—e.g., whether the act violates any relevant and operative moral precept. Because of this, an agent's subjective motive or purpose might be laudable and yet the act as a whole morally bad. As the point is often expressed in common language, "The end—i.e., the agent's motive or purpose—does not justify the means.") Considerations of b) and c) complement that of a), bringing to light other elements of goodness or badness involved in the act. In general, all three elements must be acceptable—or at least not unacceptable—for the act as a whole to be morally good. (See also the discussion at **intention**.)

determinism (n.): (1) (Also "determinacy.") A postulate of much modern (but pre-20th-century) physics, according to which in principle all events can be precisely predicted in terms of space, time, and motion. (Such a postulate appears to be incompatible with contemporary quantum theory.) (Ant: **indeterminism** (1).) (2) The philosophical position—opposed by the perennial tradition—according to which all beings, properties of beings, and events in the world are subject to natural causal necessity, and thus according to which genuine *free choice* is impossible. (Contrast **compatibilism**.) Also: "determinist" (n.), "deterministic" (adj.), "deterministically" (adv.).

development of doctrine: Process by which the Church's understanding of the content of faith evolves over time, rather than being explicitly present as a whole from the beginning. An important identifier of and commentator on this process was the 19th-century British thinker, Cardinal John Henry Newman, mentioned by John Paul II in *Fides et ratio,* #74. On the Catholic understanding, such development does not, strictly speaking, involve a *change,* or alteration, in doctrine itself; rather, it consists in the drawing out of meanings that were not included in earlier presentations of a teaching, but that are arrived at through the application of new and/or deeper insights, as well as analyses of changes in circumstances. <Current Church teaching on the extreme rarity of the justified use of capital punishment as reflecting a development of (moral) doctrine.>

diakonia (Greek n., for "service"): As used throughout Christian history, a term expressing the Church's service to the world, and individuals' service to and with the Church. (In *Fides et ratio,* #2, John Paul II spoke of the Church's "*diakonia* of the truth"—to which philosophers can make specific contributions.)

dialectic (n.): See the discussions under **dialectical** $_{(1)}$ and $_{(4)}$.

dialectical (adj.): (1) Pertaining to a method of inquiry or presentation (called "dialectic") that is rooted in discussion and exchange, rather than simple assertion. (Plato's teacher Socrates is regarded as the "father" of the dialectical method in philosophy.) (Contrast **didactic**.) (2) Pertaining to methods of justifying propositions that do not involve either deductive or empirical arguments for them. (The tradition of Aristotle applies this term especially to justifications or defenses of first *principles*—concerning which, given their primacy, deduction from prior principles is by definition impossible; and concerning which, given their universality, empirical arguments would be insufficient. In such cases justification proceeds instead via consideration of the unacceptable consequences of rejecting the propositions in question.) <A dialectical defense of the principle of noncontradiction.> (3) Characteristic of an argument such that it has the power to incline one to accept a proposition, but not to compel assent. <Aquinas's dialectical consideration of the fittingness of belief in personal resurrection.> (Contrast **demonstrative**.) (4) In the *Marxist* phrase "dialectical materialism," of or pertaining to a supposedly inexorable process in which social forces are moved by material ones, ultimately leading to the revolution of the proletariat and the ushering in of the Communist state. (Following Marx's predecessor, G.W.F. Hegel, this process itself has sometimes been referred to as "dialectic;" for Hegel, however, the process was one of spirit, rather than matter.) Also: "dialectically" (adv.), "dialectician" (n.).

dianoetic (adj., from Greek *noein,* for "to know" + *dia,* for "through"): Term coined by 20th-century Thomist Jacques Maritain to characterize the type of knowledge gained—or at least aspired to—in a *philosophical* approach to nature, by contrast with the types of knowledge characteristically achieved in the *sciences* $_{(2)}$. Such philosophical results would provide access to the *essences* of things, and thus would make possible an organization of knowledge in terms of *intelligible* necessities. (For example, traditional philosophical anthropology defines human nature as "rational animality;" this gives rise to dianoetic explanations of such properties as freedom of choice and the ability to appreciate conceptual jokes.) (See **ontological**. Contrast **perinoetic** and **ananoetic**.) Also: "dianoetically" (adv.).

didactic (adj.): Of or pertaining to a method of presentation (of information, or an argument, or a theoretical view) that proceeds in straightforward expository fashion. (Contrast **dialectical** $_{(1)}$.) Also: "didactically" (adv.).

dignity (n., Latin *dignitas,* from *dignus,* for "worthy"): (1) The quality of possessing high standing or value. For Catholic tradition, the term applies primarily to God, but it applies *analogously* to creatures—especially to human *persons,* who are made in the *image of God.* (2) The fundamental moral *precept* (i.e., "The dignity of all persons is to be fostered"), which serves as the basis for *natural rights,* as well as for the moral evaluation of certain practices. (The Vatican II document *Gaudium et spes,* #27, lists specific offenses against human dignity—e.g., subhuman working conditions, slavery, and prostitution. More recent documents of the ordinary *magisterium* have singled out in vitro fertilization and reproductive cloning as being incompatible with the dignity of human procreation.)

direct (adj.): In ethics, said of the *object* $_{(3)}$ of a *human act* (often called its "moral object," or what the act "directly accomplishes"), insofar as this is determined by the act's very *nature* $_{(2)}$. <Death as the direct object of an act of euthanasia.> (Ant: **indirect**. See as well **abortion**, **determinants** or **sources of morality**, and **principle of double effect**.) Also: "directly" (adv.).

direct (v.): To exercise the function of *authority* $_{(1)}$ in planning and/or executing a range of activities. Also: "directive" (adj. or n.).

direct realism: In *realist* epistemology and metaphysics of knowledge, the position of those Thomists (notably Joseph Owens, C.Ss.R., and, more recently, John Knasas) who emphasize—and seek to explain in philosophical terms—the fact that human knowledge does not consist in the mind's representation of reality (as is the case with a photograph), but rather in the mind's immediate grasp of reality. (Compare and contrast **critical realism**, which is compatible with this position but emphasizes the self-correcting character of human knowledge.)

discovery, order of: Proper sequence according to which truths are naturally arrived at by the human mind. <For classical Thomism, the philosophy of nature precedes metaphysics in the order of discovery, because it treats subjects more immediately available to us—namely, aspects of changing, physical, and sensible being.> (Contrast **explanation, order of**. See as well **pedagogical order**.)

discriminate (v.): To engage in a practice or practices of *discrimination*. Also: "discriminatory" (adj.).

discrimination (n.): Unequal treatment of persons (or classes of persons) who, it is alleged or implied, deserve to be treated equally. (On the perennial account, discrimination in and of itself does not necessarily involve a violation of *justice*, for there may be appropriate reasons for a particular type of unequal treatment—e.g., reasons of *merit* [but not of *race* or *gender*] in the awarding of academic honors. However, many practices involving discrimination are indeed *unjust*, some gravely so.)

dishonesty (n.): See **honesty**. Also: "dishonest" (adj.), "dishonestly" (adv.).

disobedience (n.): See **obedience**. Also: "disobedient" (adj.), "disobediently" (adv.).

disorder (n.): Condition in which there is a lack of *order* $_{(3)}$, especially in the context of *morality* and/or *political* society. <The disorder involved in the invasion of one sovereign nation by another.>

disordered (adj.): Lacking proper *order* $_{(3)}$, as said of *appetites* (both sensitive and rational) inclining people to act in ways incompatible with genuine and integral human good; also as said of *choices*, and acts resulting from choices, made under the influence of such appetites. <A disordered life—e.g., one filled with acts that intentionally harm other persons.>

disposition (n.): (1) In perennial philosophy, a term sometimes used for a *potency* deriving from the *nature* $_{(2)}$ of a being, whereby it tends to act or be acted upon in certain ways. (2) In the modern sciences, and in the philosophy of science, an observed tendency in a thing typically expressible in a conditional statement (i.e., "If *x* should happen to this thing, and all other conditions are equal, *y* will result"). (Note: There can be dispositions in sense (2) that are not—or are not known to be—dispositions in sense (1).)

distinct (adj.): In the strict usage of the perennial tradition, distinguishable as a *formal object,* although not necessarily able to *exist* independently of the other or others. <The *transcendental* property goodness as distinct from oneness or unity.> (Contrast **separate** [as an adj.] $_{(1)}$.) Also: "distinctly" (adv.).

distinction (n.): Recognition of a difference in *intelligible* features, or in the relevant *formal objects,* apart from the question of whether the intelligibilities in question can be found *existing* separately in reality. <A distinction between sensible being and physical being.> (Contrast **separation** $_{(1)}$.)

distinguish (v.): To mark a *distinction.* (Contrast **separate** [as a v.].) Also: "distinguishable" (adj.).

distributism (n.): Economic view proposing the widest possible distribution of the means of production within society. Twentieth-century distributists such as the Frenchman Hilaire Belloc based their thinking on traditional notions of *distributive justice,* especially as articulated in the encyclicals of Pope Leo XIII (*Rerum novarum* [1891]) and Pope Pius XI (*Quadragesimo anno* [1931]). Although the resulting model is regarded by many mainstream economists as impracticable, a "Society for Distributism" continues to promote it today. (Contrast both **capitalism** and **socialism**. Compare **third way**.)

distributive justice: (1) Originally, for Aristotle and other classical authors, justice in a society's assignment of honors and political offices. (2) In more recent thought, a more generalized type of justice that regulates relations between a society and its members, such that each member receives his or her due. As understood today, distributive justice is particularly concerned with the proper assignment of benefits and burdens, including ones of a financial sort. Thus, questions of *economic justice* generally fall under the heading of distributive justice. (The application of principles of distributive justice to the *world* (or *global*) *community* raises difficult questions, both theoretical and practical—especially in an age of economic globalization.)

divine (adj.): Of or having to do with God. <Attempts to articulate, in human terms, the divine "attributes.">

divine (n.): (Somewhat archaic usage.) One who studies theology, or one who is reputed to be learned in matters concerning God.

divine command ethics: Approach to ethics (sometimes called "divine command theory"), identifiable in certain late medieval thinkers (e.g., John Duns Scotus), and taken up by certain 20th-century philosophers and theologians, (e.g., the Protestant thinker Emil Brunner). By contrast with Aquinas and the perennial tradition, divine command theorists tend to root ethical considerations directly and simply in what are taken to be God's laws; moreover, they tend toward *voluntarism,* viewing law as a matter of sheer *will,* rather than as an ordinance of (divine or human) *reason.*

divine law: According to the strict usage of Catholic philosophers and theologians, ordinances concerning human acts that are specifically revealed by God through Scripture and Church tradition. (Aquinas suggested a number of reasons for the existence of specifically revealed moral precepts, in addition to those of *natural* (*moral*) *law* and *human law.* Among these reasons are: a) the weakness of the human practical intellect, especially operating in the condition of sin; b) the impossibility for human law to forbid all evil acts, given both the limitations on law enforcement's time and resources and the detrimental side effects of an overregulated society; and c) the supernatural character of humankind's ultimate end—something we can know how to pursue consciously and explicitly only by way of divine revelation.) (See **law** $_{(1)}$. See as well the discussion under **revealable.**)

docta ignorantia (Latin phrase, for "learned ignorance"): State in which the philosopher or theologian knows that he or she does not know—i.e., understands via intellectual *reasoning* that, and why, the reality of *God* is beyond human comprehension. (See **negative way**. Compare **incomprehensible.**)

double effect, principle of: In moral philosophy and moral theology, especially within the Catholic tradition, a principle recognizing that an action may have effects that are *bad* (or harmful) as well as ones that are *good* (or beneficial), and allowing for the moral *rightness* of such an action if certain conditions are met. Different writers express these conditions in slightly different ways, but the following formulations (using terms from this dictionary) are typical: a) the *object* $_{(3)}$ of the act—what it directly accomplishes by its nature—must be morally good, or at least not something in itself bad (i.e., something that violates an objective moral precept); b) the agent's *motive* or subjective *end* $_{(2)}$ must be to bring about the beneficial effect, not to bring about the harmful effect—indeed the agent must seek to mitigate the latter to the extent possible; c) the foreseen good effect must not be achieved by *means* of the bad effect; and d) the foreseen benefits of the action, taken as a whole, must be *proportionate* to the foreseen harms. (An example of an action usually regarded as morally acceptable in light of the principle of double effect is the removal of a cancerous uterus in a pregnant woman when no other remedy is available—even though such an action entails the death of the developing fetus.)

doubt (n.): (1) A state of mind in which a person entertains one or more problems about a proposition; thus a state of subjective *uncertainty.* <“Methodical doubt,” as introduced into philosophy by Descartes.> (Contrast **certainty** or **certitude** $_{(1)}$.) (2) An objective problem that arises regarding a statement proposed for belief.

doubt (v.): To neither affirm nor deny a proposition, but to suspend judgment for fear of error—ordinarily because of an awareness of relevant questions or problems concerning the proposition in question. (Sometimes, but not necessarily and not always, “doubt” suggests an inclination toward the denial of the proposition.)

doubtable or **dubitable** (adj.): Able to be doubted, as said of a proposition. (Ant: **indubitable.**) Also: “doubtability” or “dubitability” (n.).

doubtful (adj.): Character of a proposition such that it induces *doubt,* in either of the above senses. Also: “doubtfully” (adv.), “doubtfulness” (n.).

doubtful conscience: State of conscience in which the agent—even after appropriate and sustained reflection—is unable to remove all practical doubt concerning the correct course of action. (According to Catholic tradition, “A doubtful conscience [as here described] does not bind”—even in cases where, from the standpoint of *objective* $_{(1)}$ morality, the matter is one that can be definitively settled. A similar point applies to a “doubtful law”—i.e., one concerning which a person is genuinely uncertain as to whether it fulfills the characteristics of *law* $_{(1)}$.) (Contrast **certain conscience**, as well as **perplexed conscience**.)

dualism (n.): (1) A family of metaphysical views according to which reality is made up of two fundamental types of being (e.g., the *material* and the *spiritual*) or—as expressed by the early modern philosopher Descartes—“extended being” (Latin *res extensa*) and “thinking being” (Latin *res cogitans*). (Note: Dualisms—as well as their contraries, *monisms*—should be contrasted with Thomistic philosophical analyses in terms of *matter/form, potentiality/actuality,* and *essence/existence;* the latter dualities are *principles* $_{(1)}$ of being, rather than types of being.) (2) Proponents of perennial ethics sometimes use "dualism" to characterize certain contrary approaches (including those of some Catholic thinkers), which deny substantive *moral* $_{(1)}$ significance to the bodily dimension of human existence, and accordingly regard questions about the *meanings* and *ends* of human acts as being entirely dependent on human choice. (Dualists in this sense recognize *realities* as well as *values;* however, they do not accept the natural *teleology* $_{(1)}$ according to which the latter are to be specified and ordered in terms of the former.) Also, in both senses: "dualistic" (adj.), "dualistically" (adv.).

dubitable (adj., from Latin *dubitum,* for "doubt"): See **doubtable** or **dubitable.**

duration (n.): Measure of real *being* or *actuality.* For the perennial tradition, "duration" (like "being" and "actuality" themselves) is an *analogous* term. The primary members of the analogous set—as identified by the early medieval thinker Boethius (480[?]–524), and adopted by Aquinas and the later tradition—are *eternity* (the measure of God's being) and *time* (the measure of finite and especially *natural* being). (A third term, "aeviternity," is sometimes used for intermediate cases—e.g., *angels,* who are finite but purely spiritual beings, and in whom, accordingly, there is no natural change, and in particular no process of perishing.)

duty or **obligation** (n.) (1) As a general theoretical notion, a person's condition of being under some *law* $_{(1)}$, whether a part of the moral law or a law that is positively decreed by legitimate social authority. For the tradition of integral Christian wisdom, all duty or obligation ultimately is grounded in God's *eternal law*—which, as Aquinas stressed, is an ordinance of God's Reason directed to the good of the whole universe. (Note: Although the ancient Greeks had a term [*deon*] for duty as a particular type of responsibility associated with one's station in life, the generalized notion here described played no role in Aristotle's ethics. Immanuel Kant, by contrast, saw the notion of duty [or respect for law] as the *absolute* and *autonomous* foundation of all moral thinking. In much current philosophical ethics—which occurs during a period in which many thinkers share neither the classical tradition's belief in God nor Kant's sense of autonomous obligation—the nature and foundations of duty are highly contested.) (2) As applying to practical situations, what a person is required to do in a concrete circumstance in light of relevant moral precepts, human laws, personal relationships, etc. Such obligations are often correlative to (other people's) *rights;* however, this relationship is not exact—for there are obligations to God and self as well as to others. (For further discussion, see **conflict of rights and duties**.)

E

eclectic (adj. or n.): Pertaining to theorizing that draws disparate elements from various sources, with little or no concern for the coherence of the resulting whole; also a person who theorizes in this way. (In *Fides et ratio,* #86, John Paul II warned against an eclectic approach as unworthy of the philosopher's—and the theologian's—calling.) Also: "eclectically," (adv.), "eclecticism" (n.).

economic justice: Area of *justice*$_{(2)}$ falling, in the main, under *distributive justice.* Its principal topics include the proper distribution of a society's financial rewards and burdens, the obligation to make available, to the extent possible, meaningful and adequately compensated work, etc. (See the discussions under **capitalism** and **socialism**, as well as **distributism.**)

effect (n.): That which results from a *cause*—whether that cause is, according to the Aristotelian scheme, *formal, material, efficient,* or *final* in nature.

efficacy (n.): The power to exercise efficient causality, or to bring about a certain result. (Karol Wojtyla emphasized that an explicit awareness of such a power is a property of persons.) <The efficacy of collaboration by citizens of diverse political persuasions.> Also: "efficacious" (adj.), "efficaciously" (adv.).

efficient cause: An *agent* in its role of bringing about the reality of, or a feature of, something (hence also sometimes called "agent cause"); one of the four types of cause, or factors in the explanation of being and becoming, as identified by Aristotle.

egalitarian (adj. or n., from French *egalite,* for "equality"): See **equalitarian**, sometimes **egalitarian**.

ego (n., from Latin for "I"): (1) In some presentations of philosophical psychology, another name for the *subject* (2) or the *self* as the experienced source of personal activity. (2) In the theory of Sigmund Freud, one of three divisions of the *psyche;* this ego is said to serve as the "mediator" between the individual and reality.

egoism (n.): (1) (Sometimes called "psychological egoism.") Attitude that disposes one to seek one's own good, rather than the good of others. (Ant: **altruism** (1).) (2) (Sometimes called "ethical egoism.") Normative theory that commends and seeks to justify the attitude, as well as corresponding behavior, identified in sense (1). (Ant: **altruism** (2).) Also: "egoist" (adj. or n.), "egoistic" (adj.).

elementary (adj.): Pertaining to basic features or parts. <An elementary grasp of the Latin language.>

elements (n.): (1) Quantitatively and sometimes qualitatively distinguishable parts that make up a whole. Since ancient times, there have been theories of elements in the constitution of the physical world. Four basic elements typically were recognized by Greek theorists, as well as their medieval followers—earth, air, fire, and water. In the *philosophy of nature,* it is important to distinguish between elements and the *co-principles* of natural being (i.e., *form* and *matter* (3)). (2) (Metaphorically.) Constituents of any kind of whole, whether physical or not. <Elements in the process of decision-making.>

elicited (adj.): See the discussion under **appetite**.

emanate (v.): To emerge, as from an ultimate source. (See **emanation**.)

emanation (n.): A theory of the progressive emergence of reality from a single ultimate source, as articulated by the *Neo-Platonists,* and as taken over and transformed into an element of Christian theology (with the biblical God as Ultimate Source) by certain Fathers of the Church, particularly St. Augustine. (By contrast with Neo-Platonist philosophy, however, Augustine and the Christian tradition stress that Creation results from God's free choice, rather than being somehow necessitated.)

eminence (sometimes **supereminence**) (n.): The special, *analogical* mode in which *transcendental* and *pure perfections* can be predicated infinitely—i.e., without limit—of God. According to Thomistic tradition, such predication contains three elements: a) affirmation (e.g.,

"God is good"); b) negation (e.g., "God is not good in the way human beings can be good"); and c) transcendence (e.g., "God is good in a way that transcends all created being"). (Note: Unwary readers sometimes confuse the terms "eminence," "immanence," and "imminence;" as their respective definitions make clear, the three should be carefully distinguished.) Also: "eminent" (sometimes "supereminent") (adj.), "eminently" (sometimes "supereminently") (adv.).

emotion (n.): A strong movement of animal and human *affectivity* (thus a type of *passion* $_{(3)}$) arising from awareness of perceived sources of pleasure or pain, opportunities or threats, challenging circumstances, etc.; and typically including physical as well as psychic dimensions of response. <Anger as an emotion etched on a person's face.> (Related terms would be *feeling,* which refers to milder or more fleeting forms of affective movements; *mood,* which refers to longer lasting and/or deeper forms; *passion* $_{(4)}$, which refers to very strong forms; and *affective key,* which, as used by existentialist philosophers and psychologists, refers to generalized, rather than specifically reactive types of human attitude toward the world—e.g., despair or hope.) Also: "emote" (v.), "emotional" or "emotive" (adj.), "emotionally" or "emotively" (adv.).

emotivism (n.): A 20th-century theory of ethics (more strictly, of *metaethics*) and a species of *noncognitivism.* According to this theory—propounded in Great Britain by A. J. Ayer and in the United States by C. L. Stevenson—moral precepts and judgments do not contain *intellectual* content, but rather express *emotional* reactions to human acts and practices and/or seek to induce the listener to share the reactions in question. Also: "emotivist" (adj. or n.).

empathy (n., Greek *empatheia,* from *pathos,* for "feeling"): Characteristic of human persons according to which, by recognizing others as other selves, they are able in some measure to participate in others' feelings. (Philosophers such as St. Edith Stein and John Crosby have made the experience of empathy the subject of *phenomenological* investigation.) [Some psychologists, as well as philosophers influenced by them, attribute empathy to members of other species, for example, the great apes and elephants. The accuracy of such attributions depends in part on a conceptual issue, namely, whether "recognizing others as other selves" requires an act of *intellect;* but it also depends on careful study of the animals in question—which may share rather fully in relevant emotional experiences even if they do not, in the strict sense identified in this dictionary, form *concepts* of self and other.] (Compare and contrast **sympathy**.) Also: "empathic" or "empathetic" (adj.), "empathically" or "empathetically" (adv.).

empirical (adj., from Greek *empeirein,* for "to experience"): Having to do with experience (especially *sense* experience), which is an originating condition of all knowledge about the physical world. <The role of experimentation in the modern empirical sciences.> Also: "empirically" (adv.).

empiricism (n.): Philosophical position prominent in recent centuries (especially, following David Hume, in the English-speaking world), according to which all genuine knowledge—except for that which concerns relations among *ideas* $_{(2)}$—is wholly derived from, and consists simply in the organization of, *data of sense.* (See **positivism**. Contrast **rationalism**—as well as the **critical realism** of the perennial tradition.) Also: "empiricist" (adj. or n.).

empiriological (adj.): Term coined by 20th-century Thomist Jacques Maritain to characterize the concepts and methods of the modern natural *sciences* $_{(2)}$, by contrast with the *philosophy of nature.* Such a characterization stresses the fact that concepts developed in the positive sciences are ultimately resolved into sensory experience (see **resolution of concepts**), and thus the extent to which these sciences themselves are controlled by *empirical* considerations. (Note: Not all followers of Aquinas have agreed with Maritain's account. In particular, Dominicans associated with the "River Forest" school [see the discussion under **Thomism**] tend to reject any sharp contrast between the philosophy of nature and the natural sciences. It should be remarked, however, that Maritain's account—especially as applied to entire disciplines—is best understood as marking a difference in degree, rather than a strict difference in kind or order.) (Ant: **ontological**. Compare **perinoetic**.)

encyclopaedia (n.): In a specifically philosophical use, the term (sometimes capitalized) employed by Anglo-American thinker Alasdair MacIntyre to refer to a theory holding—in keeping with the editors of the ninth edition of the *Encyclopaedia Britannica* (1873 et seq.)—that all rational persons can come to agree about relevant criteria and standards for truth; and thus that, in principle, they can rationally resolve all disagreements about how things are and should be. (MacIntyre contrasts this theory with those of *genealogy* and *tradition*—especially the blending of Aristotelian and Augustinian themes characteristic of Thomist tradition.) Also: "encyclopedist" (adj. or n.).

end (n., corresponding to Greek *telos,* Latin *finis*): Goal or purpose. (1) The *intrinsic* goal or state of accomplishment appropriate to a type of *being* or *power* or *activity.* By extension, "end" in this sense also applies to the objective purposes of *natural* $_{(2)}$ institutions, for example, marriage and civil society. (See **teleology** $_{(1)}$.) (2) That for the sake of which a *human act* is undertaken. The perennial tradition distinguishes two types of end in this second sense: a) the intrinsic purpose (corresponding to (1), above) of the type of activity being undertaken (Latin *finis operis,* for "end of the act"); and b) the personal and subjective end—i.e., the conscious *motive* the agent has in undertaking the act in question (Latin *finis operantis,* for "end of the agent"). (See the discussions under **determinants** or **sources of morality**, and **means.**)

ens (Latin noun-form; from *esse,* for "to be"): See **being** $_{(1)-(3)}$.

entelechy (n., Greek *entelecheia,* literally "in-end-having"): A *natural* $_{(1)}$ being's (and especially a *living* being's) basic actuality, and thus the source of its tendency or orientation toward its proper *end* $_{(1)}$. (In his *De Anima,* Aristotle describes "soul" [Greek *psuche*] as "the first entelechy of a naturally organized body having life potentially in it.")

entitative (adj.): (1) Of or referring to *existence* or *being* $_{(1)}$ outside the mind of a knower. (Ant: **intentional** $_{(1)}$.) (2) Of or referring to the principles of *being* $_{(3)}$, (i.e., *essence* and *existence*), as studied in metaphysics—by contrast with the principles of *substance,* (i.e., *form* and *matter* $_{(3)}$), as studied in natural philosophy. <The entitative structure of all finite reality.> Also: "entitatively" (adv.).

entity (n.): A *being* $_{(1)}$.

environment (n.): The set of conditions (physical, chemical, biological, atmospheric, etc.) that affect the ecological systems of planet Earth—shaping those systems and ultimately determining whether they survive. (In recent decades, environmental ethics has become an important topic area in *applied ethics,* treating such issues as responsibility for clean air and water, the safe disposal of hazardous waste, etc.) [It is sometimes alleged that the Christian tradition—by teaching that *man* (1) has dominion over *nature* (1)—is partly responsible for the critical environmental problems that humankind faces today. However, in theory (if not always in practice), the Christian tradition has promoted the notion of dominion as responsible *stewardship;* thus, as noted by both Pope John Paul II and Pope Benedict XVI, its moral resources in fact strongly support respect for the environment.] Also: "environmental" (adj.), "environmentalist" (adj. or n.), "environmentally" (adv.).

envy (n.): (1) A movement of *passion* (3)—one that may be momentary or longer lasting—in which one is saddened or upset at another's accomplishment or receipt of a particular good. (2) The fixed, habitual *state,* listed among the seven *capital vices,* according to which a person is profoundly disposed to the reaction described in sense (1). Also: "envious" (adj.), "enviously" (adv.).

epiphenomenalism (n.): Theory holding that what is commonly believed to be mental or spiritual reality can be understood in terms of *epiphenomena.* Also: "epiphenomenalist" (adj. or n.).

epiphenomenon (n., from Greek *epi,* for "on" or "after" + *phainesthai,* for "to appear;" following the Greek, the plural form is "epiphenomena"): An object taken to be secondary to another—especially where the latter is a *sensible* (1) object—and somehow to be explained by it. [While open to properly *scientific* (2) theories of evolution, John Paul II warned against interpretations that reduce our specific properties as *persons* (1) (rationality, free choice, etc.) to functions of sensible objects (e.g., states of the brain and nervous system), and thus treat these properties as mere epiphenomena of our physical nature.]

epistemological pluralism: Philosophical position articulated by certain Thomists (in particular, Jacques Maritain and Yves R. Simon), according to which there are irreducibly diverse, although *ordered* and interconnected, modes of human knowledge—including the various natural sciences as well as the disciplines of philosophy. A key feature of these Thomists' *critical realism,* this position is opposed to various forms of *reductionism* and *positivism;* it also is opposed to the idea that philosophers can dictate either methods or concrete results to scientists and other scholars as the latter properly pursue their respective disciplines. (Note: In spite of a verbal association—see *pluralism* (2)—the present position in no way supports philosophical *relativism,* which is incompatible with the perennial tradition.)

epistemology (n.) or **theory of knowledge**: Philosophical discipline that investigates the nature and possibility of, as well as the origins and general conditions of, human *knowledge* (Greek *episteme*). (See **rationalism**, **empiricism**, **critical realism**, and **direct realism**, as well as **gnoseology**.) Also: "epistemological" (adj.), "epistemologically" (adv.), epistemologist" (n.).

equal (adj. or n., corresponding to Latin *aequus*): Being the same in some relevant respect. <The demand for equal rights. A meeting of minds among equals.> Also: "equally" (adv.).

equalitarian, sometimes **egalitarian** (adj. or n.): In *political* thought, of or pertaining to the position that all citizens are to be treated with *equality;* also, one who holds such a position. (The variant "egalitarian" stems from the French, rather than the Latin root.) An important question for equalitarian thought concerns what, specifically, a society should guarantee its members. Is this limited to equality of opportunity? Or should it also include—at least to some degree, and as far as circumstances allow—equality of actual conditions or results? Also: "equalitarianism," sometimes "egalitarianism" (n.).

equality (n., Latin *aequalitas,* from *aequus,* for "equal"): The condition or relationship of being equal. A significant application of this notion occurs in *moral* and *political* thought. (The Christian tradition has consistently maintained, even if it has not consistently put into practice, the principle that all human beings are equal by virtue of their common *dignity* as persons created in the *image of God.* In modern times, other, more *secular*—and sometimes incompatible—accounts of the principle of equality have been developed. Regarding the latter, see, for example, **liberalism** (3) and **secularism**.)

equanimity (n.): Moral *virtue* by which one is able to maintain an even temperament, even in trying circumstances. <Equanimity as an important trait for successful parenting.> (See the discussion under **fortitude**.)

equity (n.): (1) The pursuit and achievement of *justice* (2), especially in the concrete, through the wise application of relevant law—including, for the perennial tradition, *natural* (*moral*) *law.* <The wise ruler (e.g., King Solomon) as one who judges with equity.> (2) More specifically, justice pursued and achieved via attention to an accumulation of concrete cases in *human law,* which provide an evolving precedent for the settling of civil disputes between two or more parties. <Equity in the recovery of damages.> Also: "equitable" (adj.), "equitably" (adv.).

equivocal (adj.): Use of a term in two or more instances such that it has essentially diverse and unrelated meanings. <"Bank" as an equivocal term—one referring to both the side of a river and a business offering financial services.> (Contrast **univocal** and **analogical** or **analogous.**) Also: "equivocally" (adv.).

equivocity (n.): Condition of a term used in ways that are *equivocal.* (Contrast **analogy** and **univocity.**)

esse (Latin v., sometimes also used as a substantive in philosophy): (1) To *be* or to *exist.* (2) The *act of being* (sometimes also expressed in Latin as *actus essendi*) by which a thing is. (Regarding sense (2), see **being** $_{(4)}$ and **existence** $_{(2)}$.)

esse-ab (Latin phrase; also ***esse-in*** and ***esse-ad***): As articulated by contemporary American Catholic theologian David Schindler (who seeks, following 20th-century thinker Hans Urs von Balthasar, to complement but go beyond Thomistic accounts), three interrelated modes of *being* as understood in light of the doctrines of Trinity and Creation. For Schindler, being—that is, creaturely being—is first of all *esse-ab* ("being-from" or "being-as-receptivity"). It is by way of such receptivity that creaturely being also is able to manifest *esse-in* ("being-in" or "being-as-possessed") and *esse-ad* ("being for others" or "being-as-communicativity"). (See **receptivity** and **relationality.**)

essence, sometimes **quiddity** (n., Latin *essentia* and *quidditas,* from *quid est,* for "What is it?"): (1) As a principle of being, or *entitative* principle, corresponding to Aristotle's *ousia,* that whereby a thing is what it is (i.e., being in the sense of a thing's form or nature). (Contrast **existence** $_{(1)}$.) (2) As available to the mind, a system of *intelligible* features that characterize all beings of a particular type. (In the case of natural beings, such a system includes associated *potentialities,* apart from the consideration of their degrees of *actualization* in individual cases.)

essential (adj.): (1) Of or pertaining to *essence* in either sense noted above. <Rationality as an essen-

tial feature of the human person.> (2) Synonym for "basic" or "fundamental." <Essential human goods.> Also: "essentially" (adv.).

essentialism (n.): (1) A philosophy that stresses essence or "whatness" in metaphysics, and in which "being" is typically taken in a *univocal* manner. (The 14th-century Scholastic John Duns Scotus is often regarded as propounding such a philosophy.) (2) In the judgment of Etienne Gilson, a similar emphasis that occurs among certain Thomists—ones who do not appreciate Aquinas's advance upon Aristotle in emphasizing the primacy of the "act of being" or "act of existence" (Latin *esse*). (Contrast **existentialism** $_{(2)}$.) Also: "essentialist" (adj. or n.).

estimative sense: The capacity or the act (listed by Scholastic philosophers among the "internal" *senses*) involved in an animal's evaluation of a sensible object with regard to its being beneficial or harmful.

eternal (adj.): Of or pertaining to *eternity.* <God's knowledge and will as eternal.> (Contrast **temporal**, as well as **everlasting**.) Also: "eternally" (adv.).

eternal law: Ordinance of reason by which God creates and governs the entire universe of finite being, directing all things to their proper *ends* $_{(1)}$. (See **law** $_{(1)}$.)

eternity (n.): Mode of *being* that is characterized by *duration* without *change* or succession of states and by a fullness of *actuality* that literally is inconceivable to us but metaphorically can be called an "all-at-once-present." (Eternity is strictly attributable only to God, although Christian teaching speaks of humans as enjoying, through God's elevating *grace,* the opportunity to participate in eternal life.) (Contrast **time**, as well as **everlastingness**.)

ethical (adj., from Greek *ethos,* for "custom" or "character"): (1) (Neutral sense.) Of or pertaining to the discipline of *ethics.* <Principles for the ethical evaluation of warfare.> (2) (Normative sense.) Morally *good* or morally *right.* <The praiseworthiness of an ethical person or act.> Also: "ethicality" (n.), "ethically" (adv.).

ethical egoism: See **egoism** $_{(2)}$.

ethical relativism: *Metaethical* position holding not only that basic moral values, rules, etc., vary from individual to individual or group to group, but also that there is no principled manner of adjudicating among such opposed moral elements. This position is to be distinguished from "cultural relativism," which, strictly speaking, holds only the factual or sociological component of the above claim. (In his pre-Conclave address to the assembled Cardinal electors in April 2005, Cardinal Joseph Ratzinger [who would become Pope Benedict XVI] famously warned about the contemporary dangers of a "dictatorship of relativism.") (Contrast **objectivism** and **realism**, as applied to questions of morality.)

ethical theory: Reflection, at the most general level, on morality and the human good; divided into "normative theory" and "metaethics." (See the discussion under **ethics**. Contrast **applied ethics**.)

ethics (n.): Reflective and systematic study of *morality*. Ethics is divided, in terms of subject matter, into *ethical theory* and *applied ethics*. Ethical theory in turn is divided into *normative* ethics and *metaethics*—the former dealing with questions about how we ought to live, the moral rules and values we should seek to incorporate and put into practice, and the types of persons we should strive to become; and the latter dealing with second-order questions about morality, such as whether it can be said to be objective or universal. Applied ethics takes up a range of concrete topics (e.g., ones arising in relation to biomedical practices, or in the pursuit of economic justice). Ethics also is divided, in terms of its methodology, into *philosophical* and *theological*—the former treating morality in light of human nature as such and as knowable apart from explicit divine revelation; and the latter treating morality in light of human nature as understood (by Christians) to be fallen and redeemed. (Note: "Ethic" is sometimes used as a singular noun to designate a particular normative theory or principle.) (See **applied ethics** and **ethical theory**, as well as **moral philosophy** and **moral theology**.) Also: "ethicist" (n.).

ethics, Christian: (1) An alternative name for *moral theology*, especially as practiced by Protestant thinkers such as Paul Ramsey and James Gustaphson. (2) Sometimes used of *moral philosophy* in what John Paul II called the second of its three "states"—where it maintains its *autonomy* and its formal character as philosophical, while being in part inspired and motivated by Christian faith. (Thomistic moral philosophers such as the late Ralph McInerny would be Christian ethicists in this latter sense.)

eudaimonism (n., from Greek *eudaimonia* for "happiness" or "living well"): Type of ethical theory holding that the *final end* of human existence is *happiness*, however the latter notion is understood. Also: "eudaimonist" (adj. or n.).

evaluate (v.): To measure the *value* or goodness of something, especially by comparison with another thing or things and in relation to a standard. Also: "evaluation" (n.), "evaluative" (adj.), "evaluatively" (adv.).

evaluative sense: A term sometimes used for the *estimative sense*, especially as found in the specific case of human persons.

evangelize (v.): To communicate the Christian Gospel (Latin *evangelium*), either to those who have not had it proclaimed to them, or to those among whom it has had no lasting effect. (According to John Paul II [see *Fides et ratio,* #103], philosophy can play an important role in evangelization—or in what might rather be called "pre-evangelization"—insofar as it can help bring the human mind and heart to an openness to the revealed word of God.) Also: "evangelical" (adj. or n.), "evangelist" (n.), "evangelizer" (n.), and "evangelization" or—especially among Protestant authors—"evangelism" (n.).

everlasting (adj.): Without end (and, for some users of the term, without beginning), yet *temporal* (1) in nature. The ancient Greeks and their Medieval followers believed the heavenly bodies to be everlasting, and to be composed of a type of *element* different from the traditional four (earth, air, fire, and water)—an element called "quintessence" (from the Latin word for "fifth"). The term "everlasting" is sometimes used synonymously with *eternal*—although the latter, according to the perennial tradition (following Boethius, and later Aquinas), strictly pertains to a type of duration (God's) that is altogether beyond time, and thus is to be contrasted with "everlasting." [Note: This traditional understanding has been challenged by certain recent Christian writers. For example, Nicholas Wolterstorff argues—unsuccessfully, according to Thomists—that God in fact should be conceived as everlasting, that is, as temporal but without beginning or end.] Also: "everlastingly" (adv.).

everlastingness (n.): State of being *everlasting;* sometimes taken as equivalent to *eternity*—although, as with "everlasting" and "eternal" noted above, the two terms are not synonymous and in important respects should be contrasted with one another.

evidence (n.): That which stands in support of a proposition or theory; used especially in relation to *empirical* matters. <Evidence for the theory of an expanding universe.> Also: "evidential" (adj.), "evidentially" (adv.).

evident or **self-evident** (adj.): Said of propositions that can be seen to be true in light of a full and proper understanding of their constituent *concepts* or *terms.* <"All bachelors are unmarried" as self-evident. "God exists" as also self-evident—although not to us, since no one, at least in this life, understands the essence of God.> (See the discussion at ***per se nota***. Compare and contrast **analytic**, which, since it focuses on words and their meanings, would apply to the first example above, but not the second.) Also: "evidently" or "self-evidently" (adv.).

evil (n.): Not merely the lack of *good*, but the absence (i.e., a *privation* $_{(1)}$) of a good that ought to be present—e.g., blindness in an eye. Evil is commonly distinguished into "natural" or "physical" evil and "moral" evil, the latter involving bad personal acts, which result specifically from defective uses of the *will*. In Scholastic terminology, moral evil is sometimes called "evil of fault" (Latin *malum culpae*) or "evil done." (Historically, questions have been raised about the "real existence" of evil. Here the perennial tradition follows and clarifies the position of St. Augustine: evils are "real" as privations, but they do not "exist" in the sense of being themselves metaphysical *subjects* $_{(3)}$ of being.) (Compare **badness**; contrast **good** [as a n.] and **goodness**. See **problem of evil**.) Also: "evil" (as an adj.).

evolution (n.): Transformation of species of living being—the general theory accepted by the vast majority of natural scientists as best explaining the history of life on planet Earth. *Empiriological* disciplines such as biology, geology, and paleontology give accounts of evolution via factors that are physical and in principle observable, such as "random mutation" and "natural selection." [Note: Perennial *natural philosophy* (informed by *metaphysics*) recognizes what often is overlooked by the natural sciences—namely, that certain species appearing later in time share in *being* $_{(2)}$ or *actuality* in a way superior to that of predecessor species. Thus a full and proper understanding of evolution requires one to address the question, "How is it that something with more being comes from something with less being?" Whatever the types of *material* causality at work, from the standpoint of *formal* and *efficient* causality something with less of an ontological perfection cannot, of itself and *properly* $_{(2)}$, *cause* something with more of it. (That is, an increase in actuality cannot come about simply from an addition or complexification of material elements.) Thus philosophical reflection on the evolution of species gives rise to speculation about the roles of higher orders of being in the "ascent" of natural forms of life, culminating in the human or rational.] (See **creation**; compare and contrast **creationism** $_{(1)}$.) Also: "evolutionary" (adj.).

evolutionism (n.): A theory—held by some scientists (e.g., the British biologist Richard Dawkins), but clearly *philosophical* in nature—proposing that all aspects of earthly life, including the emergence of human or rational animals, can be fully and properly accounted for by evolutionary biology and the physical sciences that complement it. [John Paul II, following the lead of Pope Pius XII's encyclical *Humanae generis* (1950), alluded to this philosophical view in *Fides et ratio,* #54. In light of the preceding entry, evolutionism can be said either to ignore or to discount the questions about levels of *actuality* and *being* $_{(2)}$ raised by perennial philosophy.] Also: "evolutionist" (n.).

excellence (n., Greek *arete*): Something that completes a nature or is a perfection of that nature—in particular (although not only) human nature. Two specifically human types of excellence are recognized by the tradition of Aristotle: *intellectual* and *moral.* (Note: The Greek term *arete* also is sometimes translated as "virtue." See **virtue**.) Also: "excellent" (adj.), "excellently" (adv.).

excellence, freedom for: Human freedom as properly understood in terms of its natural *teleology* $_{(1)}$. According to accounts by contemporary moral theologians who build on the work of Aquinas (e.g., Servais Pinckaers, O.P.), human freedom is not ordered to "indifferent" or arbitrary choice, but rather to choosing the *good*—i.e., the best or most excellent good in the particular situation. (Pinckaers contrasts his account of freedom with one proposing a "freedom of indifference.")

exceptionless moral rules: Moral rules that are binding in all cases to which they genuinely apply. That there are such rules—as well as associated types of acts that are *intrinsically evil*—is affirmed by the school of Aquinas, as well as the ordinary Catholic *magisterium.* (See, in particular, John Paul II's *Veritatis splendor* [1993].) However, the matter is complex. Positive moral precepts of a very general and abstract sort (i.e., *primary precepts*) articulate duties to protect *basic goods* such as personal life, a just social order, etc. As such, these precepts are exceptionless. But, in the concrete, not all goods can be pursued equally at the same time. Moreover, when positive precepts become more particularized, they also become progressively subject to exceptions. For example, while the very general precept "Promote human life" always is to be observed, the more particular precept "Dive in and try to save a drowning swimmer" will not apply in cases in which the agent himself or herself cannot swim. Again, while certain negative precepts—e.g., "Do not steal"—hold without exception (since acts violating them always have a bad moral *object* $_{(3)}$), cases can arise in which what ordinarily would constitute a violation in fact involves an act of a different moral type. (See **change of matter** or **change of species**, and **necessity** $_{(2)}$.)

excess and defect: In the Aristotelian account of *moral virtue,* those "extremes" of choice and action between which the person of *prudence,* or practical wisdom, locates the appropriate *mean* in the particular circumstances. <A person's taking in more than four thousand calories per day, or, alternatively, less than one thousand calories per day, as, in most cases, examples of excess and defect.>

excluded middle, principle of: A basic principle of speculative thought, according to which a thing either exists or does not exist. (Strictly speaking, there is no middle ground between being and non-being: a *potential* being of whatever type remains merely in potency—and, in this sense, in *nonbeing*—until the process of *coming to be* is complete.)

exclusivism (n.): See the discussion under **pluralism** $_{(2)}$. Also "exclusivist" (adj. or n.).

exemplar (**cause**) (adj.): Species of *formal cause* in which an idea serves also as an *end* and perhaps as a *means* of agency. (The term "exemplar" has been used especially of creative ideas in the mind of God.) Also: "exemplar" (as a n.).

exist (v., corresponding to Latin *esse,* and sometimes *existere,* from Latin *ex* and *stare,* for "to stand outside of"): To be; especially to exercise *being* $_{(4)}$—with "exist" applying primarily to the metaphysical *subject* $_{(3)}$, through which parts and accidents of the reality share in being. (See the discussion under **supposit**.)

existence (n., corresponding to Latin *esse* used as a substantive; and sometimes to *existentia*—a term developed by the Scholastics for special philosophical emphasis): (1) Abstractly, the co-principle that constitutes "is-ness" in beings, as distinct from "whatness" or intelligible properties. (Contrast **essence** (1).) (2) (Also called "act of being" or "act of existence," Latin *actus essendi.*) A real being's ontologically first and ultimate *act* and *perfection,* without which none of its other modes of actuality (e.g., its characteristic features and activities) would be real. Also: "existent" (adj. or n.), "existential" (adj.), "existentially" (adv.).

existentialism (n.): (1) Family of philosophies formally developed in the 20th century (especially by atheistic writers such as Martin Heidegger and Jean-Paul Sartre) that stress the radical uncertainty and open character of our existence and take the human condition as providing important clues to the nature of all being. For Heidegger, a central concept was that of *Dasein.* Through it, he sought to express the notion of being (German *Sein*) as grasped in and through human reality. Humans, he said, have a fundamental sense of "thrownness" (German *Geworffenheit*) into the world—and it is only via reflection on this sense that one can come to understand the truth of one's human reality and, ultimately, the truth of all reality. [The concept of *Dasein* has been influential in Continental and some American thought; but it seems difficult to assimilate to the perennial tradition, both because of its partiality toward human reality and because of its subjective emphasis. Compare and contrast **being** (1)–(4).] Somewhat similarly, Sartre famously declared that "existence precedes essence"—by which he meant that humans first recognize themselves as instances of actuality, and only then come to decide (without benefit of an objective pattern or model) how they should understand and relate to that actuality. (2) As said of the thought of St. Thomas Aquinas, an interpretation propounded by 20th-century historian of philosophy Etienne Gilson, and now widely accepted, that emphasizes *existence* (2) or the "act of being" in metaphysical analyses. (Contrast **essentialism** (2).) Also: "existentialist" (adj. or n.).

ex nihilo (Latin phrase meaning "out of nothing"): Term traditionally used to characterize God's act of *Creation,* which depends on no ontologically prior reality.

experience (n.): Direct awareness by a psychological *subject* (2) of external or internal realities. (The term "experience" is broader in meaning than either *sensation* or *perception* (1), for it can refer to a person's awareness of his or her subjective motives for action, or the joys of the spiritual life—which are not instances of sensation or perception in the strict sense.) Also: "experience" (as a v.), "experiential" (adj.), "experientially" (adv.).

explanation, order of: Order of *demonstration* "propter quid"—within this order, one first articulates higher and more general causes, then proceeds by way of these to explain lower and less general causes, and then finally explains the latter causes' immediate effects. <For classical Thomism, the discipline of *metaphysics* precedes *natural philosophy* in the order of explanation.> (Contrast **discovery, order of**. See as well **pedagogical order**.)

extension (n.): As understood in modern logic, meaning as *reference* or *denotation*. (Ant: **intension**.) Also: "extensional" (adj.).

external senses: See the discussion under **sense** $_{(2)}$.

extraordinary means: See **ordinary/extraordinary means**.

extrinsic (adj.): Related to circumstances of an act or accidental features of a thing, rather than to its *nature* $_{(2)}$ or *essence*. (Ant: **intrinsic**.) Also: "extrinsically" (adv.).

extrinsicism (n.): Philosophical position, generally opposed to the perennial tradition, holding that all qualities (or, in restricted forms of the position, all qualities under consideration) have only accidental, rather than *essential* $_{(1)}$, relations to one another. <Extrinsicism regarding properties of human nature—e.g., rationality and the ability to choose what is good.> (Ant: **intrinsicism**.) Also: "extrinsicist" (adj. or n.).

fact (n.): An individual *reality,* or set of realities, in their status as *actual,* with the judgment about actuality having its ground in experience—or the equivalent of experience, such as a well-founded theory of what experience would deliver if it were possible in the particular case (e.g., that of subatomic particles). (The 20th-century Thomist Yves R. Simon distinguished "common" facts, "scientific" facts, and "philosophical" facts. Scientific facts differ from common facts in that access to the former requires specially designed and organized experiences such as occur in modern, largely *empiriologial* approaches to nature; whereas the latter are available to normal human awareness. Philosophical facts involve matters of experience of a most general sort (ordinarily too general to be of interest to the empirical sciences) that can serve as starting points for philosophical reflection; examples would be that beings exist, and that beings of our experience come into and go out of existence as well as undergo various other types of change. Among speculative philosophical disciplines, *metaphysics* requires only an awareness of common facts such as the ones just noted; other, more particular studies, such as *philosophy of nature* and *philosophy of the human person,* require contact with—and taking account of—certain scientific facts as well.) Also: "factual" (adj.), "factually" (adv.).

faculty (n.): A *power* $_{(1)}$, especially one related to *cognition* or *affectivity.* (Note: The term "faculty" at times has been held in disdain because, historically, "faculty theories" of psychology treated the powers in question—e.g., *intellect* and *will*—as though they were separate entities, and thus they did not adequately maintain the unity of the human person or other living being. In using this term, one should take care to avoid such misunderstandings.)

faith (n., Latin *fides*): (1) (As a mental *act.*) Firm adherence to a proposition in the absence of evidence necessary to remove all rational doubt. (2) (As the *object* $_{(2)}$ of such an act.) A proposition or set of propositions (sometimes called a "creed") that is adhered to in the manner described above. (3) (As a *religious* act and form of life.) A total personal response, including both *cognitive* and *affective* dimensions, to a person or a message seen as revealing the ultimate truth about the world and oneself. (See, for example, *Fides et ratio,* #13.) (4) For Christians, the *theological virtue* by which, through *grace,* one is able firmly to embrace truths that go beyond the reach of reason, on the basis of God's revealing them. Also, especially in relation to sense (3): "faithful" (adj.), "faithfully" (adv.).

faith seeking understanding (Latin *fides quaerens intellectus*): A phrase originating in St. Augustine and St. Anselm that expresses the overall goal of Christian theological reflection. The application of human *reason* is the principal means of such "seeking." (See as well **understanding of faith**.)

fallacy (n.): In logic, a defect—"formal" or "informal"—in a mode of reasoning or argument. An example of a formal fallacy, within *syllogistic* reasoning, is the failure of an argument to have a *middle term* that is properly "distributed" (or ordered) within the premises. (One instance of this fallacy—with "mortal" functioning as the middle term—would be: "All men are mortal," "All horses are mortal," "Therefore, all men are horses.") An example of an informal fallacy is "circular reasoning" (also called "begging the question," or in Latin *petitio principii*); such reasoning is defective in that what one is supposedly proving in effect is already assumed in the starting points of the argument. (Here an instance would be: "Since human persons are instances of natural being, they cannot have a spiritual dimension"—it being assumed that the natural and the spiritual are incompatible.) Other informal fallacies include arguments *ad hominem* (directed at the person making the argument, rather than at features of the argument itself), and the line of reasoning expressed in Latin as *post hoc, ergo propter hoc* (i.e., "This event follows that one, therefore it must be caused by it"). Also: "fallacious" (adj.), "fallaciously" (adv.).

false (adj.): Not *true,* especially as said of judgments and other intellectual acts, as well as their verbal articulations (e.g., hypotheses disconfirmed by the evidence). Also: "falsity" (n.), "falsely" (adv.).

falsehood (n.): A statement that is untrue. (For perennial ethics, and the Catholic tradition generally, under all ordinary circumstances—i.e., when the persons addressed ask for and/or expect to hear the truth—to knowingly say what is false constitutes a *lie* and a moral failing. But see the discussions under **exceptionless moral rules** and **change of matter** or **change of species.**)

family (n.): (1) The most fundamental type of natural human *community*—i.e., parents and their children, often called the "basic unit" of society. Rightly understood, and in the paradigm case, a family in this sense is a unique *communion of persons,* one that itself arises from an originating communion (namely, that of husband and wife). As an institution, the family is "prior" to the state, in that it derives its *nature* $_{(2)}$, its *end* $_{(1)}$, and its specific *rights* from the role it plays within the social order—a role the state and public authorities properly recognize rather than bestow, and a role they should protect by all reasonable means for the sake of both families and the larger society. (2) In a derivative but socially very important sense, any of a number of other types of communities or groupings of persons—e.g., couples or families with adopted children, single-parent families, and "blended" families involving children from the parents' prior unions—that share to some degree (in many cases quite fully) the emotional bonds and certain other characteristics of families in sense (1). Also: "familial" (adj.).

family resemblances: See the discussion under **analytic philosophy**.

Fathers of the Church: See **Patristics** or **Patrology**.

fault (n.): See the discussion at **culpability**.

fear (n.): In traditional philosophical psychology, an *irascible* passion, or emotion, arising with the awareness of a threat of suffering some harm, or losing or failing to attain some good. If not countered by other internal and/or external forces, fear leads to a retreat from the difficult situation, rather than an attempt to overcome it.

(Contrast **courage** $_{(1)}$.) Also: "fearful" (adj.).

federalism (n.): Form of *government,* typically found in large, diverse political societies (e.g., the United States), according to which *authority* $_{(1)}$ for some decisions and programs is located centrally (i.e., at the national level), while authority for others is located in the particular federated units (in this instance, the fifty U.S. states). Also: "federal" (adj.).

feeling (n.): A movement of *affectivity,* generally milder or less long-lasting than others such as *moods.* <A feeling of cold, and thus physical discomfort, after being outside on a winter's day; a feeling of relief after the successful completion of an examination.> (See the discussion under **emotion**.) [Note: This term is sometimes used more loosely to refer to a thought or judgment (e.g., one's "feeling" about a particular political issue). Perennial philosophy discourages such usage, in part out of concern for accurate expression, and in part because it can be taken to support *noncognitivism.*] Also: "feel" (v.).

feminism (n.): A general movement of thought, including philosophers and theologians as well as other scholars, which formally arose during the latter decades of the 20th century and which approaches subject matters with a special emphasis on the needs of women (and, sometimes, their children), or the perspectives of women, or both. [Note: Upholders of Catholic tradition sometimes have charged that feminism threatens a proper understanding of gender *complementarity,* and even (in the case of "radical feminism") threatens proper social order itself. For their part, many proponents of feminism have been very critical of what they take to be Catholicism's "patriarchal" understanding and treatment of women. Doubtless there is truth on both sides, and a stronger mutual appreciation of respective insights seems both possible and desirable.] Also: "feminist" (adj. or n.).

fideism (n., from Latin *fides,* for "faith"): A philosophical view according to which—contrary to Catholic tradition (see *Fides et ratio,* ##52, 55)—*religious* concerns, and more generally all *transcendent* $_{(1)}$ concerns, are to be settled by sheer "faith," unsupported and unaided by reason. Also: "fideist" (adj. or n.), "fideistic" (adj.).

fidelity (n.): A species of the cardinal virtue of *justice,* by which one is disposed to be faithful to (Latin *fidelis*), and maintain one's commitments to, another or others.

<Fidelity among spouses as a pervasive trait of a healthy and well-ordered society.> (Ant: **infidelity**.)

final cause (from Latin *finis*, corresponding to Greek *telos*, for "end"): An *end* or purpose in its role as a cause; as identified by Aristotle, one of the four causes or factors in explaining something's being or coming to be. (See **teleology** $_{(1)}$.)

final end: (1) In metaphysics, the purpose or goal of all finite activity; sometimes called the "ultimate end" or "ultimate (or 'highest') good" (Latin *summun bonum*). For the perennial tradition, this end is real and functions as such whether individual agents are aware of it or not—and, since most natural beings lack the power of understanding, most in fact are not aware of it. (*Philosophical theology* identifies the final end of the universe, including human persons, as God.) (2) In the philosophy of the human person and in ethics, that for the sake of which we humans choose all that we choose, and do all that we voluntarily do. (To will such an end is a matter of our *nature* $_{(2)}$ rather than *free choice;* that is, we cannot not will what we understand—however vaguely or even mistakenly—to be our final or ultimate good. Aristotle called our final end *eudaimonia*, and he specified it as being primarily a life of virtue. Aquinas and Catholic tradition have extended this account to ultimate *beatitude* with God.)

finality (n., from Latin *finis*, for "end"): As said of a *nature*, or a type of *power* or *act*, its being directed toward an *end* $_{(1)}$. Also, the end itself to which the thing in question is directed.

finality, principle of: A fundamental *principle* of metaphysics—namely, "Every agent acts for an end."

finis operantis (Latin phrase, for "end of the agent"): See the discussions under **determinants** or **sources of morality**, and **means**.

finis operis (Latin phrase, for "end of the act"): See the discussions under **determinants** or **sources of morality**, and **means**.

finite (adj., from Latin *finis*, in this case for "boundary"): Limited or bounded—said especially, although not only, in relation to space and time. <All beings of nature, indeed all created beings, are finite.> (Ant: **infinite**.) Also: "finitely" (adv.).

finitude (n.): State of being *finite*. (Note: The human *experience* of finitude has been an object of exploration by certain Christian phenomenologists, e.g., St. Edith Stein.)

first (adj.): See **primary** or **first**.

first principle: A fundamental, non-demonstrable starting point of reasoning, whether *speculative* (e.g., the principle of *identity*, "Each being is what it is and not another"), or *practical* (e.g., the principle of *synderesis*, "We are to do good and avoid evil").

Five Ways, the: As outlined in Aquinas's *Summa theologiae* (Part I, question 2, article 3), a set of five types of deductive *argument* by which human reason is led to affirm the existence of God. The philosophical starting points of these "ways" are, respectively, the facts of: a) change, b) efficient causality, c) the contingent (or merely "possible") existence of natural being, d) the degrees of perfection found in things, and e) the order and end-directedness within natural processes and systems. (For Aquinas and his school, one who fully and adequately grasps these arguments will see that the Five Ways constitute genuine *demonstrations*.)

foolhardiness (n.): State of "excess," rather than the virtuous *mean*, whereby a person tends to act imprudently in confronting difficult situations; sometimes also called "audacity"—although in everyday speech the latter term does not necessarily connote excess. (See the discussion under **fortitude**.) Also: "foolhardy" (adj.).

foreknowledge (n.): In theology, God's knowledge of future events. (One must exercise caution in the use of this term; otherwise, it may seem to suggest—falsely, according to the perennial tradition—that God's mode of knowledge, like our own, is temporally conditioned. See **eternity**.)

foresight (n.): (1) In the modern natural sciences, the ability to predict future events on the basis of previous experience and/or theoretical knowledge. (2) A component of the cardinal virtue of *prudence*, by which a person makes informed estimates of the consequences of actions.

form (n., Latin *forma*): (1) Principle of being according to which an individual has a specific *nature* $_{(2)}$; distinguished into *substantial* and *accidental* forms—e.g., being a rose and being red. (Strictly, in the case of physical reality, the term "nature" includes both the [type of] form and *common matter;* an actual substance, by contrast, is comprised of [individualized] form and "primary" matter [i.e., *matter* $_{(3)}$]. See **hylemorphism**.) (2) By extension, the *concept* (called "*intentional* $_{(1)}$ form") by means of which the mind comes to know a type of reality.

formal (adj.): Of or pertaining to *form,* in either sense. Also: "formally" (adv.).

formal cause: A *form* $_{(1)}$ taken in its role as a cause or explanatory factor in the being or becoming of a thing; one of the four causes as identified by Aristotle.

formal logic: The branch of logic that studies general rules among terms, propositions, and lines of reasoning—rules that hold regardless of the particular subject matter being treated. Examples would be the rules for the "distribution," or ordering of terms, in a valid syllogism; and the rules called *modus ponens* and *modus tollens* in modern propositional logic.

formal object: See **object** $_{(2)}$.

fortitude (n., Latin *fortitudo,* from *fors,* for "strength"): The *cardinal virtue*—also known as *courage* $_{(2)}$—that enables one to face challenging situations in achieving a good or avoiding a harm. (Fortitude is said to regulate *irascible* passions, as the virtue of temperance regulates *concupiscible* passions.) Scholastic philosophers have recognized the following as constituent "parts" of fortitude or as related good habits: equanimity (by which one is able to maintain an even temperament); magnanimity or "greatness of soul" (by which one is able to conceive and pursue noble goals); patience (by which one is able to moderate immediate expectations); and perseverance (by which one is able to continue with a task in spite of obstacles). Habits and attitudes incompatible with this cardinal virtue include foolhardiness, at one extreme, and cowardice at the other.

foundationalism (n.): Philosophical position holding that, in principle, all knowledge must be explicitly and rigorously grounded in *absolutes*—i.e., basic statements of sensory awareness or intellectual self-evidence. <Descartes's rationalist approach to knowledge as exemplifying foundationalism.> [Note: It may appear that John Paul II endorsed a form of foundationalism by proposing that we "move from phenomenon to foundation" (*Fides et ratio,* #83). However, it is not clear that he intended this remark to promote foundationalism in the present sense; and many thinkers of the perennial tradition, among others, reject this position. See the discussion under **epistemological pluralism**.] Also: "foundationalist" (adj. or n.).

free choice (Latin *liberum arbitrium,* for "free decision" or "judgment"): Equivalent to the possibly more common *freedom* or *liberty.* (According to some writers, "free choice"—especially as understood in light of the corresponding Latin phrase—better expresses the joint activity of *intellect* and *will* in our personal decisions and acts.)

freedom or **liberty** (n.): Property of the human *will* or *rational appetite* according to which it in principle is capable of operating without determination by physical, psychological, or social factors, but rather in response to what a person knows or rationally believes to be genuinely good. For the perennial tradition, human freedom has as its proper *end* (1) the selection and implementation of a determinate course of action, in light of its contribution to an individual's or a community's integral fulfillment. (The 20th-century Thomists Jacques Maritain and Yves R. Simon distinguished "initial freedom" from "terminal freedom." The former term refers to the native state of this property; the latter refers to a state in which, due to the presence of the *virtues,* freedom is brought to full and stable actualization—so that the will is able to regularly and easily choose the good, as this is identified by practical reason. For his part, John Paul II stressed that it is crucial for practical reason to function properly; for only such functioning will enable "the values chosen and pursued in one's life [to] be true" [*Fides et ratio,* #25]. In most persons, clearly, the actual states of both freedom and practical reason are at some point along a spectrum between "initial" and "terminal" actualization.) Freedom in the present sense is to be distinguished from, although it is related to, both *political* and *religious* freedom, or liberty. (See **excellence, freedom for**, as well as **indifference, active** or **dominating**. Contrast both **compatibilism** and **incompatibilism**, as well as **determinism** (2).) Also: "free" (adj. or n.), "freely" (adv.).

freedom, political: See **political freedom** or **liberty**.

freedom, religious: See **religious liberty** or **freedom**.

freedom for excellence: See **excellence, freedom for**.

freedom of indifference: See the discussion under **excellence, freedom for**.

friendship (n.): A relationship of mutual good will among persons; an instance of *love* (2), corresponding to the Greek notion of *philia.* (According to classical thought, as formulated by Aristotle, persons involved in a genuine friendship must in some way be equals; hence the remarkable character, from the philosophical standpoint, of the Christian proposition that *man* (1) is invited to friendship, indeed intimacy, with *God.*)

frugality (n.): A moral virtue, related to the cardinal virtue of *temperance,* by which a person regulates desires regarding the use of financial and other resources. <Frugality in one's lifestyle and choices.> Also: "frugal" (adj.), "frugally" (adv).

fulfillment (n.): (1) In Aristotle's practical philosophy, the ultimate goal of human striving (corresponding to Greek *eudaimonia,* which also is translated as "happiness"). (2) The actual accomplishment of right action, by contrast with the mere understanding of or ability to explain such action.

function (n.): In philosophy of nature and moral philosophy, a synonym for *power*$_{(1)}$, especially in the context of its actual exercise.

fundamental (adj.): Basic, foundational; also, pertaining to an object that is necessary if a given end is to be pursued. <Fundamental human needs—which, if unmet, make the achievement of fulfillment impossible.>

fundamental goods: See **basic goods**.

fundamentalism (n.): The espousal of strict and, often, literal acceptance of basic texts—e.g., those of the Bible. [Note: Christian and other religious fundamentalists typically question the positive significance of philosophy—as well as other human disciplines—in pursuing answers to ultimate questions. The perennial tradition, for its part, is opposed to fundamentalism as here understood.] (See **Biblicism**. Compare as well **fideism**.) Also: "fundamentalist" (adj. or n.).

future (n.): The aspect of temporal *duration* that, ontologically, has not been and is not now, but is to be.

gender (n.): Maleness or femaleness. The perennial tradition recognizes that aspects of the concrete status of men and women are culturally conditioned; however, it holds (along with the ordinary Catholic *magisterium*) that human *nature* $_{(2)}$—i.e., our essence as embodied *persons* $_{(1)}$—is given as male or female. Moreover, perennial thought holds that the differentiation in question has significance for *integral human good*—and thus has implications for conjugal and social morality. For example, because of women's key role in the begetting and nurturing of children, a just economic system will, if it is at all possible for the particular society, enable women to choose to remain at home, especially during children's early, formative years. On the other hand, apart from very special circumstances, persons should not receive either favorable or unfavorable treatment because of their gender in matters relating to education or professional advancement—a practice that often is termed "sexism." [Note: According to certain recent social theorists, gender in human beings (apart from sheer biological facts) is culturally "constructed," rather than representing an *ontological* difference and/or having implications for the moral and social orders. Such accounts clearly are incompatible with perennial thought.] (See **complementarity** $_{(1)}$.) Also: "gendered" (adj.).

genealogy (n.): Term used by Anglo-American philosopher Alasdair MacIntyre to refer to the approach to knowledge and practice that, following Nietzsche's *On the Genealogy of Morals* (1887), holds all fundamental perspectives to be explainable in terms of the social aspects of their origins and development. MacIntyre contrasts this approach with that of *encyclopaedia* on one hand, and *tradition* (especially Thomist tradition) on the other. (Compare **postmodernism**.) Also: "genealogical" (adj.), "genealogically" (adv.).

generate (v., corresponding to Latin *generare,* from *genus,* here meaning "birth" or "descent"): To bring into being, especially in the case of a living *substance.* Also: "generative" (adj.), "generatively" (adv.).

generation (n.): (1) The *absolute* beginning of a natural being (sometimes called "coming to be"); thus one of the two types of *substantial change.* (Ant: **corruption** $_{(1)}$.) (2) More specifically, *reproduction* in the case of living beings, and *procreation* in the case of human persons. (3) The whole set of individuals of a particular species (especially the human species) that come to be over a given period. Also, regarding sense (3): "generational" (adj.).

genuine good: See **honest good.**

genus (n.; plural form often follows the Latin *genera*): (1) In logic, a class that encompasses other, differentiated classes (i.e., *species* $_{(1)}$). <"Quadrilateral" as a genus in relation to "square."> (2) In natural philosophy and metaphysics, the fundamental modes of being, or *categories,* as identified by Aristotelian tradition. <The genera of substance, quantity, quality, etc.>

gift (n.): (1) In Christian philosophy and theology, a term stressing the utterly free, gratuitous character of God's act of *Creation,* as well as God's offer to humankind to share in the divine life. (2) In accounts especially influenced by *personalism,* a characteristic of human relations and acts (see **self-gift**) according to which—among all created beings—humans in a special way can be the *image of God.* (The notion of gift in both senses is explored in the writings of John Paul II and Benedict XVI; see especially the latter's *Charity in Truth* (*Caritas in veritate*) [2009].)

gift, law of the: A theme of *personalist* philosophers and theologians, including John Paul II—namely, that a person cannot truly be fulfilled unless he or she makes a sincere gift of self to another person or community of persons.

gifts of integrity and grace: System of gifts attributed by biblical religion (at least as interpreted by the Catholic *magisterium*) to the first humans—represented by Adam and Eve—in their original condition. Before *Original Sin,* or the "Fall" from God's grace, humankind enjoyed both a) gifts of integrity, or "praeternatural" gifts (by which they were to be preserved from certain normal effects of *nature* $_{(2)}$, for example, disease and death) and b) gifts of grace, or "supernatural" gifts (by which they were elevated to genuine *friendship* with God, a condition not naturally available to created beings).

gifts of the Holy Spirit: Set of seven spiritual gifts which, according to traditional theology (rooted in Isaiah 11), are given by the Holy Spirit to assist the faithful in coming to maturity in the Christian life: wisdom, understanding, counsel, fortitude, knowledge, piety, and fear of the Lord. (Note: Several of these spiritual gifts—as well as the "fruits" of the Spirit mentioned by St. Paul in Galatians 5—share names with natural *virtues* or *excellences*—e.g., "wisdom," "fortitude," "piety," and "chastity." The words' respective meanings in the two contexts, although related, are not the same. For example, the spiritual gift of fortitude is said to confer on the Christian a special readiness to undergo trials for the love of God and in fulfillment of God's Will. Compare and contrast this dictionary's account of **fortitude** as a cardinal moral virtue.)

globalization (n.): Economic process, or interrelated set of processes, by which the production and exchange of goods increasingly comes to involve the whole world. (See discussions under **capitalism** and **distributive justice**.) Also: "globalize" (v.).

gluttony (n.): One of the *capital vices*, a state in which a person has a fixed disposition toward overindulgence—especially regarding food and drink. (Contrast **temperance**.) Also: "glutton" (n.), "gluttonous" (adj.).

gnoseology (n., from Greek *gnosis*, for "knowledge"): An alternative name for the philosophical discipline of *epistemology*. (Some Scholastic writers have marked a distinction between the two, with "gnoseology" designating the general discipline, and "epistemology" applying more specifically to the theory of *scientific* $_{(1)}$ knowledge.) Also: "gnoseological" (adj.), "gnoseologically" (adv.).

gnostic (adj. or n., from Greek *gnosis*, for "knowledge"): Of or pertaining to, or a person who propounds, a type of *gnosticism*.

gnosticism (n., sometimes capitalized, from Greek *gnosis*, for "knowledge"): A movement of thought, or a family of such movements (both ancient and modern), claiming to possess direct and positive knowledge of God, or of other spiritual and esoteric matters. [As mentioned by John Paul II in *Fides et ratio*, #37, from the earliest times—e.g., those of St. Paul, Tertullian, and St. Iraneaus—the authentic Christian tradition has rejected Gnosticism, for it ignores the essentially received and limited character of all human truth about God's nature.]

God (n.): (1) As approached philosophically, the Absolute and Necessary Being; also the First Mover, Uncaused Cause, etc., as arrived at, for example, through Aquinas's *Five Ways.* (See as well **creation** and **eternity**.) (2) In theology, the One who, while in principle approachable through *natural* (4) reason, is made known to us personally only in *revelation* and religious tradition. (From the standpoint of philosophy, the term "God" has the same *referent* in all the monotheistic traditions; however, Christianity's understanding of the "Trinity" [Father, Son, and Spirit], Judaism's understanding of "Yahweh," and Islam's understanding of "Allah" differ from one another in significant ways.) (3) (Lowercase "g.") Any of a number of deities represented in polytheistic traditions—such as, ostensibly, Hinduism (with its figures Vishnu, Shiva, Krishna, et al.).

going out of being (sometimes hyphenated): See **corruption** (1).

Golden Rule: A moral precept—often expressed as "Do unto others as you would have them do unto you"—that is part of the common morality of most peoples and traditions. (A version of the Golden Rule is found in the teachings of Jesus. See the Sermon on the Mount, as recorded in Matthew 7, where Jesus says that such a rule, along with one prescribing the love of God, summarizes the meaning of the Jewish Law and Prophets.)

good (adj.): (1) Desirable or suitable for, or perfective of a being. <Existing as good for any being.> (2) In relation to *human nature,* able to be a part of or contribute to integral human fulfillment. <Mutually supportive relationships within a family as good.> (3) In a specific moral sense, pertaining to human *choices* or *acts* when they fulfill the *determinants* or *sources of morality.* <A just act done for the right motives and in appropriate circumstances as morally good in all respects.> (Ant: **bad**; also contrast "evil" [as an adj.; see **evil**].)

good (n.): (1) A thing that is desirable or suitable for or perfective of a being, and thus an *object* (2) of *appetite.* (Perennial philosophy distinguishes particular human goods—e.g., a happy family life—from the good "as such" or the "comprehensive good" [Latin *bonum in communi*]. The latter is the general and necessary object of the will and is involved in all voluntary acts: anything we choose is chosen precisely as something we believe will contribute to comprehensive good, however this is understood.) (2) As corresponding to the phrases "human good" and especially "integral human good," the ordered set of all those things suitable for or perfective of human nature; this includes things that are *per se* related to human fulfillment—called *honest* or "genuine" or "intrinsic" *goods* (Latin *bona honesta*)—as well as things that are *useful* and *pleasant* (which, when judiciously sought, can contribute to or add to human fulfillment). (3) In a specific *ethical*$_{(1)}$ sense, a decision or act judged positively in light of the *determinants* or *sources of morality*—e.g., a person's helping others, with a charitable motivation, in a time of special need. (Contrast **evil**.)

goodness (n.): (1) The *transcendental* perfection according to which all real beings are desirable or suitable, in appropriate respects and degrees, because of their sharing in *being*$_{(4)}$. (2) The condition shared by the various elements, with their proper internal order, that make up the integral good of *human nature.* (3) State of being good in *moral*$_{(1)}$ quality—attributable to free agents and their acts, insofar as the latter satisfy the *determinants* or *sources of morality.* (Ant: **badness**; also contrast **evil.**)

govern (v.): To regulate beings, powers, or acts—ideally with a view to achieving a recognized good. <God's governing of Creation; a human person's governing of his or her appetites; elected officials' governing of civil society.> Also: "governance" (n.), "governor" (n.).

government (n.): The agencies and mechanisms of *authority*$_{(1)}$ (i.e., executive personnel, legislative bodies, and court systems) by which, ideally, a *civil society* is directed in its pursuit of *public* aspects of the common good—e.g., the maintenance of civil order and the collection of necessary tax revenues. (Government can operate at different levels; in the United States, these include federal, state, and local levels.) (See **regime**, **nation** or **country**, and **state**$_{(2)}$.) Also: "governmental" (adj.), "governmentally" (adv.).

grace (n., Latin *gratia*): Theologically, that by which—through the free, elevating activity of God—human persons can be, and can accomplish, things not achievable according to our *nature*$_{(2)}$. (Note: In the mid-20th century, a controversy arose within Catholic thought—in connection with the work of Henri de Lubac, S.J.—over relations between grace and nature. In particular, it was asked whether nature is something actual and self-contained, which grace operates on only "extrinsically" or "externally." For the perennial tradition, the satisfactory response involves noting the following: although human nature in itself—i.e., as an *essence* (1)—is "whole" or "complete," it is not because of this closed off or impenetrable; rather, since human nature is a *spiritual* nature, it is essentially open to divine initiative, and thus to the elevating activity of grace. Compare the discussion at **obediential potency**.) Also: "gracious" (adj.), "graciously" (adv.).

grammar (n.): See **logic** (3). Also: "grammatical" (adj.).

greatest happiness principle: See **utilitarianism**.

greed (n.): See **avarice** or **greed**.

guilt (n.): Condition or state of being personally responsible for an evil done. (See the discussion of "evil of fault"—Latin *malum culpae*—under **evil**.) Such a state can be attributed either *objectively* or *subjectively*. In the former case, the attribution of guilt depends on an evaluation of a particular act in light of the *determinants* or *sources of morality*. In the latter case, guilt may be lessened (or, in fact, made greater) by a variety of individual circumstances—including non-culpable (or culpable) ignorance of the act's moral *nature* (2) and *object* (3). (Note: In modern psychology, "guilt" typically designates a subjective feeling rather than an objective state. Both usages can be recognized, as long as the above points are borne in mind.) (Ant: **innocence**. See **culpability**.) Also: "guilty" (adj.).

habit (n.): In philosophical psychology, a relatively stable disposition related to a power or appetite, according to which a human person (or other animal) typically acts in a certain manner in specific types of circumstances, or under the influence of specific types of stimuli. (See, by partial contrast, the discussion at ***habitus.***) Also "habitual" (adj.), "habitually" (adv.).

habitus (Latin n., corresponding to Greek *hexis;* plural is *habitus* [with long *u*]): This term, while often rendered into English as "habit," is best left in the Latin and then explained. For the perennial tradition, a state qualifies as a *habitus* only if it is related to objective truth or goodness and involves an element of rational direction. (Thus a *virtue* is an example of a *habitus,* while also typically involving habits—e.g., in the case of *fortitude,* a developed tolerance for physical and/or psychic discomfort.) If a human appetite or power is augmented by a *habitus,* it will be more likely to achieve its proper end; indeed, unless other factors interfere (physical constraints, inadequate information, mental disorders, etc.) it will do so without fail. There are two types of *habitus:* a) moral—e.g., the possessed virtue of fortitude or justice; and b) intellectual—e.g., the possessed knowledge of the first principles of speculative thought (identity, sufficient reason, etc.), or the axioms, postulates, and proof-procedures in Euclidean geometry.

happiness (n.): (1) (Corresponding to Greek *eudaimonia,* Latin *beatitudo.*) As noted by Aristotle, a *common sense* (2) expression for the *final end* or goal of human life. That is, a person of normal *affectivity* cannot not want to be happy, however he or she may conceive this state. Thus "happiness" also designates the ultimate human *good* (in French, suggestively, the term typically used to translate the Greek and Latin is *bonheur,* from *bon,* for "good."). Specific accounts of happiness vary considerably. Aristotle saw happiness as consisting primarily in a life of virtue, but as also requiring minimally decent physical and social conditions. Building upon this, the perennial tradition has come to understand happiness as involving an ordered set of goods, both personal and communal. Theologically considered, the human good in its fullness (expressed in Latin as *beatitudo*) comes only through sharing in the life of the Triune God, in the life to come. (2) For John Stuart Mill and other *hedonist* philosophers, the result of an act insofar as it is experienced as positive. (See **utilitarianism**.) Also: "happy" (adj.).

harm (n.): An evil suffered, precisely as suffered; thus for all beings of normal affectivity an object of *aversion* (2).

harm (v.): To bring about an *evil* in another and/or in oneself. (In the case of human persons, the evil brought about can be of various sorts: physical, psychological, social, moral, or spiritual.) <An adulterer as harming his wife, their relationship, the social order, and himself (by rendering himself morally inferior)>. Also: "harmful" (adj.).

hate (n.): A basic, negative response of appetite and affectivity to objects of *aversion* (2). (Note: Sometimes the word "hate" is used synonymously with "hatred," discussed below.) (Contrast **desire** (2) and **love** (1).)

hate (v.): (1) Most generally, to experience or exercise *hate.* (Ant: **desire** and **love** (1) [as verbs].) (2) To experience or exercise *hatred.* (Contrast **love** (2) and (3) [as verbs].) Also: "hateful" (adj.), "hatefully" (adv.).

hatred (n.): As distinct from *hate* (the basic affective response), a complex *human act* or *emotional state,* at least partially subject to reason and choice, in which one wills harm to another person or persons. (Note: What in American jurisprudence have come to be called "hate crimes" are, strictly speaking, crimes involving hatred—especially ones directed at individuals because of membership in a particular social group, e.g., being of a certain race or having a nonstandard sexual orientation.) (Contrast **love** [as a n.] $_{(2)}$ and $_{(3)}$.)

hedonism (n., from Greek *hedone*, for "pleasure"): As understood in ethics, a theory according to which all other moral considerations are reducible to questions of pleasure and pain. (Many utilitarians, including the movement's principal founders, Jeremy Bentham and John Stuart Mill, have been hedonists in this sense. However, the two terms are not equivalent, since there can be other forms of *utilitarianism*—i.e., other ways of specifying the meaning of goodness in the consequences of acts—than the one offered by hedonism.) Also: "hedonist" (adj. or n.), "hedonistic" (adj.).

Hellenization (n.): Term used primarily by critics of *classical* theology to suggest that the initial *inculturation* of Christianity via Greek and Roman intellectual categories was simply accidental—and in fact should now be overcome. (Such critics have spoken of the need to "de-Hellenize" Christianity.) [In *Fides et ratio*, #72, John Paul II declared to the contrary that, in her proper efforts to reach out to meet other cultures, "the Church cannot abandon what she has gained from her inculturation in the world of Greco-Latin thought. To reject this heritage would be to deny the providential plan of God who guides his Church down the paths of time and history."] Also: "Hellenize" (v.).

hermeneutics (n.): A type of study, formally developed in the 20th century by thinkers such as Hans-Georg Gadamer and Paul Riceour, that is devoted to the interpretation of texts—including the questions of whether, and if so how, one can determine a text's *proper* $_{(1)}$ interpretation. Many thinkers influenced by hermeneutics, including some Catholic theologians (e.g., Roger Haight, S.J.), argue that interpretation is never final, since succeeding generations of readers may have different *principles* of interpretation, as well as different cultural *horizons*. (Note: Hermeneutics is discussed in *Fides et ratio*, ##5, 55, 84, and 95. While respecting its proper place in scholarly activity, John Paul II pointed out that the "various hermeneutical approaches have their own philosophical underpinnings" [#55]; and he commended "a hermeneutic open to the appeal of metaphysics" [#95]—i.e., one anchored in the understanding of being itself, which in principle is available to all reflective persons, regardless of cultural differences.) Also: "hermeneutical" (adj.), "hermeneutically" (adv.).

heterodoxy (n., from Greek *heteros,* for "other" + *doxa,* for "teaching"): The holding of views not in keeping with accepted teachings or doctrines. (For Catholics, such teachings would especially include ones concerning faith and morals that are formally defined by the Church's "extraordinary" *magisterium.* There is controversy regarding whether, and the extent to which, a rejection of less central and/or less definitive Church teachings should be said to constitute "heterodoxy;" accordingly, one should use this term with care.) (Ant: **orthodoxy** $_{(1)}$.) Also: "heterodox" (adj.).

heteronomy (n., from Greek *heteros,* for "other" + *nomos,* for "rule"): In ethics since the time of Immanuel Kant, a condition of the will whereby it accepts moral principles from another, rather than determining such principles for itself. For Kant—and for many contemporary moral philosophers—heteronomy is a state unacceptable for rational and personal beings. (Ant: **autonomy**. See as well the discussion under **theonomy**.) Also: "heteronomous" (adj.), "heteronomously" (adv.).

hierarchy of being: According to Aquinas and his followers, the *order* $_{(2)}$ among beings, involving both their *essence* and their *existence,* in terms of *ontological* status. For example, living beings are higher (i.e., they embody and express more of *being* $_{(2)}$) than nonliving beings; and personal or spiritual beings (notably human beings) are higher than nonpersonal living beings. Purely spiritual yet created beings—the angels—are still more advanced in ontological status. And at the top of the hierarchy is uncreated, Absolute Being (i.e., God). Because of this ordered ontological status, the very terms "being," "existence," "actuality," etc., are understood as *analogous.* (Note: Although scholarly controversy surrounds the matter, Aquinas's view seems rightly contrasted with that of the later Scholastic, John Duns Scotus—and especially with that of many English-speaking philosophers today—who regard "being" as *univocal* in character, and who see no complexity or order among beings precisely in their character as beings.)

hierarchy of goods: On the Thomist understanding, the order of importance among human goods (an aspect of their *teleological structure*) as judged in light of our *final end.* For example, truth and justice are higher or more important (i.e., more central to specifically human, personal fulfillment) than sensory pleasure or even life itself. (Contrast **incommensurability thesis.**)

historicism (n.): View according to which intellectual attitudes and beliefs, including those of religion and philosophy, are inherently limited by modes of thought characteristic of the age in which they are expressed. (Compare **progressivism.**) Also: "historicist" (adj. or n.).

holy or **sacred** (adj.): Set apart from the secular by a special relation with the *supernatural.* These terms are also used of supernatural being itself—which, as famously expressed by 20th-century scholar Rudolf Otto, is experienced by religious people as "tremendous in mystery" or the "numinous." ("Sacred" is sometimes contrasted with "profane"—in the sense of "this-worldly"—as was the Hebrew Scriptures' term *kadosh.*) Also: "holiness" or "sacredness" (n.).

homicide (n., from Latin *homo* for "man" in sense (1)): See the discussions under **kill** and **murder.**

homoousios (Greek adj., from *homo,* for "same" + *ousia,* for "being," "essence," or "substance"): One in being, or one in essence or substance. (Historically, this term—like the corresponding Latin *consubstantialis*—came to have crucial significance in the articulation of Christian dogmas of the *Trinity* and *Incarnation.*)

homosexuality (n.): The condition or *state* (1) of being sexually attracted, sometimes in a very strong and apparently fixed way, to members of one's own *gender.* [As a condition, same-sex attraction—or "orientation," as it is often called—almost never is personally chosen. For perennial philosophy and traditional Catholic teaching, it constitutes an affective deficiency—one of many wounds manifested in concrete humanity following, according to theological teaching, the loss of *original innocence.* However, a homosexual condition is to be distinguished, both psychologically and morally, from specific *human acts* undertaken in line with it. Traditionally, homosexual genital acts are judged to be morally *disordered.* Still, the dignity and basic human rights of all persons must be affirmed and respected. Moreover, given the common human need for love and companionship—as well as the highly sexualized character of contemporary Western culture—many same-sex–attracted persons doubtless require heroic virtue if they are to meet the demands of chastity; and some in fact may be in a state of *invincible ignorance* regarding these demands.]

honest good (Latin *bonum honestum*): An object worthy of being chosen in its own right, because it is *perfective* of the life of human persons, or persons in a particular state; also sometimes called "genuine" or "intrinsic good." (Human motivation is typically complex; however, when persons make informed *choices,* they select and undertake acts in part because they understand them to be ordered to goods of this sort.) <Procreation as an honest or intrinsic good for a married couple.> (See further discussion at ***bonum honestum.*** Contrast **pleasant** or **pleasurable good**, and **useful good.**)

honesty (n.): Moral virtue—an aspect of *justice*—according to which one is disposed to tell the truth when asked for it. (The contrasting vice is termed "dishonesty.") Also: "honest" (adj.), "honestly" (adv.).

hope (n.): (1) In traditional philosophical psychology, a positive *irascible* passion (or emotion, mood, etc.) arising in the context of desired goods that are difficult but not impossible to attain. (Compare **courage**$_{(1)}$, which helps persons pursue such goods.) (2) As discussed by certain recent philosophers and psychologists, a generalized attitude toward the world that positively shapes one's outlook and prompts one to anticipate good (see the discussion of "affective key" under **emotion**). (3) In Christian theology, one of the three *theological virtues* (along with *faith* and *charity* or *love*$_{(3)}$)—specifically the virtue by which the soul is disposed to accept and act on the promise of sharing in God's own life. (Concerning hope in this religious sense, see Pope Benedict XVI's encyclical, *Spe salvi* [2008].) (Contrast **despair** [as a n.].) Also: "hopeful" (adj.).

hope (v.): To experience or engage in *hope,* in any of the senses indicated above. (Contrast **despair** [as a v.].)

horizon (n.): For speculative thought, especially as influenced by recent *phenomenology* and *hermeneutics,* the context and limits (or the apparent or current limits) of individual or cultural understanding. (In *Fides et ratio,* #67, John Paul II remarked that "reason needs to be reinforced by faith, in order to discover horizons it cannot reach on its own.")

human (adj.): Of or having to do with human beings, either in the *abstract* or in the *concrete.* <The specifically human meaning of sexuality.> Also: "human" (n.), "humanity" (n.), "humankind" (n.), "humanly" (adv.).

human act (Latin *actio humana,* sometimes *actus humanus*): An action that is a result of rational *deliberation* and *choice* (e.g., the acceptance of a dinner invitation), rather than an action that is compelled or done apart from the influence of reason (e.g., the natural digestion of food). The latter type of event is sometimes called by contrast an *actio hominis* or "act of a human being"—i.e., precisely not an act that is the result of a deliberate choice. According to the perennial tradition, all and only human acts (*actiones humanae*) in the strict sense are subject to *moral* $_{(1)}$ evaluation.

human being: An individual being that shares in human *nature* $_{(2)}$. Because of our status as rational and personal, humans in whatever condition have a *dignity* beyond that of other physical beings of which we are aware. [Note: Contemporary philosophers sometimes dispute whether being a human being is sufficient for being a *person*. If sense (2) of the latter term is intended, then the answer, obviously, is "No." However, if sense (1)—the ontologically more basic and ethically relevant sense—is intended, then the answer, according to the perennial tradition, is "Yes."]

human dignity: See the discussion under **dignity**.

human good: See **good** $_{(2)}$.

humanism (n.): A broad cultural movement focused on the achievements of and positive prospects for humankind. Originally, in 14th-, 15th-, and 16th-century Europe, humanism stressed the recovery of the cultural achievements of Greek and Roman antiquity. More recent forms of humanism have been diverse and, in general, less positive toward the ancients. [Note: From the beginning of this movement, there have been *secular* (and even *secularist*), as well as *Christian* (and other religious) humanists. An early representative of the latter was the Italian poet Dante (1265–1321). After the French Revolution, an extreme form of humanism arose that actively rebelled against the Church and opposed any acknowledgment of Christian revelation. Various "Humanist" societies, including those in the United States, continue this trend today. However, the possibilities of recovering a properly Christian humanism should not be overlooked. They were promoted (albeit with mixed results) in magisterial documents throughout the 20th century—including many writings of John Paul II—and they continued to be promoted, although with less enthusiasm about immediate prospects for the dominant Western culture, by Benedict XVI.]

human law: Specific ordinances of *civil law* (plus certain matters of deeply ingrained *custom*) that operate within a society. Ideally, human law involves the application or specification, for a given community at a given time, of principles of *natural* (*moral*) *law.* (For Aquinas, only those ordinances that at least cohere with natural law are to be regarded as genuine human law; "laws" that do not meet this standard are *unjust,* and in fact are instances of *violence* $_{(2)}$, rather than ordinances of reason.) (See **law** $_{(1)}$ and **positive law.**)

human nature: The *essence* shared or participated in by all human beings. Properly understood, according to perennial thought, this nature serves as a *norm* $_{(1)}$ for ethics. (Here, as often, "nature"—i.e., *nature* $_{(2)}$—should be distinguished from concrete "condition" or "state." Christian faith, with its teachings about sin and redemption, sheds light on the concrete problems of and prospects for humankind; thus theological ethics goes beyond and supplements philosophical ethics. However, the religious teachings do not negate the significance of the concept "human nature" for general moral reflection.)

human person, philosophy of: See **philosophy of the human person** or **human nature**.

human rights (sometimes **basic human rights**): See the discussion under **natural rights.**

Humean (adj. or n.): Of or pertaining to, or a person who holds, ideas and themes of the Scottish philosopher David Hume (1711–76). Following and extending the critical analyses of his predecessors, John Locke and George Berkeley, Hume became, in the theory of knowledge, a principal founder of *empiricism*—a movement that continues to be influential (especially in the English-speaking world) to the present day. In this regard, he went so far as to question whether concepts such as "cause" and "effect" are subject to rational support. In moral philosophy, Hume is credited with originating the view that one "cannot derive an 'ought' from an 'is' "—for example, even though most persons seek friendships in life, one cannot derive a moral principle that persons ought to seek friendships. (Contrast ethical *naturalism* $_{(2)}$.) Also: "Humeanism" (n.).

humility (n.): A virtue, related to the *cardinal virtue* of *temperance,* whereby one is able to develop and accept an honest understanding of oneself—including one's genuine strengths and weaknesses, gifts and limitations, etc. (Some writers associate humility with the psychological state of low self-esteem, and even with humiliation; but this virtue clearly is different from those states.) Also: "humble" (adj.), "humbly" (adv.).

hylemorphism, sometimes **hylomorphism** (n., from Greek *hule,* for "matter" + *morphe,* for "form"): The Aristotelian account of natural *substance* as composed of *co-principles* called *matter* $_{(3)}$ and substantial *form.* (By extension, "matter" and "form," and thus also "hylemorphism," can be used in analyzing realities other than physical substances—e.g., in accounts of the "matter" and "form" of a *human act.*) Also: "hylemorphic," sometimes "hylomorphic" (adj.).

hypostasis (Greek n., from *hupo,* for "under" + *histasthai,* for "to be standing"): A term with essentially the same meaning as the later Latin *suppositum*—i.e., a complete *subject* $_{(3)}$ of a nature or essence. ("Hypostasis," as well as the related notion of "hypostatic union"—figured crucially in early Church formulations of teachings on the *Trinity* [i.e., God as one Essence shared by three Hypostases or Persons] and on *Incarnation* [i.e., the Person of Christ as comprising a "hypostatic union" of two natures, *God* and *man* $_{(1)}$].) (Compare **supposit.**)

hypothesis (n.): As used in the natural *sciences* $_{(2)}$, a predictive judgment about an empirical event that will occur under a describable set of conditions. (Hypotheses are sometimes generated by more general *theories* $_{(2)}$; if the predicted events in fact occur, the hypotheses are said to be confirmed, and this in turn provides additional rational support for the theories in question.) Also: "hypothetical" (adj.), "hypothetically" (adv.).

id (n.): In Freudian theory, one of the three divisions of the *psyche* $_{(2)}$; the id is said to be the unconscious source of psychic energy derived from our instinctual needs.

idea (n., Greek *eidos*): (1) The *concept* or *intelligible species* by which the intellect to some degree knows a substantial nature or other general feature. The Greek term also was applied by the ancients to *sensible species,* by which a power of sense is in contact with physical reality. (In both cases a *form* exists *intentionally,* that is, as a modification of the power of intellect or, in the case of sensation, of the associated power of the human or animal nature.) (2) More loosely, any notion developed by the mind, whatever its supposed relation with objective reality. (3) The *exemplar* of each thing existing in the mind of God.

ideal (adj.): Of or pertaining to the perfection of a type of reality; or a being, substantial or accidental, regarded as a supreme instance of its type. <A quiet library as the ideal setting for scholarly work.> Also: "ideally" (adv.).

ideal (n.): A *good,* often abstractly expressed, that serves (or ought to serve) as a consciously accepted goal or *end* $_{(2)}$ of human striving. <A person of high ideals—truth, justice, etc.> (Compare **value** [as a n.].)

idealism (n): (1) In metaphysics and epistemology, a theory (or family of theories) holding that *reality* consists of, or exists most fundamentally as, ideas in the minds of sentient and intellectual beings—including, in some versions, God. (Contrast **realism** $_{(1)}$ and $_{(2)}$.) (2) In ethics, the possession of lofty goals—the suggestion often being that the goals in question are unrealistic or, as a practical matter, unachievable. (Contrast **realism** $_{(3)}$.) Also: "idealist" (adj. or n.), "idealistic" (adj.), "idealistically" (adv.).

identity, principle of: The first principle of *metaphysics*—and thus of all speculative thought—namely, "Everything is what it is." (Another formulation of the principle would be "What is, is; what is not, is not.") (Compare **noncontradiction, principle of**, which stands as the first principle of logic.)

ideology (n): Set of ideas governing thought and/or practice, especially (although not exclusively) in the social and political realm. <Marx's ideology of the revolution of the proletariat.> (Sometimes the term is used with a negative connotation, according to which ideologies are to be contrasted with theories having a proper philosophical or other rational grounding.) Also: "ideological" (adj.), "ideologically" (adv.), "ideologue" (n.).

idolatry (n.): Taking something other than God—in particular, a being of the physical world—to be God, and worshipping it accordingly. (The 12th-century Jewish thinker Moses Maimonides warned that any attempt to speak positively and literally of God would lead one into idolatry; thus, apart from recognizing the role of religious *metaphor* and *symbol*, he was a pure proponent of the *negative way*. Not wanting to fall into idolatry himself, and aware of the difficulty raised by his Jewish predecessor, Aquinas developed an account of positive language about God in terms of his theory of *analogy*.) Also: "idolator" (n.), "idolatrous" (adj.).

illative sense: According to the account of 19th-century British thinker John Henry Cardinal Newman (mentioned in *Fides et ratio*, #74), a faculty or act by which we sometimes come to a conclusion, or a perception of truth, without formal, logical reasoning—for example, in the case of belief in God, through the "convergence" of a variety of experiences and lines of thought. [Note: While acknowledging Newman's insight, strict Thomists insist, in apparent opposition to Newman, that God's existence is subject to *demonstration*.] (Compare **abduction**.)

illogical (adj.): Not *logical* $_{(2)}$.

illumination (n.): Prominent theme in accounts of knowledge, beginning with Plato's, that suggest we can have direct access to the intelligible features of things. (For St. Augustine, "divine illumination"—i.e., direct illumination by God—takes the place of Plato's speculation about the soul's prior acquaintance with eternal Forms.

Somewhat by contrast, Aquinas, who recruits Aristotelian notions to his *epistemology,* holds that the immediate source of illumination in natural knowledge is the individual's *agent intellect*—which, while participating in the light of the divine intellect, develops concepts rooted in the data of experience.) Also: "illuminate" or "illumine" (v).

image (n.): (1) Result of operation of the "internal" *sense* known as imagination. According to perennial philosophy, it is important to distinguish an image from an intelligible idea or concept, since the latter results from the operation of *intellect,* rather than sense itself. (2) More broadly, the result of an operation of any internal sense—e.g., an image developed from memory. <Retaining strong images of a deceased relative.> (Compare **phantasm.**) Also: "image" (as a v.).

image of God (Latin *imago Dei*): In Genesis 1, God says, "Let us create man in our own image [or likeness]." This text has been a fertile source for Christian philosophers and theologians, who have asked: In what ways can the human person, or the human community, be said to "image" (or be "like") *God?* And in what ways does our limited knowledge of God—both natural and revealed—lead to insights about the nature of *human* persons? (For the tradition of integral Christian wisdom, all persons' being created in the image of God is the fundamental ground of universal human *dignity.*)

imagination (n.): One of the "internal" *senses.* Building upon but going beyond the *common sense* $_{(1)}$, the imagination is not restricted in its synthesizing powers; thus one can imagine, without having seen or expecting to see, a winged horse or a golden mountain—although one does need to have experienced the individual elements that are brought together in such sensory objects.

immanence (n.): (1) Property of an act whereby the effect remains within the agent. (Ant: **transience** or **transitivity.**) (2) Property attributed to God, according to which, because of divine *Creation* and *Conservation,* God is present to finite reality in all individuals and at all times. (Note: Readers sometimes confuse this term with *imminence* and with *eminence;* as the entries in this dictionary make clear, the three should be carefully distinguished.) (Ant: **transcendence** $_{(2)}$.) Also: "immanent" (adj.), "immanently" (adv.).

immanence, method of: Process of reflection rooted in the interior experience of the individual person. As developed by turn of the

20th-century French Catholic philosopher Maurice Blondel, this method leads one to recognize the appropriateness—given the limitless character of human desire and the ultimate mystery of the meaning of life—of anticipating a *revelation* from God. (Note: Although Blondel did not share the perennial philosophy's metaphysical insights [and he was something of an antagonist to Thomists such as Jacques Maritain], his work exerted considerable influence on Catholic thought; in particular, the above theme was referred to with approval by John Paul II.)

immanentism (n.): Philosophical view according to which the human mind has a kind of subliminal contact with Absolute Being or God, and it periodically gives expression to this contact in sets of religious *symbols* $_{(2)}$. One who holds this view believes that such symbols (including those of Christianity and other world religions) do not function *literally* (i.e., do not express genuine concepts and judgments); thus they cannot have *truth-values* or come into *cognitive* conflict with one another. (See **postmodernism** and **religious pluralism**.) Also: "immanentist" (adj. or n.).

immaterial (adj.): Not material—either "neutrally," that is, not *essentially* material; or "positively," that is, essentially nonmaterial or *spiritual.* (The subject matter of metaphysics, being as being, is immaterial in the former way. This philosophical discipline's concepts [e.g., *being* $_{(3)}$ and *actuality*] apply to all beings—including both those that in fact are material [e.g., chemical elements and compounds], and those that come to be recognized as spiritual [e.g., human or rational souls].) Also: "immateriality" (n.), "immaterially" (adv.).

imminence (n.): As said of an event, temporal proximity to actual occurrence. <Death's imminence as justifying a withdrawal of artificial nutrition and hydration from a patient.> (Readers sometimes confuse this term with *immanence* and with *eminence;* as their respective definitions make clear, the three terms should be carefully distinguished.) Also: "imminent" (adj.), "imminently" (adv.).

immobile or **immutable** (adj.): Not subject to change. <First principles as immutable truths.> Also: "immobility" or "immutability" (n.).

immoral (adj.): Morally bad or wrong, as said of a *human act, choice,* or *intention* $_{(3)}$ undertaken in violation of one or more of the *determinants* or *sources of morality.* This term also applies to persons who are given to such acts, choices, or intentions. (Contrast both **moral** $_{(2)}$ and **amoral.**) Also: "immorally" (adv.).

immorality (n.): Condition or state of engaging in morally bad acts, sometimes on a large scale; this state may be ascribed either to individuals or to whole societies (or subgroups within a society). (Contrast both **morality** $_{(2)}$ and **amorality**. See **determinants** or **sources of morality**.)

immortal (adj.): (1) Not subject to death (Latin *mors*) or, therefore, to physical corruption. (2) (Figurative use.) Living—or destined to live, or made to live—permanently in the *minds* of succeeding generations. <The immortal words of America's Declaration of Independence.> Also: "immortally" (adv.); and, in relation to sense (2), "immortalize" (v.), "immortalization" (n.).

immortality (n.): Condition of not being subject to death; that is, once living, always alive—as long as the being remains in actual *existence* $_{(2)}$. (Compare as well the figurative use of "immortal" noted in the preceding entry.)

immutable (adj.): See **immobile** or **immutable.**

impassible (adj.): Not able to undergo change or to be affected in a strict sense. This characteristic is predicated exclusively of God. [Note: As has been discussed by writers such as W. Norris Clarke, S.J., it is a mistake—although a common one—to regard being impassible as equivalent to being unable, for example, to rejoice. God, says Clarke, rejoices at our freely chosen good acts; although in this way *contingent*, such rejoicing involves no real *change:* God happily sees from all eternity the positive responses we make to the gifts and promptings he ordains.] Also: "impassibility" (n.).

impossibility (n.): State or condition of being *impossible*, in any of the senses indicated. (Ant: **possibility**. Contrast as well **necessity**.)

impossible (adj.): (1) (Metaphysically.) Not able to be, *absolutely* $_{(2)}$; that is, such a thing's actuality would violate the *principle of identity.* (2) (Logically.) Not able to be consistently thought; that is, the proposition's truth would be incompatible with the *principle of noncontradiction.* (3) (Physically.) Not able to be the case in this universe or in the realm of physical being, as judged in light of known *laws* $_{(3)}$ of nature and/or principles of *natural philosophy.* (4) (Morally.) Not able to be morally right under any conditions; that is, the *object* $_{(3)}$ of the act involves a direct attack on a *basic good* or a violation of an applicable *moral precept.* (5) (Practically.) Not within the presumed capabilities of these agents in the present circumstances as they are understood to be. (In all of the above senses, contrast both **necessary** and **possible.**) Also: "impossibly" (adv.).

in*, *esse (Latin phrase): See the discussion under ***esse-ab.***

inalienable (adj.): Inseparable; not able to be lost, forfeited, or justifiably taken away. <Inalienable rights—e.g., the right to life or to religious liberty.> (Ant: **alienable.**) Also: "inalienability" (n.).

inanimate (adj.): Not living; said especially of a being that by *nature*$_{(2)}$ is never alive (e.g., a molecule of sodium chloride). (Ant: **animate.**)

incarnation (n., from Latin *carnis,* for "flesh"): (1) Real instance, or the process of becoming a real instance, especially in the case of living beings. (Compare **instantiation.**) (2) (With capital "I.") Central Christian mystery and teaching according to which God (the Son) became truly human, and thus according to which the *person*$_{(1)}$ of Jesus the Christ (from Greek *Christos* for "anointed") combines in a single *hypostasis* or *supposit* the two natures of *God* and *man*$_{(1)}$—an article of faith sometimes referred to as the "hypostatic union." (The doctrine of Incarnation also proposes that Christ—through his teaching, suffering, death, and resurrection, and through the sending of the Holy Spirit—makes it possible for humankind to escape the condition of *sin*$_{(3)}$ and to share in the very life of the Triune God.) Also, in both senses: "incarnate" (adj. or v.).

inclination or **tendency** (n.): A propensity to a certain type of act—whether natural, habitual, or elicited, and however conditioned by the concrete circumstances of the individual *subject*$_{(2)}$. (Philosophically, because of their bearing on the formulation of principles of *natural* (*moral*) *law,* the most important type of inclinations—insofar as these can be discerned—are the *natural inclinations* of human personal life.)

inclination, judgment by: In *practical* matters, knowledge of the good or the bad, the right or the wrong, etc., that proceeds directly from a state of *virtue,* rather than requiring a process of rational reflection. (See **affective knowledge.**)

inclusivism (n.): See the discussion under **pluralism**$_{(2)}$. Also: "inclusive" (adj.), "inclusivist" (adj. or n.).

incoherence (n.): Antonym of *coherence.* Also: "incoherent" (adj.), "incoherently" (adv.).

incommensurability thesis: By contrast with classical Thomist notions of a *hierarchy of goods,* and of goods as having a *teleological structure,* the theory espoused by Germain Grisez and some other recent Catholic thinkers (e.g., John Finnis and Robert George), according to which the *basic goods* $_{(2)}$ of human life belong to irreducibly different *orders* $_{(1)}$, with each such good recognized as being good in a distinctive manner, and with no method of comparatively evaluating, or ranking, the fundamental goods.

incommensurable (adj.): As said of two or more things, not able to be assessed according to a common *rule* $_{(1)}$. <Standardized test scores of students from diverse cultural backgrounds as often being incommensurable.> (Ant: **commensurable.**) Also: "incommensurability" (n.), "incommensurably" (adv.).

incommunicable (adj.): (1) As said of a being that is *subsistent,* not able to share its individual reality with any other being. Such beings also are not able, without loss of identity, to be subsumed into the reality of another. (These points are sometimes expressed by saying that a subsistent being, sharing in the transcendental property of *oneness* or *unity,* is "indivisible in itself and separate from all others.") As with other metaphysical properties, there are degrees of being incommunicable. Each physical substance has this property to some degree, since it is an individual whole that constitutes an instance of *matter* $_{(2)}$. Living beings, and especially animals, enjoy the property to a higher degree, since the immediate *experiences* of each individual are its own. Finally, *personal* $_{(1)}$ beings are incommunicable in the highest degree, for they can reflect upon and order themselves precisely as *selves* (see **self-possession**). (2) As said of a psychic element—e.g., a feeling or intuition—not able to be expressed to another with full intelligibility. (Ant., in both senses: **communicable** $_{(1)}$.) Also: "incommunicability" (n.), "incommunicably" (adv.).

incompatibilism (n.): As understood in recent philosophy, the thesis expressing the contradictory opposite of *compatibilism.* [Proponents of the perennial tradition regard both of these modern theses as resting on a misunderstanding. See the discussions under **compatibilism**, and **freedom** or **liberty**.]

incompatible (adj.): As said of two or more properties, unable to inhere in the same subject at the same time. <Life and death as

incompatible features of an organized body.> (Ant: **compatible**.) Also: "incompatibility" (n.), "incompatibly" (adv.).

incomplete substance: See the discussion under **substance**.

incomprehensible (adj.): Not able to be comprehended or adequately understood, at least by human persons in our present state; said especially of the reality of God. (Importantly, however—and contrary to the view sometimes suggested by theologians such as Elizabeth A. Johnson, C.S.J.—to be incomprehensible is not the same as to be simply "unknowable," or unavailable to the human intellect. For the perennial tradition, the *mystery* of God indeed exceeds our comprehension. But the human mind, through philosophical reflection, can come to know that God exists, that God is one, etc.; and it can articulate such knowledge via the *analogy of proportionality.* Moreover, docrinal formulas express the divine reality—accurately, if obscurely and incompletely—through what Maritain called the "superanalogy of faith.") Also: "incomprehensibility" (n.).

inconsistent (adj.): As said of two or more propositions or ideas, unable to be affirmed, or to be true, at the same time. <An inconsistent axiom set; a conclusion inconsistent with the argument's premises.> (Ant: **consistent**. See **contradictory**.) Also: "inconsistency" (n.), "inconsistently" (adv.).

incorporeal (adj.): Of or pertaining to realities not having a bodily nature, or not involving composition with *matter*$_{(3)}$. <Angelic natures—but not human nature—as incorporeal.> Also: "incorporeality" (n.), "incorporeally" (adv.).

incorruptible (adj.): Not subject to disintegration or dissolution. <The human soul as incorruptible.> Also: "incorruptibility" (n.), "incorruptibly" (adv.).

inculpability (n.): Opposite of *culpability.* <Although the victim died, the officer who shot him retains inculpability, since it was a tragic case of mistaken identity for which he was in no way responsible.> (For discussion of a related type of case, see **invincible ignorance**.) Also: "inculpable" (adj.), "inculpably" (adv.).

inculturation (n.): Process whereby a common but historically grounded message (including, notably, the Christian message) comes to be expressed in terms that are accessible to a new culture. (Questions about inculturation, both practical and theoretical, have been matters of widespread concern in recent decades. See the discussions under **Hellenization**, **interreligious dialogue**, and **pluralism**$_{(2)}$.)

indeterminism (n.): (1) (Also "indeterminacy.") In recent physics, the view (associated with Heisenberg's "uncertainty principle") that the precise position and the final velocity of an electron cannot be predicted simultaneously, since not all the relevant initial conditions can be ascertained without disturbing the microphenomena themselves. (Ant: **determinism** $_{(1)}$.) (2) In philosophy, the view that *human acts* are indeterminable or essentially unpredictable, and thus in that sense and for that reason are "free." [Note: Philosophers holding this view sometimes have pointed to "indeterminacy" in recent physics as supporting their position; however, this suggestion seems dubious and in any event does not bear on the question of *freedom* as understood in the perennial tradition.] (Contrast **determinism** $_{(2)}$.)

indifference (n.): Status attributed to a practical decision when two or more options are equally acceptable when judged in light of the *determinants* or *sources of morality.* (Note: Indifference as here defined neither implies nor supports an attitude of *indifferentism* in the agent.) Also: "indifferent" (adj.), "indifferently" (adv.).

indifference, active or **dominating**: As articulated by 20th-century Thomist philosophers Jacques Maritain and Yves R. Simon, the spontaneous *freedom* enjoyed by the will in its highest or "terminal" state of development; in this state the will is not determined by extraneous factors, but rather chooses with regularity and ease what the agent recognizes to be in keeping with the comprehensive *good.* (See **superdetermination.**)

indifference, freedom of: See the discussion under **excellence, freedom for.**

indifferentism (n): General attitude of unconcern about ultimate or metaphysical questions, and sometimes about moral questions as well. Often this attitude is accompanied by *skepticism.* Also: "indifferentist" (adj. or n.).

indirect (adj.): In ethics, said of an effect that is not the *object* $_{(3)}$ of an act, but that nevertheless may be relevant, under the heading of *circumstances,* in the moral evaluation of the act as a whole. (Ant: **direct**. See **determinants** or **sources of morality**, and **principle of double effect.**) Also: "indirectly" (adv.).

indirect communication: Key notion in the thought of 19th-century Danish philosopher and religious thinker Søren Kierkegaard. Given the nature and significance of human *subjectivity* $_{(1)}$, according to Kierkegaard, genuine communication among persons about matters of interiority (in particular, matters of religious faith) can only be "indirect"—since each subject has direct access only to his or her own subjectivity.

individual (n.): (1) A thing of an individuated *nature* $_{(2)}$, whether substantial or accidental (e.g., a human being, his or her height, coloring, etc.). (Syn: **particular**.) (2) A being considered in terms of the transcendental property of *oneness* or *unity*—i.e., as consistent, indivisible in itself, and distinct from every other thing. (See **incommunicable** $_{(1)}$.) (3) Among physical objects, one member of a species which (due to the presence of *quantity*) is subject to number or countability. (4) In moral considerations, the singular case—what one is to do here and now—which must be decided by a judgment of *prudence*, or rightly ordered *inclination*, rather than being completely determinable within the general discipline of ethics. Also: "individual" (as an adj.), "individuality" (n.), "individually" (adv.).

individualism (n.): (1) In political philosophy, the view that concern for the individual citizen in all respects takes precedence over concern for the community. This view in effect rejects the perennial tradition's claim that private goods may need to be sacrificed for the sake of the *common good*. (Ant: **statism** or "collectivism," which—as the other extreme—denies any intrinsic worth or moral consideration to the individual person. Compare **liberalism** $_{(1)}$. Contrast **communitarianism**.) (2) In ethics, the view that each moral agent is subject only to the dictates of his or her conscience, unencumbered by traditional standards or any objective moral order. (Compare **subjectivism**. Contrast **universalism**.)

individuate or **individualize** (v.): To cause a thing to be particular or singular. Also: "individuated" or "individualized" (adj.), "individuation" (n.).

individuating (adj.): As said of characteristics of a being, those that make it the unique, singular being it is. (Compare **incommunicable**. Contrast **communicable**, as well as **essential** $_{(1)}$.)

individuation, **principle of**: In the case of physical beings, that principle in terms of which a shared nature is individualized—i.e., matter as subject to *quantity* and thus marked off and able to be identified and counted. Individuation applies primarily and formally to *substances; concrete *accidents* are individuated insofar as they inhere in or involve relations among substances. (According to Thomists, in the case of nonphysical beings [e.g., angels], form or essence itself individuates; that is, each being in effect is its own species. Moreover, from a metaphysical point of view, the deepest type of individuation—whether a thing is physical or nonphysical—is rooted in the perfection of *subsistence,* whereby the being is able to exist on its own, rather than as a feature of another.)

indubitable (adj.): Not able to be objectively doubted. (Syn: [objectively] **certain**. Ant: **doubtable** or **dubitable**.) Also: "indubitability" (n.), "indubitably" (adv.).

induction (n.): Method by which general propositions or objects of knowledge are gathered from particular cases. (Note: For Aristotle and his medieval followers, the intellectual process called *abstraction* [Greek *epagoge;* Latin *abstractio*] in principle enabled the mind to grasp a *nature* $_{(2)}$ or *essence* via reflection on various instances, and thus allowed for "real" definition [i.e., *definition*$_{(2)}$]. In practice, however, such abstraction has proved exceedingly difficult—at least in relation to natural phenomena; and the modern *sciences*$_{(2)}$, which tend to be *perinoetic* rather than *dianoetic,* generally do not understand their inductions to be ordered to a knowledge of essences.) (Contrast **deduction**.) Also: "inductive" (adj.), "inductively" (adv.).

inequality (n.): Lack of *equality,* either objectively or in terms of perception (or both). In ethics, as well as in law and public policy, this notion applies especially to the treatment of persons (or classes of persons) who deserve to be, but in fact are not, treated equally in the particular respect in question (e.g., having access to basic education or health care)—thus raising important questions of *distributive justice.* (See also **discrimination.**)

infidelity (n.): Antonym of *fidelity;* used especially, although not only, of failure to maintain marital commitments. (In the religious context, an "infidel" fails to maintain—or to recognize—duties to God.)

infinite (adj.): Without limit or boundary. <According to some accounts—e.g., Aristotle's (but not Aquinas's)—time is said to be infinite in duration.> (Ant: **finite.**) Also: "infinitely" (adv.), "infinitude" or "infinity" (n.).

informal logic: Area of logic that deals with properties and issues other than those that can be treated formally (e.g., through syllogistic or propositional logic). A prominent topic in this area is the identification of various types of "informal" *fallacy.* (See also **material logic.**)

injustice (n.): System or act—or effect of a system or act—that does not give each person his or her due. (Ant: **justice** $_{(2)}$.)

innate (adj.): Said of a property that is present from the beginning of a thing's existence, and stems simply from its being a thing of a given *nature* (2). <The innate dignity of each human person.> (Ant: **acquired**.) Also: "innately" (adv.), "innateness" (n.).

innocence (n.): Condition in which a person is not morally responsible for evil done—either because (in light of the *determinants* or *sources of morality*) no evil in fact has been done, or because the person's involvement in the evil was not *voluntary* (i.e., it did not include knowledge of the evil and free consent). (Ant: **guilt**. Compare **inculpability**.) Also: "innocent" (adj.), "innocently" (adv.).

insight (n.): In epistemology or the theory of knowledge, an alternative term for *apprehension* or *intellection* (*simple*). (The term "insight" gained special currency with the 1957 book of this title by Catholic philosopher and theologian Bernard Lonergan, S.J., who wrote of insight that it is "the pivot between images and concepts." For Lonergan, however, the term "insight" did not necessarily imply that the effort of intellect has succeeded in capturing its object.)

instantiation (n.): In logic and philosophy, a particular case or instance of a certain type. <Instantiations of "R" in transitive relations of the form "aRb"—e.g., "being taller than."> (Compare **incarnation** (1).) Also: "instantiate" (v.).

instinct (n.): A mode of *sensory affectivity* in animals and human persons, whereby they are induced to pursue certain physical goods and avoid certain physical harms. Instincts derive from things' *natures* (3); but in human persons they are, at least according to the perennial tradition, subject to a measure of rational development and control. <The "fight-or-flight" instinct.> Also: "instinctive" or "instinctual" (adj.), "instinctively" or "instinctually" (adv.).

instrumental (adj.): Having purpose or value that is subordinate to, or in service of, some other more important or urgent good. <The instrumental value of regular dental checkups.> (Compare **useful good**.)

instrumentalism (n.): Philosophical position holding that all goods are *instrumental* goods; or that no ends or purposes have *intrinsic* value, apart from human preferences and choices. Also: "instrumentalist" (adj. or n.).

integral (adj.): Whole and integrated, that is, comprising all essential aspects in proper *order* (2). <An integral approach to promot-

ing public health.> Also: "integrally" (adv.).

integral Christian wisdom: See **wisdom, integral Christian.**

integral human good: See the discussion under **good** (n.).

integral virtue, person of: One who instantiates in his or her very selfhood the *unity* (or *interconnectedness*) *of the virtues,* and thus one who is in ideal position to exercise moral judgment. (Aristotle called such a person *phronemos*—the "man of *practical wisdom* [or *prudence*].")

integrity (n.): A state or condition of wholeness; in particular, for ethics, the state of *character* by which one consistently pursues a life of integral virtue (with the emphasis sometimes on honesty).

intellect (n., sometimes **intelligence**; from Latin *in* + *legere,* for "to read in"): (1) Power of *rational soul* by which science (especially *science* $_{(1)}$) is produced. In its use as "speculative" intellect, this power has three basic operations: a) *apprehension* or *intellection* (*simple*) of things' natures via abstraction and the formation of concepts; b) *judgment,* which affirms or denies that a thing exists, or exists in such and such manner; and c) *reasoning,* by which new knowledge is produced or existing knowledge is ordered according to logical relations. (2) The term "practical" intellect applies to the use of reason in ethics and other inquiries about things to be done, as well as in concrete prudential judgments. (Note: In either sense, when the variant "intelligence" is used, it is not to be taken as equivalent to that term as used in the *positive science* of psychology—where there is, in principle, always reference to measurable performance.) Also: "intellectual," sometimes "intellective" (adj.), "intellectually" (adv.).

intellectual (n.): A person who, by profession and/or temperament, devotes his or her life to concerns of the *intellect.*

intellectual affectivity: See **will** (n.).

intellectualism (n.): Approach to the understanding of human activity (and indeed all personal activity) that maintains the primacy of *intellect.* (Scholars sometimes speak of the "intellectualism" of St. Thomas Aquinas, for whom *law* $_{(1)}$, including *eternal law,* is always an "ordinance of reason," never merely of will.) (Contrast **voluntarism.**)

intellectual virtues: See **virtues, intellectual.**

intelligent design theory: A recent variant of *creationism* $_{(1)}$. Regarding the development of forms of life on planet Earth, intelligent design theorists argue, on the basis of probability analyses, that standard Darwinian accounts involving purely material factors (e.g., random variation and natural selection) cannot plausibly explain the present complexity of organisms. Hence the need for a theory involving "design," however this notion may be understood. (Intelligent design theory obviously is compatible with the idea of a Creator; but if it is rooted, as it is claimed to be, in *scientific* $_{(2)}$ modes of reasoning, it cannot lead to such an idea as a proper conclusion. To their credit, leading proponents of the theory—e.g., Michael Behe—recognize this point.) (See **teleology** $_{(2)}$.)

intelligibility (n.): (1) Aspect of a being that is able to become a formal *object* $_{(2)}$ of *intellect;* an abstractable *form,* whether essential or accidental. (2) (Now somewhat archaic.) A purely spiritual being, in particular, an *angel.*

intelligible (adj.): Able to become a formal *object* $_{(2)}$ of intellect.

intelligible (n.): (1) A shortened form of "intelligibility." (2) The *species* $_{(2)}$ by which—to the extent a process of *abstraction* is successful—a reality is known in its nature. (See **intention** $_{(1)}$.)

intelligible matter: The "matter" (not itself physical) focused on in pure mathematics—e.g., point, line, and number. (See **degrees** or **orders of abstraction**.)

intend (v., from Latin *intendere* for "to reach out"): To have or to exercise an *intention,* in any of the senses distinguished.

intension (n.): As understood in modern logic, meaning as *sense* or *connotation.* (Ant: **extension**.) Also: "intensional" (adj.).

intention (n., Latin *intentio*): (1) In relation to intellectual knowledge, a *being of reason*—in particular, an *intelligible species*—functioning as a "means by which" (Latin *quo*) knowledge is attained and mentally represented. (Scholastics have divided intentions into "first" intentions, which express characteristics of reality itself, and "second" intentions, which express logical characteristics of concepts of first intention, for example, being a genus or species.) (2) In relation to human acts, the agent's subjective *end* $_{(2)}$ or *motive.* (3) Derivatively, the *object* $_{(3)}$ of an act insofar as it is willed by the agent as a *means* to his or her end. (If the term "intention" is used in discussions of the morality of human acts, it is important to distinguish sense (2) from sense (3).) (See **determinants** or **sources of morality**, as well as ***praeter intentionem.***)

intentional (adj.): (1) Mode of existence in the mind, as with *sensible* or *intelligible species* $_{(2)}$, rather than in extramental reality, as with existing physical substances (which such *species* enable us to know). (Ant: **entitative** (1).) (2) Of or pertaining to either the moral *object* (3) or a *motive* for an act.

intentionality (n.): (1) Feature of cognition and choice, as well as comparable acts of sensory awareness, whereby these acts have as *objects* (2) the things known and the goods sought. (2) In *phenomenology*, as originally developed by Edmund Husserl, an essential feature of consciousness as such—namely, that it consists in a reaching out to (Latin *intendere*) objects, although it is not essentially related to any actual reality beyond itself. [Note: Students and followers of Husserl's method who have sought to bring it into contact with the perennial tradition—e.g., Roman Ingarden, St. Edith Stein, Dietrich von Hildebrand, and Karol Wojtyla—have dissented on this point, proposing instead a *realist* phenomenology according to which the mind, by way of its intentional relations, achieves contact with real being.]

interconnectedness of the virtues: See **unity** (or **interconnectedness**) **of the virtues**.

interest (n.): (1) The "matter" of a right (see **right** [n.]). (2) In capitalist economies, money earned on an investment, or charged for servicing a loan. [Note: Originally, before the nature of capitalist economies and their interactions were well developed and well understood, traditional Christian moralists (as well as Catholic Church authorities) objected, on grounds of *justice*, to the lending of money at interest—which was called "usury." As these financial systems have unfolded and been further reflected upon, this objection has been modified—not, as is sometimes suggested, simply retracted—to say that the interest charged should be proportionate to real value received by way of the loan, and that the system as a whole should serve the common good of genuine economic opportunity for all. If such conditions do not hold, the taking of interest is indeed judged to be usurious and immoral.]

interiority (n.): For *phenomenologists*, the *self* or *ego* (1), precisely as experienced.

internal senses: See the discussion under **sense** (n.) (2).

interreligious dialogue: Dialogue among the *world religions*, as well as with local indigenous religions. Both the purposes of and proper attitudes for participants in such dialogue have been subjects of controversy in the post-Vatican II period. (In *Fides et ratio* and elsewhere, John Paul II suggested a number of such purposes and attitudes. The former included, remotely, evangelization; but also the appreciation of other perspectives, a purification of one's own religious faith, and seeing how one's beliefs and practices might be expressed in the setting of a new culture. (See **inculturation**.) Regarding attitudes, in *Fides et ratio*, #72, John Paul II set out three conditions for participation in interreligious dialogue, ones he believed should be acceptable not only to Christians but to all parties: a) that all recognize "the universality of the human spirit, whose basic needs are the same in the most disparate cultures;" b) that it be understood that Catholic Christianity cannot "abandon what she has gained from her inculturation in the world of Greco-Latin thought;" and c) that, while each tradition and culture can rightly point to its "uniqueness and originality," this should not be taken as a pretext for "remain[ing] closed in its difference" or for "affirm[ing] itself by opposing other traditions.")

intrinsic (adj.): Related to the *nature*$_{(2)}$ or *essence* of a thing or act, rather than to accidental features or circumstances. (Ant: **extrinsic**.) Also: intrinsically" (adv.).

intrinsic(ally) evil: A human act that, of its nature, cannot be morally good because its *object*$_{(3)}$ itself is bad. <The deliberate taking of the life of an innocent person as intrinsically evil.> (According to the Thomist school, as well as the ordinary Catholic *magisterium,* certain types of acts are, and can be known to be, intrinsically evil.) (See the discussions under **determinants** or **sources of morality**, and **exceptionless moral rules**. Contrast **proportionalism** and **revisionism**.)

intrinsic good: See **honest good**.

intrinsicism (n.): Philosophical position holding that at least some qualities are related in *essential*$_{(1)}$ ways to other qualities and their natures. <The perennial tradition's intrinsicism regarding the relation between rationality and the capacity to develop moral virtue.> (Ant: **extrinsicism**.) Also: "intrinsicist" (adj. or n.).

intrinsic worth: The *objective*$_{(1)}$ value of a thing, apart from its being in fact desired by any particular individual or group.

intuition (n.): The immediate grasp of an object, whether *sensible* (e.g., a particular instance of a color) or *intelligible* (e.g., what it is to be a human person or a right triangle). (Jacques Maritain famously—although not to universal acclaim, even among fellow Thomists—spoke of the "intuition of being" [or "intuition of existence"] as referring to the intellect's grasp of *being*$_{(2)}$ in its analogical and inexhaustible character.) Also: "intuitive" (adj.), "intuitively" (adv.).

intuitionism (n.): The *metaethical* theory according to which moral principles, and sometimes concrete rights and wrongs, are known by immediate moral insight rather than supported by other considerations. (Note: Because of its emphasis on *synderesis* and on judgments of *conscience,* Thomistic ethics is sometimes taken to be a form of intuitionism; however, given its understanding of *law*$_{(1)}$ as an ordinance of reason, and the significance of the *natural*$_{(3)}$ for ethics, it clearly goes beyond this modern metaethical category.) Also: "intuitionist" (adj. or n.).

intuition of being: See the discussion under **intuition**.

invalid (adj.): (1) In logic, an argument, or argument form, that does not meet the standards of *validity.* (2) More loosely, an argument or position that is not regarded as acceptable or cogent. Also: "invalidly" (adv.).

invincible ignorance: State of error about moral or transcendent matters, when subjective conditions affecting an individual or group render it practically *impossible*$_{(5)}$ for them to overcome a deficient understanding and grasp the *objective*$_{(1)}$ truth of the matter. (A person who acts out of genuinely invincible ignorance is *inculpable* in relation to any objective evil done thereby.) Also: "invincibly ignorant."

involuntary (adj.): (1) Nonvoluntary; not resulting from an act of the will, but rather from either natural mechanisms or some physical or psychological constraint. <Involuntary muscle twitches; involuntary manslaughter due to acute psychic duress.> (Ant: **voluntary**.) (2) Said of an action, or, especially, a case of being acted upon, when it positively goes against what a person intends or would intend (either as a *means* or as an *end*$_{(2)}$). Also: "involuntarily" (adv.), "involuntariness" (n.).

Ipsum Esse Subsistens (Latin phrase, for "Subsistent Being Itself"): For followers of Aquinas, the favored philosophical designation for God. (Unlike finite beings and their features, Subsistent Being in no way depends upon another.)

irascible (adj.): (1) Of or related to passions of sensory appetite arising from *aggressiveness*—i.e., the drive related to difficulties that must be overcome in pursuit of objects perceived to be beneficial, or in avoidance of objects perceived to be harmful. (Contrast **concupiscible.**) (2) As said of an individual *temperament,* one that tends to be dominated by responses related to aggressiveness. Also: "irascibility" (n.).

irreplaceable (adj.): In *personalist* philosophies, a notion emphasizing the uniqueness attributable to individual human beings. (For perennial philosophy, the proper foundation for persons' being regarded as irreplaceable in this sense lies in their special manner of being *incommunicable.*) Also: "irreplaceability" (n.).

Islam (Arabic n., for "submission"—i.e., to the will of God): The religion founded in the 7th century by Mohammed and now second only to Christianity in total numbers of adherents around the world. In spite of significant differences with Judaism and Christianity, Islam identifies itself as a religion in the tradition of Abraham, and it recognizes both the Hebrew prophets and Jesus (as himself also, precisely, a prophet)—along with Mohammed as the "seal of the prophets" and receiver of the final revelation, as recorded in the Koran. Islam's name for God is "Allah;" and its adherents are called "Muslims"—from the Arabic for "one who submits." (As has been shown by David Burrell, C.S.C., and others, Muslim thinkers of the earlier Middle Ages—e.g., Ibn Sina [980–1037], known to the Latins as *Avicenna,* and Ibn Rushd [1126–98], known to the Latins as *Averroes*—served as counterparts to, and were influential upon, the great Christian Scholastics, notably Aquinas.)

J

~

journey (n.): (1) (Literally.) A physical movement or migration over considerable distance, especially by a human person or group. (2) (As a metaphor.) Common expression for the mind's progress in philosophical and religious matters, and used as such in the opening line of *Fides et ratio,* #1. (St. Bonaventure [1221–74], a contemporary of St. Thomas Aquinas, named one of his works "Journey of the Mind to God" [Latin *Itinerarium Mentis in Deum*]. For Bonaventure the existence of God is implicitly known by human beings; and such knowledge can be rendered explicit or evident via the mind's study [sustained by divine *grace*] of God's "reflections" in nature. Bonaventure's journey [or "itinerary"] thus parallels Aquinas's *Five Ways,* but without the latter's formal structure of rational *deduction.* John Paul II seemed to soften the differences between the two approaches; and this perspective continued during the pontificate of Benedict XVI, for whom Bonaventure, as well as Augustine and Aquinas, was a formative influence.)

joy (n.): (1) In traditional philosophical psychology, a *concupiscible* passion arising in the presence of a sensible good. (2) By extension, a positive affective response to the presence of an object of desire that is *intellectual* or *spiritual* in nature. <Joy in "going up to the house of the Lord."> (Syn: **delight**. Contrast **sorrow**.) Also: "joyful" (adj.), "joyfully" (adv.).

Judaism (n.): The religion originating with the ancient Hebrew people and taking as its primary sacred texts the Torah (the five books of Moses) and other Scriptures referred to by Christians as the "Old Testament." Key themes within Judaism are Creation and the Covenant with God. (The great Jewish thinker, Moses Maimonides [1135–1204], was an influential precursor of Aquinas. For a discussion of the name given to God in the Hebrew Scriptures, see ***Yahweh.***)

judgment (n.): (1) In traditional philosophical psychology, the "second" operation of *intellect,* whereby the truth of how things are is affirmed (and thus *existence* is attained by the mind) and falsity is denied or negated. Acts of judgment in this sense are sometimes referred to as "composition and division;" they involve awareness of the conformity or nonconformity of propositions with *reality.* (Regarding the other operations of intellect, see **apprehension** or **intellection** (**simple**), and **reasoning.**) (2) In ethics, the result of *practical* reasoning, which specifies what is to be done, either as a general rule or in an individual case. (Correct judgment in the latter instance involves exercise of the virtue of *prudence.*) Also: "judge" (n. or v.).

judgment of separation: See the discussion under **separation** $_{(2)}$.

juridical (adj.): Of or pertaining to the law, especially civil law (but also, for Catholics and some other religious bodies, ecclesiastical law). <A juridical person (e.g., a corporation).> Also: "juridicality" (n.), "juridically" (adv.).

just (adj.): Quality of acts or persons or social arrangements that reflect *justice* in either of its senses. (Ant: **unjust.**) Also: "just" (as a n.), "justly" (adv.).

justice (n.): (1) The *cardinal virtue* by which a person is internally directed to give another person, or his or her community, what is due. Scholastic philosophers have identified a number of virtues that are related to justice: a) truthfulness (by which one is disposed to say what one believes to be the case when asked); b) fidelity (by which one is disposed to maintain one's commitments); c) liberality (by which one is disposed to give of one's resources to satisfy needs of others); and d) piety (by which one is disposed to give proper honor to those on whom one depends—e.g., parents, country, and God). Habits and acts incompatible with the virtue of justice would include dishonesty, unjust discrimination, and disobedience to legitimate commands of authority. (2) A *common good*—or several types of common good—achievable in systems of social relationships that embody the virtue of justice. (For basic types of justice in this sense, see **commutative justice**, **distributive justice**, and **legal justice**. See also **social justice**.) (Ant: **injustice**.)

justify (v.): To give appropriate reasons, whether through formal or informal means, for one's beliefs or actions. (See **argument**.) Also: "justifiable" (adj.), "justifiably" (adv.), "justification" (n.).

just war theory: Long-standing and still developing line of reflection, especially within Christian tradition, concerning the justifiability of warfare. Historically, criteria of two sorts have been identified and characterized by Latin phrases: a) criteria related to *jus ad bellum* (i.e., justice in going to war, for example, having a just cause, being in a condition of last resort, having a genuine prospect of success, and being declared by proper authority); and b) criteria related to *jus in bello* (i.e., justice in the actual prosecution of war, for example, due proportion in the use of means and no direct targeting of noncombatants). (Note: Special difficulties arise in applying these criteria in the 21st-century context of terrorist activities and threats. For example, in many cases the most significant *agents* cannot be identified with any particular *government* or political *state;* moreover, here, perhaps more than elsewhere, there can be an extremely fine line between military interventions that respond to a morally certain "just cause" or that constitute a genuinely "last resort," and ones that positively and unjustifiably initiate activities of war.)

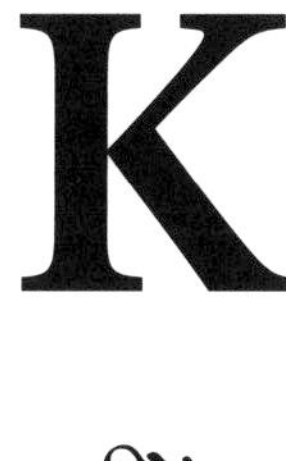

Kantian (adj. or n.): Of or related to, or a person who follows, the views of the German philosopher Immanuel Kant (1724–1804). In speculative philosophy, Kant held that we could achieve genuine knowledge—but that such knowledge was strictly limited to structured *phenomena,* together with whatever could be discovered (via the method of *transcendental*$_{(2)}$ deduction) about the intrinsic, structuring categories of the human mind. Questions that go beyond these matters—in particular, regarding the reality of God or the human soul—were, for Kant, beyond the reach of human understanding. Modern forms of *positivism, immanentism,* "symbolicism" (see **symbol**$_{(2)}$), and similar positions bear the marks of his influence. In moral philosophy, Kant stressed the *autonomy* of the human will, as well as what has come to be called a *deontological* approach to ethical issues. The latter he famously expressed in terms of the "categorical imperative," which, in contrast to "hypothetical" or conditional imperatives (which suppose particular desires on the part of agents), holds universally and without exception. Kant articulated various formulations of the categorical imperative, the most important of which inquire respectively of the relevant "maxim" or rule of action: a) Can I coherently will that everyone act in this way? b) Am I hereby treating all persons (i.e., all rational beings, including myself) as ends in themselves, rather than as mere means? Also: "Kantianism" (n.).

katabatic (adj., from Greek *katabainein,* for "to go down"): Characteristic of theological knowledge that requires the "descending" of God's *revelation* or self-disclosure (in particular, for Christians, God's self-disclosure as the *Trinity* of divine persons known through Scripture and tradition)—by contrast with theological knowledge that can be built up on the basis of *natural* $_{(4)}$ human reasoning. (Contrast **anabatic**.)

kataphatic, sometimes **cataphatic** (adj., from Greek *kata*, for "down," + *phanain*, for "to say"): Approach to God by way of words, including words that have been adapted from philosophical speculation, as well as words that have "come down" through sacred scriptures and traditions. For Christian writers, the term also characterizes the very "Word of God"—that is, Jesus Christ himself (see *Fides et ratio*, #23). (Contrast **apophatic**.)

kenosis (Greek n., for "emptying"): The self-emptying of God in Christ (see Philippians 2), a central feature of the mystery of *Incarnation*. (Mentioned in *Fides et ratio*, #93, this theme—as technically elaborated and developed—provides an example of what John Paul II called philosophy in its "third state" [see **states** (or **stances**) **of philosophy**]. He remarked that problems about the mystery of God's self-emptying are such that "a coherent solution to them will not be found without philosophy's contribution.")

kerygma (Greek n., for "proclamation"): Initial preaching of the Gospel, by contrast with teaching or instruction related to it. The aim of *kerygma* is conversion and faith; the aim of teaching or instruction is understanding. Accordingly, philosophical reason plays a role primarily in the latter. However, the very form of initial preaching can be affected by philosophical (as well as other cultural) factors; this perhaps is most evident in the opening chapter of John's Gospel, with its proclamations about Jesus as the "Word" (Greek *Logos*).

key, affective: See **affective key**.

kill (v.): To take the life of another, especially another human being. For perennial philosophy, and the ordinary Catholic *magisterium*, the *deliberate* killing of another human being—except in specifiable military, law enforcement, and judicial contexts, or in a case of true *necessity* $_{(2)}$ (where it is termed "justifiable homicide")—is *murder* and is morally wrong. (Some Catholic authors argue further that even in cases of justified killing, the *object* $_{(3)}$, strictly understood, cannot be the bringing about of the death of the other person or persons.)

knowledge (n.): An awareness of how things are. (1) Sense knowledge, which is shared by other animals, is awareness of *sensible* objects. (2) Intellectual knowledge, which is proper to rational beings, involves correct judgment related to *intelligible* objects. (Intellectual knowledge can be either *speculative* or *practical.* Ideally, for the Aristotelian tradition, both speculative knowledge and general practical knowledge are equivalent to *science* (1), or to the indemonstrable first *principles* on which such science depends.) (3) More loosely—and more commonly today—the attainment, even partial, of the mind's *objects* (2), either by way of direct acquaintance or by way of an organized set of propositions incorporating facts, hypotheses, theories, and learned opinion. (See as well **affective knowledge**.) Also: "know" (v.), "knower" (n.).

koinonia (Greek n., for "fellowship"): Biblical term for community; applied especially to the faithful who form the Church (see Acts 2). (Within Catholicism, Vatican II's emphasis on the Church as a *communion* [Latin *communio*]—with the various philosophical developments this term incorporated and in turn inspired—harks back to the original meaning of *koinonia.*)

L

labor (n.): (1) *Work*, especially manual but including other types by extension. (2) In economic systems, the human modification of goods so as to produce new or surplus value. (This term also has been used, sometimes with uppercase "L," to designate collectively the persons who actually produce such modifications.) (Contrast **capital** [as a n.].) Also: "labor" (as a v.), "laborer" (n.).

language (n.): (1) System of signs, established by convention and subject to cultural evolution, through which *communication* $_{(2)}$ takes place. The term applies primarily to human communication, but it also is used *analogously* for forms of *cognitive* and *affective* interaction shared in by certain other species. [Questions about the nature of language have been a preoccupation of philosophers during the 20th and now 21st centuries, particularly in the schools of *analytic philosophy, phenomenology,* and *hermeneutics.* The perennial tradition should profit from various insights produced, while at the same time maintaining a fundamental theme: that the use of language enables human beings to express *concepts* and *judgments* of reality.] (2) (Metaphorical use.) Said of cases in which there is a perceived relationship to communication, but no cognitive or affective interaction—e.g., "the language of DNA in our cells."

law (n.): (1) Ordinance of reason promulgated by the person(s) responsible for the good of a community. Aquinas and his school divide law in this general sense into four species: *eternal law* (God's plan of governance for the entire created universe); *natural (moral) law* (the proper regulation of human acts in light of our natural end as human, which we—through created reason, itself a participation in God's own reason—are able, in its general principles, to understand); *divine law* (strictly, norms governing human behavior that have been revealed by God through Scripture and Church tradition [although sometimes, confusingly, this term is used in a more general sense, as equivalent to "eternal law"]); and *human law* (mainly positive laws regulating behavior that are justly enacted by leaders of a society). (2) A principle of logic (e.g., the law regarding proper distribution of terms in syllogistic logic, or the rule called "modus ponens" in propositional logic). (3) A regularity of nature as grasped and systematized in the *empiriological* sciences (i.e., a "natural law" in the specific, modern sense—not to be confused with "natural (moral) law" as characterized in sense (1)).

legal justice: According to the classical understanding, the form of *justice* $_{(2)}$ whereby individuals give to the community its due, by respecting its laws (on the presumption that they are not egregiously unworthy of respect), as well as by fulfilling other duties prescribed by legitimate authority for the sake of the common good. Legal justice thus encompasses the operation of *positive law,* including its system of *punishments* for members of the community who fail to respect the law. Society's implementation of the latter is called *criminal justice.*

legal status: See the discussion under **status**.

liberal (adj. or n., from Latin *liber,* for "free"): (1) Of or pertaining to, or a person who holds, a position of *liberalism* in any of its senses. (Syn: **progressive**. Ant: "conservative;" see **conservatism**.) (2) Of or pertaining to the virtue of *liberality.* Also: "liberally" (adv.).

liberalism (n., from Latin *liber,* for "free"): (1) In social and political philosophy, the view that individual freedoms (at least tend to) override the interests of the community or *state* $_{(2)}$ when these come into conflict with one another. (Compare **individualism** $_{(1)}$ and **libertarianism**. Contrast **communitarianism**, as well as **statism** and **totalitarianism**.) (2) Regarding matters of policy and practice (and sometimes, as in the case of religion, teachings and beliefs), the tendency to support new initiatives and formulations, sometimes with a corresponding devaluation of a community's traditions. (Syn: **progressivism** (2). Ant: **conservatism.**) (3) As a general philosophical position—but one with important implications for the theory and practice of democratic government—the view that fundamental metaphysical, moral, and political questions (unlike empirical ones) cannot be settled objectively or by "public reason," and thus must be left to individual discernment and choice. (Contrast **realism**, in particular the position of perennial philosophy that there are certain knowable truths—e.g., concerning the inviolable dignity of the human person—that transcend the empirical realm and should serve as a rational basis for the organization of society.) (4) An attitude or position that favors the freedom of individuals to seek their proper fulfillment, without excessive societal interference. (Note: One can hold to liberalism in this last sense without being a liberal in any of the first three senses. In fact, most recent proponents of the perennial tradition, as well as the Catholic moral tradition generally, can be characterized in precisely this way.)

liberality (n.): The virtue—an adjunct to the cardinal virtue of *justice*—by which one is disposed to give of one's resources to satisfy the needs of others. <Contributing to disaster relief efforts as an exercise of liberality.> (See **liberal** (2).)

liberation (n.): The act by which, or state of affairs according to which, a person or a people is freed from a condition of bondage or subservience. (The term also is used by analogy in nonpolitical contexts, as in "liberation from ignorance.")

liberation from being: Phrase used by Catholic *postmodernist* philosopher Jean-Luc Marion, who sees the traditional notion of *being* (3) as unduly limiting for an appreciation of ourselves and God, and who champions the more self-involving New Testament language of God as "Love." [For the tradition of integral Christian wisdom, there is no incompatibility between these two forms of language; and Marion's objections to the term "being" seem ill-conceived—at least if one recognizes the primacy of *actuality* over *potentiality,* and the centrality of being among the *transcendental* perfections. Nevertheless, Marion has delivered a bracing challenge to traditional thought, especially to anyone who (in spite of Thomist teaching to the contrary) tends toward a static and *univocal* understanding of the term "being."]

liberation theology: Form of moral and social theology developed in the latter half of the 20th century, especially by thinkers in Latin America (e.g., Fathers Gustavo Guttierrez and Leonardo Boff). Sensitive to the injustice done by economic and political leaders throughout much of the hemisphere, liberation theologians adapted and applied certain *Marxist* ideas in developing their vision of a proper social order—without (at least as they themselves understood their project) succumbing to Marx's collectivism, materialism, and atheism. [However, Vatican authorities warned against aspects of this project, and sometimes seemed even to question its motives. Although liberation theology as a movement has waned, important issues concerning it remain unresolved.]

libertarian (adj. or n.): Of or pertaining to, or a person who holds, a version of *libertarianism.* <Libertarian approaches to health care policy.> (Ant: **communitarian**. Compare **liberal** $_{(1)}$.)

libertarianism (n.): Social and political theory according to which the rights of individual citizens in general have primacy over the interests of the community or state. (Often this type of theory stresses independence in financial matters; it thus leads to policy proposals that severely limit government power in taxation and other matters related to economic justice.) (Syn: **individualism** $_{(1)}$; see as well **liberalism** $_{(1)}$. Ant: **communitarianism.**)

liberty (n., Latin *libertas* for "freedom"): See **freedom** or **liberty**.

libido (n.): (1) In Sigmund Freud's psychoanalytic theory, the structure of instincts and urges in the human being, in particular the sex drive. [Note: While they do not challenge the therapeutic value of many of Freud's analyses, traditional Catholic thinkers question his underlying theory of human nature. In particular, whereas Freud regards the instinctual structure in question as, quite simply, a product of *nature* $_{(1)}$, these thinkers recognize the actual *state* $_{(1)}$ of human urges as constituting a falling away from the *natural* $_{(3)}$ orientation of our sense inclinations—a falling away that, theologically, bespeaks the effects of *sin.*] (2) As used in some recent presentations of Scholastic philosophical psychology, a synonym for **concupiscence**.

lie (v.): To represent as true what one knows or believes to be untrue. The injunction against lying is traditionally regarded as an *exceptionless moral rule.* (The complexities of the latter notion apply here; thus, for example, to utter what is false as part of one's role in a drama simply is not a case of lying. Recently, some writers within the perennial tradition have argued that certain other types of cases—e.g., saying what is untrue in order to protect innocent life—can be justified in terms of *necessity* (2), somewhat as can appropriating another's property in a case of true emergency. However, more rigorously Thomistic scholars note that the latter case involves a change in the moral nature of the act, in light of the *universal destination of goods*: that is, in extreme circumstances appropriating another's property does not constitute genuine theft [see **change of matter** or **change of species**]. They further argue that—whatever the circumstances—no comparable account would be plausible in a case of deceiving through an untruth. However this may be, it should be noted that Aquinas himself would judge lying in such circumstances as a moral failing, but a minor one [a "venial" rather than a "mortal" sin]: strictly speaking, the act should not be done, but it would not, by itself, preclude progress in the moral life or achievement of one's final end. For critical discussion of this issue, see, for example, the work of Lawrence Dewan, O.P.) Also: "lie" (as a n.), "liar" (n.).

life (n.): (1) Condition of, or an instance of, a natural being that is alive—i.e., one whose formal, organizing principle enables it to be spontaneous and self-moving, or to bring about *change* in itself. (This principle was called *psuche* by Aristotle, and *anima* by Aquinas; both terms are typically translated into English as *soul*.) (2) In an important *analogous* usage, "life" applies to all cases in which beings *actualize* themselves—including angels and God—even if there is, strictly speaking, no change or motion in the being. Also: "live" (v. or adj.).

life, beginning of: An important question ("How are we to understand and mark the point at which a living organism begins to be?") that, as applied to specifically human life, has implications for issues in *applied ethics* and *positive law*—in particular, issues of abortion and embryonic stem cell research. For the perennial tradition, human life—understood ontologically, rather than empiriologically—begins when a specifically human *form* or rational *soul* organizes *matter* (3) so that the resulting individual is able to carry out vital activity on its own. Without in any way seeking to justify abortion, Aquinas—writing centuries before the discoveries of modern embryology—supposed that this occurred at some point well after what is today known as fertilization. According to most, although not all, contemporary Thomists (as well as the common, but not definitive teaching of the Catholic Church), the point of successful fertilization—when a viable human zygote with its own genetic complement comes to be—provides the most reasonable marker for the beginning of individual human life. (An exception to this account would occur in the case of identical twinning. Here it may be supposed that the second individual comes to be after a certain number of cell divisions, at which time a portion of the matter comprising the original individual is reorganized by a new human form or rational soul.)

life, right to: Negatively, the right of a human being not to be killed; positively, a right to develop and maintain one's life, and to have a fair share in society's resources in pursuit of this goal. Since life is the human good on which all others depend, the right to life (at least in its negative form) is, for traditional philosophy and theology, the most fundamental of the *natural rights.*

life, sanctity of: Character of human life as sacred, as revealed, for example, in Jewish and Christian scriptures; thus also a *principle*$_{(2)}$ for much religiously inspired or potentiated ethics. (For example, from the standpoint of natural morality, murderers and unjust aggressors "forfeit" their *right* to life. According to many Christian ethicists, however, the principle of the sanctity of life requires that, if at all possible, nonlethal means be developed to address even the gravest problems of social order. See the discussions under **culture of death/culture of life**, and **death penalty**.)

limitations of rights: See **rights, limitations of**.

linguistic philosophy: See **analytic philosophy**.

literal (adj.): Said of uses of language in which terms both express meaning directly and express meaning that results from human *cognition* (i.e., from experience, abstraction or concept formation, and judgment). In the tradition of Aquinas, such uses of language are grouped under three headings: *univocal, equivocal,* and *analogous.* (Note: In a related but different usage, Scripture scholars sometimes refer to the "literal" sense of a biblical passage—i.e., what the author or authors directly intended—by contrast with other types of senses, called *spiritual senses.* Importantly, however, such spiritual senses can be conveyed through what, philosophically, are literal uses of language, as well as through *metaphorical* uses of language.) Also: "literally" (adv.), "literalness" (n.).

literalism (n.): A tendency to take texts (especially sacred texts) literally, and only literally—by contrast with interpretations that also recognize *spiritual senses,* as well as the use of *symbol* and *metaphor.* (Literalism of course also is opposed by noncognitivist approaches, according to which the texts in question have only symbolic meaning.) (Compare **Biblicism** and **fundamentalism**.) Also: "literalist" (adj. or n.).

locomotion (n.): *Change* or movement from place (Latin *locus*) to place.

logic (n.): (1) In the Aristotelian tradition, the art of defining and reasoning, including the development of formal rules of thought as well as "material" or topic-related considerations. (Also typically treated are matters of *informal logic,* for example, fallacies in everyday reasoning.) The ideal of Aristotelian logic is the achievement of knowledge by way of *demonstration,* in particular through syllogistic reasoning. (See **deduction** and **induction**, as well as **material logic**.) (2) For modern "symbolic" logic, the study of formal, propositional systems themselves, in abstraction from applications and material considerations. (Properly understood, this second approach to logic is different from, but—from the standpoint of formal reasoning—not opposed to the first. See, however, the discussion at **x** (logical symbol).) (3) In *analytic philosophy,* a feature of a term's use, sometimes also called its "grammar," that has implications for its association (or nonassociation) with other terms—such that, if these implications go unrecognized, they can lead the unwary philosopher into misunderstandings. <The logic of normative terms such as "good" or "right" as differing from the logic of empirical and descriptive terms such as "wet" or "yellow.">

logical (adj.): (1) Of or having to do with the discipline of *logic,* or with *intentions* $_{(1)}$ developed and systematized by the mind. (Contrast **ontological**.) (2) Said of reasoning that correctly follows appropriate formal rules. (Ant: **illogical**.)

logical positivism: See the discussion under **positivism**.

logicism (n.): Philosophical position, prominent in the English-speaking world in the mid to late 20th century, according to which metaphysical discussions are reducible to considerations of formal logic. (See discussion at **x** (logical symbol).)

logos (Greek n. for "word" or "account"): (1) Principle or ultimate account, especially of the whole cosmos, as sought by the ancient philosophers. (2) (Often capitalized.) In the context of Christianity, as originally inculturated in the Greco-Latin world, a designation for God—in particular God as Son. (See, for example, the prologue to the Gospel of John.)

love (n.) (1) Most generally, the fundamental response of appetite to objects of desire and/or attraction; also such an object itself. In this general sense all beings can be said to have "loves." (Compare **desire**. Contrast **aversion** and [natural] **hate**.) (2) Specifically human love, which takes various forms (in spouses, parents and children, etc.) and involves various *powers* and *acts*. In the case of romantic love, this includes both *sensory* (including emotional) and *rational* or *personal* aspects of our nature. Such love comprises both Greek *eros* (which is possessive and acquisitive, and especially seeks fulfillment of sensory desire), and Greek *philia* (which seeks the good of the other for his or her own sake). According to integral Christian wisdom, romantic love is ultimately ordered to the *communion of persons* constituting marriage and the family. (3) Within Christianity, *God*'s love (Greek *agape*, Latin *caritas*)—i.e., *charity* $_{(3)}$—which humans are called, by grace, to share in and imitate. (For a modern exposition, see Benedict XVI's inaugural encyclical, *Deus Caritas est* [2006].) Also: "love" [as a v.], "loving" (adj.), "lovingly" (adv.).

lust (n.): (1) In a general and neutral sense, the appetite for sexual pleasure—one aspect of *concupiscence.* (2) In a more specific sense, the habitual tendency (listed among the seven *capital vices*) toward an inordinate desire for and pursuit of sexual pleasure. Also: "lust" [as a v.], "lustful" (adj.), "lustfully" (adv.).

M

~

magisterium (Latin n., from *magister,* for "teacher;" sometimes rendered without italics; sometimes capitalized): Highest teaching authority in the Roman Catholic Church—either the bishops speaking as a body with the pope, as in the documents of the Second Vatican Council (as well as earlier ecumenical councils); or the pope when he invokes the privilege of speaking *ex cathedra* (Latin for "from the chair" [sc. of Peter]) on a matter of faith or morals. This term also applies to the common, if less definitive teachings of the pope and the bishops in communion with him. (The former exercise of authority is sometimes called the "extraordinary" magisterium, the latter the "ordinary" magisterium.) Also: "magisterial" (adj.).

magnanimity (n.): Moral *virtue* by which one is enabled to conceive and pursue noble goals; sometimes called "greatness of soul." (See the discussion under **fortitude**.) Also: "magnanimous" (adj.), "magnanimously" (adv.).

man (n.): (1) (Corresponding to Latin *homo.*) Human *nature* $_{(2)}$, or all human beings, considered precisely from the standpoint of their sharing in human nature. Thus, the *philosophy of the human person* also has been called the "philosophy of man." (2) (Corresponding to Latin *vir.*) A male member of the human race. (Note: Contemporary linguistic sensitivities, inspired by concern over the status of women, sometimes discourage the use of "man" in the first sense; however, it still figures prominently in some expressions of philosophy and theology, as well as in official Church teachings. If the difference between the two meanings of "man" is observed, no obstacles to correct understanding need occur.) (Regarding sense (2), contrast **woman.**)

manifestation (n.): A feature of things insofar as it is available to powers of awareness, especially sense awareness (when thus restricted, the term is equivalent to *phenomenon*). Also: "manifest" (v.).

man of practical reason (Greek: *phronemos*): According to Aristotelian accounts of moral *virtue,* the person (or *man* (1)) who has *prudence,* and who thus is able to determine with accuracy the proper *mean* between extremes in a particular case.

marital (sometimes **conjugal**) (adj.): Of or having to do with *marriage.* (Thus, strictly in light of this dictionary's entry on the latter term, the phrases "marital (or conjugal) relationship" and "marital (or conjugal) act" refer to relationships and to acts, especially acts of sexual intercourse, engaged in by couples who have entered into the state and institution of marriage.)

marital and sexual ethics: A field of *applied ethics* with many important issues for Catholic tradition, some examples of which are listed here. a) Does the practice of *contraception* by a married couple fall within the range of proper respect for the *ends* (1) of marriage and human (i.e., personal) sexuality? Or must birth regulation or control, if it is to be morally acceptable, be pursued by means of *natural family planning?* The Church's "ordinary" *magisterium* continues to hold and promote the latter position, sometimes with increasing vigor. b) Which reproductive technologies can be used to assist infertile couples in ways consistent with proper respect for the *dignity* of human life and procreation? Surely some technologies can, while others cannot—but which, and why? c) Might the *personalist* emphasis that is being infused into the perennial tradition open philosophical "space" for reconsidering the morality of nonmarital sexual acts, perhaps including homosexual acts? Or would such a development involve an unacceptable *dualism* (2) about human acts, as popes and traditional moral thinkers so far have firmly maintained?

market economy: See the discussion under **capitalism.**

marriage (n.): The institution, *natural* (3) in origin, but commonly regulated by *positive law,* in which a man and a woman are united to form a unique *community* of love, as well as to provide a proper context for the *procreation* and rearing of children that may result from their union. (For Catholic Christianity, the marital union and associated civil contract can be elevated by *grace* to the level of a *sacrament*, namely, matrimony.) [Note: According to this account, the general nature of marriage is ontologically prior to any determinations by the state. However, continuing debates and *de facto* legal developments in certain U.S. jurisdictions—as well as in certain other Western countries—have led to pressure on the perennial tradition, and on the Catholic Church, to recognize a second sense of the term "marriage," one whose *extension* would include all relationships recognized as marriages by local law and public policy (thus including, in some cases, homosexual relationships). Whether this second meaning—which would eliminate (or radically alter) the *natural* $_{(3)}$ basis for the term "marriage"—should be accepted as legitimate is likely to be an issue for some time.]

Marxist (adj. or n.): Pertaining to, or one who holds, positions developed by Karl Marx (1818–83). (A variant term, "Marxian," sometimes is used of those who study the writings of Marx without necessarily holding his positions.) Influenced by the writings of G. W. F. Hegel (1770–1831), Marx transformed his predecessor's idea of *dialectic* from idealist to materialist terms; he argued that the dynamic of history is ordered by facts of economic life, with the final stage involving a revolution of the proletariat (working class) and an ensuing classless society. [Marx's writings were influential on the movement called *liberation theology*. However, due to his atheism, as well as to the human degradation wrought by 20th-century Communist regimes claiming him as their inspiration, Catholic authorities have remained cool or even hostile to Marx, although they have recognized and adapted some of his notions—e.g., that of *alienation*.] Also: "Marxism" (n.).

material (adj.): Of or pertaining to *matter*, in any of its senses. Also: "materially" (adv.).

material cause: That which undergoes and survives a change from one form or state to another—thus *matter* $_{(1)}$ in its role as a cause in things' being and becoming. One of the four types of causes or factors in explanation, as identified by Aristotle.

materialism (n.): (1) (Sometimes also called "physicalism.") A philosophy, or family of philosophies, according to which all reality is composed of and subject to the conditions of physical matter; or according to which all references to "mind," "soul," or "spirit" can, in principle, be reduced to physical terms (e.g., those of brain chemistry). [Note: Certain recent philosophers and theologians (e.g., the Protestant thinker Nancey Murphy) have undertaken to develop a coherent but "non-reductive" physicalism (at least with regard to finite reality, including the human person)—one that they believe is compatible with Christian tradition. However, it does not seem that such a position can be assimilated within perennial philosophy and theology. See, for example, the discussion under **spirit**.] (2) In ethics, a position identifying all human goods with physical goods; or a lifestyle that reflects such a position. Also: "materialist" (adj. or n.), "materialistic" (adj.), "materialistically" (adv.).

material logic: As understood by Scholastic writers, the branch of logic devoted to evaluating nonformal factors in defining and reasoning. (Thus, while *formal logic* treats, for example, general rules governing validity in syllogisms, material logic instead treats topics related to particular subject matters—i.e., the particular *category* [or, more strictly, "predicament"] into which a term falls, or the specific character of a *demonstration* as being either *quia* or *propter quid*.)

material object: See the discussion at **object** (2).

mathematics (n.): The formal discipline, or set of disciplines, related to *quantity*. From the standpoint of logic and epistemology, these disciplines involve the "second" *degree* (or *order*) *of abstraction*. Also: "mathematical" (adj.), "mathematically" (adv.).

matter (n.): (1) Most generally, the underlying subject of physical change, whether substantial or accidental—e.g., the bronze or marble that becomes, through the sculptor's art, a statue. (2) "Signed" or "designated" or "marked-off matter" (Latin *materia signata*)—i.e., physical reality insofar as it is characterized by quantity. Matter in this sense is the principle of countability and measurability in the physical realm. (See **principle of individuation**.) (3) "Prime" or "primary" or "first matter" (Latin *materia prima*)—also sometimes called "protomatter," "undifferentiated materiality," or the "matter-matrix"—i.e., the co-principle of substance consisting in sheer *potentiality* for physical form. (It is necessary to recognize such a principle, according to the tradition of Aristotle, if one is to give an adequate philosophical account of *substantial change*.) (Contrast **form**. See **hylemorphism**. See as well **common matter**.)

mean (n.): In the Aristotelian theory of *moral virtue,* that concrete *object*$_{(3)}$ of choice, or that *human act,* which—by contrast with either of two "extremes"—is appropriate for the agent in the particular circumstances. This object or act is sometimes referred to as the "golden mean." <*Temperance* as enabling one to choose the mean regarding pleasures—i.e., avoiding both an excessive pursuit of sensual goods and a life devoid of pleasure altogether.> (The notion of a mean must be very carefully applied. As suggested above, it depends on particular features of persons and their situations; moreover, it corresponds to what would be chosen by the individual in question if he or she employed the virtue of *prudence* [or *practical wisdom*], bolstered by other relevant *moral virtues.* Thus, for example, a normal, healthy adult may choose to enjoy one or two alcoholic drinks during an evening. For that person, this is his or her mean, and to act accordingly is a manifestation of the virtue of temperance. But for a person with the disease of alcoholism, the only appropriate choice is no intoxicating drink at all. And prudence may dictate a similar decision for a person seeking to overcome the *vice* of drunkenness.)

meaning (n.): (1) In general philosophical usage, the *sense* and/or the *reference* of a word (or phrase or statement). (2) (Corresponding to Latin *ratio.*) As used by some proponents of perennial philosophy, the *essence* or set of intelligible features of a type of reality designated by a term. (3) Related to sense (2), especially in the context of morality, the objective significance (including the *end*$_{(1)}$) of a type of *human act* or *power.* <Respect for the true meaning of human sexuality.> Also, in sense (1), "meaningful" and "meaningless" (adj.).

meaning of life: Fundamental question, asked by sages in all cultures and historical periods, regarding the ultimate significance of human existence. (John Paul II noted this question in *Fides et ratio,* #1; he also spoke of a "crisis of meaning" as afflicting modern and postmodern humanity [#81]. For him, it was part of the philosopher's task to combat skepticism about life's ultimate meaning, while at the same time articulating the truth that, from a purely *natural*$_{(4)}$ standpoint, such meaning remains a *mystery.* Here John Paul II's thinking was informed by the Vatican II document *Gaudium et spes* [see especially ##12 and 22]; it also perhaps reflected the influence of the turn-of-the-20th-century French philosopher Maurice Blondel. Blondel, a Catholic, is not explicitly mentioned in *Fides et ratio,* presumably because he did not see himself [nor was he seen by others] as directly contributing to the perennial tradition; however, his principal philosophical efforts were devoted to elaborating a theme related to the above point: namely, that the supremely human act of questioning the meaning of one's life is ordered to the object of religious *faith*—more specifically, to God's "answer" to the philosophical search in the person of Jesus Christ.) (See **destiny, human**, as well as **immanence, method of.**)

means (n.): A *human act* insofar as it is ordered to attaining an *end* (or *ends*) $_{(2)}$. For the act to be morally good, the agent's end in this sense (Latin *finis operantis,* also called *motive* or subjective purpose) must be good, and the means also must be good—i.e., morally appropriate and, so far as human judgment can predict, likely to be effective. Part of moral appropriateness in a means lies in its not going against an intrinsic end (Latin *finis operis*) of the type of act being undertaken, and thus not going against an objective moral precept. (This point of perennial ethics is reflected in the common saying, "The end [i.e., motive or subjective purpose of the act] does not justify the means [i.e., a means that violates an objective moral precept].") (See **determinants** or **sources of morality**.)

measure (n.): A means or criterion of judgment for thought or action. (The term is used by analogy with the calculation of quantity in physical beings.) Some measures are subject to a "higher" measure, and some are not. Regarding the latter type of case, the mind of God is said to be a "measuring measure" only; the human mind, by contrast, is said to be both a "measuring measure" (i.e., it articulates standards for judgment) and a "measured measure" (i.e., it itself must—if its judgments are to be correct—conform to *objective* $_{(1)}$ truth). Also: "measurable" (adj.).

mechanism (n.): Philosophical position associated with *materialism* $_{(1)}$, according to which, at least in principle, all real change can be reduced to changes in material realities in keeping with laws of physical motion. Also: "mechanistic" (adj.), "mechanistically" (adv.).

mediating institutions: See the discussion under **civic** or **civil society**.

memory (n.): (1) An "internal" *sense* whereby an image is recalled and serves as a medium of *intentional* $_{(1)}$ existence for an object no longer having *entitative* $_{(1)}$ existence, or at least not present to the observer.

(With the activity of memory, according to the perennial tradition, the soul—especially the reflective, human soul—begins, in the words of Pierre-Marie Emonet, to "breathe above time;" that is, it is no longer restricted to an awareness of the here and now.) (2) A memory image itself.

mental (adj.): Of or having to do with *mind.* Also: "mentally" (adv.).

mental word (Latin *verbum mentis*): See **concept**.

mercy (n.): An internal disposition or attitude of kindness and forgiveness. Although not traditionally listed as a *virtue,* mercy can be associated with *temperance,* insofar as it "tempers" righteous anger and the pursuit of retribution, especially in assigning punishment for wrongdoing. (For Christian tradition, the model of mercy is God the Father—who does not abandon humankind in its sin but generously provides the means of new and everlasting life.) Also: "merciful" (adj.), "mercifully" (adv.).

merit (n.): (1) In ethics, the condition of being responsible for, and thus worthy of moral approval for, a good choice made and/or a good act done. (See **determinants** or **sources of morality**. Contrast [objective] **guilt**.) (2) In the vast majority of societies, a factor in determining the distribution of material goods, in particular financial compensation. (The question arises as to whether, from the standpoint of normative *ethics,* merit is a suitable factor—that is, whether it can figure in the *just* distribution of a society's material goods. According to the perennial tradition, individual action and accomplishment indeed can play a role in a just system of distribution, as long as there is roughly equal access to the means of developing and displaying such merit, and as long as the *basic needs* of all members of society are in some way addressed within the overall system.) (See **distributive justice** $_{(2)}$.) Also, in both senses: "meritorious" (adj.).

meritocracy (n.): Form of government in which decision-making power is concentrated in persons of *merit* $_{(2)}$.

metaethics (n.): Branch or dimension of ethical theory that does not address *normative* issues themselves, but rather focuses on questions that go "beyond" (Greek *meta*) such issues by taking them as the formal *objects* $_{(2)}$ of inquiry—e.g., by asking: "Do moral judgments have a kind of objectivity; and, if so, what account should be given of it?" and "What is the meaning of the terms 'good' or 'bad,' 'right' or 'wrong,' etc., as used in a moral context?" Also: "metaethicist" (n.), "metaethical" (adj.), "metaethically" (adv.).

meta-philosophy (n.): See the discussion under **methodology**. Also: "meta-philosophical" (adj.).

metaphor (n.): A use of language, characteristic of poetry but also common in everyday life, in which the meaning of a term is "carried beyond" (from the Greek roots *meta* + *pherein*) its original context. The term thus comes to be used in a special, nonliteral sense, rather than directly expressing a concept that results from an act of *cognition*. The use of metaphor is associated with "symbolic" language (see discussion at **symbol**)—especially when an everyday word is used in a novel way to express a matter of special depth or mystery. [Note: For some purposes, certain authors, even within the perennial tradition, classify metaphor as a species of *analogy*. However, strictly speaking, metaphor involves the human mind creatively imposing an order among meanings, rather than—as with analogy—appealing to a known or supposed ontological relationship.]

metaphorical (adj.): Of or pertaining to *metaphor*. <In a metaphorical presentation by the poet Apolinaire, the Eiffel Tower is addressed as a shepherd surrounded by bleating sheep.> (Compare and contrast **analogical** or **analogous**.) Also: "metaphorically" (adv.).

metaphysics (n., sometimes "philosophy of being" or "first philosophy"): The philosophical discipline that is most basic or "first" in the *order of explanation*—although not, at least for perennial philosophy, in the *order of discovery*. Metaphysics investigates being just as being (i.e., *being* $_{(3)}$, Latin *ens inquantum ens* or *ens secundum quod est ens*), along with being's properties, principles, and causes. It culminates in philosophical theology (i.e., *theology* $_{(1)}$), which approaches God as First Cause and Absolute Being, and which considers the world's relations to God in light of concepts developed via common human experience and reason. [Note: Some contemporary philosophers, especially of the *analytic* school, treat under the heading of metaphysics topics which, strictly speaking (for the Aristotelian tradition), belong to *philosophy of nature* (e.g., the topic of time).] Also: "metaphysical" (adj.), "metaphysically" (adv.), "metaphysician" (n.).

metascience (n.): (1) Reflection on, and especially the logical analysis of, *science* $_{(2)}$. (2) According to a usage proposed by Benedict Ashley, O.P., a more appropriate label for the discipline of *metaphysics*—

more appropriate in that this discipline, focused on being as such, goes beyond not only what today is called "physics," but beyond all studies or "sciences" of nature. (Note, however, this dictionary's discussion at **science** $_{(1)}$.)

methodology (n.): In recent philosophy and theology (as well as the natural sciences and other disciplines), a study that takes the discipline's own presuppositions, methods, and types of results as formal objects of investigation. (In the case of philosophy, such a study is sometimes called "metaphilosophy.") Also: "methodological" (adj.), "methodologically" (adv.), "methodologist" (n.).

middle term: See the discussion under **syllogism**.

milieu (French n.; plural in English often follows the French *millieux*): The setting, especially the *social* setting, of a process or historical event; in relation to philosophy, the setting in which a particular view or theory emerges. <The milieu of war-torn Europe, out of which existentialism developed.>

militarism (n.): Inordinate reliance on force of arms to protect a nation's standing in the international order—or to try to influence or affect that order. Also: "militaristic" (adj.), "militaristically" (adv.).

mind (n., Latin *mens*): General name for powers and operations of the *soul*—especially the *rational* soul—that are involved in knowledge, both speculative and practical. Mind is attributable, at least *analogously,* to other species of animals because of their (various types and levels of) *sense* knowledge; it is not literally attributable to inanimate objects. (Thus, in particular, mind is not attributable to products of technology such as computers—for, at least as presently constituted, such machines are not living wholes, and therefore they are not animated by single substantial forms of any sort.) [In recent decades, especially in the English-speaking world, a discipline called "philosophy of mind" has emerged. Although it has resulted in important analyses, from the standpoint of perennial philosophy this discipline forms a part—often, as practiced, a highly truncated part—of the *philosophy of the human person* or *human nature.*]

miracle (n.): An action or event that goes beyond the *natural* $_{(4)}$ powers of the agents involved, and is attributed to a higher power. (According to Christian tradition, the purposes of God—who is First Cause of all being and activity—are, for the most part, achieved by way of "secondary" causes, that is, agents that are beings of *nature* $_{(1)}$. But this need not be the case and, in genuine miracles, it is not the case; that is, here God acts without intermediary.) Also: "miraculous" (adj.), "miraculously" (adv.).

miscarriage (n.): The loss of a developing fetus through natural causes involving the maternal-fetal biological system. (See the discussion under **abortion**.)

mixed perfection: Property or actuality that is essentially bound up with *matter* $_{(2)}$ and material conditions—e.g., color, shape, and physical gender. (Such properties, although manifold in the physical world, are not capable of being predicated formally and literally of God—or of any other purely *spiritual* being.) (Contrast **pure perfection** and **transcendental** $_{(1)}$.)

mixed science (Latin *scientia media*): A body of knowledge in which the subject matter is physical, but the "form" or mode of explanation is mathematical. <Optics and astronomy as *scientiae mediae* familiar to the Ancients.> (Note: Much of what today is called "natural science" [i.e., *science* $_{(2)}$] is of this "mixed" sort.)

mobile (adj.): Changing; subject to physical motion. <The cosmos as comprising the realm of mobile being.>

moderate realism: See the discussions under **conceptualism** and **realism**.

modernism (n.): A 19th-century theory that held religion to be the result of humankind's subliminal experience of the divine, with different forms of religion (including Christianity) representing diverse attempts by humankind to articulate such experience by way of *symbols* $_{(2)}$. [Note: This theory influenced a group of Catholic thinkers in the late 19th and early 20th centuries. What is called the "Modernist Crisis" in the Church centered around the formal condemnation of this movement in 1907 by Pope Pius X (in the documents titled *Lamentabili* and *Pascendi*). Today, modernism is much more diffuse, but its effects are widespread. (See this dictionary's entries on **immanentism** and **religious pluralism**, as well as on **symbol** $_{(2)}$.) John Paul II mentioned modernism in *Fides et ratio*, #87, in connection with his call for Christian philosophers to reject *historicism* and support theologians in their efforts to explore the *objective* $_{(1)}$ content of Christian teaching.] Also: "modernist" (adj. or n.).

modes of signification: See **signification, modes of**.

Molinist (adj. or n.): Of or pertaining to, or a person who holds, ideas and themes of Luis de Molina, S.J. (1535–1600). Molina perhaps is best known for his account of human *free choice* in relation to God's knowledge of future events. By contrast with strict Thomists, he held that God's eternal knowledge of what humans will choose to do is not a direct but rather a "middle knowledge"—which, since it involves a generic understanding of what human persons would do under any possible set of circumstances, in no way involves restrictions on individuals' actual choices. Similarly, for Molina, God's grace aids the human will but in no way determines a person's concrete decision-making. Variations on such controversies about free will continue to the present day. Also: "Molinism" (n.).

monism (n.): A family of philosophical views according to which all reality is made up of one fundamental type of being (e.g., matter or spirit). (Contrast **dualism**—as well as the perennial philosophical account of reality in terms of proportional structures of essence and existence.) Also: "monist" (adj. or n.), "monistic" (adj.).

monogenism (n.): See the discussion under **polygenism**. Also: "monogenist" (adj. or n.).

monotheism (n.): A tradition of religious or philosophical thought that subscribes to belief in a single *God.* (See **theism**. Contrast **polytheism.**) Also: "monotheist" (adj. or n.), "monotheistic" (adj.).

mood (n.): A deep and/or long-lasting *affective* response. (See the discussion under **emotion.**)

moral (adj., from Latin *mos* for "custom"): (1) Of or pertaining to *morality.* (Contrast **amoral** and **nonmoral good.**) (2) As said of a person, an intention, a free act, etc., having a positive moral quality—as judged in light of the *determinants* or *sources of morality.* (Contrast **immoral.**) Also, in both senses: "morally" (adv.).

moral (n., used especially in plural form "morals"): A person's or a society's values, standards of behavior, etc.

moral community: As spoken of in much recent English-language moral philosophy, the totality of beings having *rights* or moral *status.* [Note: According to some ethical theorists (e.g., Mary Ann Warren and Michael Tooley), this set of beings is equivalent to the set having actual *duties* or *obligations*—thus excluding from the moral community human fetuses, the irreversibly comatose, etc. Such an understanding clearly conflicts with the perennial tradition, for which the moral community would include all *persons* $_{(1)}$.]

moral good: The type of *good* that is specifically achievable in *human* *acts*—i.e., acts that result from *free choice* and that fulfill the *determinants* or *sources of morality.* (Contrast **nonmoral good**, as well as moral **evil.**)

morality (n.): (1) The set of practices and judgments, together with their underlying principles, that guide an individual's or social group's action in pursuit of the good; thus, in its general features, the subject matter of *ethics* as a reflective discipline. (Contrast **amorality**.) (2) Those practices and judgments of morality in the first sense that are evaluated positively—i.e., judged to be morally sound or correct. (Contrast **immorality**.)

moral law: Law that binds the human conscience in matters of *choice* and *action.* For followers of Aquinas, and the Catholic tradition generally, moral law is available to us in two ways: through *natural (moral) law* and *divine law.*

moral object: See **object** (3), as well as **determinants** or **sources of morality**.

moral philosophy: The search for wisdom in the *practical* order, by contrast with the *speculative* order. Moral philosophy involves reflection aimed at answering questions about the human good, about how we ought to live, and/or about the types of persons we should strive to become. As philosophical, this study proceeds via reflection on the *natural* (3) ends of the human person and his or her acts, insofar as these in principle can be known by all, regardless of religious faith and/or cultural factors. (Viewed from the standpoint of Christian *revelation,* moral philosophy just by itself—given our *de facto* status as fallen and redeemed—is inadequate to the completion of its formal task of telling us, in all respects, "how we ought to live." The fullness of moral wisdom is available only through religious faith and moral theology. This is not to say, however, that philosophy cannot make independent and substantive contributions to moral reflection, contributions that are of special importance in the context of a *pluralistic society.* Controversy about whether moral philosophy somehow depends upon, or is "subordinated to," moral theology involved prominent 20th-century participants in the perennial tradition—e.g., Jacques Maritain, Mortimer Adler, and Ralph McInerny.)

moral precept: A *norm* or *rule* expressing a general directive for right and wrong action, and in light of which more particular directives may be formulated. For the Thomist school, and the tradition of integral Christian wisdom more generally, precepts are discerned by way of both *natu-*

ral (*moral*) *law* or reflective reason, and *divine law* or revelation and authoritative Church teaching. Precepts often are divided into "primary" and "secondary" (and, for some authors, "tertiary," etc.). Primary precepts of natural law are most general; they hold for and—at least in principle—are equally knowable by all human beings. (See **primary precepts of natural (moral) law** and **synderesis**.) Secondary precepts specify or apply the primary ones; they typically hold contingently and "for the most part" (Latin *ut in pluribus*), rather than always and necessarily. By way of illustration, "Justice is to be pursued in human relationships" and "The intrinsic ends of human sexuality are to be respected" are primary precepts of natural (moral) law; they find application in such secondary precepts as "Hiring practices should consider equally all qualified applicants" and "Sexual relationships should promote a couple's striving for unity." Moral precepts also are divided into "positive" and "negative." The preceding examples all express positive precepts. Negative precepts would include "Innocent life should not be directly taken" and "One should not steal another's goods." Certain negative precepts, particular as well as general, hold universally (i.e., in all cases to which they genuinely apply). (See **exceptionless moral rules**.)

moral relativism: See the discussion under **ethical relativism**.

moral sense (sometimes also called "moral intuition"): According to certain modern ethical theorists, a power attributed to human beings by means of which we apprehend values and other moral data—whether or not such apprehension reflects moral reality. (No term originating in the perennial tradition functions in quite this way; however, a rough equivalent for the school of Aquinas would be the combination of *synderesis* [the immediate awareness of the most general moral precepts] and right *conscience* [the ability to apply moral precepts to questions of concrete action].)

moral status: See the discussion under **status**.

moral theology: An approach to or system of ethical thought, or a moral wisdom, rooted at least in part in what is held by a believing community to be divinely revealed—e.g., for Catholic Christians, through Scripture and Church tradition. (See **ethics**, **ethics, Christian**, and **moral philosophy**.)

moral virtues: See **virtues, moral**.

motion (Latin *motus*) or **movement** (n.): Change in the very general sense of a continuous, measurable alteration. Although in everyday English the term "motion" applies primarily to *locomotion,* in Aristotelian philosophical usage it applies to any kind of *accidental* change in a being of nature (including movement from place to place, but also changes in any of the other categories of accident—*quantity, quality, relation,* etc.).

motive (n.): A person's *end* $_{(2)}$, or subjective purpose, in performing an act—sometimes referred to as the *finis operantis* (Latin for "end of the agent"), as distinguished from the *finis operis* (Latin for "end of the act," in keeping with the act's natural *teleology* $_{(1)}$). <A proper motive can increase the moral goodness of an already good act—e.g., giving to charity.> (See **determinants** or **sources of morality**.)

movent (n.): (Now somewhat archaic.) Term for a being that is moved by or undergoes change through the agency of another.

mover (n.): A being that brings about a change in another; an *efficient cause.* <God as the First (i.e., ontologically primary) Mover of the entire cosmos.>

murder (n.): An intentional killing of another human being that goes against right order in human relationships, as reflected in *natural* (*moral*) *law* and various systems of *human law.* (Note: The *killing* of another person, or a homicide, is not necessarily a case of murder, because under certain specifiable conditions—e.g., the taking of a combatant's life in a just war, or an assailant's life in a case of self-defense when no lesser means will be effective—the acts in question do not offend against right order. [See, however, the discussion under **culture of death/ culture of life**.])

Muslim (adj. or n.): See **Islam**.

mystery (n., Greek *musterion,* Latin *mysterium*): Realm of intelligibility that is "hidden from view," either because of the weakness or inattentiveness of our intellects, or because of the difficult character (sometimes *supernatural* character) of the subject matter, or both. Philosophy seeks to penetrate the realm of *natural* $_{(4)}$ mystery (e.g., the nature of *being, goodness, truth,* etc.), by means of common human *experience* and reflective *reason.* Additionally, Christian philosophy, in what John Paul II called its "third state," seeks to assist theology in the latter's attempts to articulate—to the extent possible for human minds—*supernatural* mysteries expressed in *revelation* and accepted as part of religious faith. (A "mystery" as here defined should be distinguished from a "problem"—i.e., something that in principle admits of final and complete human resolution, such as a question properly pursued via the methods of the natural *sciences* (2).)

mystic (n.): One who practices, or is given to, *mysticism.* Also (now somewhat archaic): "mystic" (as an adj., i.e., as equivalent to "mystical").

mystical (adj.): (1) Of or having to do with *mysticism.* <A sense of merging with the Absolute as common to various types of mystical experience.> (2) As said of a quality or attribute, one which, due to the sublime nature of the reality in question, is expressed via terms that do not bear their ordinary or literal meaning. <The "Mystical Body of Christ"—a traditional expression for the Church.> Also: "mystically" (adv.).

mysticism (n.): Mode of apprehending God or the immaterial realm not by *reasoning,* nor by *faith* (3), but by a direct if obscure experiential awareness.

myth (n.): (1) Technically, a story presented in one category of terms—e.g., great heroes, with their trials and triumphs—which, although not literally corresponding to historical facts, conveys insight into the human condition or expresses some aspect of a people's self-understanding. <The ancient Greek myth of Sisyphus.> (2) According to a common but very different usage, an account of things believed by some people to be factually true, but known or reasonably assumed to be false. <The myth (in the judgment of most contemporary philosophers) of "the given," that is, of absolutely uninterpreted or unmediated *sensory data* as possible objects of investigation.> Also: "mythic" or "mythical" (adj.), "mythically" (adv.).

narrative ethics: A recent approach to ethics that stresses moral insight gained from a person's or a group's historical experience, and in particular from the written articulation of that experience.

nation or **country** (n.): A people or large-scale *civil society*, ordinarily one that has recognized geographical boundaries and is organized into a *state* $_{(2)}$, with *governmental* structures, as well as other types of institutions (educational, cultural, religious, economic, etc.). <Canada is the nation just north of the U.S. border.> (Note: The present concepts are difficult to mark off with precision. There can be states without nations [e.g., Vatican City], and, arguably, nations without states [e.g., Kurdistan]; moreover, a single nation may be divided into more than one sovereign state [e.g., Korea].) Also: "national" (adj.), "nationalize" (v.), "nationally" (adv.).

nationalism (n.): In contrast to proper *patriotism* (which is a species of the moral virtue of *piety*), an inordinate concern about the good of one's own country, to the neglect of the good of other peoples and nations, and/or the neglect of one's country's responsibilities vis-à-vis global society. Also: "nationalistic" (adj.), "nationalistically" (adv.).

natural (adj.): Of or having to do with *nature*, in its various senses. (1) Existing in or characterizing the physical world as such, sometimes as opposed to the results of human creativity and production (contrast **artificial**). (2) Features of a *being* or *power* or *act*, etc., that are determined by its *essence,* as opposed to features that depend upon events in the internal or external environment (contrast **conditional**), or that derive from human decision and agreement (contrast **conventional**). (3) In accord with the *end*$_{(1)}$ of a being of nature—in particular, human nature—or the ends of its specific powers or acts (contrast **unnatural**$_{(3)}$). (4) Within the power and activity range of beings of nature (including human nature) as such, as opposed to both what is other than nature (e.g., mathematical objects and relations) and what is beyond nature—i.e., God and created pure spirits, as well as the *final end* to which, by grace, human persons are called (contrast **supernatural**). Also: "naturally" (adv.), "naturalness" (n.).

natural family planning: Method, or a family of methods, of regulating conception that do not, for Catholic magisterial teaching, involve sexual acts performed in such a way, or in a context so altered, as to frustrate their natural *ends*$_{(1)}$—as is judged to be the case in *contraception.* (Methods of natural family planning have dramatically improved over recent decades; they typically focus on monitoring biological indications of fertility [i.e., ovulation]. If conception is desired according to a couple's family planning, sexual intercourse is undertaken accordingly; if conception is not desired, the couple refrains from sexual intercourse during the fertile period.)

natural inclinations: A special application of *natural*$_{(3)}$ to philosophical anthropology and ethics; according to the perennial tradition, the structure of *basic goods,* as well as the primary precepts of the *natural (moral) law,* can be articulated via reflection on these natural tendencies of human, personal life. (Aquinas groups such inclinations into three categories: a) those shared with all natural beings [e.g., the inclination to preserve one's existence]; b) those shared with other animal species [e.g., the inclinations to reproductive activity and education of the young]; and c) those specifically human in nature [e.g., the inclinations to life in organized society, to knowledge of the truth—including the truth about God—and to reflective pursuit of the good]. Although our rational and personal nature relates specifically to inclinations at level c), it also penetrates and shapes our human inclinations at the other two levels.)

naturalism (n.): (1) The general philosophical view that holds all of reality to be exhausted by the order of *nature* $_{(1)}$. (2) In ethical theory, one of a variety of positions holding that we can recognize moral truths through reflection on facts of nature, especially human nature. (The natural law accounts of Aquinas, and the tradition of integral Christian wisdom generally, would constitute forms of naturalism in this second sense.)

naturalistic fallacy: Term used by certain modern ethical theorists (beginning with the early 20th-century British philosopher G. E. Moore) to express the thesis that moral propositions cannot be reached by valid reasoning from propositions expressing only matters of natural or scientific (i.e., *empiriological*) fact. [Note: Since the Thomistic account of *natural* (*moral*) *law* is rooted in *ontological* rather than empiriological considerations, and since it speaks of the *natural* in senses (2) and especially (3), rather than sense (1), it does not—contrary to some scholarly opinion in the English-speaking world—involve this fallacy.]

natural (**moral**) **law**: Rational ordinances for the direction of human acts, ultimately traceable to the mind of the Creator, which reflect the *natural* $_{(3)}$ structure of human *teleology* $_{(1)}$, and which, at least in principle, can be grasped at the most general level by all human beings. (According to Aquinas, such a grasp of moral precepts is possible because human practical reason, properly functioning, is a *participation* in the Creator's eternal reason.) (See **law** $_{(1)}$, **primary precepts of natural** (**moral**) **law**, and ***synderesis***.)

natural law theory: Approach to ethics, prominent within the perennial tradition, that locates a source of moral rules in what is taken to be *natural* (*moral*) *law*.

natural philosophy: See **philosophy of nature**.

natural rights: A range of *rights* (also called "human rights" or "basic human rights") that—according to recent formulations within the perennial tradition—accrue to human beings simply by virtue of their nature and dignity as *persons* $_{(1)}$, rather than by virtue of their citizenship, their achievements, or any other conditions of acquisition (as is the case with other types of rights, called "acquired" rights). For Thomists, natural rights are ordered in terms of the *teleological structure of human goods*. Thus, the right to *life* is the most fundamental of these rights, while the right to *religious liberty* is the highest or most central to specifically human fulfillment. [Note: The present account of natural rights contrasts sharply with accounts reflective of *liberalism* $_{(3)}$.]

nature (n., Latin *natura*): (1) The whole *order* of physical being (Greek *phusis*), or being that is changing and observable (Latin *ens mobile seu sensibile*), including powers and activities of, and relations among, beings within this order. (2) The *essence* of a natural *being* (or *power* or *act,* etc.)—i.e., the set of intrinsic intelligible features that mark the being as one of a certain type—by contrast with its *state* or *condition* or *circumstances,* and also by contrast with features that are due to human *convention* or *choice* $_{(2)}$. (For example, to be capable of speech expressing judgments is due to our rational nature; but to be able to speak English or Spanish, etc., is due to circumstance and convention.) (3) The *principle* $_{(1)}$ of a being's operations, due to which the being itself, as well as its proper powers and acts, are intrinsically ordered to respective *ends* $_{(1)}$. (4) By contrast with *grace,* what a being (in particular, a human being) is and is able to accomplish according to its given essence, apart from special divine assistance or elevation.

necessary (adj.): (1) (Metaphysically.) What must be *absolutely* $_{(2)}$; that is, the thing's non-actuality would violate the *principle of identity.* (2) (Logically.) What must be *true;* that is, the negation of the proposition in question would be incompatible with the *principle of noncontradiction.* (See **evident or self-evident** and **tautology**.) (3) (Physically.) What must be the case in this universe or in the realm of physical being; that is, the opposite would violate known *laws* $_{(3)}$ of nature or principles of *natural philosophy.* (4) (Morally.) What must be chosen and done if the *integral human good* is to be pursued and if applicable precepts of *moral law* are to be respected. (5) (Practically.) What must be expected to happen, in light of all reasonable assumptions about the agents and circumstances involved. (In the five senses listed above, contrast the parallel senses of both **impossible** and **possible.**) (6) As used in the phrase "Necessary Being," not able not to *exist* (in particular, supposing this marks a real contrast, having this perfection in and of itself, rather than from another)—a predicate uniquely applicable to *God* $_{(1)}$. (Ant: **possible** $_{(6)}$.) (7) As used in the phrases "necessary condition" and "hypothetically necessary," what must be the case if something else is to be the case. Also: "necessarily" (adv.).

necessary and sufficient conditions: An approach to definition by way of identifying exact conditions for the instantiation of a concept, or the occurrence of a property or state of affairs. (This approach has been popular in the English-speaking world, especially within *analytic philosophy,* since the middle decades of the 20th century. It seeks rigor by articulating *truth-conditions* for the proposition expressing the state of affairs in question. In particular, *p* is said to be a "necessary condition" for *q* if and only if *q* cannot be true unless *p* is true; and *p* is said to be a "sufficient condition" for *q* if and only if *p* cannot be true unless *q* is true.)

necessity (n.): (1) The condition or state of being *necessary,* in any of the senses distinguished in that entry. (Contrast both **impossibility** and **possibility**.) (2) In ethics, the term "necessity" has an additional, quite different, meaning beyond that of being morally necessary (i.e., *necessary* $_{(4)}$): namely, a concrete existential condition (a "state of necessity") that renders inapplicable a moral rule that otherwise would be relevant—for example, a life-threatening fire in one's home and the availability of a neighbor's water supply, but not one's own (in relation to the moral rule "Do not steal another's property"). (Strictly speaking, on the perennial tradition's ethical analysis, such extraordinary circumstances do not—as many suppose—justify the violation of a moral precept; rather, they change the moral nature of the act in question. Thus, in terms of the above example, appropriating the neighbor's water supply in such circumstances simply would not be a case of stealing.) (See **change of matter** or **change of species**, and **exceptionless moral rules**.)

negate (v.): See **deny** or **negate**.

negation (n.): See **denial** or **negation**.

negative way (Latin *via negativa*): Term designating the approach to knowledge and language about God by way of saying "what God is not"—e.g., that God is infinite (which is to say, not finite), uncaused, unchanging, atemporal, etc. The negative way is sometimes also called the "way of remotion;" that is, in undertaking this approach one "removes" properties that are in no way attributable to God.

Neo-Platonic (adj.): Of or relating to a form of late Hellenistic philosophy that was a revival of Platonic ideas, and that was represented most fully by Plotinus (204–70). Plotinus developed a theory of necessary "emanations" from the ultimate principle of reality (which he called "the One")—with lower stages of reality constantly flowing from higher stages. In their original form, Neo-Platonic positions often were incompatible with Christianity; but writers such as St. Augustine and (Pseudo-) Dionysius—and through them the great medieval Scholastics—adapted certain Neo-Platonic themes in developing their philosophical and theological frameworks. (See, e.g., **participation** $_{(1)}$.) Also: "Neo-Platonist" (adj. or n.), "Neo-Platonism" (n.).

Neo-Thomism (n.): See the discussion under **Thomism**. Also: "Neo-Thomist" (adj. or n.), "Neo-Thomistic" (adj.).

New (or **Evangelical**) **Law**: For Christians, the principles governing human action as revealed in the person and Gospel (Latin *Evangelium*) of Jesus, who is acknowledged as the Christ (from the Greek for "annointed") and the Son and Word of God. (Contrast **Old Law**.)

new natural law theory: Designation given to a recent approach to ethics—especially its treatment of *basic goods* and its *incommensurability thesis*—that was developed by Germain Grisez and certain associates (John Finnis, Robert George, et al.). The phrase itself was introduced by more Thomistically-oriented critics of the movement, notably Russell Hittinger.

nihilism (n., from Latin *nihil,* for "nothing"): Philosophical position holding that human life and the world are purposeless or totally without intrinsic meaning; attributable to some forms of *materialism* and *scientism,* as well as to *existentialism* of the atheistic variety. (The late 19th-century German philosopher Friedrich Nietzsche is sometimes cited as a proponent, or a precursor, of the position.) Also: "nihilist" (adj. or n.), "nihilistic" (adj.), "nihilistically" (adv.).

nominalism (n.): Philosophical position, developed in the Middle Ages but also influential today, according to which nothing in extra-mental reality grounds our universal concepts or "names" (Latin *nomina*). (Perennial philosophy holds to the contrary that although, as a universal, an *essence* [e.g., *man* $_{(1)}$] has existence only in the mind, the concept can be grounded—and in cases of successful *apprehension* is grounded—in common intelligible features of real existing things [in this case, individual human beings].)

(See **universals, problem of**; contrast **conceptualism** and **realism.**) Also: "nominalist" (adj. or n.), "nominalistic" (adj.), "nominalistically" (adv.).

nonbeing (n.): (1) A pure nothingness in the sense that it could not exist, either in reality or in the mind; a metaphysical and logical impossibility. (2) That which, although it could exist, does not at present actually exist. (The 20th-century Thomist Yves R. Simon noted that this latter sense of "nonbeing" applies to *potency,* as a kind of "nonbeing that is." In terms of this dictionary, to be in potency is to be an instance of *being* $_{(1)}$ but not *being* $_{(2)}$.)

noncognitivism (n.): Philosophical view, or family of views, holding that certain types of putative judgments and beliefs in fact involve no genuinely cognitive content or understanding. Noncognitivism's primary target has been *metaphysics.* Other prominent targets include normative ethics (as with *emotivism*) and religious beliefs (as in "symbolicism," discussed at **symbol** $_{(2)}$; and in some versions of *fideism.*) Also: "noncognitive" (adj.), noncognitively (adv.), "noncognitivist" (adj. or n.).

nonconscious (adj.): Not *conscious.* (See **subconscious** and **unconscious,** as well as **preconscious** or **precognitive.**)

noncontradiction, principle of: The first, indemonstrable *principle* of logic and theoretical knowledge—namely, "Nothing can be both affirmed and denied of the same subject at the same time and in the same respect." This principle can be regarded as a corollary of the metaphysical *principle of identity.* (Somewhat confusingly, it also is sometimes referred to as the "principle of contradiction.")

nonmoral good: A good which, in and of itself, does not possess moral value (e.g., health, education, etc.)—by contrast with a *moral good,* that is, one that can be achieved only in and through *choices* and *human acts* that accord with the *determinants* or *sources of morality* (e.g., deciding to take appropriate steps to maintain one's health, or to achieve an education, etc.).

non-reductive physicalism: See the discussion under **materialism.**

nonvoluntary (adj.): Not *voluntary,* in the neutral sense of failing to meet one or both of the criteria for voluntary action. (Note: A nonvoluntary action, or undergoing of action, is not necessarily *involuntary* $_{(2)}$.) Also: "nonvoluntarily" (adv.), "nonvoluntariness" (n.).

noosphere (n.): See **Teilhardian.**

norm (n.): (1) A *rule, measure,* or other *criterion* to which a power or action must conform if it is to reach its proper *end* $_{(1)}$—for example, the rules of thought (i.e., logical and metaphysical *principles* $_{(2)}$) that must be followed if the *intellect* is to attain a discursive knowledge of truth; and the rules of conduct (i.e., genuine *moral precepts*) that must be followed if the *will* is to make proper choices about action. (2) In the *positive sciences,* a statistical regularity noted in the behavior of things.

normal (adj.): (1) In the positive and primarily *empiriological* sciences, falling within the range of cases that fit a "statistical norm" (i.e., a *norm* $_{(2)}$). <It is normal for males to be physically stronger than females.> (2) In philosophical and especially *ontological* disciplines, a set function in keeping with the *nature* $_{(2)}$ in question. <It is normal that lions be carnivorous.> (3) In *ethics,* an action, or a tendency toward action, that is in accord with a power's *natural* $_{(3)}$ end. <It is normal for a speaker to intend to communicate the truth.> (Note: Confusion about these various senses adversely affects discussion in *applied ethics*—especially, in recent years, concerning sexual practices. For example, in most populations, some incidence of homosexuality is normal in sense (1); but this does not answer the question of whether it is normal in sense (3).) (Ant: **abnormal.**) Also: "normalcy" (n.), "normally" (adv.).

normative (adj.): A type of judgment, rule, or general theory about human acts that goes beyond the description of behaviors to an evaluation of their goodness, rightness, or obligatoriness. (See **ethical theory** and **ethics**, as well as **prescriptive.**) Also: "normatively" (adv.), "normativity" (n.).

noumenon (Greek n., now Anglicized, from *nous,* for "mind;" plural in English follows Greek *noumena*): See the discussion under **phenomenon** $_{(1)}$.

nutritive (adj.): See **vegetative** (sometimes **nutritive**).

O

obedience (n.): The acceptance and carrying out of legitimate dictates of *authority.* Such obedience is ordinarily a matter of *justice* and *duty*—e.g., of minor children in relation to their parents, of citizens in relation to *government* authorities, and of all human beings in relation to the Creator and the *natural* (*moral*) *law* inscribed in our natures. (However, just as there are limitations on rights, so also there is no actual duty to obey one who has illegitimately usurped authority; nor is there a duty to obey a person in authority who demands that one do something morally wrong.) Also: "obedient" (adj.), "obediently" (adv.).

obediential potency: In traditional Christian theology, an openness (strictly speaking, a type of *passive potency*) within human nature to be disposed to *supernatural* ends—in particular, to *beatitude.* (On this account, it is not given with human nature as such to be able even to aspire to personal communion with God; such an aspiration and its fulfillment requires divine elevation, although one that works on genuine features of our humanness. Compare the discussion at **grace**.)

object (n.): (1) In the most general sense, synonymous with "thing." (2) In philosophical psychology, a *reality* (or a *potential* reality) that attracts a power of knowledge or appetite. Objects in this sense are sometimes divided into *material* objects (i.e., things as concrete wholes—for example, this particular apple), and *formal objects* (i.e., the specific *natures* $_{(2)}$ or aspects of things that attract the powers in question—for example, this particular apple as something that might satisfy my hunger). (Contrast **subject** $_{(2)}$). (3) In ethics (where it is spoken of as the "moral object"), what is directly accomplished according to the essential character of an act—e.g., in a case of euthanasia, the killing of the patient. (In relation to sense (3), see **determinants** or **sources of morality**.)

objectification (n.): In personalist philosophies, the treating of a *self* or *subject* $_{(2)}$ as an *object* $_{(1)}$ or thing to be used. <The objectification of human beings as a pervasive problem in modern societies.>

objective (adj.): (1) Of or having to do with being itself, or an instance or aspect of being itself, rather than our experience of it—e.g., an act's objective moral character. (Ant: **subjective**.) (2) Pertaining to the mode of existence proper to an object of experience or thought just as such (i.e., *intentional,* by contrast with *entitative,* existence). Also: "objectively" (adv.).

objective (n.): Goal or end—ordinarily in the sense of "end of the agent" (Latin *finis operantis*)—of a human act.

objectivism (n.): Regarding philosophical accounts in both the speculative and practical orders, a synonym for *realism* $_{(1)}$. (Ant: **subjectivism**. Contrast as well **relativism**.)

objectivity (n.): (1) A being's status as an *object* $_{(2)}$, rather than a *subject* $_{(2)}$. (2) A cognitive standpoint from which one seeks to know things just as they are (i.e., in their true essential and accidental features), insofar as it is possible to do so. <The importance of objectivity in newspaper reporting.>

obligation (n.): See **duty** or **obligation**. Also: "obligatory" (adj.).

Ockhamist (adj. or n.): Of or pertaining to, or one who follows the late Medieval Scholastic William of Ockham (c. 1285–1349). By contrast with Aquinas, Ockham held a form of *voluntarism* in ethics; and he was a *nominalist* regarding the significance of universal terms. In keeping with the latter position, even today the principle called "Ockham's Razor" is appealed to in arguments against "inflationary" metaphysics (i.e., metaphysics that recognizes more types of reality than is thought to be warranted). This principle, also called the "principle of parsimony," often is expressed as *entia non sunt multiplicanda praeter necessitatem* ("Entities are not to be multiplied beyond necessity")—although this precise formulation seems not to appear in Ockham's own writings.

Old Law: For Christians, directives regarding the moral life given through Moses and the Hebrew scriptures, that is, the "Old Testament." (Contrast **New** (or **Evangelical**) **Law**.)

oligarchy (n.): In the tradition of Aristotle, political rule by those with inherited sources of power (position, wealth, etc.), and according to which the ends served tend to be those of the rulers themselves rather than, as they should be, *common goods* of the people as a whole—i.e., goods such as justice in the assignment of social benefits and in the exchange of material goods. (Compare **aristocracy** $_{(2)}$; contrast **democracy**, as well as **aristocracy** $_{(1)}$.)

Omega point: See **Teilhardian**.

omnipotence (n., from Latin *omnia*, for "all" + *potential*, for "power"): Property according to which God can do all that it is *possible* $_{(1)}$ to do. Also: "omnipotent" (adj.), "omnipotently" (adv.).

omniscience (n., from Latin *omnia*, for "all" + *scientia*, for "knowledge"): Property according to which, for the perennial tradition, God knows in an *eternal* manner all that is, including individuals and events in the physical world, past, present, and future. Also: "omniscient" (adj.), "omnisciently" (adv.).

one and the many, the: Metaphysical problem and theme explored in Western philosophy since the time of the pre-Socratics: How is it that beings, although differentiated in various ways, all can be identified as beings? (Among recent Thomist writers, this question—and the role of *participation* $_{(1)}$ in a proper response to it—has especially been emphasized by W. Norris Clarke, S.J.)

oneness or **unity** (n.): A *transcendental* property of being, according to which every being is a consistent, integral whole, indivisible in itself and distinct from all other beings as long as it remains the same being. (For those who also list "being something definite" [Latin *aliquid*] among the transcendentals, certain of the above features—in particular, that of being distinct from all other beings—might be said to relate to that property rather than to oneness or unity.) Also: "one" or "united" (adj.), "unit" (n.).

ontological (sometimes **ontic**) (adj.): Having to do with *being* $_{(1)}$ or the way things are, sometimes by contrast with the way things manifest themselves (i.e., their *empiriological* features). *Metaphysics* is the discipline chiefly concerned with ontological matters; however, in relation to the being of the physical world, the *philosophy of nature* and the modern natural *sciences* (2) have their own ontic significance—although some aspects of the latter seem purely empiriological in nature. <Ontological categories; the ontological status of the human embryo.> Also: "ontologically" (adv.).

ontological argument: In *philosophical theology,* a type of argument according to which God, when properly conceived or defined, can be seen to exist—and exist necessarily—in *reality,* apart from further inquiry. (Ontological arguments for God have been proposed at least since the time of St. Anselm [1033–1109], who defined God as "that than which nothing greater can be conceived." But such arguments often have been rejected, including by Aquinas, who noted that they presuppose what cannot plausibly be maintained: namely, that the human mind is able to arrive at a proper *definition* (2) of God.)

ontology (n.): The part of the discipline of metaphysics that seeks to articulate the fundamental types and categories of *being* (1)—e.g., *substances* and their *accidents,* the relations between parts and wholes, etc.

onto-theology (or **onto-theo-logy**) (n.): Term used to characterize traditional philosophical and theological approaches to God by certain of their *postmodern* critics—e.g., at least for a time, the French Catholic thinker Jean-Luc Marion. Marion affirmed that "God is, exists;" but, he added, "that is the least of things." Rather than trying to fashion an understanding of God via the concept of *being,* the Church should, he argued (as suggested in 1 John 4), focus on the revelation of God as *love.* [Note: While many of their claims about the perennial tradition fall wide of the mark, the critics of "onto-theology" raise an important caution, connected with what this dictionary lists as *essentialism* (2).] (Compare **liberation from being**.)

operation (n.): Synonym for *activity,* an instance of "second" *act* in a being. (Although for many purposes the terms are used interchangeably, "operation" sometimes stresses that the act is *proper* (2) to the being in question, while "activity" sometimes carries the connotation that it is the result of *free choice.*)

optimism (n.): General outlook or attitude toward the world, and especially toward human events, characterized by the expectation of good results. (Note: Optimism is not equivalent to the theological virtue of *hope,* which can function in the absence of *natural* (4) expectations of good.) (Ant: **pessimism**.) Also: "optimist," (n.), "optimistic" (adj.).

order (n.): (1) A broad realm of *being*$_{(1)}$ or of a type of *object*$_{(2)}$, with this term often marking a contrast between one such realm and another. <The practical vs. the speculative order; various orders of good (ontological, moral, instrumental, etc.).> (2) A kind of unity, or quasi-unity or relationship, that results from a principled association of two or more objects. <The order in analogous sets; the order between the human genders; the order between a power and its end.> (3) Proper relationship or set of relationships capable of being brought about through the good exercise of human agency—e.g., within a city or among nations.

order (v.): (1) To bring about an *order*$_{(2)}$. <An account that orders various uses of the term "good."> (2) To exercise proper political or other authority with a view to achieving and maintaining *order*$_{(3)}$. <A government's ordering of its systems of taxation and welfare so as to provide for the basic needs of all its citizens.> Also: "orderly" (adv.).

ordered (adj.): As said of two or more things, having a specifiable relationship or *order*$_{(2)}$, whether by nature or by convention. <The human mind as naturally ordered to the understanding of real being. The three branches of the U.S. government as constitutionally ordered to their respective roles.>

order of discovery: See **discovery, order of**.

order of explanation: See **explanation, order of**.

ordinary/extraordinary means: In biomedical ethics, contrasting terms used in the moral assessment of *means* to preserve life. Such a means is called "ordinary" if it satisfies two criteria: a) it offers a reasonable hope of benefit to the patient (considered as a whole person); and b) it involves no unreasonable or excessive burden. A medical means that fails to meet one or both of these criteria is thereby judged "extraordinary." Whether a specific type of means—e.g., a heart bypass operation, or the undertaking of chemotherapy—is ordinary or extraordinary will in part be determined by the individual circumstances of the case. According to traditional Catholic teaching, if a means of preserving life is ordinary, it is morally obligatory; if it is extraordinary, it is not morally obligatory, although it may, depending on the circumstances, be morally acceptable. (Unfortunately, medical professionals sometimes use the same pair of terms to mark the level of technical challenge, or the frequency of occurrence, of a specific procedure at a particular health care institution. The resulting differences in meaning can be a source of misunderstanding in discussions between physicians and health care ethicists.)

organ (n.): (1) A functional part of a living being or organism. <The skin as the organ of touch.> (2) (Metaphorical use.) The public agent of an organizing force or social movement. <Certain media outlets as organs of propaganda.>

organic (adj.): (1) Of or having to do with *organs* or *organisms*. (2) Analogously, manifesting an *order* $_{(2)}$ that is in some way similar to that found within organisms. <An organic account of a particular historical movement.>

organism (n.): A *living* being, usually composed of diverse organs, but having a single principle of substantial unity—i.e., for the Aristotelian tradition, a *soul* (Greek *psuche*) of the relevant type. (Unlike the parts of a continuum [which, although distinct, are functionally identical], and unlike the parts of a machine [which, although functionally differentiated, are not related to one another so as to comprise a unified substance], the parts of an organism are both diversified in function and ordered by a substantial principle to a single overall end or good.)

original innocence: As presented by biblical religion—or at least by traditional Catholic Christianity—the elevated condition enjoyed by the first human persons (represented in the book of Genesis by Adam and Eve). In this condition—before *sin* entered the world—original humanity enjoyed *friendship* with God, along with a system of "praeternatural" and "supernatural" gifts. (See **gifts of integrity and grace**.)

Original Sin (also called "the Fall"): As presented by biblical religion, and depicted in the story of Adam and Eve eating the forbidden fruit (said in Genesis to be fruit "of the tree of the knowledge of good and evil"), the decision by original humanity to defy God's Knowledge and Will as it was made known to them. With sin came the loss of the *gifts of integrity and grace*, and a wounded condition of *human nature* itself. Consequently, the pursuit of the human good—even in its *natural* $_{(3)}$ dimensions—is more difficult than it otherwise would have been, even in a supposed (although never actual) state of "pure nature."

original solitude: See the discussion under **solitude**.

orthodoxy (n. from Greek *orthos,* for "right" + *doxa,* for "belief"): (1) Positions in keeping with, or constituting, accepted or definitive teachings. (For Catholics today, these especially would include teachings on faith and morals defined by the Church's "extraordinary" *magisterium*). (Ant: **heterodoxy.**) Also: "orthodox" (adj. or n.). (2) When written with a capital "O," the term typically designates those Christian churches which share the substance of Catholic belief—as well as valid sacraments, priestly orders, and ordained episcopate—but which have not been in formal communion with Rome since the Great Schism of 1054. Also: "Orthodox" (adj. or n.).

orthopraxis (n., from Greek *orthos* for "right" + *praxis* for "activity"): In keeping with accepted or mandated practice(s). [Note: Some Christian theologians have undertaken to treat orthopraxis apart from concerns about *orthodoxy.* However, as Joseph Ratzinger long ago emphasized, a *separation* of the two would not have been recognized within the early Church.]

otherness (n.): Difference; as used in recent philosophy, especially *phenomenology* and *existentialism,* the term implies a difference of major human significance—as in the experience of strangers, those of very different cultures, etc. (See **xeno-**.)

ownership (n.): Relation expressed by *positive law,* according to which a person or group of persons has a right to a particular *property* $_{(3)}$ or other resource. With ownership ordinarily comes a right of use; however, the latter fails to hold in cases where the owner is incapable of a proper use of the resource, or where another person, or the state (with a view to the common good), has a strict need to appropriate the resource. (See **necessity** $_{(2)}$, as well as **universal destination of goods**.)

P

pacifism (n.): Philosophical or theological position opposed to *war* as a matter of strict *principle* (2). (Note: Throughout its history, Christianity has given rise to expressions of pacifism. While supporting the right of individual citizens to embrace pacifism as a matter of conscience, perennial philosophy, and the Catholic moral tradition generally, also recognize the *justice* (2) of engaging in armed conflict under certain specified conditions. See the discussion under **just war theory**.) Also: "pacifist" (adj. or n.).

paganism (n.): Worship of gods other than the one, true God (as in the polytheisms of ancient cultures); also, the worship of physical things as gods. In the contemporary context, pervasive attitudes (sometimes collectively referred to as "neo-paganism") that involve seeking one's ultimate fulfillment through physical things, even if these things can be called objects of "worship" only in an extended or metaphorical sense. (See **atheism** (2) and **materialism** (2).) Also: "pagan" (adj. or n.).

pain (n.): A direct negative experience, in any of its various types and modes, but especially those involving the *senses*. Objects threatening pain, apprehended precisely as such, are objects of *aversion* for all persons of normal affectivity. (Ant: **pleasure**.) Also: "painful" (adj.), "painfully" (adv.).

panentheism (n.): See the discussion under **pantheism**. Also: "panentheist" (adj. or n.).

panpsychism (n., from Greek *pan*, for "all" + *psuche*, for "soul"): Theory that all things in nature are animated or enjoy some type of experience. (Versions of this theory are found in the religions of *animism;* it also has had philosophical adherents—most notably, among modern thinkers, Gottfried Leibniz (1646–1716).) (See as well **vitalism**.) Also: "panpsychist" (adj. or n.).

pantheism (n., from Greek *pan,* for "all" + *theos,* for "god"): Theory, or family of theories, holding that all things are divine, and/or that God and the world are identical. (This position is to be distinguished from the somewhat rarer view called "panentheism," according to which the world is partially, but only partially, identifiable with God—that is, the reality of God encompasses the world, but goes beyond it.) Also: "pantheist" (adj. or n.), "pantheistic" (adj.).

parenthood (n.): The state of having initiated, through *procreation,* new human life and a unique *communion of persons* (i.e., a new *family* (1)). In the personalist account elaborated by John Paul II, parenthood—properly understood and practiced—involves a special type of human imaging of God (in which, for Roman Catholic theology, the Holy Spirit is said to "proceed" from the mutual love and self-giving of the Father and the Son). That is, the woman becomes a mother through the gift of self to her husband; and the man becomes a father through the gift of self to his wife; and the child proceeds from their mutual, self-giving love. (Note: Just as there are other, related groupings that can analogously be called *families,* so there are other, related relationships that can analogously be called "parenthood.") Also: "parent" (n.), "parental" (adj.).

parenthood, responsible: Phrase used in Pope Paul VI's *Humanae vitae* (1968) to designate the appropriate regulation of conception and birth in family life. (See **birth regulation** or **control**, and **natural family planning**.)

Parousia (Greek n., from *ousia,* for "being" or "essence"): Literally meaning "arrival" or "presence," this term has been used since ancient times to name the biblical second coming of Christ, with its attendant judgment and final transformation of the physical world.

parsimony, principle of: See the discussion under **Ockhamist**.

part (n.): (1) Component of a physical being, whether integral and constituent (e.g., its substantial form); or material (e.g., a hand or a foot). (2) (Metaphorical.) A distinguishable aspect of a *spiritual* being (e.g., intellect and will in the human soul), or of a *being of reason* (e.g., the middle term in a syllogism). (Contrast **whole**.) Also: "partial" (adj.), "partially" or "partly" (adv.).

participate (v.): To share in a property that belongs primarily and *per se* to another—e.g., the brush being used participates in the painter's art. Metaphysically speaking, all beings participate in the *transcendental* properties, which belong primarily to, and are enjoyed *per se* by, God. Also: "participative" (adj.).

participated theonomy: See the discussions under **autonomy** and **theonomy**.

participation (n.): (1) The condition or state according to which a being shares in a quality belonging primarily and *per se* to another. (That physical and limited beings thus share qualities with the eternal order was a fundamental position developed by Plato and the Neo-Platonics, and taken over, albeit with qualifications, by Augustine and Aquinas.) <Human wisdom as a participation in God's wisdom.> (See **transcendental** (1) and **pure perfection**.) (2) In personalist anthropology and ethics (notably the philosophical writings of Karol Wojtyla), the condition of a person properly related to society in all essential dimensions—and thus able to fulfill himself or herself as a personal whole within the larger whole of the community. (Contrast **alienation** (2).)

particular (n.): Concrete instance or example of a nature or form—or, by extension, a type of situation. <Moral particulars as needing to be decided by judgments of prudence.> (Syn: **individual** (1). Ant: **universal**.) Also: "particular" (as an adj.), "particularly" (adv.).

particularism (n.): In recent philosophy (especially ethics) in the English-speaking world, the position that individual cases (e.g., what are called "moral particulars") comprise the whole of the relevant reality (in this case, moral reality). [This position restates and develops aspects of the Aristotelian view about *prudence* and moral judgment; however, it seems to preclude any role for more general elements of perennial moral philosophy—e.g., the importance of developing moral *virtues*, and recognizing the precepts of *natural (moral) law*.]

partnership (n.): See the discussion under **community**.

passing away: In its philosophical usage, antonym for **coming to be**.

passion (n., Latin *passio*, from *patior*, for "to undergo"): (1) One of the nine categories of *accident* identified by Aristotelian tradition; passivity, being acted upon (contrast **action** (1)). (2) A *change* considered in relation to the subject or the thing undergoing change (contrast **action** $_{(2)}$). (3) A movement or response of *sensible appetite* or *affectivity,* with typical bodily manifestations, in animals and human beings. Although difficult to identify and enumerate with precision, passions and appetites in this general sense are traditionally divided into *concupiscible* (such as hunger, thirst, and sexual desire, which arise in relation to objects of pleasure and pain), and *irascible* (such as natural courage and fear), which arise in relation to objects deemed beneficial or harmful, in circumstances that present challenges to their pursuit or avoidance. (See as well **emotion**.) (4) Some writers also use the term "passion" more restrictively for a very strong affective response (e.g., rage)—a psychological state that, in human persons, severely limits the possibilities of developing and/or exercising *free choice.* Also: "passionate" or (somewhat archaic) "passional" (adj.), "passionately"(adv.).

passive (adj.). Pertaining to being acted upon or affected by another being, or to *undergoing* or *suffering.* (Contrast **active.**) Also: "passiveness" or "passivity" (n.), "passively" (adv.).

past (n.): In the order of temporal *duration,* that which, in terms of its *entitative* status, at one time has been, but is not now and will not be again.

patience (n.): Moral *virtue* by which one is enabled to moderate immediate expectations, and to anticipate the eventual acquisition of a good or the ending of a harm. (See the discussion under **fortitude.**) Also: "patient" (adj.), "patiently" (adv.).

patriotism (n., from Latin *patria,* for "homeland"): Respect for, and willingness to contribute to the good of, one's *nation* or *country.* Thus a species of the virtue of *piety.* (Contrast **nationalism.**) Also: "patriot" (n.), "patriotic" (adj.).

Patristics or **Patrology** (n., from Latin *pater,* for "father"): Study of the early Christian figures called the "Fathers of the Church." (These Fathers—who, as John Paul II noted in *Fides et ratio,* ##37–41 and 74, first brought Christianity into systematic contact with Western philosophical thought—are recognized by the Church as having given expression to *orthodoxy* during its formative stages. They are divided into two groups: the Latin Fathers and the Greek Fathers. Among the Latins were St. Irenaeus, Tertullian, and St. Augustine; among the Greeks were St. Justin, St. Clement of Alexandria, Origen, St. Gregory of Nazianzus, and Dionysius [sometimes called "Pseudo-Dionysius the Areopagite"]. In *Fides et ratio,* #85, John Paul II noted that the Fathers were early contributors to the "great tradition"—which philosophy now is called upon to help renew and revitalize.) Also: "Patristic" (adj.).

peace (n.): (1) In a common but narrow sense, the absence of open conflict, especially conflict involving violent force of arms. (Ant: **war.**) (2) More fully and more positively, the "tranquility of order" (Augustine's *tranquilitas ordinis*)—a most important *common good* within a society or community, including the *world* (or *global*) *community.* (3) Psychological state in which there is an "inner" order or harmony. <The search for peace of mind.> Also: "peaceful" (adj.).

pedagogical order: The *normal* (2) order in which—due to features of the respective subject matters as well as typical processes of the human mind—a set of disciplines is best able to be learned. <According to tradition, prudent pedagogical order involves some study of the philosophy of the human person before undertaking the study of philosophical ethics.> (See as well **discovery, order of**; and **explanation, order of.**)

per accidens (Latin phrase): By way of *accidental* or contingent features; accidentally or contingently. (Contrast ***per se.***)

perceive (v.): To recognize an object that comes to awareness by way of *sensation.* (But see as well **perception** (2).)

perception (n.): (1) Awareness of an object by way of *sensation.* Often, in the case of human perception, there is implied some degree of recognition of the object's *nature,* and thus involvement of the *intellect.* <Perception of a figure as triangular.> [As noted by 20th-century Aristotelian Mortimer J. Adler, in other animals perception is bound up with sense memory, as well as with powers of generalization and the discrimination of differences—none of which require *concepts,* properly speaking. Thus it is important, but it can be difficult, to distinguish human perception from that in other higher animals; and, not surprisingly, some philosophers and psychologists regard these animals (mistakenly, according to the perennial tradition) as sharing in the life of intellect.] (2) Sometimes, through an extended use, this term denotes a broader mode of awareness—and thus is equivalent to *experience.* (For example, Hans Urs von Balthasar spoke of the need for a "perception" of the beauty of Creation.)

perennial philosophy (Latin *philosophia perennis*) or **perennial tradition**: As understood within Catholic thought, and as understood in this dictionary, a name for the philosophical tradition, incorporating insights of Plato and especially of Aristotle, that came to fruition (although not final completion) in the work of St. Thomas Aquinas. According to 20th-century Thomist Jacques Maritain, the word "perennial" indicates this philosophy's inherent need to renew itself in the intellectual climates of successive ages. John Paul II spoke similarly of an "enduringly valid philosophical tradition;" and in *Fides et ratio,* #85, he added that this tradition now must come to include "the fundamental achievements of modern and contemporary thought." Although associated with Catholic Christianity, the perennial philosophy, precisely as *philosophy,* does not appeal in its argumentation to specifically religious or theological teachings; moreover, its adherents hold this philosophy to be in principle intellectually available, indeed intellectually compelling, to persons of any age and culture. [Note: In 1946, the British writer Aldous Huxley published a book with the title "The Perennial Philosophy." However, in the case of Huxley and those who have followed him, this expression promotes a rather different—and dubious—theme: namely, that the content of the world's major religions and mystical traditions can be reduced to certain common principles, which together make up the "philosophy" they propose to call "perennial."] (For further discussion of perennial philosophy, see this volume's Introduction, especially notes 4 and 7.)

perfect (v.): To complete or make whole, ordinarily along some particular line of achievement or good. <Seeking to perfect one's reading knowledge of Medieval Latin.> Also: "perfect" (as an adj.), "perfectly" (adv.)—although the latter terms sometimes carry a connotation of completeness in all possible respects, as in "Perfect Being" (i.e., God).

perfection (n.): (1) In speculative philosophy, an *actuality* or completeness of a being, existing in proportion to that being's essence; sometimes divided into *mixed, transcendental,* and *pure perfections.* (2) In practical philosophy, a designation for the objective end or goal of human activity, that is, the highest degree of personal fulfillment. (Compare **happiness** and **beatitude.**) (3) In the unique case of God, *Absolute* Perfection, or perfection involving the fullness of Actuality beyond all temporal process.

perfectionism (n.): Position in political philosophy that supports a society's direct involvement—with or without the mechanisms of the *state* $_{(2)}$—in the moral betterment of its citizenry. Recent writers in the perennial tradition who have articulated forms of perfectionism are Robert George and Christopher Wolfe. (Ant: **antiperfectionism.**) Also: "perfectionist" (adj.).

perfective (adj.): Productive of an appropriate fullness or completeness of actuality in a thing. (Syn: **good** [as an adj.] $_{(1)}$.)

perfect society: See **complete or perfect society.**

perinoetic (adj.): Term coined by 20th-century Thomist Jacques Maritain to designate the kind of knowledge typically gained in the natural *sciences* $_{(2)}$—a knowledge of what circumscribes or lies about (Greek *peri*) an *essence,* without penetrating to the core of that essence itself. (It has been a matter of controversy among Thomists to what extent the pursuit of knowledge of *nature* $_{(1)}$ should retain the Aristotelian ideal of organization in terms of essences or necessary intelligible relations. Apart from very general truths developed in the *philosophy of nature* and the *philosophy of the human person,* it has proved extremely difficult for any discipline to give more than perinoetic knowledge of natural being.) (Contrast **dianoetic** and **ananoetic**. See **empiriological.**) Also: "perinoetically" (adv.).

permanence (n.): Condition of being in which there is, in the relevant respect, no alteration. (As Aristotle notes in the first book of the *Metaphysics,* the relationships between permanence and its opposites—that is, various types of *change*—have occupied Western speculative philosophy since the time of the pre-Socratics Parmenides and Heraclitus. The former held that being, in spite of appearances, in reality must be one and unchanging; while the latter held that all things are constantly in processes of change. (Aristotle and the perennial tradition have developed precise notions of *actuality* and *potentiality* in the attempt to satisfactorily address the issues.) Also: "permanent" (adj.).

perplexed conscience: State of conscience in which an agent, even after sustained reflection, is radically *uncertain* as to the moral correctness of a proposed course of action, or as to what, in the particular case, he or she should do. (Contrast **certain conscience**, as well as **doubtful conscience**.)

per se (Latin phrase, literally "through itself"): By way of *essential* $_{(1)}$ features or the very being of a thing; essentially. (Contrast ***per accidens***.)

per se nota (Latin phrase, literally "known through itself"): Characteristic of *propositions* whose truth is knowable by way of the *essences* that correspond to their constituent terms. *Per se nota* propositions traditionally are distinguished into two categories: knowable "in themselves" (Latin *secundum se*), and knowable "to us"(Latin *quoad nos*)—i.e., knowable to given individuals or to human persons as such. For example, according to the school of Aquinas, the truth of the proposition "God exists" is *per se nota* in itself, but not to any human person, for the human intellect cannot form a proper *definition* $_{(2)}$ of—i.e., know the essence of—God. (In light of the above distinction, the idea of *per se nota* propositions can be seen as comparable to, but not the same as, the more recent idea of *analytic* $_{(2)}$ statements.)

perseverance (n.): Moral *virtue* by which one is enabled to continue with a task in spite of obstacles. (See the discussion under **fortitude**.) Also: "perservering" (adj.), "perseveringly" (adv.).

person (n., Latin *persona*): (1) For the perennial tradition, as expressed in the formula developed by Boethius (480[?]–524), "an individual *supposit* of a rational nature." A person in this sense—whether physical (in particular, human) or purely spiritual (e.g., angelic or divine)—will be a special type of metaphysical *subject* $_{(3)}$, as distinguishable from a psychological *subject* $_{(2)}$. (Note: Reflection on implications of the doctrine of *Trinity* has led recent proponents of integral Christian wisdom, including Cardinal Joseph Ratzinger, to take *relationality* as an essential feature of personhood.) (2) An individual who manifests the developed traits and abilities associated with human, personal life (e.g., self-awareness, deliberate choice and action); thus, a psychological *subject* $_{(2)}$. (Note: In this second sense, neither human fetuses, nor newborns, nor the profoundly retarded, nor the comatose would count as persons—although all would count as persons in the first sense. Inattention to this point leads to confusion in the practical order, particularly in certain discussions of biomedical ethics.) (3) In an extended sense, a *juridical* subject (e.g., a corporation) that is able to participate in contracts and other legal instruments.

personal (adj.): Of or pertaining to *persons,* in either of the two primary senses indicated. Also: "personally" (adv.).

personalism (n.): A family of philosophies, arising in the 20th century, that stress the unique features of human personal and interpersonal life—e.g., relationality, authentic dialogue and self-giving love, as well as human dignity and solidarity as bases of ethics. Influential early personalists include the Jewish thinker Martin Buber, as well as the Christian thinkers Emmanuel Mounier and Gabriel Marcel. [The perennial tradition can profit from—and in fact already has profited from—an influx of personalist thinking, while at the same time being able to offer the latter something it often lacks: an articulated metaphysical foundation.]

personality (n.): (1) The group of psychic characteristics, variously interrelated, that characterize an individual. (In the theory of Sigmund Freud, the most basic elements of personality are *id, ego,* and *superego.* See **psyche** $_{(2)}$.) (2) Sometimes used as a synonym for **personhood** $_{(1)}$.

personhood (n.): (1) the status of being a *person* $_{(1)}$—i.e., being an individual *supposit* of a rational nature. (2) As understood by many contemporary moral philosophers, especially in the English-speaking world (e.g., Mary Ann Warren and Michael Tooley), equivalent to having membership in the *moral community*—which, for these thinkers, is determined by the possession of the developed traits and abilities characteristic of *persons* $_{(2)}$.

pessimism (n.): General outlook on the world, especially on human events and cultural conditions, characterized by the expectation of bad results. (It is important to distinguish *metaphysical* from *moral* pessimism. The former holds that, in the very nature of things, good cannot come about—a position incompatible with traditional metaphysics, as well as with the theological virtue of *hope.* The latter holds only that the achievement of true and lasting good by human beings is something very difficult and rare—a position that may simply reflect clear-sighted moral awareness, and one that is compatible with Christian hope.) Also: "pessimist" (n.), "pessimistic" (adj.), "pessimistically" (adv.).

phantasm (n.): In traditional philosophical psychology and theories of knowledge, a sensory image, in particular one developed via *internal sense.* (Correct *insight* related to phantasms by the *agent intellect* enables human persons to develop a conceptual understanding of reality as originally presented through the senses. Moreover, having thus formed certain *intelligible species,* we then can re-relate the concepts involved to particular sensible objects, a process the Scholastics called *conversion to phantasms* [Latin *conversio ad phantasmata*]. In this way we are able to apply general judgments to *individual* material existents.)

phenomenalism (sometimes **sensationism**) (n.): A modern theory of knowledge according to which what is truly knowable is restricted to what is presented through the powers of sense (i.e., particular phenomena). In one form, phenomenalism grows out of the long-prevailing *empiricism* in English-speaking philosophy. Another form of phenomenalism is that of the French *existentialist* philosopher Jean-Paul Sartre, who wrote, "Being is nothing but the closely joined series of its manifestations." [In either form, this theory of knowledge clearly is incompatible with the perennial tradition. See the discussion at **phenomenon** $_{(1)}$.] Also: "phenomenalist" (adj. or n.).

phenomenology (n.): Philosophical method developed in the early decades of the 20th century that—in the words of its originator, German philosopher Edmund Husserl (1859–1938)—seeks to get to "the things themselves," (i.e., for phenomenologists, objects of investigation precisely as they appear in *experience,* apart from intervening conceptual apparatus or assumptions about their status in *reality*). This method has been variously refined and elaborated by Husserl's students and followers—e.g., the French philosopher Maurice Merleau-Ponty. (A number of Catholic thinkers have also made contributions to phenomenology: for example, Max Scheler [who for a time was Catholic], St. Edith Stein [the famous Jewish convert], Roman Ingarden, Dietrich von Hildebrand, Karol Wojtyla, and Robert Sokolowski.) [Note: Phenomenologists have made welcome advances, especially in exploring the interior life of human *subjectivity* $_{(1)}$. However, as *Fides et ratio,* #83 emphasizes, if this methodology is to have a proper philosophical grounding, it must be complemented by a *realist* metaphysics. Otherwise, it is likely to, and in Husserl's own case actually did—lead to *idealism* $_{(1)}$.] Also: "phenomenological" (adj.), "phenomenologically" (adv.).

phenomenon (Greek n., now Anglicized, from *phainesthai,* for "to appear;" plural form follows Greek *phenomena*): (1) A feature of things insofar as it is available to a power of *sensation;* an appearance or sensory manifestation. <Auditory and visual phenomena.> [Note: For the Aristotelian tradition, the sensory manifestations of things are starting points for the knowledge of physical reality. However, Aristotelians also hold that such manifestations can, to some extent, be rendered intelligible through the process of *abstraction.* Thus the perennial account of knowledge is to be contrasted with *phenomenalism,* as well as with the influential theory of the German philosopher Immanuel Kant (see **Kantian**). The latter proposed that our knowledge of physical reality is genuine, but limited to the organization and analysis of phenomena through our inherent "forms of sensory intuition" (which prompt us to recognize objects as conditioned by space and time) and "categories of the understanding" (which prompt our conviction that, for example, every event has a cause). Things as they are in themselves—i.e., apart from all phenomena—he referred to as "noumena" (from Greek *nous* for "mind"); the latter designation is somewhat ironic, since Kant held, precisely, that noumena cannot be objects of knowledge.] (2) For phenomenologists, an object, or range of objects, precisely insofar as it is consciously experienced and thus subject to philosophical investigation. <The phenomenon of moral responsibility.>

philosophia perennis (Latin phrase): See **perennial philosophy** or **perennial tradition.**

philosophical anthropology: See **anthropology** $_{(1)}$.

philosophical psychology: See **psychology** $_{(1)}$.

philosophical theology: See **theology** $_{(1)}$, as well as the discussions under **metaphysics** and **philosophy of God.**

philosophy (n., from Greek *philia,* for "love" + *sophia,* for "wisdom"): (1) The search for *wisdom* (literally and etymologically, the "love of wisdom")—traditionally divided into *speculative* philosophy and *practical* philosophy (with *logic,* or the art of defining and reasoning, serving as an indispensable tool for both branches). In modern times, many particular areas of philosophy (especially speculative philosophy) have been recognized: philosophy of art, of history, of language, of mathematics, of science, etc. (2) As sometimes contrasted with the modern natural *sciences* $_{(2)}$, a set of rational disciplines that employ *ontological* rather than *empiriological* modes of thought. (3) As contrasted with sacred theology (i.e., *theology* $_{(2)}$), a set of disciplines that, while culminating in discourse about God, proceed by way of reflection on common human experience, rather than formally appealing to religious revelation. Also: "philosopher" (n.), "philosophical" (adj.), "philosophically" (adv.).

philosophy of God: A variant term for *philosophical theology.* Traditionally understood as the culmination of *metaphysics,* but now often treated as an additional subject area, this part of philosophy considers topics such as the possibility of natural knowledge of the existence of God; what properly can be said of God and how the terminology is to be understood (e.g., via the theory of *analogous* language); the world's relations with God (especially as expressed in the notions of *creation* and *providence*); the *problem of evil;* and the idea of a *revelation* from God.

philosophy of mind: See the discussion under **mind.**

philosophy of nature or **natural philosophy**: Discipline that investigates mobile or *changing* being and its properties, principles, and causes—as well as related topics such as the nature of *time* and *space.* (A principal developer of the philosophy of nature during the medieval period, as *Aristotelian* texts were being reintroduced into the West, was Aquinas's teacher, St. Albert the Great [1206–80].) [Note: In spite of certain overlapping concerns—and at times inevitable tensions—there in principle should be no real conflict between a correct natural philosophy and the reliable results of the *positive sciences* of nature. Indeed, the two types of disciplines should complement and condition one another. See the discussions at **epistemological pluralism**, and **degrees** or **orders of abstraction.**]

philosophy of the human person or **human nature**: Somewhat loosely organized philosophical discipline, in which our human reality is studied in its integral nature, through the application of principles drawn from both the philosophy of nature and metaphysics. Topics include our *nature* $_{(2)}$ (as rational or personal animals); our *powers* (both cognitive and affective); and our *activities* (including the specifically personal activities of *intellectual knowledge, free choice,* and life in organized *society,* as well as our openness to *transcendence*). Finally, this discipline considers what can be known of our ultimate *destiny* (especially the question of the human soul's *immor-*

tality). For the perennial tradition, insights from the philosophy of human nature contribute to the articulation of normative theory in ethics. (Compare **anthropology** $_{(1)}$ and **psychology** $_{(1)}$.)

physicalism (n.): (1) See **materialism** $_{(1)}$. (2) In recent moral theology, a term used by *revisionists* in claiming that traditional moral teachings, especially regarding sexual issues, place undue emphasis on the bodily aspects of human acts. (Regarding sense (2), see as well the discussion under **biologism**.)

physics (n., from Greek *phusika*, for "things of nature"): (1) Name given by Aristotle to all natural studies, both what has come to be known as *science* $_{(2)}$ and the more abstract discipline called the *philosophy of nature*. (2) Today the term is usually taken restrictively to refer to studies of reality that are most fundamental from the standpoint of *matter* $_{(2)}$, while also being to a large extent mathematical in form. (See **mixed science**.) Also: "physical" (adj.), "physically" (adv.), "physicist" (n.).

piety (n., Latin *pietas*): A species of the cardinal virtue of *justice*, by which one is disposed to give proper honor to those on whom one depends or has depended in a fundamental way—e.g., parents, country, God. Also: "pious" (adj.), "piously" (adv.).

place (n.): In Aristotelian natural philosophy, that feature of physical being in terms of which each thing is locatable in relation to others and can be specified and measured as such. (Note: Aristotle and his medieval followers held that things have *natural* $_{(3)}$ places. Although this latter notion may have continuing value in philosophical discussions of the *teleology* of natural being, it no longer is used in *scientific* $_{(2)}$ modes of explanation.) (See also **space**.)

Platonic (adj.): Said of philosophical positions developed in the *Dialogues* of Plato (428[?]–347 BC) or otherwise attributed to him—or to later philosophies influenced by him. Prominent Platonic themes include the distinction between sense and intellectual knowledge; the separate existence of Forms of reality (in which the realities of this world are said to "participate," and which themselves become objects of knowledge through a process of "recollection" that is stimulated by the soul's contact with sensible reality but ultimately reliant on its prior awareness of the Forms in its original, pre-physical state); a strict dualism of body and soul, with the former functioning as a kind of shell or even prison of the latter; and the equivalence of virtue with moral knowledge and of vice with moral ignorance. (Note: During much of the 20th century, Thomistic scholars tended to downplay Platonic influences on Aquinas in favor of the obvious Aristotelian ones. In recent decades, however—with the reemphasis on, for example, the theme of *participation* $_{(1)}$ in Aquinas's metaphysics—the importance of Plato has been more fully recognized.) (See as well **Neo-Platonic.**) Also: "Platonism" (n.), "Platonist" (adj. or n.).

pleasant or **pleasurable good** (Latin *bonum delectabile*): A good that attracts human or animal desire because of the *pleasure* it promises. For the perennial tradition, a pleasurable good is truly a good; however, it is a lesser good than (and accordingly may need to be sacrificed in favor of) other, more intrinsically fulfilling human goods, such as *knowledge* and *moral virtue.* (Contrast **honest good** and **useful good.**)

pleasure (n.): A positive experience that is a direct object of *concupiscence,* in any of its types and modes, but especially in the order of the senses. In themselves and other things being equal, objects promising pleasure are objects of *desire.* (Ant: **pain.**) Also: "pleasurable" or "pleasant" (adj.).

plenitude (sometimes **plentitude**) (n.): Fullness of *actuality* or *perfection* $_{(1)}$; state of *abundance.* (The notion of plenitude applies primarily and properly to God. But it also applies *analogously* to finite being; thus, for example, the human *will* can be said to be in a state of plenitude insofar as it is ideally and fully developed, and therefore makes choices in light of a recognition of the requirements of objective good.)

pluralism (n.): (1) Diversity or plurality in certain fundamental beliefs and practices. (Recent articulations of perennial thought typically recognize such pluralism up to a point; they do not, however, endorse *relativism*—or what John Paul II called "undifferentiated pluralism." Some moral and social truths are of such overall importance as to require that public behaviors be at least minimally in accord with them; still, it is possible (and socially prudent) to accept certain ideas and behaviors that one judges to be wrong. See the discussion under **tolerance.**) (2) (In the context of world religions.) The position, often called "religious pluralism," according to which not only are the various religions of humankind irreducibly diverse in fact; they are also so bound to cultural suppositions and experiences as to make any common evaluation of them impossible. As a consequence, no religion can be characterized as *objectively* (1) "true" or "correct," or "superior" to any other; alternatively, various religions are to be regarded as equally "true" or "correct." (Proponents of pluralism in this sense—e.g., John Hick—typically contrast their position with both "exclusivism" [which holds that one particular religion is true or correct and all others are simply false and unrelated to human salvation] and "inclusivism" [which holds that while one religion is primary, and responds to authentic revelation, persons of other traditions and indeed all persons of good will can, albeit unknowingly, reach ultimate fulfillment through its means]. On this analysis, the Catholic view, as articulated in documents of Vatican II and elaborated by recent popes, is considered a version of "inclusivism.") Also: "pluralist" (adj.).

pluralistic society: A society whose laws and practices recognize a legitimate diversity of belief and practice among its members—especially regarding matters of religion, and even, to some degree, regarding fundamental matters of morality. (See the discussions at **liberalism** (3), as well as at **pluralism** (1) and **tolerance**.)

political (adj.): Of or related to a *polity*. (In everyday use, however, the term can apply to various forces within a civil society, as well as to processes of government at different levels.) Also: "politically" (adv.).

political freedom or **liberty**: Within civil society, a person's (or group of persons') condition of being at liberty to openly express views about, and to play some role in the development of, governmental structures, laws, and policies. (For the perennial tradition, this condition is a *natural* (3) feature of life in political communities.)

political liberalism: See **liberalism** in its various senses, all of which have relevance for political contexts. (Following an influential book with this title by John Rawls, the term has come to be applied especially to liberalism in the third sense.)

political realism: In political theory and policy analysis, a special application of "realism" according to which decisions about strategies and tactics (e.g., in international affairs) are to be based on the "realities" of the situation—i.e., the various geopolitical forces involved—as they affect the national interest. [Note: In this usage, "realism" has a meaning somewhat contrary to that of *realism* (2) as it applies to political questions;

according to the latter usage, which is common in perennial philosophy, political realities can and should be assessed in all their relevant features, including (most importantly, for Catholic tradition) their impact on human dignity and the global common good. Thus, the use of the present term requires caution.]

politics (n.): Concrete workings and interactions within a *polity*, as these affect issues of leadership and policy making. (Note: As with **political**, this term applies to diverse types of interactions and to various levels of government.)

polity (n., from Greek *polis*, for "city"): A large-scale *civil society*, especially as considered in terms of its governmental structures. Polities can properly take a variety of concrete forms—e.g., *democracy* and its alternatives—depending on times and circumstances, as well as the will of the people.

polygenism (n.): Theory, rooted in evolutionary biology and paleontology, that members of the human species emerged at slightly different times and in different regions of the Earth. [Depending on the theory's interpretation, it may—but also may not—be compatible with perennial philosophy of the human person, as well as acceptable to orthodox Christian faith. The strict opposite of polygenism would be "monogenism," the view that all human beings are descended from a single, original couple. However, it is not clear that the latter view (although suggested by the biblical story of Adam and Eve) is a fixed feature of Catholic belief—for both the philosophical interpretation of polygenism (which may prove compelling as an *empiriological* account) and the theological interpretation of the book of Genesis are subject to legitimate continuing study.]

polytheism (n.): Belief in many gods. (Polytheism is often attributed to certain Eastern religions—in particular, to Hinduism. But close study and reflection have led scholars to conclude that, at least sometimes, the "many" in these religions serve as *symbols* for a single, ultimate God.) (Contrast **monotheism**. See as well **theism**.) Also: "polytheist" (adj. or n.), "polytheistic" (adj.).

population policy: Set of positive laws and other instruments by which a society—especially a nation, but by extension the world community (acting through, for example, the United Nations)—seeks to regulate, in light of environmental and resource concerns, the number and relative density of the human populations for which it is responsible. [Note: From the standpoint of integral Christian wisdom, the *end* (2) of population policy, depending on concrete conditions as they develop, may be a good and even compelling one; but serious moral questions arise about frequently proposed *means*—in particular, abortion and forced (or virtually forced) sterilization.]

positive law (from Latin *posita,* for "things set down"): Ordinances of reason duly developed and promulgated by those responsible for a particular human society. (See **civil law**; compare also **human law**.) In light of what Christian tradition takes to be specific *revelation* regarding human acts, theologians sometimes speak of "divine positive law," in addition to human positive law. (See **divine law**.)

positive sciences (from Latin *posita,* for "things set down"): Another name for the natural and experimental *sciences* (2) plus, on some accounts, the disciplines of *mathematics.* (See also **empiriological**.)

positivism (n.): Originally developed by 19th-century Frenchman August Comte, a philosophical position holding that all genuine human knowledge follows the methods of the *positive sciences.* "Logical positivism," popular among many German- and English-speaking philosophers from the 1930s through the 1950s (e.g., Rudolf Carnap and other members of the "Vienna Circle," as well as A. J. Ayer in Great Britain), held further that all cognitively meaningful language is reducible to language referring to sense experience. Also: "positivist" (adj. or n.), "positivistic" (adj.), "positivistically" (adv.).

possibility (n.): Condition or state of being *possible,* in any of the senses indicated. (Ant: **impossibility**. Contrast as well **necessity**.)

possible (adj.): (1) (Metaphysically.) Able to be; that is, the thing's actuality would not violate the *principle of identity.* (2) (Logically.) Able to be consistently thought; that is, the proposition's truth would not be incompatible with the *principle of noncontradiction.* (3) (Physically.) Able to be the case in this universe or in the realm of physical being, as judged in light of known *laws* (3) of nature and principles of *natural philosophy.* (4) (Morally.) Able to be morally right, depending on the agent's motive and the circumstances; that is, the act's *object* (3) does not directly attack a *basic good* or violate *moral law.* (5) (Practically.) Within the presumed capabilities of the agents in question in the circumstances as they are understood to be. (In all of the above senses, contrast counterpart senses of **impossible** and **necessary**.) (6) As used in the phrase "possible being," that which—if it exists—might not exist, and depends for its existence on another being or beings. (Syn: **contingent** [in the first sense]. Ant: **necessary** $_{(6)}$.) Also: "possibly" (adv.).

possible intellect (Latin *intellectus possibilis*): The human intellect insofar as it is able to be *actuated* via intelligible *species* $_{(2)}$ of things, and thus to achieve, via concepts, some understanding of those things' natures or essences. (See ***species expressa***. Contrast **agent intellect**.)

postmodernism (n., sometimes hyphenated): Philosophical movement during the latter half of the 20th century (associated with Jacques Derrida, Michel Foucault, and others), according to which the supposed certainties that animated *rationalism* in modern philosophy are things that are irretrievably past, and all knowledge is embedded in particular viewpoints or forms of discourse (and thus is unable to be ultimately—i.e., rationally—grounded). [Note: John Paul II recognized (*Fides et ratio,* #91) that "the currents of thought which claim to be postmodern merit appropriate attention." Some aspects of the movement (e.g., the rejection of *rationalist* approaches) are quite compatible with the perennial tradition; however, other aspects (e.g., the general challenge to *realist* thought) are not, and thus call for a careful philosophical response. (It should be added that certain prominent Christian thinkers outside the perennial tradition—e.g., the Frenchman Jean-Luc Marion and the American H. Tristram Engelhardt—accept many tenets of postmodernism. Engelhardt, for example, says that the *realism* and *objectivism* of Aquinas and his followers should be given up in favor of recognizing an "irreducible" and "rationally contested" plurality of approaches both to knowledge and to the practical organization of life—with Christian orthodoxy being included among the available approaches.)] Also: "postmodern" or "postmodernist" (adj. or n.).

potency or **potentiality** (n.): Not *real* being, but *capacity* for such being, according to some mode or perfection—existence, operation, etc. (Like "act" and "actuality," the present terms are predicated in an *analogical* manner across all of being—except in the case of God, who alone among real beings is without potency and is fully Act. At the other end of the spectrum of being, *matter*$_{(3)}$ is sheer potentiality for physical form.) It is important to distinguish two types of potency: a) "*active* potency," which is a *power*$_{(1)}$ or internal disposition whereby a type of being is able to become or to do or to make something (e.g., a human fetus's potency to develop rational awareness); and b) "*passive* potency," whereby a type of being is able to *undergo* certain changes, or to be acted upon by others in certain ways (e.g., a fetus's potency to be aborted, whether spontaneously or by human choice).

potential (adj.): Said of a *being*$_{(1)}$ or a *perfection*$_{(1)}$ not now in existence, but one that may come into existence, because of the passive and especially the active *potencies* present due to the *natures*$_{(2)}$ of the things in question. [Note: The meaning of "potential" is thus different from—and stronger than—that of being merely physically or metaphysically *possible.* This point is often misunderstood or overlooked in discussions of the status of human embryos and fetuses. For the tradition of integral Christian wisdom, such entities are potential (not merely possible) *persons*$_{(2)}$ because they are actual *persons*$_{(1)}$.] Also: "potential" (as a n.), "potentially" (adv.).

poverty (n.): (1) In economics and ethics, a condition of destitution or near-destitution—a condition which, supposing it is not one for which the individual is morally responsible (or has chosen via a religious vow), and supposing political authorities are able to eliminate it, is incompatible with the *natural right* to share in the material goods of the world. (2) In speculative philosophy, a condition according to which a thing lacks a quality or perfection, or has it only to a limited degree. (Regarding sense (2), contrast **abundance** and **plenitude**.)

poverty of being: Phrase used by some recent Thomists (e.g., Pierre-Marie Emonet) to accentuate the lack of self-sufficiency of beings of nature—a point that grounds Aquinas's *Five Ways* of reasoning to God.

power (n.): (1) In speculative philosophy, an "active" *potency*, or principle of action stemming from a thing's *nature*$_{(2)}$; the immediate formal source of an activity or operation. Powers are attributed especially to living beings. <Nutrition and growth as vegetative powers; sensation and self-movement as animal powers; intellect and will as rational powers.> (Syn: **faculty**.) (2) In ethics and social philosophy, having the ability (whether by right or by sheer might) to undertake certain actions and bring about certain results, often including a measure of control over other persons and their destinies. <The rightful power of duly elected officials.>

practical (adj.): (1) Of or concerned with action, or things to be done or to be made, rather than with how things are. Although they contain theoretical elements, both *art* and normative *ethics* are in this sense practical rather than speculative disciplines. (2) Pertaining to the use of *reason* or *intellect* to pursue knowledge about what is to be done. (Within the realm of the practical, the 20th-century Thomist Jacques Maritain distinguished the "speculatively practical" from the "practically practical." The former would include moral philosophy, which in part is directed toward understanding and explanation. For Maritain, only the latter—which is directed strictly toward choice and action—is to be regarded as fully practical.) (Contrast **speculative.**) Also: "practically" (adv.).

practical reason: Use of reason as described in **practical** $_{(2)}$.

practical syllogism: Type of formal reasoning about things to be done, the *conclusion* of which takes the form, "Therefore, this is what I or we must do (or not do)." For example (with the first two statements as *premises*): "Basic health care is a human right; accordingly, insofar as a society can provide it for all its citizens, it has a moral obligation to do so. The United States could provide basic health care for all through a reallocation of health care expenditures, plus moderate and attainable additional funding. Therefore, the United States must work toward providing basic health care for all its citizens." (See **command.**)

practical wisdom: See the discussion under **wisdom.**

practice (n.): (1) See ***praxis.*** (2) As discussed by certain social theorists, as well as certain *analytic philosophers,* an underlying social form that helps render intelligible a human act or use of words.

praeter intentionem (Latin phrase): In the discussion of human acts, a consequence that may be foreseen, but is "beside" (or "outside" or "beyond") the agent's *intention,* as this term is used in sense (2) (i.e., as referring to the subjective purpose or *end* $_{(2)}$ of the act), and sometimes sense (3) (i.e., as referring to some effect of the act that is not included in its moral *object* $_{(3)}$). (The manner of determining, especially in complex cases, the exact scope of "moral object," and thus whether a particular consequence can be characterized as *praeter intentionem* in the relevant sense, has been subject to debate among contemporary Thomists—e.g., Steven A. Long and Martin Rohnheimer.)

praeternatural (sometimes **preternatural**) **gifts**: See the discussion under **gifts of integrity and grace**.

pragmatism (n.): Philosophical school—especially prominent in late 19th- and early 20th-century America, but continuing in influence today—which takes usefulness or workability, rather than a supposed *objective* truth, as the *criterion* for accepting ideas and judgments. (Important historical pragmatists were C. S. Pierce, William James, and John Dewey. The movement has been continued through the work of Richard Rorty and others.) Also: "pragmatic" (adj.), "pragmatist" (adj. or n.).

praxis (Greek n.): (1) Deliberate activity, the end of which lies outside the will of the agent—thus "practice," by contrast with "theory" (Greek *theoria*), the end of which (i.e., understanding) is achieved within the intellect itself. For the perennial tradition, if praxis is to conform to the *good,* it must accord with a correct understanding of human nature and its *ends* $_{(1)}$. (2) In Marxist and some recent existentialist usage, the fundamental practical reality through which *man* $_{(1)}$ comes to understand, or to create, his own nature.

preambles of faith (Latin *praeambula fidei*): Truths which, although revealed in Scripture and Church tradition, are not part of the content of *faith* $_{(2)}$ in the strict sense because in principle they are available to human reason and thus do not need to be accepted solely on God's authority. (For Thomists, such truths would include that God exists, that God is one, that human nature has a spiritual dimension, and that human acts are ordered to an ultimate end.) Although they are available to reason, such truths are both very difficult to attain yet necessary for *salvation;* thus it is appropriate that they have been revealed and form part of the content of faith in the broader sense. In fact, apart from those with a relevant philosophical background, most Christian believers do accept them simply as matters of faith. (Compare the discussion under **revealable**.)

precept, moral: See **moral precept**.

preconscious or **precognitive** (adj.): As used by perennial philosophers such as Jacques Maritain, characteristic of the deepest sources of knowledge and choice—ones that do not reach the level of explicit consciousness, yet are aspects of our intellect's natural affinity for the true, and our will's natural affinity for the good. <The will's preconscious tendency toward comprehensive good.> Also: "preconsciously" or "precognitively" (adv.).

predicament (n): For this term's special use within Scholastic logic, see the discussions under **category** and **predicate** (v.)

predicate (n.): Term in a proposition that modifies the *subject*$_{(1)}$; also, by extension, a feature or concrete form that thereby is attributed to a being or beings.

predicate (v.): To attribute a feature or concrete form (in any of the *categories,* which in the context of *logic*$_{(1)}$ are traditionally called the "predicaments") to a being or beings. Also: "predicable" (adj.).

premise (n.): Statement in an argument—especially a formal, deductive argument—that is asserted to be true and that serves as a basis for arriving at the argument's *conclusion.* (See **validity** and **soundness.**)

premoral goods: See the discussion under **proportionalism.**

pre-philosophical (sometimes **pre-reflective**) (adj.): Understandings of reality that are rooted in and expressed in the language of *common sense*$_{(2)}$, prior to any formal or technical elaboration.

prescind (v.): To ignore certain features of an issue or object in order to focus on another or others. <To prescind from the question of the agent's motive.> (Compare **abstract** (v.)$_{(1)}$.)

prescriptive (adj.): Evaluative or normative in force, by contrast with judgments or accounts that are *descriptive.* <Ethics as ordered to prescriptive judgments; the experimental sciences as not so ordered.>

prescriptivism (n.): A variant of noncognitivist metaethics, made popular by British philosopher R. M. Hare, according to which normative statements are neither mere descriptions of acts, nor logically derivable from mere descriptions, yet have a force that goes beyond that identified by *emotivists*—namely, prescribing (or forbidding) certain forms of behavior. [Note: The perennial tradition itself recognizes the prescriptive force of normative statements, while at the same time insisting that moral judgments can, and should, be subject to a properly cognitive elaboration.] Also: "prescriptivist" (adj. or n.).

present (n.): (1) In the order of temporal duration, that which is now. (2) The term is also used *metaphorically* in relation to God, whose duration is *eternal,* and for whom past, present, and future (the stages of temporal duration) are encompassed in an all-at-once "present"—with the quotation marks indicating that God's mode of existence and awareness, as they are in themselves, lie beyond *literal* human description.

pride (n.): (1) A proper satisfaction in one's genuine accomplishments. (2) A fixed state of inordinate self-esteem, according to which a person is disposed to regard his or her own worth, or importance, as being virtually without boundaries. Understood in this second sense, pride traditionally has been identified as a *capital vice,* and indeed as the ultimate source of all the vices. (Contrast **humility**.) Also: "prideful" (adj.).

***prima facie* duty**: In certain *deontological* theories of ethics (especially that of the early 20th-century British philosopher W. D. Ross), a notion that qualifies the apparent *absolutism* of Immanuel Kant by holding that our actual duty in a given situation is arrived at through a consideration of all moral rules that apply to that situation. The latter, for Ross, are expressions of *prima facie* (Latin for "at first glance") duty—with one's actual duty emerging (to borrow the language of physics) as a resultant of the various forces of *prima facie* duty.

primary or **first** (adj.): Pertaining to what comes or exists before others. (Note: In philosophical contexts, this term usually has a primarily ontological significance, not simply—if at all—a temporal one. This point is important for the correct interpretation of, for example, Aquinas's initial two arguments for the existence of God at the beginning of the *Summa theologiae* [see **Five Ways, the**].) (Ant: **secondary**.)

primary precepts of natural (moral) law: The starting points of thought about matters of right action, as these can be discerned by human practical reason functioning with the appropriate *habitus* of first principles (see **synderesis**). (Aquinas spoke of these precepts as following a threefold order of *natural inclinations;* but he did not attempt to develop an exhaustive list of such inclinations or the associated precepts. His followers through the centuries have offered a variety of accounts. The following might be mentioned as norms typically proposed as primary, positive precepts of natural law: "Human personal life is to be promoted and integrally maintained." "The physical world is to be treated responsibly." "The ends of human sexuality are to be respected." "Truth is to be sought and communicated." "Justice is to be pursued in human relations and communities." "God's sovereignty is to be acknowledged.") The primary precepts of natural law are sometimes said to be ordered to the preservation and promotion of *basic goods* of human existence. Ordinarily, they are applied by way of more particular or "secondary" precepts, and ultimately by way of specific judgments. For example, the primary precept about treating the world responsibly has implications for the ethical evaluation of proposals regarding genetic engineering—namely, that proposals likely to promote natural *ends* $_{(1)}$ of human life (e.g., the use of intellect) without compromising other natural ends (e.g., the ability to form personal relationships) are, to this extent, morally good. (See also the discussions under **moral precepts** and **natural (moral) law.**)

prime matter (also called "primary" or "first" matter): See **matter** $_{(3)}$, as well as **protomatter.**

principal (adj., Latin *princeps*): First or leading, often with the implication that other things follow from the one in question. Also: "principally" (adv.).

principle (n., Greek *arche;* Latin *principium*): (1) That from which something comes to be. <Form and matter as principles of a physical substance.> (2) That in terms of which something comes to be known or judged. <The principle of noncontradiction ("Nothing can be both affirmed and denied of the same subject at the same time in the same respect") as the first principle of logic and theoretical knowledge; the principle of *synderesis* ("Good is to be done and promoted, and evil avoided") as the first principle of practical knowledge.> Also, regarding sense (2): "principled" (adj.).

principle of causality: See **causality, principle of.**

principle of double effect: See **double effect, principle of.**

principle of excluded middle: See **excluded middle, principle of.**

principle of finality: See **finality, principle of.**

principle of identity: See **identity, principle of.**

principle of individuation: See **individuation, principle of.**

principle of noncontradiction: See **noncontradiction, principle of.**

principle of parsimony: See the discussion under **Ockhamist.**

principle of subsidiarity: See **subsidiarity** (sometimes **autonomy**), **principle of.**

principle of sufficient reason: See **sufficient reason, principle of.**

principle of totality: See **totality, principle of.**

principle of utility: See **utilitarianism.**

principlism (n.): In ethics, a methodology stressing the importance of beginning with an articulation of moral principles, then proceeding to the application of principles to cases. (Contrast **casuistry**, although—at least for the perennial tradition—an emphasis on principles is not necessarily incompatible with some recourse to the direct comparison of cases. See, on this point, **prudentialism**.) Also: "principlist" (adj. or n.).

privacy, **right to**: Positive legal right identified by the United States Supreme Court in *Roe v. Wade* (1973) and its progeny, according to which, in intimate and personal matters (including the question of whether to bear a child), individuals' private choices are to be respected, with no unreasonable government interference. Although not explicitly enumerated in the U.S. Constitution, the Court asserted that such a right is part of a "penumbra" implicitly entailed by rights that are enumerated. [Note: From the standpoint of the present dictionary, this court finding involves a questionable assimilation of the *personal* to the *private;* moreover, if consistently applied, it would severely limit the state's ability to restrict individual behavior even when the *common good* of society is at stake.]

private (adj.): Of proper concern only to the individual or individuals involved in the action, relationship, etc. Also: "privately" (adv.).

privation (n., Latin *privatio*): (1) Absence or lack in a being, especially the absence of something that normally characterizes an instantiation of the specific type of being in question. <Blindness as a privation in a human being or other sighted animal.> (2) A principle or starting point in the analysis of *change*—that is, the absence of the form that is to be brought about in a particular subject. <Lack of discernible shape as a privation in a block of marble to be sculpted; lack of prudence as a privation in a still-youthful character.> Also: "privative" (adj.).

problem of evil: A challenge to most forms of *theism,* which hold that God is all-good, all-knowing, and all-powerful. As expressed by the 18th-century Scottish skeptic David Hume, if all these qualities are to be predicated of God, "Whence then is evil?" (For a discussion of formal responses to the problem of evil, see **theodicy**.)

problem of universals: See **universals, problem of**.

process thought: A 20th-century approach to philosophy and theology, associated especially with the Anglo-American philosopher

Alfred North Whitehead (1861–1947) and his students and followers (e.g., Charles Hartshorne and John B. Cobb). (For a variant of process thought arising within Catholicism, see **Teilhardian**.) Whitehead and contemporary process thinkers have held that the fundamental concepts for understanding natural being should be "process" and "event," rather than, as for Aristotle and the Scholastics, "substance." [Note: In spite of the above, some recent Thomist thinkers—e.g., W. Norris Clarke, S.J.—have sought to take elements of process thought and incorporate them into the perennial tradition, while at the same time retaining essential features of the classical accounts of being and intelligibility.]

procreation (n.): The process by which human beings cooperate with God in the bringing about of new *personal* (i.e., rational and spiritual) life. [Note: This cooperation obviously involves the human sexual function; thus the word "procreation" is sometimes used interchangeably with *reproduction.* However, the latter term treats human generation as a process or event in the biological order entirely parallel to sexual generation in other species. While for most *scientific* $_{(2)}$ purposes this usage is acceptable, in the context of the *philosophy of the human person* and *ethics,* it ignores both the spiritual nature of the human soul and the full significance of human love and parenthood. Thus, in relation to the latter disciplines, perennial philosophy and Catholic tradition more generally maintain a distinction between the two terms.] Also: "procreative" (adj.), "procreatively" (adv.).

progress (n.): Movement toward an actual or assumed goal. (In the expression "human progress," there is an implicit if vague reference to an ultimate *state* $_{(1)}$ or ultimate *norm* of humanity.)

progressive (adj. or n.): Of or pertaining to a person, or a movement, that favors novelty and experimentation. (Syn: **liberal** $_{(2)}$, especially in relation to public policies, practices, or, in the case of religion, the formulation of beliefs. Ant: "conservative"—see **conservatism.**)

progressivism (n.): (1) A family of views according to which later developments in human thought and practice are probably or even necessarily better than what preceded them; or according to which, at least in the long run, humankind inevitably makes *progress.* (Compare **historicism.**) (2) In social and political thought, as well as in religion, the tendency to support new ideas or initiatives. (Syn: **liberal-**

ism $_{(2)}$. Ant: **conservatism.**) Also: "progressivist" (n.).

prohibition (n.): A negative moral rule or command.

proof (n.): (1) In the strict sense, a *sound* deductive argument—i.e., one characterized by *true* premises and a *valid* form. (Sometimes the term "proof" is also taken to imply that the argument is recognized as sound by some particular person or group of persons. On such accounts, while "soundness" would be a purely *logical* notion, "proof" would also express a *psychological* element.) (Compare **demonstration.**) (2) More loosely, an argument or evidential showing that establishes a given proposition beyond all practical doubt. Also: "prove" (v.).

proper (adj.): (1) In both general and philosophical usage, a synonym for "correct" or "according to a strict interpretation." (2) In speculative philosophy, relating to either a *property* $_{(2)}$ of, or the formal *object* $_{(2)}$ of, a particular *nature, power, habitus,* or type of *act.* (3) In ethics, a synonym for morally *right,* as said of a human act, or some aspect of it, when judged in light of the *determinants* or *sources of morality.* Also: "properly" (adv.).

property (n.): (1) As commonly understood, and in the positive *sciences* $_{(2)}$, equivalent to "feature" or "characteristic." <A concentration of slow-twitch muscle fibers as a property found in most distance runners.> (2) More strictly and in philosophical usage, a type of feature or characteristic that follows specifically from a being's *nature* $_{(2)}$. <The power of intelligent speech as a property of human life; the ability to respond to pleasurable and painful stimuli as a property of animal life.> (3) In moral and political philosophy, a good that belongs by *right* to a person or group of persons. <The property to be distributed at a probate hearing.> (Regarding the third sense, see **ownership.**)

proportion (n.): Originally signifying a mathematical relationship, this term is used in philosophy to signify an order or adequation within being, or among a term's meanings. <The proportion between a being's essence and the intensity of its sharing in existence; or between a type of act (e.g., intellection) and its proper object (i.e., the formal nature of a thing).> (See as well **proportionality, analogy of.**) Also: "proportional" or "proportionate" (adj.); "proportionally" or "proportionately" (adv.).

proportionalism (n.): A 20th- and now 21st-century development in Catholic moral theology (especially since Vatican II) led by such figures as Joseph Fuchs, S.J.,

Louis Jannsens, Richard McCormick, S.J., and Charles Curran. According to proportionalists, goods and evils related to moral choice are, taken in the abstract, simply "premoral." Thus, by contrast with the traditional Catholic approach to evaluating *human acts* (see **determinants** or **sources of morality**), these theorists hold that judgments about moral good or evil can be made only after considering an act in all its relevant features—including the agent's subjective purpose or *motive,* as well as the act's (premorally) good and bad *consequences.* [Note: Although it has attracted many adherents, this movement consistently has been rejected by the Church's ordinary *magisterium* as incompatible with its teachings about *exceptionless moral rules* and *intrinsically evil* acts. (See, e.g., John Paul II's *Veritatis splendor* [1993].) The proportionalist approach also has been subjected to criticism by moral theologians and philosophers such as Servais Pinckaers, O.P., Martin Rohnheimer, Benedict Ashley, O.P., Kevin O'Rourke, O.P., Germain Grisez, Christopher Kaczor, and William E. May.] Also: "proportionalist" (adj. or n.).

proportionality, analogy of: Type of analogy in which the diverse meanings of a common term nevertheless stand in a proper *order* $_{(2)}$ to one another, because the things they name manifest some type of proportional relations. For example, the term "living" follows the analogy of proportionality in its application to plants, animals, human persons, and God, since the life of plants is to the being of plants as the life of animals is to the being of animals; etc. *Transcendental* terms and the perfections they signify (e.g., "being," "truth," and "goodness") also manifest this type of analogy. (Contrast **attribution, analogy of**, as well as **metaphor**. See **participation** $_{(1)}$.)

proportionate reason: In ethics, the measuring of an act in terms of its proportion of good and harmful consequences, as judged by *right reason.* For moral philosophy and theology in the perennial tradition, the concern about proportion in an act's effects arises only if it is seen that the act is good (or at least not evil) in its very nature or moral object (i.e., its *object* $_{(3)}$). (In this regard, contrast the methodology of **proportionalism**, as well as **teleology** $_{(3)}$.)

proposition (n.): Linguistic expression of a *judgment* or the formal content of a judgment—i.e., what is affirmed or denied. Also: "propositional" (adj.).

propositional logic: Branch of modern formal logic that, by contrast with the logic of terms (or of the *syllogism*), focuses on relations among propositions or statements. Among the important rules of propositional logic are *modus ponens* and *modus tollens.* Regarding the former: if it is the case that *p* implies *q*, and *p* is affirmed, then *q* also must be affirmed. Regarding the latter: if it is the case that *p* implies *q*, and *q* is denied, then *p* also must be denied. (See as well **necessary and sufficient conditions**.)

propter quid (Latin phrase): See the discussion under **demonstration**.

protomatter (n.): As introduced by Thomistic natural philosopher William Wallace, O.P., a term equivalent to "prime matter" (Latin *materia prima;* see **matter** $_{(3)}$). Through the use of this term, Wallace sought to clarify and avoid confusions about the philosophical concept of matter in relation to modern scientific theories, including ones dealing with subatomic particles.

providence (n.): (1) (Sometimes with capital "P.") God's eternal plan for, direction of, and care for finite reality, manifested by things in their various types moving toward their natural *ends* $_{(1)}$, and also including those events that, from the standpoint of natural philosophy, are called *chance* $_{(1)}$. (2) Analogously, the planning, directing, and caring that other rational beings—in particular human persons—exercise over their lives and other matters for which they are responsible. Also: "provident" (adj.), "providential" (adj.), "providentially" (adv.).

proximate (adj.): Immediate, as said, for example, of the last member in a chain of causality. (Contrast **remote**.) Also: "proximately" (adv.).

prudence (n.): The *virtue*—which has both intellectual and moral dimensions—by which a person knows how to live well and how to apply reason rightly in matters of choice and action. As it relates to very general matters of human living, this virtue is also called *practical wisdom.* Prudence is taken by classical writers, including Aristotle and St. Thomas, to be one of the four *cardinal virtues.* (Scholastic philosophers have identified a number of constitutive "parts" of prudence, as well as related good and bad habits. Parts of prudence would include caution [by which one exercises appropriate care in decision-making], and foresight [by which one is able to make informed estimates of the consequences of actions]. Habits or vices inimical to prudence would include rashness of judgment on one hand, and indecisiveness on the other.) Also: "prudential" (adj.), "prudentially" (adv.).

prudentialism (n.): An approach to ethical reasoning formally articulated by theologians Benedict Ashley, O.P., and Kevin O'Rourke, O.P. This approach incorporates key elements of perennial philosophy: namely, the use of "right reason" in light of the integral human good; the development of the virtues; and the careful application of principles or precepts to cases. (Contrast strict **principlism** and strict **casuistry**, as well as **proportionalism**.) Also: "prudentialist" (adj. or n.).

psyche (n., from Greek *psuche,* for "soul"): (1) In philosophical psychology, the powers of *soul* that impinge upon human awareness and activity—in particular, the cognitive and affective powers of *rational* soul (including ones that are either *subconscious* or *unconscious,* and ones that are *preconscious*)—together with their interactions. (The term applies *analogously* to the associated powers of *sensitive* soul that characterize much animal life.) (2) In psychoanalytic theory, the fundamental basis of *personality,* analyzed by Freud in terms of "id," "ego," and "superego." Also: "psychic" (adj.), "psychically" (adv.).

psychological egoism: See **egoism** $_{(1)}$.

psychology (n.): Study of the nature, powers, and activities of the *sensitive* and *rational souls* and of the living beings animated by such souls. (1) *Philosophical* psychology proceeds primarily from data of common human experience; it seeks *ontological* judgments about the soul's nature and proper powers (e.g., in the case of human persons, intellect and will). (2) *Positive* psychology (or psychology in a modern *scientific* $_{(2)}$ sense) is a discipline that primarily employs *empiriological* methods, including controlled experimentation; it has complex (and sometimes disputed) points of overlap with both the physical sciences and philosophy. [Note: Relations among the terminologies of the two types of psychological disciplines are often difficult to clarify and assess. For example, traditional philosophical psychology's notions of *concupiscible* and *irascible* appetites (supposing they are well-grounded) might be expected to have counterparts in positive psychology. But here—as in other cases arising on both sides—it is not obvious what these counterparts are. Moreover, the two disciplines ought in principle to complement and strengthen one another; however, due to a relative lack of communication between philosophers and scientific psychologists, there in fact has been little progress along this line. In the renewal of the "enduringly valid tradition" for which John Paul II called, fuller communication between these two disciplines (and between both of them and relevant aspects of *theology*) should be an important objective.] Also: "psychological" (adj.), "psychologically" (adv.).

public (adj.): A matter that concerns a *community,* especially an organized *political* community at whatever level of generality (local, state, federal, etc.). (According to the perennial tradition, some *personal* choices can be of public, not merely private, interest. The question of precisely how and where to draw lines between private and public—e.g., regarding matters of sexuality—has become a major policy issue in many *civil societies,* including the United States.)

public philosophy or **theology**: Systematic approach, rooted in common human experience and reason, or in revelation—or in both—to such public issues as the maintenance of proper order within human society, relations between individual liberties and the common good, etc.

punishment (n.): An evil suffered by one who offends against a *law* $_{(1)}$, in light of a judgment by competent *authority* $_{(1)}$. For the classical tradition, punishment is ordered to three purposes: a) the reestablishment of justice in relationships; b) the correction of the offender himself or herself; and c) (in the specific case of *human law*) the protection of human society, through deterrence of crime and at least temporary isolation of offenders. (Compare **sanction**.)

pure perfection: Property or actuality that does not depend for its existence on matter or material conditions, and that cannot be found in them as in a proper *subject* $_{(3)}$. (Thus, in human persons, intelligence and freedom are properties of the rational *soul,* not, strictly speaking, of the bodily composite.) Since they are not intrinsically limited by matter, pure perfections can exist in an infinite state; thus they can, within the bounds of *analogy* (see **eminence**, sometimes **supereminence**), be formally predicated of God—by whom they are enjoyed in an *absolute* manner. (Contrast **mixed perfection** and **transcendental** $_{(1)}$.)

purpose (n.): An *end* in either of its philosophical senses; thus sometimes—but not always—equivalent to subjective *motive.* Also: "purposeful" (adj.).

qua (prep., from Latin *qua,* for “in which” or “as which”): As, just as, or just insofar as. <Being *qua* being as the subject of metaphysics.> (See **absolutely** $_{(1)}$.)

quality (n.): (1) One of the nine categories of *accident* identified by the tradition of Aristotle. This category includes aspects of reality that are available to the external *senses* (i.e., color, sound, taste, smell, or feel), as well as other aspects analogously related to these—e.g., intellectual knowledge, which, as a type of reality, is a potential quality of the *rational* soul. (2) In common usage, “quality” can refer to any accident of a being; in this latter sense the term is synonymous with everyday words such as “attribute” and “feature,” and it functions irrespective of the Aristotelian category into which the accident in question falls. Also: “qualitative” (adj.), “qualitatively” (adv.).

quantification (n.): See discussion under **x** (as a logical symbol).

quantity (n.): One of the nine categories of *accident* identified by the tradition of Aristotle. This category includes features of physical reality such as divisibility into parts and measurability. <Being of a certain size and weight as aspects of quantity found in all beings of nature.> (Note: Although in concrete cases quantity is always bound up with sensible features, when the mind develops properly mathematical concepts [e.g., number, line, or triangularity], it abstracts from “sensible” matter altogether and focuses on “intelligible” matter. See **degrees** or **orders of abstraction**.) Also:

"quantitative" (adj.), "quantitatively" (adv.).

quia (Latin conjunction): See the discussion under **demonstration**.

quiddity (n.): See **essence**.

quintessence (n.): See the discussion under **everlasting.**

quod est vs. ***quo est***: Latin expressions marking the metaphysical distinction between "what is" and "that by which it is." *Substance* is a primary instance of "what is." Substantial *form* is "that by which" a being is a substance as well as an instance of a particular natural kind. *Existence* $_{(2)}$ is "that by which" any being, substantial or accidental, is, *absolutely.*

R

race (n.): Grouping of humans that share a genetic stock, typical physical features, and often cultural interests and characteristics identifying them as a people or nation. (The term "ethnicity" is similar in meaning, but stresses the aspects of nationality and culture and does not necessarily imply underlying genetic factors.) Also: "racial" (adj.), "racially" (adv.).

racism (n.): Conscious or unconscious *hatred* of those of another race and/or a desire to see them harmed or disadvantaged. Often deeply rooted in the human *psyche,* racism affects social life in virtually every country that has a racial mix; and it leads to many types of *discrimination* toward individuals and groups—ones that ordinarily constitute grave *injustices.* Also: "racist" (adj. or n.).

rage (n.): See the discussion under **passion** $_{(4)}$.

raison d'etre (French phrase, literally "reason of the being"): (1) Reason, ground, or *justification* of the reality of a given *being* $_{(1)}$. (The French phrase is sometimes retained in philosophical expositions in English.) (2) A translation of the Latin *ratio entis,* a phrase meaning *essence.*

random (adj.): Of or concerning events that either result from the accidental intersection of two lines of natural causality, or that cannot be predicted due to the impossibility of having a complete and simultaneous understanding of the relevant antecedent conditions. <Random variation as a factor in species evolution.> (See **chance** (n.).)

ratio entis (Latin phrase for "[formal] reason of a being"): Phrase sometimes retained in English expositions of perennial philosophy, corresponding to *essence.* (See **reason** $_{(3)}$.)

rational (adj.): Of or pertaining to activities of *soul* typical of human personal life with its powers of *intellect* and *will.* (According to integral Christian wisdom, human rationality marks the lowest order of *spiritual* being. A sign of this is that, apart from the understanding of first *principles* and matters of direct *perception,* human knowledge requires inductive and deductive *reasoning.*) (See as well **sensitive** and **vegetative soul.**) Also: "rationally" (adv.), "rationality" (n.).

rational affectivity: See **will** (n.).

rationalism (n.): Family of views, represented in all time periods but especially prominent in the period called "modern philosophy" (beginning with René Descartes in the early 17th century). These views propose that all knowledge and reliable guidance for life are to be rooted strictly in our rational powers—which can have, according to many rationalists, universal (or nearly universal) insight. [Note: The perennial tradition, following Aristotle's experiential and realist approach to knowledge, seeks to avoid the extremes that characterize both rationalism and its contraries.] (Contrast **empiricism**; see as well the discussion under **postmodernism.**) Also: "rationalist" (adj. or n.).

Rawlsian (adj. or n.): Of or related to, or a person who holds, principles and themes of the American philosopher John Rawls (1921–2002). In such works as the extremely influential *A Theory of Justice* (1971) and the later *Political Liberalism* (1993), Rawls explored the nature of *distributive justice,* as well as the foundations of *democracy.* Regarding the former, he stressed the notion of justice as fairness, together with the consequent need for social institutions that do not perpetuate the giving of social and economic advantages to some persons at the expense of others on the basis of morally irrelevant factors—e.g., race, gender, or inherited wealth. In grounding his theory of justice, Rawls appeals to a hypothetical "original position," in which the *social contract* is entered into by participants under a "veil of ignorance;" that is, no one knows any particulars about his or her own race, gender, economic status, etc. In such a condition, Rawls notes, all would be motivated to agree to a system that is just or fair. [Note: In recent years, certain scholars—e.g., Paul Weithman—

have explored relations between Rawls's philosophy and the Catholic social tradition. Parallels have been suggested, for example, with the work of the mid-20th-century American theologian John Courtney Murray, S.J. However, in the end, Rawls's articulation and defense of *liberalism* $_{(3)}$, and its implications for democratic society, make a full assimilation of his ideas by perennial thought seem out of the question.]

real (adj.): (1) Synonym for *actual,* as said of a being or beings. <A real job opening—not one still awaiting budgetary approval.> (Contrast **potential.**) (2) Synonym for *entitative,* also as said of a being or beings. <A real encounter—not one that is imagined.> (Contrast **intentional** $_{(1)}$—although intentional beings themselves have a mode of reality, one that is mind-dependent [see **being of reason**].) Also: "really" (adv.).

realism (n.): (1) In metaphysics, the position that certain types of things—e.g., physical objects, natures, moral values, or transcendent beings—are realities. (An extreme form of metaphysical realism is often attributed to Plato—namely, the view that separately existing Forms correspond to our universal terms and concepts. By contrast, the perennial tradition is said to hold a "moderate" realism, according to which forms have a universal character only in the mind, although our general concepts have a basis in individual realities.) (Ant: **antirealism.** Contrast as well **nominalism.** See the discussion at **conceptualism.**) (2) In the theory of knowledge as practiced in the perennial tradition, the position, or range of positions, according to which the human mind is able to make contact with and understand the real (i.e., *actual* being) and according to which our judgments can and typically do have a degree of *objective* $_{(1)}$ truth or *adequation* to reality. In addition to realism regarding the knowledge of being, there also is *moral* $_{(1)}$ realism, which holds that there can be appropriate kinds of objectivity in judgments regarding good or bad, or right or wrong, *human acts.* (Compare **critical realism** and **direct realism.** Contrast **antirealism, idealism** $_{(1)}$, and **liberalism** $_{(3)}$, as well as ethical **noncognitivism, relativism,** and **subjectivism.**) (3) In relation to concrete moral and especially political issues, sometimes said in contrast with *idealism* $_{(2)}$, insofar as realism identifies goals judged to be achievable in practice and/or identifies means judged likely to be effective. (Compare

political realism.) Also: "realist" (adj. or n.), "realistic" (adj.), "realistically" (adv.).

reality (n.): A thing, or the set of all things—that is, all things having *being* $_{(4)}$ (Latin *esse*), either in themselves or as features of other beings.

Real Presence: Doctrine of Catholic Christianity regarding the unique reality of Christ in the sacrament of the Eucharist. As expressive of a religious *mystery,* this doctrine is subject to indefinitely many theological insights; but traditionally it has received a primary type of elucidation in terms of the philosophical notions of *substance* and *accidents.* That is, at the words of Consecration ("This is my body. . ."; "This is my blood. . . ."), the substance of the bread and wine offered at Mass is wholly changed into the substance of the glorified Christ (true God and true Man), while the appearances (i.e., all the perceptible "accidents") of bread and wine remain. This change is, in the words of the Council of Trent (1551), "fittingly and properly called transubstantiation." (A classical theological formulation of the teaching was developed by Aquinas in part III of *Summa Theologiae.* See also documents of Church councils beginning with the Fourth Lateran Council [1215] and extending to Vatican Council II [*Sacrosacanctum concilium*]; and see encyclicals by Popes Pius XII, Paul VI, and John Paul II, culminating in *Ecclesia de eucharistia* [2003].)

reason (n., Latin *ratio*): (1) The "third" act of *intellect,* by which knowledge is developed and organized according to the methods of logic. (Regarding the other two acts of intellect, see **apprehension** or **intellection** (**simple**) and **judgment**.) (2) More generally, the intellect itself or its three acts taken as a whole. <*Faith and Reason*—the English title of John Paul II's 1998 encyclical.> Also, related to both senses: "reason" (as a v.), "reasoning" (adj. or n.). (3) An *intelligible* feature of a *nature* $_{(2)}$ or *essence;* or, derivatively, the meaning of a term that designates such an intelligible feature.

receptivity (n.): According to a development of Aquinas's thought by contemporary Catholic thinkers such as W. Norris Clarke, S.J., and David Schindler, an openness that characterizes all being, and that therefore is itself to be regarded as a kind of *transcendental.* [Note: This development has not been accepted by all Thomists. Some have argued, for example, that receiving is essentially passive rather than active, and thus that the quality in question cannot be a genuine perfection of being as such, since in God there is no passivity or potency. A solution perhaps lies in distinguishing two senses of "receptivity," in light of which when the term expresses being "open" or "welcoming," it does not necessarily designate a metaphysical *potency.* Used in this sense, the term "receptivity" (like the term "duration") would be *analogous,* with the implication of potency (like the implication of temporal passage in the case of "duration") applying only to receptivity in natural beings.]

rectified appetite: Condition or state in which the *affective* powers of the human soul are brought under the direction of practical *reason.* (This state is important for right living because to judge correctly concerning moral matters—especially at the level of the concrete case—requires not only the recognition of *basic goods* and *moral precepts,* and the ability to exercise *practical reason,* but the possession of properly ordered appetites as well.)

rectitude, **moral**: (1) An upright *character.* (Contrast **turpitude**, **moral.**) (2) Moral quality of a *human act* that flows from such a character. (Syn: **rightness, moral.**)

reduction (n.): (1) According to general philosophical and scientific usage, a process by which a complex *whole* is broken into ("reduced" to) its component *parts.* (2) For perennial philosophy, also a process by which an *effect* is traced to its proper *principles* or *causes.* Also: "reductive" (adj.), "reductively" (adv.).

reductionism (n.): Philosophical position according to which all elements of one order can be reduced to, and explained within, that of another. (A prime example involves *materialism* or *physicalism,* which often—although not always—holds that all references to mental qualities can, in principle, be eliminated in favor of explanations that refer only to physical realities. Contrast "nonreductive" views discussed under **materialism.**) Also: "reductionist" (adj. or n.).

reference (n.): In modern logic, the *object* $_{(1)}$, or range of objects, to which a term applies (sometimes also called the term's "denotation" or "extension"). <The reference of "Morning Star" is the same as that of "Evening Star"—i.e., both expressions denote the planet Venus.> (Contrast **sense** $_{(1)}$.) Also: "referent" (n.), "referential" (adj.), "referentially" (adv.).

reflection (n.): Thinking that involves formal inquiry, and thus the intellectual activities of *abstraction,* *judgment,* and *reasoning.* In reflection, a person seeks to become aware of *truth* $_{(2)}$, or of the conformity (or nonconformity) of propositions with *reality.* Also: "reflective" (adj.), "reflectivity" (n.), "reflectively" (adv.).

reflexivity (n.): In accounts deriving from *phenomenology* (including that of Karol Wojtyla), the type of awareness that is aware of itself. (Insofar as this type of awareness is conditioned by *reflection,* it is a specifically *personal* characteristic; see **self-awareness**. However, less complete forms of reflexivity also occur in other animal species, especially, it seems, among the great apes.) Also: "reflexive" (adj.), "reflexively" (adv.).

regime (n.): Form of *government,* especially of a *state.* Also, the particular government currently in power, with its unique, *individuating* features.

relation (n.): One of the nine categories of *accident* distinguished within the tradition of Aristotle: one being as referred to another (or others). Relations can be either *real* or *logical* (in Latin, *secundem rationem*). <A proposition of the form "*x* is the effect of *y*" expresses a real relation, while a proposition of the form "*x* is a species of which *y* is the genus" expresses a logical relation.> Also: "relational" (adj.).

relationality (n.): (1) In *personalist* developments of the perennial tradition, the feature of real beings whereby, in order to complete themselves as beings, they turn to others. (For strict Thomists, "relationality" designates a type of "second act" in beings [Latin *agere* or doing], rather than belonging to "first act" [Latin *esse* or being]. See, however, the discussion of *esse ad*—"being-for-others"—in the entry ***esse-ab.***) (2) In a philosophically informed *semiotics,* the distinguishing feature of human signs whereby they relate to realities as understood.

relativism (n.): Position of philosophers and others who hold not only that cultures or subcultures, and even individuals, have diverse views of reality (including moral and religious reality); but also that there is no principled means by which any one such view can come to be regarded as superior to the others. (See **ethical relativism** and **pluralism** $_{(2)}$. Ant: **universalism**. Contrast as well **realism** $_{(2)}$.) Also: "relativist" (adj. or n.), "relativistic" (adj.), "relativistically" (adv.).

religion (n., from Latin *ligare,* for "to bind"): (1) Set of beliefs, relations, and activities by which people are united, or regard themselves as being united, to the realm of the *transcendent* (often, although not always, with a focus on Absolute Being or God). (See **faith** $_{(3)}$ and **worship**.) (2) For the tradition of Aquinas, "religion" also names a *natural virtue* (one that in principle is able to be recognized and developed by all) involving respect, gratitude, and love for God as Source of all being—as well as openness to the possibility of *revelation.* Also: "religious" (adj.), "religiously" (adv.).

religious indifference (or **indifferentism**): Belief or attitude that it is not important to try to arrive at religious truth—stemming either from a disinterest in or rejection of religion in general, or from a belief that all particular religions are equal in value. (Compare **indifferentism**. See **relativism** and **pluralism** $_{(2)}$.)

religious liberty or **freedom**: The freedom to choose, out of one's own developed *cognitive* and *affective* states, which religious tradition to embrace, or whether to embrace a religion at all. (From the standpoint of integral Christian wisdom, religious liberty is a *basic good* and a *natural right.* Indeed, it is the highest in importance of these, since ultimate human fulfillment ideally comes through the free embracing and living of the Gospel message. For the definitive modern Catholic account of this matter, see the Vatican II document *Dignitatis humanae.*)

religious pluralism: See **pluralism**, particularly sense (2).

remote (adj.): Prior to another, but not immediately prior, especially as said of a member in a chain of causality. (Use of this term may—or may not—imply *temporal,* in addition to *ontological* priority.) <The formation of galaxies as a remote cause of energy on planet Earth; the properly functioning electrical coil as a remote cause of water in a kettle becoming hot.> (Contrast **proximate.**) Also: "remotely" (adv.).

remotion, way of: See **negative way**.

remotion from matter: See the discussion under **degrees** or **orders of abstraction**.

reproduction (n.): The process by which members of a biological species continue the concretized existence of their natural *form.* (Of special interest to the *philosophy of the human person* and *ethics* is reproduction in the human species. Here the process is given the name *procreation* because, for perennial philosophy [as well as for Catholic magisterial teaching], it involves the coming to be of a *personal, spiritual* being—something that cannot be accounted for by purely physical or biological factors.) Also: "reproductive" (adj.).

resolution (Latin *resolutio*) **of concepts**: As articulated by 20th-century Thomists Jacques Maritain and Yves R. Simon, a procedure by which different types of concepts—and thus also different cognitive approaches to natural being—can be recognized as belonging primarily either to the modern natural *sciences*$_{(2)}$ or to *philosophy.* In the former case, concepts are traced to elements that are *empiriological* in nature; in the latter case, concepts are traced to elements that are *ontological* in nature. (One and the same "material" *object*$_{(2)}$ of study might be treated in either or both ways. For example, the concept "human being" as resolved into elements such as "bipedal" and "having a brain of such-and-such a typical size" belongs to the natural sciences; whereas "human being" as resolved into elements such as "able in such-and-such respects to be self-actuating" belongs to philosophy.)

resolve (n.): A firm intention regarding some future *deliberation* and/or *human act;* also, the ability to form such an intention. <A person of great resolve.> Also: "resolute" (adj.), "resolutely" (adv.).

resolve (v.): (1) To make a firm commitment to some future *deliberation* and/or *human act.* <To resolve to amend one's life.> Also: "resolution" (n.). (2) To undertake a *resolution of concepts.*

responsibility (n.): (1) A correlate of rightly held *power*$_{(2)}$, according to which persons with such power (e.g., the ability to control or influence events—and especially other people's destinies) are obliged to exercise it wisely, and with a view to genuine *good*$_{(1)}$. (2) (Sometimes called "moral responsibility.") Condition according to which meritorious or unmeritorious behavior (and/or the results of such behavior) are personally assignable to a given individual or group. Also: "responsible" (adj.), "responsibly" (adv.).

restitution (n.): Return of a particular good or goods, or repayment in other terms, as dictated by the virtue of *justice*—and sometimes as specified by *positive law.*

resurrection (n., often capitalized in relation to the Easter event): Belief of orthodox Christians that on the "Last Day" the bodies of those who have died in Christ will "be raised" (as was Christ's own body after crucifixion) to unending, glorified life. [Philosophically speaking, there can be no compelling argument for this belief, although certain thinkers (including Aquinas and many of his followers) hold that there are sound arguments for the *immateriality* and thus *immortality* of the human soul. Regarding resurrection itself, the Christian philosopher must maintain a respectful silence—while at the same time being prepared to refute arguments that purport to show the doctrine's incoherence, as well as to articulate concepts (*matter, soul, actuality,* etc.) that can be useful in formulations of the doctrine.]

retributive justice: Justice in *punishments* assigned by competent authorities for violations of law, especially *positive law.* (See **legal justice** and **criminal justice**.)

reveal (v.): To make known or to make manifest. In Christian and other religious traditions, the term is applied especially to supernatural *mysteries.* <The God of love as revealed in the person of Jesus Christ.>

revealable (adj., from Latin *revelabilia*): As articulated by 20th-century scholar Etienne Gilson, Aquinas's category for truths that, since they bear directly on the knowledge of God and the means of human salvation, could have been revealed by God. (Relations between the "revealable" and the "actually revealed" are complex. For, in addition to truths that can be known only by revelation and in fact have been revealed [e.g., the Trinity of Persons in God], there are truths that are revealable, and in fact have been revealed, although strictly they need not have been revealed. [These truths St. Thomas called *preambles of faith*—namely, that God exists, that God is One, etc. In principle they can be discovered in metaphysics or philosophical theology.] From the other side of the relationship, there may be truths that are revealable, and that could only be known by revelation, but have not actually been revealed by God. What these might be, of course, we cannot know. Thus, as stressed by Gilson, these two categories of truths—the revealed and the revealable—need to be carefully distinguished.)

revelation (n.): Teaching, or the original basis of teaching, accepted in faith as coming from God and containing truths beyond the reach of natural reasoning. For orthodox Christian tradition, revelation—what actually has been revealed—includes all the truths that are required to be known for personal *salvation.* (Some Protestant writers also speak of "natural revelation" in a way that roughly corresponds to St. Bonaventure's *Journey of the Mind to God,* or—if emphasis is placed upon formal activities of reason—to St. Thomas's *Five Ways.*) Also: "revelatory" (adj.).

revisionism (n.): Movement involving certain recent moral theologians who are critical of classical Christian ethics, at least as represented in the teachings of the ordinary Catholic *magisterium.* In the words of one of the movement's chief proponents, Charles Curran, revisionism typically holds "an *autonomous* ethic, the charge of *physicalism* [i.e., what this dictionary identifies as *physicalism* $_{(2)}$] made against accepted Catholic teaching in sexual and medical ethics, . . . and the ethical theory of *proportionalism.*" (For accounts of these various elements, see the respective entries in the present volume.) Other proponents of revisionism include theologians Lisa Sowle Cahill, Todd A. Salzman, and Michael G. Lawler. Also: "revisionist" (adj. or n.).

right (adj.): Correct or proper. The term sometimes, but not always, carries a *moral* $_{(2)}$ connotation. <A right moral act. Use of right reason.> (Ant: **wrong** [as an adj.].) Also: "rightly" (adv.), "rightness" (n.).

right (n.): In ethics and political and legal theory, that which is owed to some *person* (or *community* of persons), or that to which a person or community has a legitimate claim—whether by nature, statutory or judicial decree, agreement or promise, concrete circumstance, etc. Rights are distinguished into a number of types. The terms used to designate them are not always uniform, even within the perennial tradition; but the following accounts are representative: a) "natural" rights, or basic "human" rights, are ones enjoyed by all persons due to their sharing in a rational and spiritual nature called to pursue the good (e.g., the rights to life and to religious freedom); b) "legal" rights, especially *civil rights,* are ones that citizens enjoy as members of a particular organized society (e.g., in the United States, the rights to vote and to free assembly); and c) "acquired" rights, which may or may not be specified in particular human laws, are ones that persons come to have because of particular relationships or events (e.g., the undertaking of marriage, with its associated rights, as well as duties, in relation to each other and to children that may issue). Rights often are further distinguished into "positive" and "negative" (i.e., rights to actually enjoy particular goods vs. rights not to be interfered with in the pursuit of these goods) and into "alienable" and "inalienable" (i.e., able vs. not able, as a matter of principle, to be taken away). <The natural right to religious freedom

as inalienable; the constitutional right to own firearms as alienable.> (See as well **rights, limitations of** and **rights, structure of.**) Also: "rightful" (adj.), "rightfully" (adv.).

rightness, moral: Correctness in matters of *choice* and *human acts.* (Syn: **rectitude, moral**. Ant: **wrongness, moral**. See **determinants** or **sources of morality**.)

right reason (Greek *orthos logos,* Latin *recta ratio*): The *intellect*'s "third" power and act (i.e., reason or reasoning), insofar as it is used in a correct manner. In accord with the term's origination in *Stoicism,* "right reason" often relates in particular to the use of *practical* reason, and thus signifies correct processes of thought, and correct judgments, about what is to be done or avoided. (See **moral precept**, **rectified appetite**, and **ultimate practical judgment**.)

rights, limitations of: Limitations on "positive" rights (see the discussion under **right** [n.]), when viewed in light of all relevant features of the concrete situation. For example, taken in the abstract, there is a basic right to a decent minimum of health care. But in context this right may be limited—e.g., when a particular society is too poor for such a guarantee to be made to its citizens; or when a natural disaster has occurred that temporarily requires the concentration of health care resources. (Sometimes the point about limitations of rights is expressed by saying that while persons retain the actual "right" in such circumstances, they do not, at least temporarily, enjoy the "use" of this right.)

rights, structure of: Components of, or factors in the analysis of, rights. As typically articulated in Scholastic tradition, these are four in number: "subject," "term," "matter" (sometimes "object"), and "title." The subject is the person who has the right (e.g., all citizens of the country); the term is the formal nature of the right (e.g., the right to a fair trial); the matter is the good which the right protects or secures (e.g., just treatment of those accused); and the title is the basis for claiming the right (e.g., it is guaranteed by the United States Constitution).

right to life: See **life, right to**.

right to privacy: See **privacy, right to**.

Roman Catholicism: See the discussion under **Catholicism**.

rule (n.): (1) Generally, a *measure* or means of measurement. (2) In ethics, a *moral precept* that is to be applied in practical deliberation leading to choice and action. (3) In political philosophy, the type of *regime* or form of *government* developed by a society—democracy, single party rule, kingship, etc.

rule (v.): (1) To govern. <God rules the world. The United States is ruled by a tripartite system—involving legislative, executive, and judicial branches.> (2) To measure. <Custom, sometimes backed by positive law, rules what is acceptable social behavior among a given people.>

S

~

sacrament (n.): In the understanding of Catholic Christianity, a practice instituted by Christ, the significance of which is raised to the *divine order* and which confers what it symbolizes. (For example, in the sacrament of Baptism *Original Sin* is removed—"washed away"—in the practice involving water; and in sacramental Marriage husband and wife are joined irrevocably by God through their exchange of vows and physical union.) Also: "sacramental" (adj.), "sacramentally" (adv.).

sacred (adj.): See **holy** or **sacred**.

salvation (n.): The *final end* for human persons, as specified in Christian teaching; thus a concept equivalent in function to Aristotle's *eudaimonia* ("happiness" or "fulfillment"), but with the added note that this state is *supernatural* and cannot be achieved without God's gracious, saving action. (See **beatitude**.)

sanction (n., Latin *sanctio,* from *sancire,* for "to fulfill"): A punishment or reward that safeguards the character of *law,* and thus guarantees its holiness (Latin *sanctitas*). As there are different types of law, so there are different types of sanction. *Human* positive law enacts various systems of *punishment* for those who violate it; *divine* law is sanctioned by the promise of *beatitude* and the threat of ultimate separation from God. In the case of *natural* (*moral*) *law,* the very *order* $_{(2)}$ of natural and human reality provides the fundamental sanction: one who makes good moral choices thereby becomes a better person and proceeds toward his or her fulfillment, while one who makes bad moral choices proceeds in the reverse direction.

sanctity of life: See **life, sanctity of.**

sapiential (adj., from Latin *sapientia,* for "wisdom"): Having to do with *wisdom,* the traditional goal of philosophy. <According to John Paul II (*Fides et ratio,* #81), philosophy must recover its "sapiential dimension.">

Scholastic (adj. or n., from Latin *schola,* for "school"): (1) Pertaining to the medieval philosophers and theologians known as "Schoolmen"; also, such a thinker himself. In *Fides et ratio,* #74, John Paul II mentions, as a "great triad" of Scholastics, St. Anselm, St. Bonaventure, and St. Thomas Aquinas. Although in certain respects there were significant differences among the medieval schools, the common term "Scholastic" is warranted by the distinctive style of inquiry shared by them all—a style that emphasized commentary on traditional problems and texts, rigorous disputation, and logical precision. (2) (Sometimes Neo-Scholastic.) Pertaining to followers of medieval schools from the late 19th century to the present day; or such a thinker himself or herself. Also: "Scholasticism" and "Neo-Scholasticism" (n.).

school (n.): Within philosophy and other disciplines, a community of scholarship (comprising teachers and students, often across generations) that maintains a well-defined approach to issues and/or a common set of core theses. Schools often are associated either with a particular center of study (e.g., the "Oxford school" of *analytic philosophy*) or with one or a few principal thinkers (e.g., the "Scotist school," after the late medieval Scholastic John Duns Scotus). (A school can be contrasted with a *tradition,* with the latter term ordinarily designating a somewhat broader movement of thought. However, this distinction is not exact. Thomism, for example, is alternatively called a "school" or a "tradition"—and it is called both by John Paul II in different sections of *Fides et ratio.* Moreover, taken as a tradition, it can be seen to comprise several differing schools, as indicated in this dictionary's entry for **Thomism.**)

science (n., Latin *scientia*): (1) Originally, and according to the Aristotelian ideal, explanatory knowledge in the form of conclusions *demonstrated* by way of principles and causes, which are mentioned in the premises of the reasoning. (In this sense, "science" includes *metaphysics* and other philosophical disciplines, as well as sacred *theology,* whose formal principles are objects of *faith* $_{(2)}$). (2) As commonly understood today, by contrast with philosophy and theology, any of various "positive" studies of nature (from Latin *posita,* for "things set down") that employ primarily *empiriological,* including experimental, methods. Also: "scientific" (adj.), "scientifically" (adv.).

scientism (n.): A recently articulated but widely held (either explicitly or implicitly) philosophical view claiming that all genuine knowledge is to be achieved through the methods of the *positive sciences.* [Note: This view, expressed by writers such as Richard Dawkins, is clearly at odds with perennial philosophy, as well as with theology understood as a cognitive discipline. For this and other reasons, it is important to mark a clear distinction between scientism and genuine *science* $_{(2)}$—the latter of which Thomism, and the Catholic tradition more generally, strongly supports.] (Compare **naturalism** $_{(1)}$ and **positivism**. See as well the discussion under **evolutionism**.) Also: "scientistic" (adj.).

Scotist (adj. or n.): Pertaining to the teachings or the school of John Duns Scotus (1265–1308), or one who holds such teachings. Sometimes called the "subtle" Doctor, Scotus introduced many novel notions into Scholastic philosophy (e.g., *haecaeitas* or "thisness," from Latin *haec,* for "this"). He disagreed with Aquinas regarding the proportionately shared character of *being* $_{(2)}$, and he seems to some scholars—although not all—to have held that "being" is a univocal term. (Compare **essentialism** $_{(1)}$.) Also: "Scotism" (n.), "Scotistic" (adj.).

secondary (adj.): Pertaining to what comes after, or exists in dependence upon, another or others. *Scholastic* philosophers, including Aquinas and his school, have developed accounts of secondary causes, by contrast with the "First Cause" (i.e., God). (From a rather different perspective, certain modern philosophers spoke of secondary qualities, by contrast with what they took to be "primary qualities"—i.e., ones in principle subject to quantitative specification.) (Ant: **primary** or **first**.)

secular (adj., from Latin *saecula* for "ages"): Properly belonging to the order of *temporal* reality, or things of this world, by contrast with things (or dimensions of things) that are *eternal* or specifically religious. <Secular reasons, in addition to religious ones, for supporting the traditional understanding of marriage.> Also: "secularity" (n.).

secularism (n.): General perspective—often prevailing in contemporary Western societies—according to which all matters of genuine human interest are reducible to factors related to the *temporal* world. (Note: A theory, or a form of government, can be *secular*—and can be understood and embraced as such—without a person's subscribing to secularism as here defined. Thus, within the perennial tradition, Jacques Maritain, Yves R. Simon, and theologian John Courtney Murray, S.J., all developed powerful analyses in support of secular [but not secularist] democratic government.) Also: "secularist" (adj. or n.).

secularization (n.): Process by which matters that formerly had been arranged or settled by religious authority come to be recognized as properly belonging to the temporal order, and thus subject to determination by, for example, the natural sciences or autonomous political processes. [In itself, and regarding many matters—e.g., the organization of civil society—the process of secularization is entirely *natural* $_{(3)}$ and *normal* $_{(2)}$. However, if it is carried to the extreme and universalized, secularization leads to the above-mentioned *secularism,* from which it should be carefully distinguished.] Also: "secularize" (v.).

self (n.): The individual, personal subject, or the "I." In the case of human selves, there are three distinct dimensions: a) the organic self (one's body or integrated physical being as one perceives it); b) the psychological self or *ego* $_{(1)}$ (the experienced source of personal activity); and c) the metaphysical self (the underlying ontological basis for the characteristic activities of human nature and, by analogy, any personal nature). (Regarding dimension c), see **subject** $_{(3)}$ and **supposit.**)

self-awareness (n.): Consciousness of oneself as a *subject* $_{(2)}$. (This state, unlike, for example, *self-possession* and *self-transcendence,* seems to be shared in various degrees by certain other animal species.)

self-determination (n.): As understood by *personalist* philosophers, the shaping of oneself (i.e., as a *subject* $_{(2)}$) that a person progressively undertakes as author of his or her own actions.

self-gift (n., also sometimes "self-donation"): As understood by personalist philosophers, especially ones inspired by the Christian notion of *agape,* an act by which one who is in possession of his or her (psychological) self makes a *gift* of that self to another person or to a community. (See **gift, law of the.**)

selfhood (n.): The *status* of being a *self,* in the relevant organic, psychological, and/or metaphysical dimensions.

self-possession (sometimes **self-appropriation**) (n.): A human subject's mastery over the dynamism of the will, and thus in a most important sense over his or her *self* (in dimension b), that is, as the experienced, personal source of one's own acts. Such a state constitutes a goal—perhaps never fully achieved in this life—of moral striving. <Self-possession as prerequisite for self-giving.> Also: "self-possessed" (adj.).

self-realization (n.): (1) The goal of all natural striving; in rational beings, equivalent to personal fulfillment. [Note: Contrary to some interpretations, self-realization in human beings need not—and according to the perennial tradition cannot—involve neglecting the good of others.] (2) As a type of *ethical theory,* one that tends to reduce all moral considerations to ones related to personal fulfillment—however such fulfillment is conceived.

self-transcendence (n.): In philosophical anthropology, especially as developed by *personalist* thinkers, the *property* $_{(2)}$ of human beings whereby we are able to (and in fact are drawn to) go beyond ourselves—thus making possible *community* with other persons, as well as openness to the *transcendent.* Also: "self-transcendent" (adj.).

seminal principles (Latin *rationes seminales*): The *forms* of things (including the human body) that, according to a view suggested by St. Augustine, were present by divine wisdom in a seminal or potential condition at the beginning of the created universe and then evolved into actuality over time. [Note: Some writers take this as an early Christian anticipation of the scientific theory of *evolution,* or at least as a vehicle for the philosophical interpretation of evolution. However, if one accepts the Aristotelian account of primary matter (i.e., *matter* $_{(3)}$) as pure passive *potentiality* for physical form, it would seem that the supposition of forms being present in a "seminal condition"—in addition to being difficult to comprehend—is unnecessary for the philosophical and theological accommodation of properly *scientific* $_{(2)}$ evolutionary theory.]

semiotics (n.): The theory of the nature, role, and use of *signs.* An interdisciplinary field of scholarship associated primarily with linguists and anthropologists, it also is one with profound philosophical dimensions. [Many scientists, as well as representatives of other traditions of philosophy, regard the human use of signs as merely a complex extension of their use by other animals; in recent decades, however, perennial philosophy—led by writers such as John Deely—has restated insights of Aquinas and his commentators (especially John of St. Thomas, or Poinsot); and it has argued that the essential *relationality* and *intentionality* of human signs shows that a philosophically informed semiotics will recognize the distinctiveness of human thought and understanding.] Also: "semiotic" (adj. or n.).

sempiternity (n., from Latin *semper* for "always"): *Eternity,* with the emphasis on God's mode of existence as being without beginning and without end. (Contrast **everlastingness**, which, although sometimes taken to be equivalent, is generally understood by contemporary thinkers to involve a temporal mode of existence.)

sensation (n.): Mode of *experience* by which a subject (animal or human) becomes aware of things in its environment through modifications of the "external" *senses.*

sensationism (n.): See **phenomenalism**.

sense (n.): (1) In modern logic, what a term expresses (sometimes also called its "connotation" or "intension"), as this might be captured in a verbal or nominal *definition.* <The sense of "Morning Star" is different from that of "Evening Star."> (Contrast **reference**.) (2) A cognitive power that operates by way of a physical organ and that makes possible a knowledge of natural beings in their sensible features. These powers often are divided into the five "external" senses (touch, sight, hearing, taste, and smell); and the "internal" senses (the *common* or "central" or "unifying" sense, which synthesizes the data of external sense so as to enable sensory awareness of whole objects, plus *imagination* and *memory*—as well as, in relation to the operation of appetite, the *estimative sense*).

sense (v.): To exercise one of the "external" or "internal" powers of *sense* (2).

sense or **sensory data**: See **data of sense**.

sense appetite: See the discussion under **sensible** (2).

sensible (adj.): (1) Pertaining to features of things (e.g., colors) that are available to the *senses* (contrast **intelligible**). (2) (Sometimes also *sensory* or *sense* [as an adj.].) Related to bodily nature, and specifically animal nature, as said, for example, of certain cognitive powers, as well as certain appetites and passions. Also "sensibly" (adv.), "sensibility" (n.).

sensible matter: See the discussion under **degrees** or **orders of abstraction**.

sensitive (adj.): Said of the type of *soul,* or power or operation (e.g., sensation, instinct, and locomotion) that is typical of animal life and shared by humans. (Note: The present philosophical use is to be distinguished from a common use according to which the term characterizes a person of delicate sensibility.)

sensus communis (Latin for "common sense"): See **common sense** $_{(1)}$, as well as the discussion of "internal" senses at **sense** (n.) $_{(2)}$.

sensus plenior (Latin for "fuller sense"): See **spiritual sense.**

separate (adj.): (1) Existing independently. <This particular tree as separate from that one.> (Contrast **distinct.**) (2) As used in the phrase "separate [or "separated"] substances," existing apart from *matter* $_{(3)}$. <Angels as separate substances.> Also: "separately" (adv.).

separate (v.): To divide in *reality,* not simply in *concept.* <According to the biblical prophecy, to separate the sheep from the goats.> (Contrast **distinguish.**)

separation (n.): (1) Act of judging that diverse formal intelligibilities are not merely distinguishable from one another, but can exist independently of one another in the concrete order. (Contrast **distinction.**) (2) As used in the phrase "judgment of separation" by certain recent followers of Aquinas (especially those influenced by the 20th-century scholar Etienne Gilson), the judgment that being is not restricted to physical being—a judgment giving rise to the formal object of metaphysics, namely, being just as being (Latin *ens qua ens*).

seven deadly sins: See the discussion under **vices, capital.**

sex (n.): See the discussions under **gender** and **procreation.** Also: "sexual" (adv.), "sexuality" (n.), "sexually" (adv.).

sexism (n.): See the discussion under **gender.** Also: "sexist" (adj. or n.).

sexual ethics: See **marital and sexual ethics.**

sign (n.): A linguistic or other type of thing used to represent something else. (1) Most signs are instrumental and conventional; that is, they function in service of the purposes of the users, and—if communication is to be effective—they suppose agreement as to how the signs are to be interpreted. (Some use of such signs also is manifested in certain other animal species—e.g., dolphins and the great apes.) (2) Other signs are, in the language of the perennial tradition, "formal"; that is, they signify types of reality according to their very essence. Signs of this sort—unique to human persons—are *concepts.* (3) Scholastic writers also have spoken of "natural" signs, where there is a physical or psychophysical connection between the sign and the thing signified. <Tears as a sign of sadness.> Also: "sign" (as a v.).

signification, modes of (Latin *modi significandi*): Semantical notion introduced by medieval logicians, for whom a term's "signification" (Latin *significatio*, roughly corresponding to "sense") was contrasted with its "supposition" (Latin *suppositio*, roughly corresponding to "reference")—with different "modes" possible in each case. (In his discussion of how human language can be used positively of God, Aquinas notes that a term's different modes of signification are vehicles for its *analogous* use; thus we can, in the case of *transcendental* and *pure perfections*, apply the associated terms properly—although not *univocally*—both to creatures and to God.)

signify (v.): To use a thing (word, picture, gesture, etc.) to represent something else. Also: "significative" (adj.).

simple (adj.): (1) As said of a *being* or a *concept*, not composite or not made up of parts. (2) As said of a *character* trait, the quality of being unassuming and unpretentious.

simple apprehension: See **apprehension** or **intellection** (**simple**).

simplicity (n.): State of being *simple*, in either sense noted above.

sin (n.): (1) An *objective* $_{(1)}$ *moral wrong*, especially insofar as such an action or state of affairs is seen as an offense against God. (2) Human beings' culpable failure to follow God's law, whether this is made known through *natural* (*moral*) *law* or *divine law*, or both. (See **culpability** and **guilt**.) (3) In orthodox Christian theology, the condition of humankind following *Original Sin*—with the resulting compromise of our powers of intellect and especially will, and the train of behaviors against God and our fellow humans that followed. (See **gifts of integrity and grace**.) Also: "sin" (as a v.), "sinful" (adj.), "sinfully" (adv.).

situation ethics: An *antinomian* approach to morality, one stressing the uniqueness of each moral situation. (In the 1960s, the American Protestant theologian Joseph Fletcher elaborated a famous version of situation ethics, which was rooted in a straightforward, unnuanced understanding of the ancient Christian precept "Love, and do as you will.")

skepticism (n.): Philosophical position that questions whether there is *objective* $_{(1)}$ human knowledge or truth, and/or questions whether it is possible to establish that there is such knowledge or truth. Skepticism can be generalized or can take a particular form—e.g., regarding *moral* (1) or *religious* knowledge. Also: "skeptic" (n.), "skeptical" (adj.), "skeptically" (adv.).

sloth (n.): One of the seven *capital vices,* a state that goes beyond a mere tendency to laziness (with which it is often associated). In Aquinas's analysis, sloth (Latin *acedia*) involves a kind of sorrow at and even loathing of one's human condition—a state that precludes, or at least hinders, the development of authentic personal goals and choices. Also: "slothful" (adj.), "slothfully" (adv.).

sobriety (n.): A species of the cardinal virtue of *temperance,* whereby one is able to make correct decisions regarding the use of intoxicating substances. Also: "sober" (adj.).

social (or **societal**) (adj.): Of or having to do with the *natural inclination* toward organized communal life, or with *societies* that result from this inclination. (The variant "societal" is sometimes used more strictly with the latter connotation.) Also: "socially" (adv.), "sociality" (n.), "socialization" (n.).

social contract (**theory**): A theory of certain modern philosophers (e.g., Thomas Hobbes and, at least arguably, John Locke), according to which human social relations, as well as duties and obligations, are founded upon the free agreement of the various individuals involved. [This theory is to be contrasted with that of the perennial tradition, which holds that certain types of community, including civil society, are products of *nature* (3).] (For a recent version of social contract theory, see **Rawlsian.**)

social ethics: Broad field of *applied ethics* concerned with moral issues involving societies as wholes (rather than issues involving only individuals and smaller groups). Prominent topics in social ethics include the nature of human rights; the fair distribution of benefits and burdens across a citizenry; the ethics of economic systems; civil freedoms (e.g., freedom of speech) and their limits; criminal justice and the ethics of punishment, including capital punishment; and proper approaches to formulating public policy, especially regarding issues on which there is principled disagreement among citizens (e.g., in the United States, whether forms of legal status should be extended to same-sex couples).

socialism (n.): An economic system in which there is centralized, public control of the means of production and distribution. [Note: Considered from the standpoint of perennial ethics, such a system can have merits—e.g., it can, at least in principle, effectively attend to matters of economic justice and the proper distribution of goods. However, actual examples of socialist systems are widely regarded as having suffered from significant practical difficulties—e.g., depression of economic initiative and enterprise, and overreliance of individuals on the state.] (Contrast **capitalism**. See as well **distributism** and **third way**.) Also: "socialist" (adj. or n.).

social justice: Matters of *justice* $_{(2)}$ within societies and, increasingly, the world as a whole. Two main concerns of social justice are the promotion of economic and other types of *distributive justice,* and the development of fair and effective systems of *legal justice.*

society (n.): A *community* as formally organized, with structures of *authority* $_{(1)}$ for promoting the *common good.* Like the term "community," "society" covers human groupings of different levels and types—including *families* as well as *civil societies* at various levels (e.g., cities, states or provinces, countries, and even the international community, with the last partially organized through the mechanisms of the United Nations). Scholastic thinkers have drawn a distinction between "perfect" and "imperfect" societies, with the former—if there are any such within the *secular* and *political* orders—consisting of organized communities that have within themselves the means necessary to serve all the basic needs of their peoples.

Socratic (adj.): Pertaining to the views, and especially to the methods, of Plato's teacher, Socrates, who left no writings but who appears as the major protagonist in Plato's *Dialogues.* ("Socratic method" usually designates an approach to teaching and learning in which there is steady dialogue and give-and-take among the participants; the teacher thereby hopes to help the student come to grasp important points on his or her own.) (See **dialectical** $_{(1)}$.)

solidarity (n.): As articulated by John Paul II (e.g., in *Centesimus annus* (1991)), the virtue, related to the cardinal virtue of *justice,* whereby a person is committed to the authentic good of his or her fellow humans—both within a particular society and in the world as a whole—and accordingly seeks concrete ways to assist in the bringing about of such good.

solitude (n.): Condition of being alone. (In John Paul II's developed teaching on marriage, the term "original solitude" is used in the interpretation of the biblical story of human creation: Adam—representing either human *gender*—realizes his aloneness, and wishes for another, Eve, who will be *complementary* to himself, and with whom he can form a unique *communion of persons.*)

sophism (n.): An argument with the appearance of strength, but one which, on closer inspection, is seen to suffer from formal or informal *fallacies.* Also: "sophist" (n.), "sophistical" (adj.), "sophistically" (adv.).

sophistry (n.): (1) Practice of developing arguments that are *sophisms.* (2) (Somewhat archaic.) Synonym for **sophism**.

sorrow (n.): (1) In traditional philosophical psychology, a *concupiscible* passion (pain or distress) at the loss of, or failure to attain, a sensible good. (2) More generally, as with the contrasting affective elements *delight* and *joy,* a response of pain or distress at the loss of, or failure to attain, any object of desire—whether the object and the response are sensory, intellectual, and/or spiritual. <Sorrow at one's having fallen short of achieving holiness.> Also: "sorrowful" (adj.).

soul (n.): For Aristotelian tradition, the first or fundamental *act* of a living body as an instance of natural being; specifically, the substantial *form* of such a body, by which *matter* $_{(3)}$ is organized so as to be an individual of a given type, with characteristic powers to perform a range of vital functions. These functions, and thus soul itself, are distinguished into three general types: *vegetative, sensitive,* and *rational* (or *spiritual*). [Notes: a) Sometimes, especially in the case of human beings, "soul" is popularly used to designate an individual's psychic dimensions, by contrast with "body" in the sense of an individual's physical dimensions. However, the fundamental philosophical contrast is between the two *co-principles* of a living substance—form and matter—as discussed at the beginning of this entry. If care is not taken to keep these points in mind, discussions of soul and body—and of their interrelations—tend to become badly confused. b) Perhaps surprisingly at first, in the overall context of *hylemorphism,* the "reality" of soul is not a matter of genuine controversy. As Aquinas explicitly noted, real issues arise as to whether human soul is *spiritual* in nature and whether—although not a complete substance—human soul nonetheless in some way is "itself a thing" and "subsists." (See the discussion under **subsistence**.)]

soundness (n.): As understood in logic, a property of *deductive arguments* that have both *truth* in their premises and *validity* in their form. The conclusion of a sound argument, thus understood, is true of logical necessity. Also: "sound" (adj.), "soundly" (adv.).

sovereignty (n.): Characteristic of a *state* $_{(2)}$ that has its own organizing principles and structures and is not under the direct *authority* of any other political entity. Also: "sovereign" (adj. or n.).

space (n.): For natural philosophy in the tradition of Aristotle, the feature of physical being according to which each such being can be identified as occupying a *place*—and, as such, can be located and measured in relation to other such beings. (Note: Space as here understood is very different from the idealized expanse ["absolute space"] supposed by early modern scientific theories—an idealization that, with the success of relativity theory, is now recognized to have been part of the prior scientific model itself, rather than to have represented an aspect of real being.) Also: "spatial" (adj.), "spatially" (adv.).

species (n.): (1) In logic, the narrowest unit in the classification of terms. (Contrast **genus** $_{(1)}$.) (2) (Latin *species,* corresponding to Greek *eidos.*) In philosophical psychology and epistemology, a purely "presentative" form (as it was called by Jacques Maritain)—that is, a modification of *sense* or *intellect* whose very essence is to enable one, through the activity of the relevant cognitive power, to be aware of a sensible quality or an intelligible nature. (See **idea**.) (3) In biology, a classification of *organisms* falling immediately below "genus," one whose members are characterized by the possibility of interbreeding and other *empiriological* features.

species expressa (Latin phrase): In Thomistic philosophy of human knowledge, the *species* $_{(2)}$ ultimately resulting from the process of intellectual *abstraction.* The intelligible form thus "expressed" becomes an explicit *concept* or "mental word," whose mode of existence is as a qualitative determination of the intellect. (See **possible intellect**.)

species impressa (Latin phrase): In Thomistic philosophy of human knowledge, the "impressed" *species* $_{(2)}$, that is, the initial result of the intellect acting on sensory data and abstracting an intelligible form. (See **agent intellect**.)

speciesism (n.): Name sometimes used to characterize the view—which is a key element of Christian as well as a number of other moral traditions—that human beings enjoy a particular *dignity* or moral *status.* (This name has been introduced by opponents of the view [e.g., Peter Singer]; these opponents generally take some actualized trait—e.g., the ability to communicate, or to have "interests" of a certain sort—as a *necessary and sufficient condition* for moral status. They then argue that not all members of the human species have this trait, while certain members of other species do have it. Thus, they conclude, according special moral status to human beings as such involves a wrong comparable to *racism* or *sexism*. For the perennial tradition's response, see the discussions at **human being** and **person**.) Also: "speciesist" (adj. or n.).

speculative (adj.): (1) Of or concerned with knowledge (especially knowledge of a high *degree* or *order of abstraction*) that is pursued for its own sake as perfective of the intellect. (This type of knowledge also is termed "theoretical." However, in philosophy the goal of intellect is not—as in "theoretical" physics and other natural *sciences* $_{(2)}$—greater comprehensiveness in accounts of natural fact; rather, it is knowledge of real being that constitutes *demonstration* by way of first principles. Thus one must be careful not to confuse "theories" of the two sorts.) (2) Pertaining to uses of intellect or reason that are directed toward speculative knowledge. (In both senses, contrast **practical**.) Also: "speculation" (n.), "speculatively" (adv.).

speech, power of: As traditionally understood, a *property* $_{(2)}$ of human beings by which we can share the content of our *concepts, judgments*, and *reasonings* with others. [Note: Certain key figures of 20th-century *analytic philosophy*, e.g., Ludwig Wittgenstein and J. L. Austin, stressed that there are many "uses" of language, or many types of "speech-act"—a variety that is not easily or appropriately reduced to, for example, "communicating what one understands to be true." Moreover, it seems clear that members of certain other animal species can participate in some (not all) of these linguistic activities or uses of signs—comforting, correcting, warning about perceived dangers, etc. These points should be accepted by the perennial tradition; but they should be seen as supplementing, not contradicting, the account of speech articulated in this entry.]

spirit (n.): (1) A being that exists or can exist apart from matter. In a human person, identical with (rational) *soul*, itself a subsistent being whose act of existence (*esse*) actuates the whole human *composite* throughout one's life as a natural being. (See the discussion at **subsistence**.) (2) Sometimes understood as applying specifically to the higher powers of rational soul (*intellect* and *will*), especially insofar as these are open to the infinite, and insofar as their proper activity culminates in natural *mystery*—to which (according to Christian faith) God responds via revelation.

spiritual (adj.): Of or pertaining to *spirit* or *spirituality.* Also: "spiritually" (adv.).

spirituality (n.): In theology and religious literature, the interior relationship—always able to be further perfected during this life—of a human person with transcendent reality. (Christianity, as well as certain other religions, embraces various forms of spirituality.)

spiritual sense (also ***sensus plenior***, Latin for "fuller sense"): As understood by Scripture scholars whose work reflects what John Paul II called the "great tradition" (*Fides et ratio,* #85), a type of meaning contained in biblical passages that goes beyond the intention of the human authors (sometimes referred to as the "literal sense") and that conveys something of the fullness of God's message. The category of the spiritual sense historically has been subdivided into the "typological" (according to which one is able to more deeply appreciate one biblical event in light of another, earlier or later, event), the "tropological" (according to which one is able to discern the moral significance of a Scriptural passage for one's own life), and the "anagogical" or "eschatological" (according to which one is led to grasp something of the ultimate mystery of God and our relationship with God). (Importantly, in some cases what the biblical scholar or theologian recognizes as a type of "spiritual" sense is expressed through what the philosopher calls—with a different meaning—a "literal" use of language, in particular, that of *analogy;* whereas in other cases a spiritual sense is expressed through what the philosopher calls "metaphorical" or "symbolic" uses of language.)

state (n.): (1) The concrete existential condition of an individual being (substantial or accidental), by contrast with that being's *essential*$_{(1)}$ characteristics. <The state of a human being's health.> (2) An organized *civil society,* one having concrete instruments of *government* and claiming *sovereignty.* <The United States of America, but not its fifty federated political units, as a sovereign state.> (Regarding (2), compare **nation.**)

states (or **stances**) **of philosophy** [**in relation to Christian faith**]: A key notion in John Paul II's *Fides et ratio,* ##75–77, according to which there are three concrete, existential conditions (or instances of *state* $_{(1)}$) in which philosophy can properly be practiced: a) philosophy prior to hearing and accepting the Christian message; b) philosophy in its Christian state (i.e., *Christian philosophy*); and c) philosophy as it is taken up by and formally contributes to sacred *theology.*

statism (n.): Position in political philosophy—sometimes called "collectivism" and consistently rejected by Catholic tradition—holding that the person or citizen exists for the good of the whole (i.e., the *state* $_{(2)}$ or the "collective"), rather than vice-versa. (See **totalitarianism**. Contrast **communitarianism**, as well as **individualism** $_{(1)}$ and **liberalism** $_{(1)}$.) Also: "statist" (adj.).

status (n.): How beings are to be regarded or treated, in the context of a particular type of inquiry. It is common to distinguish three types of status in the present, philosophical sense: a) "Ontological status" concerns how a being is to be understood *metaphysically* (e.g., whether it has existence on its own, or only as a part or feature of another); b) "Moral status" concerns whether, and to what extent, a being enjoys *moral* $_{(1)}$ standing, or merits consideration in the ethical evaluation of acts; c) "Legal status" concerns how a being should be treated, or the specific rights that it has (or should be recognized as having), within a particular system of *positive law.* (Note: Diverse questions about the "status" of human embryonic and fetal life, as well as lives of medical patients in comatose and other severely compromised states, can fall under all three headings.)

stealing or **theft** (n.): The appropriation of another's property against his or her reasonably presumed will, an action that violates *natural (moral) law.* (However, given the *universal destination of goods,* not all appropriations of another's property constitute genuine cases of stealing. See **change of matter** or **change of species**, **exceptionless moral rules**, and **necessity** $_{(2)}$.)

stewardship (n.) A moral concept and principle present in Christian (and certain other religious) accounts of ethics. According to this principle, human beings, as rational creatures, are to take responsible care of and, as appropriate, make creative use of the goods of the physical world—e.g., through advances in *technology.* However, creativity must be limited by respect for the essential features of, and the genuine good of, the world of nature (including our own *nature* $_{(2)}$), as given by the Creator. (This principle serves as a religious basis for *environmental* concerns, as well as for concerns in biomedical ethics about certain forms of genetic engineering.)

Stoicism (n.) A prominent school of ancient philosophy, centered in Greece and later in Rome, during the period of the founding of Christianity. (As noted in *Fides et ratio,* #36, Stoicism was encountered in some form by St. Paul during his journey to Athens [see Acts 17].) Principal representatives of "Early," "Middle," and later "Roman" Stoicism were, respectively, Chrysippus (3rd century BC), Cicero (1st century BC), and Epictetus (1st–2nd centuries). Much emphasis within Stoicism was placed on *practical* philosophy. Additionally, while some proponents of this school spoke of "breath" or "soul" (Greek *pneuma,* Latin *spiritus*), all were *materialists* in their accounts of the cosmos, and they tended to treat the whole of physical reality as akin to a comprehensive organism. (In spite of this obvious incompatibility with biblical religion, Stoicism contributed to the development of Christian reflection through its notions of *right reason* (Greek *orthos logos,* Latin *recta ratio*) and, by way of Cicero, *natural* (*moral*) *law* (Latin *lex naturalis*).) Also: "Stoic" (adj. or n.).

structure of rights: See **rights, structure of.**

structure of the human act: Series of cognitive and appetitive operations that, in a fully *human act,* are involved in the pursuit of a good. As typically characterized, the operations in question are, in sequential order: a) willing the good in question; b) anticipating the enjoyment of the good; c) intending this good as concretely achievable, supposing the availability of some appropriate means; d) preliminary consent to one or more prospective means as ways the good might be pursued; e) use of various human powers to comparatively evaluate the prospective means; and, finally, f) concrete choice—which in turn is followed by action.

Suarezian (adj. or n.): Related to the teachings and school of thought associated with Francisco Suarez, S.J. (1548–1617). A figure who bridged the Medieval and Modern periods, Suarez was a Scholastic who exercised influence on Descartes and even on Kant. Contrary to Aquinas and *Thomism,* Suarez held that there is no real distinction between *essence* $_{(1)}$ and *existence* $_{(1)}$ in creatures, although there is what he called a "modal" distinction. Moreover, for Suarezians (again, in more or less conscious opposition to Thomists), the proper subject matter of metaphysics is not real *being* $_{(3)}$, but rather the "objective concept of being." Also: "Suarezianism" (n.).

subalternate (adj. or v.): Character of two (or more) disciplines such that one provides at least some of the principles for the other (or others). <The science of optics as subalternate to mathematics.> (Note: The 20th-century Thomist Jacques Maritain stirred controversy among Catholic thinkers—still unresolved, in the judgment of many—when he proposed that, in order for *moral philosophy* to be adequate to its formal task of providing guidance toward our actual human *end* $_{(1)}$, this discipline (unlike the purely *speculative* branches of philosophy) must be "subalternated" to (moral) theology. To Maritain, this seemed the inevitable consequence of the fact that our ultimate end—namely, *beatitude* or a sharing in the life of the Trinity—can be recognized only by faith.) Also: "subalternation" (n).

subconscious (adj.): Said of certain powers and operations of the animal (and especially the human) *soul* that do not reach the level of explicit awareness—although modern psychotherapeutic techniques are designed precisely to bring the content of some of these operations into such awareness. <Subconscious desires affecting human acts.> (Contrast both **conscious** and **unconscious**. See as well **nonconscious**.) Also: "subconscious" (as a n.) or "subconsciousness" (n.), "subconsciously" (adv.).

subject (n.): (1) In logic, the thing about which something is said. <The subject of a proposition of the form "S is P."> (Contrast **predicate** [as a n.]). (2) In psychology, both philosophical and positive, another name for the *self*, as the experienced source of activity. <The perceptions of the individual subject.> (Ant: **object** $_{(2)}$.) (3) In metaphysics, that which primarily exercises *being* $_{(4)}$ or *existence* $_{(2)}$ (ordinarily, as a complete *supposit*). <This existing tree, considered precisely as a unified subject, including its trunk, leaves, etc.> (4) In ethics, the bearer of a *right* (n.), by contrast with the right's "term," "matter," and "title." <A child as the subject of a natural right to care and nurture.> (Regarding sense (4), see **rights, structure of**.)

subjective (adj.): Having to do with the psychological *self*'s experience of, responsibility for, or personal reaction to an aspect of reality—rather than the aspect of reality itself. <The agent's degree of subjective guilt for a wrong action.>

(Ant: **objective** $_{(1)}$.) Also: "subjectively" (adv.).

subjectivism (n.): A type of *epistemological* theory, found in both ancient and modern times, holding that matters of truth and falsity, and/or moral rightness and wrongness, are entirely determined by personal judgment, rather than by any correspondence to or "adequation" with *objective* $_{(1)}$ reality. (Ant: **objectivism.** Compare **relativism.**) Also: "subjectivist" (adj. or n.).

subjectivity (n.): (1) In psychology, and in 20th-century *personalism* and *phenomenology* (as well as certain precursors of these movements such as the 19th-century Danish thinker Søren Kierkegaard), interiority as experienced by a *subject* $_{(2)}$, in particular by a human person. (2) In perennial metaphysics, sometimes used as equivalent to *subsistence* (and accordingly called "metaphysical subjectivity").

subordinate (adj.): Of or pertaining to what is dependent upon another or others. <A series of causes, each of which is subordinate to the preceding one in terms of its actual exercise of causality.> (Compare **secondary.**) Also: "subordination" (n.).

subsidiarity (sometimes **autonomy**), **principle of:** In *social ethics,* a principle holding that decisions regarding local practical matters are best made by those immediately involved in the situation; and that the role of the *state* $_{(2)}$ in such cases is to provide appropriate assistance (Latin *subsidium*), rather than itself attempting to formulate concrete directives. (Contrast **statism** and **totalitarianism.**) Also: "subsidiary" (adj. or n.).

subsist (v.): To have or exercise the perfection of *subsistence.*

subsistence (n.) *Act* or *perfection* of a being whereby it exercises individual *existence* $_{(2)}$ on its own and thus is separate in being from all others. Among purely physical beings, things subsist only as complete *substances.* By contrast, *accidents* do not subsist; rather, they exist by virtue of inhering in substances. (Notes: a) On the Thomist account, certain powers and acts of rational *soul*—namely, those of intellect and will—are not, strictly speaking, powers and acts of the whole human *composite.* Here, that is, the soul acts on its own. Thus, while not a complete substance, human soul nonetheless subsists, and it can exist in a "separated" state [i.e., a state separated from bodily conditions]. Also, for the Thomist, the person [the whole metaphysical "supposit"] has existence via the subsisting soul. b) In the historical development of perennial philosophy, certain

Thomists elevated subsistence to a metaphysical *principle* $_{(1)}$ on a par with *essence* and *existence*. Today, the vast majority treat subsistence as a mode or perfection of being, but not, properly speaking, as a metaphysical principle.) (See **incommunicable** and **supposit**. Compare the discussion under **individuation, principle of**.) Also: "subsistent" (adj.).

substance (n., Latin *substantia*): For the Aristotelian tradition, the first *category* of being: that which is primarily and in itself, rather than as an *accident* or feature of another—thus, for example, the being of the rose itself, rather than the being of the rose's color or its shape. That there is substantial being, and that it is ontologically primary, is grasped via reflection on the fact that beings of nature retain a unity and identity over time although they change in particular features. Natural substance is a composite of "primary" matter (i.e., *matter* $_{(3)}$) and substantial *form;* these accordingly are called the *co-principles* of substance. (Notes: a) In its philosophical usage, "substance" refers to a being as a center of act and intelligibility—rather than, as in the term's everyday usage [including its usage in the empirical sciences], a physical reality from the standpoint of its tactile properties and/or its material or chemical composition. b) The present account applies to what Aquinas, following Aristotle, sometimes calls "first" substance; these philosophers also speak of "second" substance—what Aristotle usually intends by *ousia*—that is, being as "whatness" or *essence*. c) Purely spiritual but finite beings—i.e., *angels*—exist as complete substances [or, more strictly, as complete *supposits* of existence] without matter. However, as noted in the preceding entry, although human or rational souls enjoy *subsistence*, they are not in this way complete; rather, as forms they are ordered toward matter as the condition of their full actualization. Human life, properly speaking, is incarnated. In light of this, our souls are sometimes referred to as "incomplete substances.")

substantial (adj.): Of or pertaining to *substance*. Also: "substantially" (adv.).

substantial change: The coming into being and going out of being of an individual, natural *substance*—events sometimes referred to as *generation* and *corruption*. (Note: The word "change" can mislead the unwary here, since it typically conveys a sense of gradual alteration over time—whereas alterations of *substantial* form, strictly and in themselves, are instantaneous, although they involve natural processes and thus gradual alterations of various sorts [e.g., in the case of human "corruption" or death, the shutting down of the cardiovascular system].)

suffer (v.): See **undergo** or **suffer**.

sufficient condition: See the discussion under **necessary and sufficient conditions**.

sufficient reason, principle of: A first principle of metaphysics, namely: "Everything that is, insofar as it is, has a sufficient reason for its being." This principle is similar to, but more comprehensive than, natural philosophy's *principle of causality.* (Note: Some Scholastic authors use the phrase "principle of causality" *analogously* for both the physical and the metaphysical principle; however, the distinction in terminology seems important. For example, God's Essence ["What God Is"] is sufficient reason for God's Existence; but, strictly speaking, God has no cause.)

suicide (n.): As a human act, the deliberate taking of one's own life. (Note: Often there is doubt as to whether an event termed a "suicide" in fact resulted from genuine *deliberation* and *choice.*)

summum bonum (Latin phrase, sometimes capitalized, for "ultimate [or 'highest'] good"): See **final end** $_{(1)}$.

superabundance (n.): See **abundance** (sometimes **superabundance**).

superdetermination (n.): Term used by 20th-century Thomists Jacques Maritain and Yves R. Simon to characterize the *will* at its highest state of actualization—in which it is committed to the genuine and comprehensive *good,* and thus can exercise dominating causality in practical judgments and make truly free decisions.

superego (n.): In Freudian psychoanalytic theory, the part of the *psyche* $_{(2)}$ by which a person, beginning in early childhood, subconsciously internalizes the rules and values of parents and the broader society, and by which he or she is internally rewarded with feelings of approval or punished with feelings of guilt. [Note: The notion of superego can be compared with the traditional notion of *conscience;* however, Freudians tend to ignore the possibility of *objectivity* $_{(2)}$ in moral awareness, as well as the role of *reason* in moral judgment.]

supereminence (n.): See **eminence** (sometimes **supereminence**).

supererogatory (adj.): In modern moral philosophy, a category of good acts that goes beyond ones that are morally required. For example, most ethicists recognize a general obligation to be concerned about the welfare of others; but, from the standpoint of philosophical reason, acts of radical Gospel *charity* go beyond this. <Giving away one's worldly possessions to benefit the poor as morally supererogatory.> Also: "supererogation" (n.).

supernatural (adj.): Related to a *being* or *power* or *act* beyond the order of nature as such. (Contrast **natural** $_{(4)}$. See **grace** and **obediential potency.**) Also: "supernaturally" (adv.).

supernatural gifts: See the discussion under **gifts of integrity and grace**.

supersensible (adj. or n.): Of or pertaining to beings that are *transcendent* $_{(1)}$, and thus beyond all ability to be sensed; also such a being itself. <God and other spiritual beings as supersensible.>

superstition (n.): A belief or practice that is without rational basis—indeed, one that can be shown to go against reason—but one that nevertheless may be deeply embedded in the psyche of a person or culture. (Religious superstitions can be seen as corruptions of genuine religion: the latter involves accepting as a matter of *faith* $_{(3)}$ things that cannot be naturally known or proved—but not things that can be shown to be irrational.) Also: "superstitious" (adj.), "superstitiously" (adv.).

supposit (Latin *suppositum*, from *sub*, for "below" + *ponere*, for "to place") (n.): An individual *subject* $_{(3)}$ of existence that subsists as a complete instance of a nature or essence. In relation to rational beings, supposit is equivalent to *person* $_{(1)}$. (Compare ***hypostasis***. See the discussion under **subsistence**.)

supposition (n.): (1) Statement accepted as true in the context of, and for the sake of, inquiry. <The supposition of absolute velocity.> (2) In medieval logic, a notion roughly corresponding to "reference." (See the discussion at **signification, modes of**.)

syllogism (n.): Type of deductive reasoning, formally articulated by Aristotle in the book *Prior Analytics*, in which two *premises* (called "major" and "minor") contain three terms that are ordered (or "distributed") in such a way as to lead necessarily to a *conclusion* containing two of them. The third term, which logically connects the two that appear in both the premises and the conclusion, is called the "middle term." An example of a *valid* form of syllogism (with "M" as the middle term, and "S" and "P" as the terms that respectively form the subject and predicate of the conclusion) would be: "All M is P; all S is M; therefore, all S is P." (As an instantiation of this form, consider "animals" for M, "human beings" for S, and "mortal" for P.) Also: "syllogistic" (adj.), "syllogistically" (adv.).

symbol (n., from Greek *symbolon,* for "token" or "pledge"): (1) In the most general sense, a thing that refers or points to another type of reality. (In this sense, natural beings, according to traditional theology, can be regarded as symbols of God.) (2) More particularly, and more commonly today, a word or other sign that is used by convention (but not, in the typical case, by way of expressing a cognitive *concept*) in order to communicate a matter of special depth or value or mystery. (Often the symbol [e.g., a nation's flag] is said to participate in the very reality that is symbolized—in this case, what the nation stands for, has accomplished, and hopes to achieve. Moreover, the symbol is said to express this reality—and to open up corresponding depths of the human soul—in a way that no *literal* term or conceptual expression could. Thus, according to the influential 20th-century Protestant thinker Paul Tillich, one should never say "only a symbol"; rather, one should say "not less than a symbol.") [Note: As applied to religious language, such an account, while acceptable and even illuminating as far as it goes, runs the risk of falling into what may be termed "symbolicism"—i.e., a form of *noncognitivism* (incompatible with integral Christian wisdom) according to which all statements about God, and the spiritual realm generally, can involve only non-literal uses of terms. On this view (apparently held by Tillich himself, as well as by Catholic writer Roger Haight, S.J.), religious language cannot express conceptual *knowledge,* even by way of *analogy,* and thus cannot have genuine *truth-value.*] Also: "symbolic" (adj.).

symbolicism (n.): See the discussion under **symbol**$_{(2)}$.

sympathy (n., from Greek *pathos,* for "feeling"): The ability, or the exercise of the ability, to feel "with" (Greek particle *syn*) another being, as said especially—although not only—of human persons. <Genuine sympathy for the poor.> (Compare and contrast **empathy**, which involves apprehension of the other as another self.) Also: "sympathetic" (adj.), "sympathetically" (adv.).

symphonic (adj.): Term used by Swiss Catholic theologian Hans Urs von Balthasar to express his vision of truth. (With this term von Balthasar emphasized the dynamic and organic character that should mark Christian teaching—by contrast with what, in his experience, was a flat and lifeless form of Scholasticism.)

synderesis (Latin n., from Greek *synteresis,* for "spark of conscience"): The *habitus* of first principles of practical reason, which should ground all thinking about matters of action. According to Aquinas, the *absolutely* first practical principle is "Good is to be done and promoted, and evil avoided." Other practical principles—in particular the *primary precepts of natural (moral) law*—are illustrations or exemplifications of this one. (As in speculative knowledge, a genuinely first principle can be defended but not strictly proven—i.e., demonstrated in terms of more basic concepts and judgments.) [Note: Questions arise concerning the conditions *de facto* necessary for sharing this *habitus,* and concerning the extent to which it in fact is shared by all normal human persons, as maintained by strict Thomist accounts. Compare **invincible ignorance**.]

synthesis (n.): (1) In relation to sensory data, the unifying function of the internal sense referred to by Scholastics as the *common sense* (Latin *sensus communis*) or "central" sense. (2) In relation to conceptual knowledge, the process whereby the mind goes from an abstract notion (for example, "being") to an understanding of the multiplicity and complexity of the things that specify and instantiate that abstract notion. (In this sense, contrast **analysis** $_{(2)}$.) Also: "synthesize" (v.).

synthetic (adj.): (1) Related to some process of *synthesis.* (2) According to a usage popularized by Immanuel Kant, type of statement that cannot be known to be true simply from an understanding of the meanings of its terms, but requires further experience or reflection for its confirmation. <"Bachelors tend to be unhappy" as a synthetic statement.> (In both senses, contrast **analytic**.) Also: "synthetically" (adv.).

systematic (adj.): Characteristic of approaches to knowledge that emphasize organization and hierarchy among truths. (Thinkers can undertake a systematic approach without claiming to have, or even attempting to have, a complete and final "system." As discussed and as commended in *Fides et ratio,* Thomist thought may be regarded in precisely this way: that is, as being highly organized but at the same time open to enrichment by other philosophical approaches, as well as by developments in the natural sciences and other fields of intellectual culture.) Also: "systematically" (adv.).

T

~

tautology (n.): A proposition that can be known to be true simply by virtue of its form. Sometimes the term is more restrictively applied only to compound propositions that have this property—e.g., propositions of the form "Either *p* or not-*p*." (Compare and contrast **analytic** $_{(2)}$, **evident** or **self-evident**, and **per se nota**.) Also: "tautological" (adj.), "tautologically" (adv.).

techne (Greek n.): Skill or know-how. See the discussion under **art** $_{(2)}$.

technology (n., from Greek *techne*, for "skill"): Application of the modern physical and, increasingly, biological sciences to address human needs or desires. [For perennial thinkers, the development of new and effective technologies is, in general, to be welcomed. However, critical questions sometimes arise concerning: a) whether genuine needs are being identified and met; and b) whether the development and use of particular technologies properly assist in the pursuit of *integral human good*—or whether, on the contrary, they violate an aspect of that good (as would be the case, for example, in efforts at human cloning).] Also: "technological" (adj.), "technologically" (adv.).

Teilhardian (adj.): Of or pertaining to the thought of Teilhard de Chardin, S.J. (1881–1955). Teilhard was a paleontologist by training, in addition to being a philosopher and theologian. His thought was daring and controversial; not surprisingly, he has been both admired and maligned by fellow Catholic thinkers. For example, Teilhard took terms originating in the Bible (see Rev. 21, where Christ is identified as the Alpha and the Omega, or the beginning and the end, of Creation) and developed the notion of "Alpha and Omega points" in expressing his theological vision. According to this vision, the Alpha point represents the first instant of Creation, and the Omega point represents its evolutionary fulfillment, sometimes conceived by Teilhard as the full embodiment of Christ in global society. Another of his neologisms was "noosphere" (compare "atmosphere," "biosphere," etc.), by which he intended the final stage of evolutionary development, in which the ability to think rationally (Greek *noein*) emerges. (Compare **process thought**.)

teleological (adj.): Of or pertaining to *teleology,* in any of the three senses specified. (In relation to the third sense, contrast **deontological**.) Also: "teleologically" (adv.).

teleological structure of human goods: In Thomistic accounts of the human good, the structure—or set of structures—according to which goods are *ordered* to one another. Two orders in particular are distinguished: first, as to which goods are more basic or fundamental, in the sense of being necessary if other goods are to be enjoyed; and second, as to which goods are higher or more important, in the sense of fulfilling our specifically human, or personal, powers and acts. The most fundamental good would be life itself. The highest good would be one's personal relationship with God. (See **hierarchy of goods** and **conflict of rights and duties**. Contrast **incommensurability thesis**.)

teleology (n., from Greek *telos,* for "end" or "purpose"): (1) For perennial philosophy generally, the view that each being is naturally ordered (in Aristotle's terminology, via its *entelechy*) toward respective types of fulfillment, with implications for the proper *ends* (1) of human acts. (See **final cause**.) (2) In philosophical theology, a type of reasoning to God (exemplified in the fifth of Aquinas's *Five Ways*) that begins with the end-directedness and order within the universe and concludes to God as transcendent, universally ordering Intelligence. (Note: As formally *philosophical,* such teleological arguments do not stand or fall with recent efforts by some scientists [and religious writers] to present *intelligent design* as the *scientific* (2) theory that most plausibly accounts for the development of the natural world.) (3) In recent moral philosophy, any type of *normative* theory that emphasizes the consequences of actions as the key to their moral evaluation. (Regarding sense (3), contrast **deontology**.)

temperament (n.): The feature of *personality* comprising an individual's typical *emotional* and other *affective* responses to various types of experience. (Note: Aspects of temperament figure into *character;* the latter, however, also includes *virtues* the individual may develop—or fail to develop.) <An easygoing temperament; a highly irascible temperament.>

temperance (n.): The *cardinal virtue* that enables the making of right choices regarding food, drink, sex, and other matters involving pleasure or physical satisfaction. Temperance operates by regulating the movements of *concupiscible* appetite—and, by extension, other modes of desire and aversion. (Compare *fortitude* in relation to movements of *irascible* appetite.) Species of temperance include moderation of diet (concerning food), sobriety (regarding intoxicating substances), chastity (regarding sexual desires and acts appropriate to one's state), and frugality (regarding the use of financial and other resources). A related virtue involving a higher order of personal satisfaction is *humility* (by which one "tempers" one's self-image through an honest understanding of self, with one's strengths and weaknesses, gifts and limitations, etc.). Among vices and tendencies contrary to temperance are gluttony, habitual drunkenness (i.e., the *moral* state, as distinct from the disease-state known as alcoholism), and *lust* (2) (i.e., the *capital vice* so designated). Also: "temperate" (adj.), "temperately" (adv.).

temporal (adj.): (1) Of or related to *time.* (2) Of or related to this world by contrast with things that are unchanging or that belong to the *spiritual* order. (Contrast **eternal**. Compare, especially in relation to sense (2), **secular**.) Also: "temporality" (n.), "temporally" (adv.).

Ten Commandments: Name given by biblical religions to the commandments received by Moses on Mount Sinai (see Exodus 20). (Within Catholic tradition, the Ten Commandments are generally said not only to express divine *positive law,* but also to contain in a virtual manner the principles of *natural (moral) law.*)

tendency (n.): See **inclination** or **tendency**.

term (n.): (1) As generally understood in logic and philosophy, a word or phrase expressive of a *concept.* (2) In relation to a human *right,* its formal nature.

theft (n.): See **stealing** or **theft**.

theism (n., from Greek *theos,* for "God"): (1) Generally, belief in or affirmation of God. (Contrast **atheism** as well as **agnosticism**. See **monotheism** and **polytheism**.) (2) More specifically, a formally developed philosophical (i.e., metaphysical) account in which the reality of God and of the world's relations to God are articulated. (3) Also sometimes understood as equivalent to *deism* (a view incompatible with integral Christian wisdom). Also: "theist" (adj. or n.), "theistic" (adj.), "theistically" (adv.).

theocracy (n.): Form of government according to which the *state* $_{(2)}$, or the civil order, comes under the direct sway of the *spiritual* order, with leaders from the latter (e.g., imams or priests) formulating matters of *human law* and public policy precisely with a view to satisfying religious commandments. Also: "theocratic" (adj.), "theocratically" (adv.).

theodicy (n., from Greek *theos,* for "God" + *dike,* for "judgment" or "right"): A rationally structured response to the *problem of evil,* via an account that undertakes to maintain God's goodness despite the experience of widespread evils in the world. (Among proponents of the perennial tradition, theodicies typically proceed in two stages. First, it is argued that evil in itself, although real as a *privation,* is not a *subject* $_{(3)}$ of existence; thus it cannot be characterized as a direct object of Creation. [Thus God does not *create* evil.] Secondly, regarding evils as actually experienced, a distinction is drawn between "evil suffered" or "evil of loss" and "evil done" or "evil of fault." [This distinction is roughly equivalent to that between "natural evil" and "moral evil" made by many modern writers.] In relation to this point, it is argued that evils suffered are the natural by-products of other things' fulfilling themselves—e.g., carnivorous animals' satisfying their need for food—and that evils done are the results of *free choices* by human beings. Thus in neither case can the evils, precisely as evils, be directly attributed to the action of God.) [Not surprisingly, these and other approaches to theodicy have been the subject of much discussion and debate. It remains an important question whether, or to what extent, theodicy can be successful in purely *philosophical* terms—that is, terms involving reference only to common human experience and reflection, without any formal appeal to *revelation*—e.g., concerning *Original Sin* and concerning God's offer of unending life in Christ.]

theological virtues: See **virtues, theological**.

theology (n., from Greek *theos,* for "God" + *logos,* for "word" or "account"): Systematic study of God and of the world's—especially humankind's—relations with God. (1) Philosophical theology, as the ultimate stage of *metaphysics,* approaches God as *Necessary*$_{(6)}$ Being, and as absolutely First Cause and Final End of all finite being. (2) Sacred theology (Latin *sacra doctrina*)—i.e., "theology" as commonly understood—studies God and our relations with God by way of principles drawn from *revelation,* while also incorporating relevant knowledge from other disciplines (including, at least for Catholic tradition, the disciplines of philosophy).

theology of the body: Name given to the fully developed teaching of John Paul II on *marital and sexual ethics.* This teaching incorporates both the theory of *natural* (*moral*) *law* and *personalism,* and it sets them in a context of reflection on the *communion of persons* formed by man and woman as revealed in biblical sources—especially the Creation accounts in Genesis. (See also the discussion under **parenthood.**)

theonomy (n., from Greek *theos,* for "God" + *nomos,* for "rule"): The condition of being subject to the rule of God. [Many philosophers, following the lead of Immanuel Kant, object to this notion as involving a type of *heteronomy;* they say that authentic moral life depends on the rational agent's self-rule. (See *autonomy*$_{(2)}$). However, Christian thinkers (including John Paul II) have argued to the contrary that—properly appreciated in its full context—genuine autonomy precisely involves "participated theonomy;" that is, an individual's personal recognition of the precepts of *natural* (*moral*) *law* constitutes a kind of sharing in God's eternal ordering of the universe.] Also: "theonomous" (adj.), "theonomously" (adv.).

theory (n., Greek *theoria,* from *theorein,* for "to view" or "to understand"): (1) In philosophy as well as in common usage, a broad understanding (especially a *speculative* understanding) of things. <The theory of human nature and origins.> (Contrast ***praxis.***) (2) In the modern *sciences*$_{(2)}$ of nature, a very general statement or set of statements (sometimes highly mathematical in form) that provides an explanatory context for a broad range of empirical facts—and that can be used to generate *hypotheses* about new possible facts, which, if confirmed by experience, provide additional rational support for the overall explanation in question. <The "Big Bang" theory of the origin of the cosmos.> Also: "theoretical" (adj.), "theoretically" (adv.), "theorist" or "theoretician" (n.).

theory of knowledge: See **epistemology** or **theory of knowledge.**

thing (n., Latin *res*): (1) A being that is actual by way of *entitative* (especially physical and substantial) existence. (2) By extension, anything that can be named and discussed, that is, anything having *entitative* or *intentional* existence (whether physical or spiritual, and whether substantial or accidental in nature). Thus molecules of water, propositions, and angels all can be called "things" in this extended sense. (In light of this, some Scholastics list "thing" or *res* among the *transcendental* perfections of being.)

third way: Name sometimes given to a supposed economic system that would stand as a hybrid or middle position between *capitalism* and *socialism.* Although primarily associated with writers such as the German/Swiss social theorist Wilhelm Röpke, and with European center-left political movements, proposals of a *third way* are seen by some commentators—although not by others—to be promoted in modern Catholic social encyclicals, including those of John Paul II. Controversy about this matter, which in part depends on the precise understanding of "capitalism" and the extent to which it (or the "market economy") is subject to regulation by public authority, has continued in light of Benedict XVI's *Caritas in veritate* (2009). (Note: The present term obviously applies as well to the third of Aquinas's five arguments for the existence of God, as outlined at the beginning of the *Summa theologiae* [see **Five Ways, the**].) (Compare **distributism.**)

Thomism (n.): Designation for the tradition of thought that embraces central concepts and principles of St. Thomas Aquinas (1224/5–74). Recognized historical masters of Thomism include Thomas de Vio, better known as Cajetan (1469[?]–1534), and John of St. Thomas, also called Jean Poinsot (1589–1644). The variant "Neo-Thomism" has been applied to 20th- and now 21st-century developments of this tradition. However, many of the thinkers involved (including Jacques Maritain) eschewed this label, preferring to be called simply "Thomists." Within the overall tradition, several recent schools can be distinguished: a) "existentialist Thomism," or "the Gilson school" (after Etienne Gilson, who stressed the importance for Aquinas of the "act-of-being" or "act-of-existence"—i.e., *esse* or *being* $_{(4)}$); b) the "River Forest school" (associated with the Dominican house of studies in River Forest, Illinois, which emphasized the Aristotelian dimension of Thomism, especially the need for a renewed philosophy of nature, together with the possibilities of synthesizing this branch of philosophy with the modern natural sciences); c) the "Laval School" in Canada (associated with Charles De Koninck, who also pursued natural philosophy and who famously defended the idea of the common good against what he perceived as personalist thinkers' tendencies to diminish it); and d) the "Lublin school" (centered at the University of Lublin in Poland, where Karol Wojtyla was a professor of ethics during the early years of his career, and where scholars energetically undertook efforts to incorporate themes from phenomenology and personalism, while holding fast to the primacy of traditional metaphysics as articulated by M. A. Krapiec, O.P.). (See also **analytic Thomism** and **transcendental Thomism.**)

Thomist (sometimes **Thomistic**) (adj.): Pertaining to *Thomism,* or to a person who holds concepts and principles of Aquinas. St. Thomas's principal intellectual enterprise involved an effort to synthesize the (then recently recovered) thought of the ancient philosopher Aristotle with orthodox Christian teaching and reflection, as transmitted by the Scriptures, the writings of the Church Fathers (especially St. Augustine), and later sources. In *Fides et ratio,* John Paul II devoted two full sections (##43–44) to Aquinas's achievements; he commented that the Church rightly has regarded him as a "model" for philosophical and theological thought. (Certain recent scholars—a minority—now prefer the term "Thomasian" when referring to actual writings and positions of St. Thomas himself, by contrast with the broader tradition that derives from his work.) Also: "Thomist" (as a n.), "Thomistically" (adv.).

time (n.): In natural philosophy in the tradition of Aristotle, a measure of the physically changing as such, numbered as to before and after. Given the different types of change or motion, the different systems of numbering, and the range of human interests, there naturally are different systems of time: seconds, minutes, hours; appearances of the moon and seasons of the year; etc. (Recent Thomists such as W. Norris Clarke, S.J., have reflected on implications of relativity theory in physics, as well as on psychological dimensions of time as revealed by phenomenological investigation.) (Contrast **eternity**. See as well **duration**.)

title (n.): See the discussion under **right** (n.).

tolerance (n.): A virtue of life in *civil society,* one that involves and applies all of the *cardinal virtues.* Certain behaviors—e.g., *murder*—are clearly destructive of fundamental human rights and/or the public order; as such they are not to be tolerated, and virtually all organized societies in fact prohibit them. But other behaviors (as well as attitudes, beliefs, etc.) are less destructive, or less clearly destructive, and in these cases—even when one is convinced that, in principle, the acts should be seen as evil by all—the attempt to impose a standard of behavior (let alone an attitude or belief) often will produce very harmful social side effects, as well as inhibit people's progress toward freely and intelligently embracing the good. Thus some degree of tolerance of views and practices to which one is personally opposed is essential in any viable *pluralist* society. [This account, it may be noted, is squarely rooted in the perennial tradition as articulated, for example, by Jacques Maritain; it does not involve an acceptance of *ethical relativism* or *liberalism* $_{(3)}$—positions that support social and political tolerance on quite different bases.]

totalism (n.): Variant term for **totalitarianism.**

totalitarianism (n.): A system of government—or of less formal but still effective modes of social influence—in which decisions and concrete programs are developed universally rather than locally, by a single centralized authority (or other, comparable source of influence); and in which the good of the whole society is held in all cases to supersede the rights of individuals. (See **statism**. Contrast **communitarianism** and the **principle of subsidiarity**, as well as **liberalism** $_{(1)}$.) Also: "totalitarian" (adj. or n.).

totality, **principle of**: Moral principle—articulated by theologians, but having general philosophical content—according to which, if necessary for the life or psychic integrity (the "totality") of the person in question, lower powers of human personhood (e.g., normal digestive or urinary functions) can be altered or even sacrificed. [Note: The principle of totality has sometimes been appealed to by theologians who dissent from the teaching of *Humanae vitae* (1968) regarding *contraception.* Pope Paul VI anticipated this appeal, and he pointed out in the encyclical that such a principle cannot be used to justify acts that are *intrinsically evil*—which, he argued, contraceptive acts are.]

tradition (n., Latin *traditio,* from *tradere,* for "to hand on" or "transmit"): A broad movement of thought—one comprising generations of teachers and students, and sometimes accommodating a of variety of approaches, all in pursuit of a common intellectual goal. In this sense, John Paul II spoke (*Fides et ratio,* #85) of the need to continue, and to renew, the "great tradition" of thought that begins with the ancients, includes the contributions of medieval Scholastics such as Aquinas, and seeks to incorporate the genuine achievements of modern and contemporary thought. (A distinction often is drawn between tradition and the generally narrower notion of *school.* In practice, however, this distinction is not exact, and the choice of terms sometimes depends upon context. Moreover, the notion of "tradition" itself can be used in a narrower sense; thus scholars sometimes speak, for example, of "Catholic traditions" [plural], to distinguish, for example, typically Dominican from typically Jesuit or Franciscan approaches to theology or the spiritual life.) (In relation to the philosophical work of Alasdair MacIntyre, contrast **encyclopaedia** and **genealogy**.) Also: "traditional" (adj.), "traditionalist" (n.), "traditionally" (adv.).

transcendence (n.): (1) Most generally, a property of beings or realities (including aspects of human reality) that are not limited by the material or physical. <Spiritual natures as enjoying transcendence.> (2) More particularly, property whereby God is said to supersede all limits and to be totally "other" than the world. <God's ability to be intimately present at all times, and to each created thing, as entailing God's transcendence.> (Contrast **immanence** $_{(2)}$.) Also: "transcendent" (adj.), "transcendently" (adv.).

transcendental (adj.): (1) Of or related to a property of *being* $_{(3)}$ as such, and thus proportionately shared by each individual, whatever its category and whether it is physical or spiritual, etc. The transcendental properties are commonly listed as *being, oneness* or *unity, truth, goodness,* and, by many authors, *beauty.* Some also include "being a definite something" (Latin *aliquid*) and even, simply, "being a thing" (Latin *res*). The recent Thomist, W. Norris Clarke, S.J., promoted "agency" or "being active" as a distinct transcendental perfection. Within the bounds of analogy (see **eminence**, sometimes **supereminence**), the transcendental properties can be formally predicated of God, by whom they are enjoyed in an *absolute* manner. (Contrast **mixed** as well as **pure perfection**.) Also: “transcendental” (as a n.). (2) Pertaining to an approach to speculative philosophy, typified by the German philosopher Immanuel Kant, that begins with human experience as such and then, through reflection, articulates what is judged to be the mind’s essential contribution to that experience. (For Kant, this included certain innate principles and categories according to which data of sense are organized.) Also: “transcendentally” (adv.).

transcendental Thomism: Name given to a movement of thought, notably including the 19th-century Jesuit Joseph Maréchal (whose philosophical works are not yet available in English), and 20th-century Jesuits Karl Rahner and, in some respects, Bernard Lonergan. These thinkers and their followers have sought to revitalize certain themes of Aquinas (e.g., the human intellect’s openness to the infinite) by using *transcendental* $_{(2)}$ methods. [Critics of transcendental Thomism within the perennial tradition typically express the concern that, as proved to be the case with Kant, it seems impossible to support an adequate philosophical *realism* through such methods. But Lonergan, among others, held that such a concern can be overcome.]

transience or **transitivity** (n.): Property of an act whereby the effect takes place in a being other than the agent. (Ant: **immanence** $_{(1)}$.) Also: “transient” or “transitive” (adj.), “transiently” or “transitively” (adv.).

transitivity (n.): (1) See **transience** or **transitivity**. (2) In modern formal logic, the property of a relation R such that if aRb and bRc, then aRc. <The relation “larger than” displays transitivity.> Also: “transitive” (adj.), “transitively” (adv.).

transubstantiation (n.): See **Real Presence**.

Trinity, the (n.): Central Christian doctrine affirming three *persons* $_{(1)}$—together with their interrelations—in God: God the Father, God the Son, and God the Holy Spirit. The doctrine of the Trinity is a classic example of a truth about God that humans could know only by *revelation*, not by *natural* $_{(4)}$ reason. Still, particular formulations of this doctrine depend on theologians’ application of philosophical concepts such as *being, hypostasis,* and *supposit.* (For recent discussions that reflect the tradition of Aquinas, see, for example, works by Giles Emery, O.P., and Matthew Levering.) Likewise, the pursuit of this and similar theological tasks can prompt insights into related philosophical matters. (See, in this regard, the discussion under ***esse-ab.***) Also: "Trinitarian" (adj.).

truth (n.): (1) One of the *transcendental* properties of being, according to which anything real has *intelligible* characteristics. (2) In relation to activities of the intellect operating speculatively, the conformity or "adequation" (Latin *adequatio*), of the mind with the way things are, as this is achieved in correct *judgment.* (3) In relation to matters of human action (where the perennial tradition sometimes speaks of "practical truth"), conformity of the *will* with the dictates of *right reason.* Also: "true" (adj.).

truth-conditions: Conditions under which a proposition is true (or not true), expressed either in terms of the type of conformity noted at *truth* $_{(2)}$ or, as by modern logicians, in terms of the truth or falsity of an incorporated proposition or set of propositions. Regarding the latter, if *P* is the state of affairs expressed by the proposition "*p*," then "*p*" is true if and only if *P*, and "Not-*p*" is true if and only if "*p*" is false. Further, the compound proposition "either *p* or *q*" is true if and only if either "*p*" is true or "*q*" is true. (See as well **necessary and sufficient conditions.**)

truthfulness (n.): A cognate of the cardinal virtue of *justice,* whereby one is disposed to say what one believes to be the case when legitimately asked, even in difficult circumstances. Also: "truthful" (adj.), "truthfully" (adv.).

truth-value: Term developed by modern logicians to indicate a *proposition*'s being true or being false.

turpitude, **moral**: Condition in which a person is totally lacking in positive moral *character.* (Contrast **rectitude, moral** $_{(1)}$.)

tyranny (n.): Form of government or regime that serves the private interests of the governing class (the "tyrants") rather than the *common good.* (Considered abstractly, *democracy* is clearly opposed to tyranny. However, in the concrete, even democratic polities—if not animated by a proper respect for *human rights* and the *natural (moral) law*—can devolve, as John Paul II noted [see *Evangelium vitae* (1995)], into subtle forms of tyranny.)

ultimate end or **good**: See **final end**.

ultimate practical judgment: The final judgment of practical intellect about a concrete matter, one that takes the form "Such-and-such is to be done (or not done)." As proposed to the *will* of the person(s) involved in the situation, this judgment is also called a *command* (in Latin, *imperium*).

uncaused (adj.): Existing and acting without being dependent on any cause; said properly only of the *absolutely* $_{(2)}$ First Cause (i.e., God). (Note: "Uncaused" is to be distinguished from "self-caused;" the latter designates *change* or *motion* as originating from within a thing's *nature* $_{(3)}$—and thus applies in respective ways to all living but finite beings.) (Compare **aseity**.)

uncertain (adj.): Subjectively experienced as, or objectively marked by, the impossibility of a firm judgment, at least in the present circumstances. <An uncertain witness; an uncertain outcome.> (Ant: **certain**. Compare **doubtful**.)

uncertainty (n.): Subjective or objective state marked by lack of firm judgment, due to possibility of error. <Uncertainty as to the proper method for solving an equation. "An objective uncertainty held fast in an appropriation-process of the most passionate inwardness"—a philosophical account of Christian faith offered by 19th-century Danish thinker Søren Kierkegaard.> (Ant: **certainty** or **certitude**. Compare **doubt** [as a n.].)

unconscious (adj.): (1) Unable, either temporarily or permanently, to enjoy (or to be brought to) a psychic state of *consciousness*. (Compare **nonconscious**.) (2) In the theory of Sigmund Freud, pertaining to deep motivations that fail to reach consciousness. (Contrast both **conscious** and **subconscious**, as well as **preconscious** or **precognitive**.)

unconscious (n.): In the theory of Sigmund Freud, deep aspect of the *psyche* $_{(2)}$ that affects behavior without any possibility of reaching a level of explicit awareness in the *subject* $_{(2)}$. (Contrast **conscious** [in its occasional use as a n.] and **consciousness**, as well as "subconsciousness," listed under **subconscious**.)

unconsciousness (n.): State in which a person, or an animal, suffers a loss of *consciousness*. (Unlike simple nonconsciousness—which characterizes, for example, chemical compounds and statues—unconsciousness is a *privation*.)

undergo or **suffer** (v., corresponding to Latin *patior*): To be acted upon by another. <With the change of seasons, deciduous trees undergo a loss of their leaves.> (Contrast **act** [as a v.].)

understanding (n.): (1) (Corresponding to Latin *intellectus*.) The *habitus* of first principles of the speculative reason—e.g., the principles of *identity* ("Each being is what it is"), of *sufficient reason* ("Everything that is, insofar as it is, has a sufficient reason for its being"), and of *finality* ("Every agent acts for an end"). (2) More generally, the achievement of knowledge or correct awareness of any sort, especially in relation to the explanation of conditions and events, but also in relation to the meaning of words and texts. Also: "understand" (v.).

understanding of faith (Latin *intellectus fidei*): Phrase used by the medieval Scholastic St. Anselm to speak of the role of philosophically trained reason in theology—namely, to develop, as John Paul II put it (*Fides et ratio*, #42), "explanations which might allow everyone to come to a certain understanding of the contents of faith." For Anselm, reason or intellect is spurred on in this task because it "must seek that which it loves [i.e., the truth about God]." (See as well **faith seeking understanding**.)

unethical (adj.): Not ethical (i.e., morally *wrong*), as judged in terms of an explicit or presumed standard. (Ant: **ethical** $_{(2)}$. Compare **immoral**. Contrast **moral** $_{(2)}$.) Also: "unethically" (adv.).

unicity (n.): Uniqueness.

unity (n.): See **oneness** or **unity**.

unity (or **interconnectedness**) **of the virtues**: The idea that all of the essential *moral virtues* must in some measure be possessed by a person if he or she is to judge and act rightly over a lifetime of typical human circumstances. (For example, a person with *fortitude* or *courage* (2) will act bravely in challenging situations; but if that person does not also possess the virtue of *justice,* he or she cannot be counted on to exercise courage only in ways that preserve social order. Likewise, without *prudence,* the person may needlessly endanger his or her life, as well as that of others.)

universal (adj. or n.): (1) (As an adjective.) Able to be predicated of many—i.e., all things of a specific *formal* character. <"Round" signifies a universal feature of rings, buttons, tires, etc.> (2) (As a noun.) Formal character or *essence* that can be thus shared. <Humanness as a universal shared by Americans, Europeans, Africans, etc.> (Ant: **particular**. See as well **universals, problem of**.) Also: "universality" (n.), "universally" (adv.).

Universal Declaration of Human Rights: Document developed by the fledgling United Nations organization in 1947, and subsequently ratified by a majority of member *states* (2). Coming after the defeat of *totalitarian* forces in World War II, the document expresses a ringing endorsement of human rights, individual and community freedoms, and the obligations of states to provide for the needs of their citizens. It continues to be appealed to today. (Note: The Thomist philosopher Jacques Maritain was a member of the committee that drafted the Universal Declaration. Afterward, he remarked that while the committee readily agreed on a range of rights, freedoms, and obligations, there was—not surprisingly—much less unanimity concerning the general philosophical principles that underlie these moral points.)

universal destination of goods: In modern Catholic social teaching—which incorporates insights of the perennial philosophy—a moral principle according to which the resources of the earth are intended for the good of all people. (Because of this, although systems of "private" *property* (3) are morally acceptable—and ordinarily the most effective means to certain individual and common goods—such systems are never to be understood as conferring *absolute* rights of ownership.)

universalism (n.): In ethics, the position that at least some moral principles, rules, etc., apply to all human beings. (Contrast **ethical relativism** and **individualism** (2).)

universals, problem of: A prominent topic for medieval philosophers, and one of continuing relevance today: What is the precise nature of universal terms and concepts, and of the realities they designate? (See **conceptualism**, **nominalism**, and **realism**.)

univocal (adj.): Use of a term, in relation to several individuals, such that it has the same meaning—and, ideally, expresses the same cognized *essence*—in each instance. Examples abound in the natural sciences. <"*Homo sapiens*" as a univocal term.> (Contrast **equivocal** and **analogical** or **analogous**.) Also: "univocally" (adv.).

univocity (n.): Condition of a term used in a *univocal* manner. (Contrast **equivocity** and **analogy**.)

unjust (adj.): Not *just*. Also: "unjustly" (adv.).

unmoved (adj.): Pertaining to a reality not itself moved or changed (although it may bring about movement or change in others); said primarily and most properly of the *absolutely*$_{(2)}$ First Mover (i.e., God).

unnatural (adj.) (1) Not *natural*$_{(1)}$ (i.e., *artificial*). (2) Not possible or achievable in light of the *nature*$_{(2)}$ of a thing, or in light of pertinent concrete conditions. (3) In moral philosophy and theology, inclinations and/or freely chosen acts that go against the *end*$_{(1)}$ of human existence, or against the significance of a *natural*$_{(3)}$ power or type of act. (Note: A particular act—e.g., the implantation of a medically necessary feeding tube—can be "unnatural" in sense (1) without being "unnatural" in sense (3); the reverse also is the case. Such points can be important for topics in applied ethics.) Also: "unnaturally" (adv.), "unnaturalness" (n.).

use (n.): In ethics, a freely chosen *activity* involving a human power, thus one that is open to moral assessment in light of that power's proper *teleology*, as well as overall human good. <A bad use of the ability to drive a car—e.g., to assist in a bank robbery.>

use (v.): To treat something as an object to be manipulated for human purposes. <According to common moral wisdom, as well as sound philosophical reflection, it is not right to use other people simply as a means to one's own ends.>

useful good (Latin *bonum utile*): A good that is worthy of choice, not simply (if at all) for itself, but as a means to something else. For example, financial wealth is a useful good, insofar as it enables one to live well and do good for one's fellow human beings. (The exercise of moral virtue may require one to forego a useful good, especially if, in the concrete context, it is incompatible with an important good that is worthy of choice in itself.) (Contrast **honest good**, as well as **pleasant** or **pleasurable good**.)

usury (n.): See the discussion under **interest** $_{(2)}$.

utilitarian (adj. or n., sometimes capitalized): (1) Of or pertaining to, or a person who holds, the ethical theory of *utilitarianism.* (2) Sometimes the term is used more broadly of any approach to life or activity that focuses on matters of perceived usefulness, apart from questions of intrinsic value.

utilitarianism (n., sometimes capitalized): A species of *teleological* $_{(3)}$ ethics, originally developed by mid-19th-century British philosophers Jeremy Bentham and John Stuart Mill, and later by Henry Sidgwick, among many others. Classical utilitarianism holds to the "principle of utility," or "greatest happiness principle." According to this principle, as articulated by Mill, the goodness or badness of an act is to be judged in light of its consequences, as measured in terms of aggregate happiness and unhappiness. By "happiness," Mill specifies pleasure, which for him is subject to qualitative as well as quantitative measures. He also emphasizes that all those affected by the act are to be considered in the calculation of its consequences. (Later utilitarian theorists have offered a range of alternatives and/or refinements to the basic theory. An important example is the distinction between "act" and "rule" utilitarianism. The former holds that the locus of the measurement of happiness and unhappiness should be the consequences of individual acts; the latter holds that at least sometimes the locus should be the consequences of general practices or types of acts.)

validity (n.): As understood in logic, a property of *deductive* arguments whose *premises* and *conclusion* are related in such a way that, if the former are true, the latter also must be true. (See as well **soundness**.) Also: "valid" (adj.), "validly"(adv.).

value (n.): (1) A thing, concrete or abstract, insofar as it is perceived or accepted as a *good.* <A person's fundamental values.> [Note: The term "value" is often used by contemporary social theorists in abstraction from the question of whether the thing valued is adequately perceived or rightly accepted, and indeed from the question of whether matters of value can be *objective* $_{(1)}$ at all. Thus the term is disdained by some followers of Aquinas and the Catholic tradition more generally. But other Thomists (e.g., Jacques Maritain) have held that "value" is to be related to questions of genuine good, by way of the desirability or suitability or perfective character of the thing in question. Moreover, on many *personalist* accounts (including that of Karol Wojtyla), a good becomes a properly human or personal good only when and insofar as it is, in fact, valued.] (2) In modern formal logic, an item that can instantiate a variable. <In a statement of the form "aRb," if "R" is taken to be "is taller than," then values for "a" and "b" that yield a true statement would be "Washington Monument" and "Jefferson Memorial," respectively.>

value (v.): To perceive or accept something as a good. Also: "valuable" (adj.), "valuation" (n.).

value neutrality (sometimes hyphenated): Characteristic often attributed to the *positive* or *empiriological* as well as the *mathematical* sciences, insofar as they are pure instances of these types: by way of possessing this characteristic, they supposedly neither express nor imply judgments of *value.* (However, controversy arises—especially in relation to the social sciences—over whether there in fact can be completely value-neutral empiriological disciplines, at least if these are taken to have *practical* bearing. For in order to have such a bearing, a discipline must incorporate, or suppose, views about relevant *ends* $_{(1)}$ or *goods.*)

vegetative (sometimes **nutritive**) (adj.): Type of *soul,* or power or operation (e.g., nutrition and growth), typical of plant life and shared by higher types of organisms as well. (See **sensitive** and **rational.**) Also: "vegetation" (n.).

vengeance (n.): The application of punishment, or the desire to apply punishment, for its own sake (i.e., precisely in order to bring *harm* to the other person)—ordinarily as a response to perceived wrongs that have been suffered. [Vengeance in this sense has no place in perennial philosophical ethics—let alone in Christian ethics—and it is to be distinguished from proper concern for *retributive justice.*] Also: "vengeful" (adj.), "vengefully" (adv.).

vice (n.): An *inclination* or, especially, a *habit* according to which an individual tends toward doing moral evil. (As persons should develop moral virtues, so also they should, as far as possible, eliminate vices—e.g., by avoiding circumstances that stimulate the growth and exercise of such habits.) Also: "vicious" (adj.).

vices, capital (from Latin *caput,* for "head" or "source"): Those vices that are regarded as the sources of all others. Traditionally these are identified as seven: *pride* (said to be the primary or ultimate source), *avarice* or *greed, gluttony, lust, sloth, envy,* and *anger.* The first four represent disorders of *concupiscible* appetite, or other types of desire; the latter three represent disorders of *irascible* appetite, or other types of response to challenging circumstances. (Sometimes the capital vices have been called the seven deadly sins—although strictly, at least for Aquinas, the qualities in question are not themselves "deadly" [or "mortal"]. However, if they are allowed to go uncorrected, they indeed can lead to deadly sin.)

violence (n.): (1) A use of force—especially in the context of human conflict—that produces physical harm to persons or things.

(2) More generally, anything that causes harm or disorder, whether physical, psychological, social, etc. (Given the harm thereby caused, *human acts* involving violence must meet stringent criteria if they are to be morally justified. See, for example, the discussion under **just war theory**.) Also: "violent" (adj.), "violently" (adv.).

virtual (adj.): (1) Synonym for *potential,* especially applicable to cases in which the related *actuality* is almost present, either qualitatively or temporally, or both. (Note: As used in the phrase "virtual reality"—in the context of modern electronic technology—this term perhaps should be said to function *metaphorically* in relation to the present sense.) (2) Special mode of presence for a quality or *perfection* that is actual in beings of a lower order and that cannot by its very nature be actual in a being of a higher order—but which, because of a relationship of ontological dependency between the two, must in some way be attributed to the latter. For example, and in particular, *mixed perfections*—i.e., purely physical perfections involving dimensionality, color, etc.—cannot actually be present in God; but because God is First Cause of all being, such perfections are sometimes said to be present in God in a virtual manner. (Contrast **transcendental** and **pure** perfections, which—because they are either not essentially bound up with matter, or not bound up with matter at all—are in some way actually present in God.) Also: "virtually" (adv.).

virtue (n., from Latin *virtus,* originally meaning "power"): A *habitus* or stable disposition, intellectual or moral, that enables ("empowers") a person to pursue regularly and with ease an appropriate *object* $_{(2)}$ or *end* $_{(1)}$—i.e., some type of knowledge in the case of an intellectual virtue, or right action in the case of a moral virtue. (Note: In some contexts, the Greek word *arete* is translated as "virtue," but in others it is translated as "excellence." In the latter contexts, the meaning of *arete* is broader and the word can apply to a perfection of any nature—e.g., health in an animal—not specifically and exclusively human nature.) (See succeeding entries regarding various types and categories of virtue—**cardinal**, **intellectual**, **moral**, and **theological**.) Also: "virtuous" (adj.), "virtuously" (adv.), "virtuousness" (n).

virtue epistemology: An approach to certain recent questions in epistemology, as pursued in the *analytic* tradition, which makes use of the classical notion of *excellence* or *virtue* (Greek *arete*). (For example, the known quality of a person's habitual attention to detail provides a warrant for the credibility of his or her recollection about a situation—e.g., in the context of courtroom testimony.)

virtue ethics: An approach to moral philosophy that emphasizes the need to develop and employ excellences of *character.* In the latter decades of the 20th century, Alasdair MacIntyre and others brought this Aristotelian element back to the forefront of general philosophical discussion. [Note: A "pure" virtue ethics would reduce all morally significant factors to matters of virtue, and thus would not be adequate to the full ethical theories of Aristotle and the perennial tradition.]

virtues, cardinal (from Latin *cardo,* for "hinge"): The specific virtues on which, according to classical accounts, the whole of the moral life depends. Traditionally these are numbered as four—*prudence, justice* $_{(1)}$, *fortitude* (or *courage* $_{(2)}$), and *temperance.*

virtues, intellectual: Types of stable disposition or *habitus* that promote excellence in intellectual functioning. Such virtues strengthen the power of *intellect* itself, rather than the will or sensible appetite; they thus empower a person to pursue objects of knowledge with relative assurance. Examples would include an understanding of theoretical principles, whether of metaphysics or of some more particular philosophical or scientific discipline; as well as practical wisdom or prudence (also listed as a moral virtue), insofar as this *habitus* enables one to reason well about practical matters, especially ones related to the moral life.

virtues, moral: Types of stable disposition or *habitus* that consist in excellences of *character.* Moral virtues may modify primarily either the *will* (as in the case of justice and fidelity) or some aspect of *sensible appetite* (as in the case of temperance and chastity). According to Aristotle's account, moral virtues facilitate the choice and pursuit of the *mean*—i.e., that concrete object or action that is appropriate for this agent in these circumstances. (Scholastic thinkers have developed a variety of *systematic* accounts of the moral virtues. Such accounts typically involve setting out the four *cardinal virtues,* then showing that other virtues, habits, and dispositions constitute "parts" and species of these four [e.g., equanimity and perseverance in relation to fortitude], or are ancillary and cognate to them [e.g., caution and foresight in relation to prudence].)

virtues, theological: Specific excellences, available only through

God's *grace* (and thus sometimes said to be "infused," rather than naturally developed), that define and make possible the Christian life. Following St. Paul (see 1 Corinthians), they traditionally are numbered as three—*faith, hope,* and *charity* (or love in the sense of *agape*).

vitalism (n.): View holding that objects, especially animate objects, operate from a vital force within their natures—although not necessarily, as with *animism,* a force that includes intentionality and choice. (Aristotle's account of *psuche* or soul as substantial form, whereby living beings undertake their characteristic activities—e.g., nutrition and growth—can be considered a form of vitalism; indigenous beliefs, including those of Native American religions, often extend vitalism so as to attribute such forces to inanimate natures.)

volition (n.): Act of the *will,* particularly the intending of an *end* (2) to be achieved through human action. (Compare and contrast **choice**.) Also: "volitional" (adj.), "volitionally" (adv.).

voluntarism (n.): Philosophical approach, or family of approaches, holding that the *will* (Latin *voluntas*)—in humans as well as in God—acts prior to or apart from *intellect* in the selection of goods or ends, and in the development of moral precepts. (Contrast **intellectualism**.) Also: "voluntarist" (adj. or n.), "voluntaristic" (adj.).

voluntary (adj.): Resulting from a free act of the *will,* rather than from any necessity or constraint (whether an external constraint such as coercion, or an internal constraint such as a psychic disorder). The criteria for voluntary action are: a) *knowledge* (i.e., knowledge of the *nature* (2) and *object* (3) of the act, together with awareness of relevant *circumstances*); and b) free *consent.* (Ant: **involuntary**.) Also: "voluntarily" (adv.), "voluntariness" (n.).

war (n.): Open conflict between communities (in particular, although not only, organized *states* $_{(2)}$), ordinarily involving *violence* or force of arms. Since the time of St. Augustine, Christian thinkers (as well as, more recently, the ordinary Catholic *magisterium*) have developed accounts of the conditions under which war, in spite of the evils that are entailed, can be morally justified. (See **just war theory**. Contrast **pacifism.**) Also: "(go to) war" (v.).

wealth (n.): An accumulation of financial and other material goods. (Neither Christian revelation nor perennial philosophy condemns the accumulation of wealth as such—although both warn against the dangers of *avarice* or *greed.* They stress, however, that the goods of this world are to be used for the benefit of all, with consequent moral requirements for wealthy individuals and societies, as well as particular duties for those charged with articulating and promoting standards of *distributive justice.*) (See **universal destination of goods**.) Also: "wealthy" (adj. or n.).

Weltanschauung (German n.): Worldview or fundamental way of conceiving and understanding the world. [Note: This notion, originally developed by 20th-century European philosophers and cultural commentators, is illuminating; but it must be treated with caution since those who speak of *Weltanschauungen* (plural) often exhibit tendencies toward *historicism* or *relativism.*] (See as well **deconstructionism**.)

whole (n.): A unit or unity, especially one that is composed of *parts*—e.g., an organism. <Appropriate

means of medical treatment must offer benefit to the patient as a whole.> Also: "wholly" (adj. or adv.), "wholeness" (n.).

will (n.): The *power,* proper to rational or spiritual beings, that enables such beings—in particular, human persons—to pursue the good as known or judged to be good, rather than simply acting by way of instinct or passion or emotion. (Will is thus sometimes referred to as "rational" or "intellectual" affectivity.)

will (v.): The *act* (i.e., willing a particular end or good) that is the initial element in a series of cognitive and appetitive operations that comprise the *structure of the human act.* (Sometimes the verb "will" is applied to the whole series of operations, culminating in concrete *choice.*) Also: "willing" (adj.), "willingly" (adv.), "willingness" (n.).

will to power: A notion made famous by late 19th-century German philosopher Friedrich Nietzsche, who used it to characterize what he regarded as the fundamental drive of human existence—a drive suffocated, in his view, by traditional religious faith. [By contrast, in *Fides et ratio,* #90, John Paul II referred to a "destructive will to power;" and he suggested that this attitude (as well as a contrary attitude also found in contemporary societies—namely, a "solitude without hope") could ultimately be traced to the neglect of being and truth—specifically, the being and truth of the human person.]

wisdom (n., Greek *sophia,* Latin *sapientia*): The goal of philosophy as traditionally understood—a comprehensive understanding of ultimate matters. For perennial thought, wisdom involves true intellectual *knowledge* of things by way of their highest causes and principles. Wisdom can be divided into two broad dimensions: a) *speculative* wisdom, or ultimate knowledge concerning how things are; and b) *practical* wisdom, or ultimate knowledge concerning how we human beings should act, the goods we should pursue, and the types of persons we should strive to become. (Catholic tradition also speaks of *theological* wisdom—which requires as premises certain statements accepted in faith; and *mystical* or infused wisdom, which is beyond rational articulation and can be enjoyed only as a direct gift from God.) (Compare **contemplation**.) Also: "wise" (adj. or n.), wisely" (adv.).

wisdom, integral Christian: The type of articulated wisdom—especially promoted within Catholic tradition—in which, as expressed by Cardinal Avery Dulles, S.J., "theology and philosophy are harmoniously integrated to the advantage of both and the detriment of neither." (The tradition of integral Christian wisdom corresponds to the "great tradition" referred to in *Fides et ratio,* #85—from which, according to John Paul II, philosophers should draw inspiration, as well as make fresh contributions.)

Wisdom literature: Those books of the Hebrew Bible (Job, Psalms, Proverbs, Ecclesiastes, The Song of Solomon, The Wisdom of Solomon, and Sirach [or Ecclesiasticus]) that constitute the *sapiential* portion of the ancient scriptures—and therefore provide continuing inspiration and subject matter for *philosophy* in what John Paul II called its "second" state—i.e., as practiced by the Christian thinker.

woman (n.): An adult female human being. (Contrast **man** $_{(2)}$. See as well the discussion under **gender**.)

wonder (n.): The common human drive to understand or know, especially in a comprehensive way and with regard to matters of the greatest depth and/or *mystery.* Wonder of this sort is taken by Aristotle and his followers to be the originating impulse of all philosophy. Also: "wonder" (as a v.).

word (n., corresponding to Greek *logos,* Latin *verbum*): (1) A sound or a written character that functions as a unit of linguistic communication (see **speech, power of**); for perennial philosophers, the most important and distinctive human linguistic function is the expression of *concepts* and *judgments.* (2) (Sometimes called "mental word" [Latin *verbum mentis*].) The *intelligible species* itself that is articulated by means of language. (3) (Usually capitalized.) In Christian *kerygma* and theology (see John 1), the "Word of God" through whom the world comes to be and who becomes incarnate in Jesus Christ.

work (n.): Human activity directed to an *extrinsic* purpose or end (i.e., one not identical with the activity itself). Work can be physical or mental. (The 20th-century Thomist Yves R. Simon noted that this term does not encompass the philosophical and theological activities of *contemplation,* in which the end is *intrinsic;* however, a great deal of work may be involved as a prelude to, or a cognate of, these self-justifying activities.) Work can be directed toward an individual end or a communal end, or both; moreover, the worker's *subjective* motivation in undertaking the activity need not coincide with the *objective* $_{(1)}$ end of the activity as such—although, as with all appropriate human action, such an end must not be directly opposed. Ideally, work is one important source of human fulfillment. (See, however, **alienation** $_{(2)}$.)

world (n.): (1) The planet Earth. (2) The entire universe or *cosmos.* (3) The *world* (or *global*) *community.* (4) In certain theological contexts, the realms of nature (especially human nature) and culture, insofar as these are fallen (see **Original Sin**) and not yet fully redeemed.

world (or **global**) **community**: The whole of humanity, with its complexity and diversity of social organization, taken as a *communion of persons,* and thus as having *common goods,* the need for *distributive justice,* etc. (A special concern in applying this notion arises from the fact that, on the perennial understanding, an authentic community must have a structure of *authority.* Accordingly, in spite of shortcomings of the United Nations organization as presently constituted, a philosophically informed global perspective must include hope for the success of this or some successor organization. For a recent discussion from a theological perspective, see Pope Benedict XVI's encyclical *Caritas in veritate* [2009].)

world religions: Religions that, although they originated in a particular place and time, have come to enjoy—or to aspire to—a universal audience and significance. In addition to Christianity, Judaism, and Islam, world religions in this sense would include Hinduism, Jainism, and Sikhism (originating in India); Buddhism (originating in India but quickly spreading to East Asia and beyond); and perhaps Confucianism and Daoism (originating in China). Sometimes world religions are contrasted with "indigenous" ones (e.g., various Native American religions and Shinto in Japan), as well as with *animisms* or religions of nature. However, the boundaries of these categories are not exact. (In *Fides et ratio,* #104, John Paul II expressed the hope that philosophy can be a vehicle for mutual understanding among adherents of diverse religions.)

worship (n.): Acknowledgment of another's (in particular, God's) special *status* and *dignity,* together with appropriate practices of adoration and devotion. (For the tradition of Aquinas, that human beings should worship—in the general sense of acknowledging the Creator—is a precept of *natural* (*moral*) *law,* whether or not it is explicitly recognized as such. Awareness of specific, prescribed forms of adoration and devotion can come only from *revelation.* In light of this, practices of the various monotheistic religions can be regarded philosophically as specifying particular forms of the universal and natural duty to acknowledge the One on whom the world depends.) Also: "worship" (as a v.).

worth (n.): Actual *value* $_{(1)}$. <The infinite worth of the human person, as proclaimed by Christianity.>

wrong (adj.): Incorrect or improper; said especially, although not exclusively, in relation to moral matters. (Ant: **right** [as an adj.]. Compare **unethical**. See as well **determinants** or **sources of morality**, and **intrinsic**(**ally**) **evil**.) Also: "wrong" (as a n.), "wrongful" (adj.), "wrongness" (n.).

wrongness, moral: Failure to achieve correctness in a matter of *choice* or *human act,* as judged in light of the *determinants* or *sources of morality.* (Compare **badness** or **evil** [in the moral senses of these terms]. Ant: **rightness, moral**. Contrast also **rectitude, moral**.)

x (logical symbol): In modern formal logic, a symbol used in the "quantification" of statements—i.e., in the expression of the range of instances (either "universal" or "particular") to which what is *predicated* applies. Thus: "(x). . . ." expresses a universal statement (i.e., "For all x, ..."); while "(∃x). . . ." expresses a particular statement (i.e., "For some x, . . . ;" or "There is at least one x such that. . . ."). [Note: Many contemporary philosophers, especially in the English-speaking world, have taken this feature of modern formal logic to entail that the very meaning of *being* or *existence* is reducible to quantificational factors. Typical expressions of this view are: "Existence is not a predicate;" and "To be is to be the value of a variable." From the standpoint of perennial philosophy, modern logic as a formal system (or systems) is unexceptionable; however, such an interpretation of being itself is both gratuitous and philosophically mistaken. (See the distinction of senses under **being**, especially (4) vs. (5).)]

xeno- (particle, from Greek *xenos* for "strange"): A combining word-form signifying *otherness*—including individual otherness, but especially otherness of race or culture, and even, more recently, of species. (The experience of "the other" has been an object of investigation in *phenomenology.* The notion of otherness also has become relevant in *applied ethics:* for example, "xenophobia" signifies a morally inappropriate (and, in the strict sense, pathological) fear of persons of another race or culture; while "xenotransplantation" refers to the biomedical practice of replacing human tissues or organs with those of other animals—a practice that calls for reflection on the concrete implications of respect for human *dignity,* as well as on the proper treatment of other animals themselves.)

Yahweh (Hebrew n.): Term designating *God* in the Hebrew scriptures. The Jewish people came to believe that they were enjoined from speaking or writing the holy name of God (see Exodus 3 and 20). The word "Yahweh" renders "YHWH"—a transliteration of the set of four letters (sometimes referred to as the "tetragrammaton") used by ancient biblical writers to designate the One they recognized as the Creator and the Author of the Covenant. (As introduced in the first Exodus passage noted above, "YHWH" is connected with the Hebrew verb *hayah,* which means "to be"; thus arguably there is a deep affinity between the biblical *Yahweh,* the "I AM" who sends forth Moses, and Aquinas's philosophically conditioned expression for God, namely, "Subsisting Being Itself" [Latin *Ipsum Esse Subsistens*].)

Z

zeal (n.): Strong positive *affection* (1), especially in relation to *intellectual* or *spiritual* goods. This affection moves a person to attain what he or she loves, and to remove obstacles to such attainment. (Note: Although related to "zeal," the word "zealot," at least in ordinary usage, has a somewhat different sense—one suggesting that the person in question manifests an extremeness in thought or action.) Also: "zealous" (adj.), "zealously" (adv.), "zealousness" (n.).

Zeitgeist (German n.): Literally, "spirit of the time." This term—which, from the standpoint of the perennial tradition, involves a *metaphorical* or *symbolic* (2) use of the word "spirit" (*Geist*)—treats a whole age (or the people of an age) as if it (or they) were animated by a single soul. The prime indication of this spirit of the time is seen in certain ideals or intellectual tendencies that predominate—for example, "rationalist optimism" during much of the 18th and 19th centuries (as noted in *Fides et ratio*, #91), and a culture of secularism and individual freedom, as well as unreflective recourse to technology, today.

zygote (n.): See the discussion under **life, beginning of**.

BIBLIOGRAPHY

I. Works by St. Thomas Aquinas in English

For a comprehensive list of Aquinas's works, along with brief synopses, see Jean-Pierre Torrell, O.P., *Saint Thomas Aquinas,* vol. 1, *The Person and His Work,* rev. ed., trans. Robert Royal (Washington, D.C.: The Catholic University of America Press, 2005). The website "Thomas Aquinas in English," maintained by Thérèse Bonin at http://www.home.duq.edu/~bonin/thomasbibliography.html, also is quite useful. (Note: In relation to both section I and section II of this bibliography, see as well the websites listed in the introduction, note 5.)

Within each of the five categories below—theological syntheses, commentaries on Aristotle, other philosophical commentaries, disputations, and additional philosophical works—Aquinas's writings, as indicated by the dates in parentheses, are listed in the approximate order of their Latin composition. (In several cases, the dates either are not precisely known or are matters of continuing scholarly dispute. For discussion, see the volume by Jean-Pierre Torrell, O.P., cited above.)

A. Theological Syntheses

1. *Scriptum super libros Sententiarum* (Composed 1252–56, with revisions 1265–66):

"Excerpts from the Commentary of Thomas Aquinas: Commentary on the Second Book of the Sentences of Master Peter Lombard, Distinction 44." Translated by Michael P. Molloy. In *Civil Authority in Medieval Philosophy: Lombard, Aquinas and Bonaventure.* Lanham, Md.: University Press of America, 1985.

Commentary on the Sentences, Book 4, distinction 15, question 4. Translated by Simon Tugwell. In his *Albert & Thomas: Selected Writings.* New York: Paulist Press, 1988.

"How We Know One Simple God by Many Concepts," and "God as Goal of Human Living." (Book 1, distinction 2, question 1, article 3; and Book 4, distinction 49, question 1, both incomplete.) Translated by Timothy McDermott.

In *Thomas Aquinas, Selected Philosophical Writings.* Oxford: Oxford University Press, 1993.

Aquinas on Creation: Writings on the "Sentences" of Peter Lombard, Book 2, distinction 1, question 1. Translated by Steven E. Baldner and William E. Carroll. Toronto: Pontifical Institute of Mediaeval Studies, 1997.

"The Nature of Theology: Commentary on *Sentences 1, Prologue*" and "The Six Days of Creation: Commentary on *Sentences 2.2, d. 12.*" Translated by Ralph McInerny. In his *Thomas Aquinas, Selected Writings.* Harmondsworth, England: Penguin, 1998.

Thomas Aquinas's Earliest Treatment of the Divine Essence: Scriptum super Libros Sententiarium, Book 1, Distinction 8. Translated by E. M. Macierowski. Binghamton, N.Y.: Center for Medieval and Renaissance Studies and Institute for Global Cultural Studies, 1998.

On Love and Charity: Readings from the Commentary on the Sentences of Peter Lombard. Translated by Peter Kwasniewski. Washington, D.C.: The Catholic University of America Press, 2008.

2. *Summa contra gentiles* (1259–65):

Of God and His Creatures: An Annotated Translation (with Some Abridgement) of the Summa contra gentiles of Saint Thos. Aquinas. St. Louis: B. Herder, 1905.

The Summa contra Gentiles. 5 vols. Translated by Laurence Shapcote. Reprint, New York: Benziger, 1928–29.

On the Truth of the Catholic Faith (Summa Contra Gentiles). 5 vols. Translated by Anton C. Pegis, James F. Anderson, Vernon J. Bourke, and Charles J. O'Neil. Reprint, Notre Dame, Ind.: University of Notre Dame Press, 1975.

3. *Summa theologiae* (or *theologica*) (1266–73; unfinished):

The Summa theologica. 2nd rev. ed. 22 vols. Translated by the Fathers of the English Province. London: Burns, Oates & Washbourne, 1912–36. Reprint, 5 vols., Westminster, Md.: Christian Classics, 1981.

Summa theologiae. 60 vols. (Latin and English facing texts). Translated by Thomas Gilby et al. New York: McGraw-Hill, 1964–73. (Note: This is often referred to as the "Blackfriars edition.")

Treatise on Law: The Complete Text, Summa Theologiae I-II, Questions 90–108. Translated by Alfred J. Freddoso. South Bend, Ind.: St. Augustine's Press, 2009. (This is the first volume of a projected complete translation of the *Summa theologiae,* to be published by St. Augustine's Press.)

"My Translation of the *Summa Theologiae,*" on Alfred J. Freddoso's website. Translated by Alfred J. Freddoso. E-text, with commentary, in progress. http://www.nd.edu/~afreddos/.

(Note: In addition to the above, there are many other partial translations of the *Summa theologiae,* either published as abridgements or included in more comprehensive volumes.)

B. Commentaries on Aristotle

1. *Sententia super De anima* (1267–68):
Commentary on Aristotle's De Anima. Translated by Kenelm Foster and Silvester Humphries. Reprint, Notre Dame, Ind.: Dumb Ox Books/St. Augustine's Press, 1994.
Commentary on Aristotle's De Anima. Translated by Robert C. Pasnau. New Haven, Conn.: Yale University Press, 1999.
2. *Sententia de sensu et sensato; Sententia de memoria et reminiscentia* (1268–69):
Commentaries on Aristotle's "On Sense and What Is Sensed" and on "On Memory and Recollection." Translated by Edward M. Macierowski and Kevin White. Washington, D.C.: The Catholic University of America Press, 2005.
3. *Sententia super Physicam* (1268–69):
Commentary on Aristotle's Physics. Translated by Richard J. Blackwell, Richard J. Spath, and W. Edmund Thirlkel. Reprint, Notre Dame, Ind.: Dumb Ox Books/St. Augustine's Press, 1999.
4. *Expositio libri Peri hermenias* (1270–71):
"How Words Mean: Exposition of *On Interpretation,* 1–5." Translated by Ralph McInerny. In his *Thomas Aquinas, Selected Writings.* Harmondsworth, England: Penguin, 1998.
On Interpretation. Translated by Christopher Martin. In his *The Philosophy of Thomas Aquinas: Introductory Readings.* London: Routledge, 1998.
Commentary on Aristotle's On Interpretation. Translated by Jean Oesterle. Reprinted with a new introduction by John O'Callaghan. South Bend, Ind.: Dumb Ox Books/St. Augustine's Press, 2008.
5. *Expositio libri Posteriorum* (1271–72):
Commentary on Aristotle's Posterior Analytics. Translated by Richard Berquist. South Bend, Ind.: Dumb Ox Books/St. Augustine's Press, 2008.
6. *Sententia libri Ethicorum* (1271–72):
Commentary on Aristotle's Nichomachean Ethics. Translated by C. I. Litzinger, O.P. Reprint, Notre Dame, Ind.: Dumb Ox Books/St. Augustine's Press, 1993.
7. *Sententia libri Politicorum* (1269–72; unfinished):
"Thomas Aquinas: *Commentary on the Politics.*" Translated by Ernest L. Fortin and Peter D. O'Neill. In *Medieval Political Philosophy: A Sourcebook.* Edited by Ralph Lerner and Muhsin Mahdi. New York: Free Press of Glencoe, 1963.
Commentary on Aristotle's Politics. Translated and with a preface by Richard J. Regan. Indianapolis, Ind.: Hackett Publishing Co., 2007.
8. *Sententia super Metaphysicam* (1270–72):
Commentary on Aristotle's Metaphysics. Translated by John P. Rowan. Reprint, Notre Dame, Ind.: Dumb Ox Books/St. Augustine's Press, 1995.

9. *Sententia super librum De caelo et mundo* (1272–73; unfinished):
Exposition of Aristotle's Treatise on the Heavens. 2 vols. Translated by Fabian R. Larcher and Pierre H. Conway. Columbus, Ohio: College of St. Mary of the Springs, 1964.

C. *Other Philosophical Commentaries*

1. *Expositio super librum Boethii De Trinitate* (1257–59; unfinished):
Commentary on the De Trinitate of Boethius. Vol. 1, *Faith, Reason, and Theology.* Vol. 2, *The Division and Methods of the Sciences.* Translation, introduction, and notes by Armand Maurer. Toronto: Pontifical Institute of Mediaeval Studies, 1986–87.
2. *Expositio in librum Boetheii De hebdomadibus* (Date uncertain; not before1259):
"How Are Things Good? Exposition of *On the Hebdomads* of Boethius." Translated by Ralph McInerny. In his *Thomas Aquinas, Selected Writings.* Harmondsworth, England: Penguin, 1998.
An Exposition of the "On the Hebdomads" of Boethius. Translated by Janice L. Schultz and Edward A. Synan. Washington, D.C.: The Catholic University of America Press, 2001.
3. *Expositio super Dyonisium De divinis nominibus* (Date uncertain; not before 1261):
On the Divine Names. Translated by Hannes Jarka-Sellers. Washington, D.C.: The Catholic University of America Press, forthcoming.
4. *Expositio super librum De causis* (1272):
Commentary on the Book of Causes. Translated by Vincent A. Guagliardo, Charles R. Hess, and Richard C. Taylor. Washington, D.C.: The Catholic University of America Press, 1996.
The Exposition of the Book of Causes, 1–5. Translated by Ralph McInerny. In his *Thomas Aquinas, Selected Writings.* Harmondsworth, England: Penguin, 1998.

D. *Disputations*

1. *De veritate* (1256–59):
Truth. 3 vols. Translated by Robert W. Mulligan, James V. McGlynn, and Robert W. Schmidt. Reprint, Indianapolis, Ind.: Hackett Publishing Co., 1994.
"The Meanings of Truth: *Disputed Question on Truth,* 1"; "On the Teacher: *Disputed Question on Truth,* 11"; and "On Conscience: *Disputed Question on Truth,* 17." Translated by Ralph McInerny. In his *Thomas Aquinas, Selected Writings.* Harmondsworth, England: Penguin, 1998.

2. *De quodlibet I–XII* (1256–59; 1268–72):

Quodlibetal Questions 1 and 2. Translated by Sandra Edwards. Mediaeval Sources in Translation 27. Toronto: Pontifical Institute of Mediaeval Studies, 1983.

The Quodlibetal Questions (Selections). Translated by Paul Vincent Spade. Stillwater, Okla.: Translation Clearing House, 1983. Available at http://philosophy.okstate.edu/.

Disputed Question on the Soul's Knowledge of Itself. Translated by Richard T. Lambert. Stillwater, Okla.: Translation Clearing House, 1987. Available at http://philosophy.okstate.edu/.

Quodlibets. Translated by Eileen Sweeney and Sandra Edwards. Washington, D.C.: The Catholic University of America Press, forthcoming.

3. *De anima* (1265–66):

The Soul. Translated by J. P. Rowman. St. Louis: B. Herder, 1949.

Questions on the Soul. Translated by James H. Robb. Milwaukee: Marquette University Press, 1984.

4. *De potentia* (1265–66):

"On the Divine Simplicity: *Disputed Question of the Power of God*, 7." Translated by Ralph McInerny. In his *Thomas Aquinas, Selected Writings*. Harmondsworth, England: Penguin, 1998.

On the Power of God. Translated by Laurence Shapcote. Reprint, Westminster, Md.: Newman, 1952; and Eugene, Ore.: Wipf and Stock, 2004.

On Creation. [*Quaestiones Disputatae De Potentia Dei, Q. 3*]. Translated with introduction by S. C. Selner-Wright. Washington, D.C.: The Catholic University of America Press, 2011.

5. *De spiritualibus creaturis* (1267–68):

On Spiritual Creatures. Translated by Mary C. Fitzpatrick and John J. Wellmuth. Milwaukee: Marquette University Press, 1949.

6. *De caritate* (1268–72):

On Charity (De caritate). Translated by Lottie H. Kendzierski. Milwaukee: Marquette University Press, 1960.

7. *De malo* (1266–72):

On Evil. Translated by John A. and Jean T. Oesterle. Notre Dame, Ind.: University of Notre Dame Press, 1995.

On Evil. Translated by Richard Regan. Edited with introduction and notes by Brian Davies. Oxford: Oxford University Press, 2003.

8. *De virtutibus cardinalibus* (1271–72):

Disputed Questions on Virtue: Quaestio disputata de virtutibus in communi; Quaestio disputata de virtutibus cardinalibus. Translated by Ralph McInerny. South Bend, Ind.: St. Augustine's Press, 1998.

The Cardinal Virtues: Aquinas, Albert, and Philip the Chancellor. Translated by R. E. Houser. Toronto: Pontifical Institute of Mediaeval Studies, 2004.

The Cardinal Virtues. Translated and edited, with an introduction and glossary, by Richard J. Regan, S.J. Indianapolis, Ind.: Hackett Publishing Co., 2005.

Disputed Questions on Virtue. Translated by Jeffrey Hause and Claudia Eisen Murphy. Introduction and commentary by Jeffrey Hause. Indianapolis, Ind.: Hackett Publishing Co., 2009.

9. *De virtutibus in communi* (1271–72):

On the Virtues in General. Translated by Robert P. Goodwin. In his *Selected Writings of Thomas Aquinas: The Principles of Nature, On Being and Essence, On the Virtues in General, On Free Choice.* Indianapolis, Ind.: Bobbs-Merrill, 1965.

Disputed Questions on Virtue: Quaestio disputata de virtutibus in communi; Quaestio disputata de virtutibus cardinalibus. Translated by Ralph McInerny. In his *Thomas Aquinas, Selected Writings.* Harmondsworth, England: Penguin, 1998.

Disputed Questions on Virtue: Quaestio disputata de virtutibus in communi; Quaestio disputata de virtutibus cardinalibus. Translated by Ralph McInerny. South Bend, Ind.: St. Augustine's Press, 1998.

Disputed Questions on Virtue. Translated by Jeffrey Hause and Claudia Eisen Murphy. Introduction and commentary by Jeffrey Hause. Indianapolis, Ind.: Hackett Publishing Co., 2009.

E. Additional Philosophical Works

1. *De ente et essentia* (1252–56):

Aquinas on Being and Essence: A Translation and Interpretation. By Joseph Bobik. Notre Dame, Ind.: University of Notre Dame Press, 1965.

On Being and Essence. 2nd rev. ed. Translated by Armand Maurer. Toronto: Pontifical Institute of Mediaeval Studies, 1968.

On Being and Essence. Translated with introduction, notes, and commentary by Peter King. Indianapolis, Ind.: Hackett Publishing Co., 2009.

2. *De principiis naturae* (1252–56):

On the Principles of Nature. Translated by Robert P. Goodwin. In his *Selected Writings of St. Thomas Aquinas: The Principles of Nature, On Being and Essence, On the Virtues in General, On Free Choice.* Indianapolis, Ind.: Bobbs-Merrill, 1965.

On the Principles of Nature. Translated by Timothy McDermott. In his *Thomas Aquinas, Selected Philosophical Writings.* Oxford: Oxford University Press, 1993.

Aquinas on Matter and Form and the Elements: A Translation and Interpretation of the De Principiis Naturae and the De Mixtione Elementorum of St. Thomas

Aquinas. By Joseph Bobik. Notre Dame, Ind.: University of Notre Dame Press, 1998.

3. *De regno ad regem Cypri* (a.k.a. *De regimine principum*) (1257; unfinished):

On Kingship to the King of Cyprus. Translated by Gerald B. Phelan and I. T. Eschmann. Toronto: Pontifical Institute of Mediaeval Studies, 1949.

On Kingship, or, The Governance of Rulers. Translated by Paul E. Sigmund. In his *St. Thomas Aquinas on Politics and Ethics: A New Translation, Backgrounds, Interpretations.* New York: Norton, 1988.

4. *De mixtione elementorum* (Date uncertain; before 1270):

On the Mixture of the Elements, to Master Philip. Translated by Paul Vincent Spade. Stillwater, Okla.: Translation Clearing House, 1983. Available at http://philosophy.okstate.edu/.

Aquinas on Matter and Form and the Elements: A Translation and Interpretation of the De Principiis Naturae and the De Mixtione Elementorum of St. Thomas Aquinas. By Joseph Bobik. Notre Dame, Ind.: University of Notre Dame Press, 1998.

5. *De unitate intellectus contra Averroistas* (1270):

On the Unity of the Intellect against the Averroists (De Unitate Intellectus Contra Averroistas). Translated by Beatrice H. Zedler. Milwaukee: Marquette University Press, 1968.

Aquinas against the Averroists: On There Being Only One Intellect. Translated by Ralph M. McInerny. West Lafayette, Ind.: Purdue University Press, 1993.

6. *De aeternitate mundi contra murmurantes* (1271):

On the Eternity of the World (De aeternitate mundi). Translated by Cyril Vollert, S.J. In St. Thomas, Siger de Brabant, and Bonaventure, *On the Eternity of the World.* Translated by Cyril Vollert, S.J., et al. Milwaukee: Marquette University Press, 1964.

On the Eternity of the World against the Grumblers. Translated by Mary T. Clark. In her *Aquinas Reader.* Garden City, N.Y.: Image Books, 1972.

On the Eternity of the World against the Murmurers. Translated by Ralph McInerny. In his *Thomas Aquinas, Selected Writings.* Harmondsworth, England: Penguin, 1998.

7. *De substantiis separatis* (1271; unfinished):

Treatise on Separate Substances. Translated by Francis J. Lescoe. West Hartford, Conn.: St. Joseph College, 1959. E-text edited by Joseph Kenny, O.P. Available at http://www.josephkenny.joyeurs.com/CDtexts/SubstSepar.htm.

8. *Compendium theologiae* (1265–67, 1272; unfinished):

The Compendium of Theology. Translated by Cyril Vollert, S.J. St. Louis: B. Herder, 1947. Reprinted with editorial revisions as *Light of Faith: The Compendium of Theology.* Manchester, N.H.: Sophia Institute, 1993.

II. Recent Commentaries and Elaborations on Perennial Themes

Adler, Mortimer J. *The Conditions of Philosophy.* New York: Atheneum, 1965.

———. *How to Think about God.* New York: Collier Books, 1991.

———. *The Difference of Man and the Difference It Makes.* Introduction by Deal W. Hudson. New York: Fordham University Press, 1993.

———. *The Time of Our Lives.* Introduction by Deal W. Hudson. New York: Fordham University Press, 1996.

Aersten, Jan A. *Medieval Philosophy and the Transcendentals: The Case of Thomas Aquinas.* Leiden and Boston: Brill Academic Publishers, 2004.

Anscombe, G. E. M. *Intention.* Oxford: Oxford University Press, 1958.

Anscombe, G. E. M., and Peter Geach. *Three Philosophers.* Ithaca, N.Y.: Cornell University Press, 1961.

Ashley, Benedict M., O.P. *The Ashley Reader: Redeeming Reason.* Naples, Fla.: Sapientia Press of Ave Maria University, 2006.

———. *The Way toward Wisdom: An Interdisciplinary and Intercultural Introduction to Metaphysics.* Notre Dame, Ind.: University of Notre Dame Press, 2006.

Ashley, Benedict M., O.P., and Kevin O'Rourke, O.P. *Health Care Ethics,* 4th ed. Washington, D.C.: Georgetown University Press, 1997.

Balthasar, Hans Urs von. *My Work: In Retrospect.* Translated by Brian McNeil. San Francisco: Ignatius Press, 1993.

———. *Theo-Logic: The Truth of God.* 3 vols. Translated by Adrian J. Walker. San Francisco: Ignatius Press, 2001, 2004, and 2005.

Benestad, J. Brian. *Church, State, and Society: An Introduction to Catholic Social Doctrine.* Washington, D.C.: The Catholic University of America Press, 2011.

Bobik, Joseph. *Veritas Divina: Aquinas on Divine Truth.* South Bend, Ind.: St. Augustine's Press, 2001.

Bourke, Vernon J. *Ethics: A Textbook of Moral Philosophy.* New York: The Macmillan Co., 1966.

Bradley, Denis J. M. *Aquinas and the Twofold Human Good.* Washington, D.C.: The Catholic University of America Press, 1997.

Braine, David. *Reality of Time and the Existence of God.* Oxford: Oxford University Press, 1988.

———. *The Human Person: Animal and Spirit.* Notre Dame, Ind.: University of Notre Dame Press, 1992.

Brock, Stephen. *Action and Conduct.* Edinburgh: T & T Clark, 1998.

Burrell, David, C.S.C. *Aquinas: God and Action.* London: Routledge and Kegan Paul, 1979.

———. *Knowing the Unknowable God: Ibn-Sina, Maimonides, Aquinas.* Notre Dame, Ind.: University of Notre Dame Press, 1986.

Cahalan, John C. *Causal Realism*. Lanham, Md.: University Press of America, 1985.

Cajetan (Thomas de Vio). *Commentary on St. Thomas Aquinas on Being and Essence*. Translated by Lottie H. Kendzierski and S.J. Wade. Milwaukee: Marquette University Press, 1965.

Carlson, John W. *Understanding Our Being: Introduction to Speculative Philosophy in the Perennial Tradition*. Washington, D.C.: The Catholic University of America Press, 2008.

Cessario, Romanus, O.P. *Introduction to Moral Theology*. Washington, D.C.: The Catholic University of America Press, 2001.

———. *The Moral Virtues and Theological Ethics*. 2nd ed. Notre Dame, Ind.: University of Notre Dame Press, 2009.

Ciapalo, Roman T., ed. *Postmodernism and Christian Philosophy*. Washington, D.C.: American Maritain Association/The Catholic University of America Press, 1997.

Clarke, W. Norris, S.J. *Person and Being*. Milwaukee: Marquette University Press, 1993.

———. *Explorations in Metaphysics*. Notre Dame, Ind.: University of Notre Dame Press, 1994.

———. *The One and the Many*. Notre Dame, Ind.: University of Notre Dame Press, 2001.

———. *The Philosophical Approach to God: A New Thomistic Perspective*. 2nd ed. New York: Fordham University Press, 2007.

———. *The Creative Retrieval of St. Thomas Aquinas*. New York: Fordham University Press, 2009.

Colvert, Gavin T., ed. *The Renewal of Civilization: Essays in Honor of Jacques Maritain*. Washington, D.C.: American Maritain Association/The Catholic University of America Press, 2010.

Connell, Richard J. *From Observables to Unobservables in Science and Philosophy*. Lanham, Md.: University Press of America, 2000.

Conway, Pierre. *Faith Views the Universe: A Thomistic Perspective*. Edited by Mary Michael Spangler. Lanham, Md.: University Press of America, 1997.

Copleston, F. C. *Aquinas*. London: Penguin, 1961.

Crosby, John. *The Selfhood of the Human Person*. Washington, D.C.: The Catholic University of America Press, 1996.

———. *Personalist Papers*. Washington, D.C.: The Catholic University of America Press, 2004.

Cunningham, Lawrence S., ed. *Intractable Disputes about the Natural Law: Alasdair MacIntyre and Critics*. Notre Dame, Ind.: University of Notre Dame Press, 2009.

Dauphinais, Michael, and Matthew Levering, eds. *John Paul II & St. Thomas Aquinas*. Naples, Fla.: Sapientia Press of Ave Maria University, 2006.

Dauphinais, Michael, Barry David, and Matthew Levering, eds. *Aquinas the Augustinian.* Washington, D.C.: The Catholic University of America Press, 2007.

Davies, Brian. *Aquinas.* London and New York: Continuum, 2002.

———, ed. *Aquinas's Summa Theologiae: Critical Essays.* Lanham, Md.: Rowman and Littlefield, 2006.

Deely, John N. *What Distinguishes Human Understanding?* South Bend, Ind.: St. Augustine's Press, 2002.

———. *Intentionality and Semiotics: A Story of Mutual Fecundation.* Scranton, Pa.: University of Scranton Press, 2007.

De Koninck, Charles. *The Writings of Charles De Koninck.* Vols. 1 and 2. Edited and translated by Ralph McInerny. Notre Dame, Ind.: University of Notre Dame Press, 2008 and 2009.

Dennehy, Raymond. *Reason and Dignity.* Washington, D.C.: University Press of America, 1981.

Dewan, Lawrence, O.P. *Form and Being.* Washington, D.C.: The Catholic University of America Press, 2006.

———. *Wisdom, Law, and Virtue.* New York: Fordham University Press, 2008.

De Wulf, Maurice. *The System of Thomas Aquinas.* Mineola, N.Y.: Dover Publications, 1959.

———. *Scholasticism Old and New: An Introduction to Scholastic Philosophy, Medieval and Modern.* Reprint, Whitefish, Mont.: Kessinger Publishing, 2008.

DeYoung, Rebecca Konyndyk, Colleen McCluskey, and Christina Van Dyke, eds. *Aquinas's Ethics: Metaphysical Foundations, Moral Theory, and Theological Context.* Notre Dame, Ind.: University of Notre Dame Press, 2009.

Di Blasi, Fulvio. *God and the Natural Law: A Rereading of St. Thomas Aquinas.* South Bend, Ind.: St. Augustine's Press, 2006.

Di Noia, J. A., O.P. *The Diversity of Religions: A Christian Perspective.* Washington, D.C.: The Catholic University of America Press, 1992.

Doig, James C. *Aquinas on Metaphysics.* The Hague: Martinus Nijhoff, 1972.

Doolan, Gregory T., ed. *Aquinas on the Divine Ideas as Exemplar Causes.* Washington, D.C.: The Catholic University of America Press, 2008.

———, ed. *The Science of Being as Being: Metaphysical Investigations.* Washington, D.C.: The Catholic University of America Press, 2010.

Dougherty, Jude. *Western Creed, Western Identity: Essays in Legal and Social Philosophy.* Washington, D.C.: The Catholic University of America Press, 2000.

Dulles, Cardinal Avery, S.J. *The Splendor of Faith: The Theological Vision of Pope John Paul II.* Rev. ed. New York: Crossroad, 2003.

Emery, Giles, O.P. *Trinity in Aquinas.* Naples, Fla.: Sapientia Press of Ave Maria University, 2003.

Emonet, Pierre-Marie, O.P. *The Dearest Freshness Deep Down Things.* Translated by Robert R. Barr. New York: Crossroad, 1999.

———. *God Seen in the Mirror of the World.* Translated by Robert R. Barr. New York: Crossroad, 2000.

———. *The Greatest Marvel of Nature.* Translated by Robert R. Barr. New York: Crossroad, 2000.

Fagothey, Austin, S.J. *Right and Reason.* 2nd ed. Reprint, Rockford, Ill.: Tan Books and Publishers, Inc., 2000.

Finnis, John. *Fundamentals of Ethics.* Washington, D.C.: Georgetown University Press, 1983.

———. *Moral Absolutes: Tradition, Revision, and Truth.* Washington, D.C.: The Catholic University of America Press, 1991.

———. *Aquinas: Moral, Political, and Legal Theory.* Oxford: Oxford University Press, 1998.

Flannery, Kevin L. *Acts Amid Precepts: The Aristotelian Logical Structure of Thomas Aquinas's Moral Theory.* Washington, D.C.: The Catholic University of America Press, 2001.

Foster, David Ruel, and Joseph W. Koterski, S.J., eds. *The Two Wings of Catholic Thought: Essays on Fides et ratio.* Washington, D.C.: The Catholic University of America Press, 2003.

Fuller, Timothy, and John P. Hittinger, eds. *Reassessing the Liberal State: Reading Maritain's Man and the State.* Washington, D.C.: American Maritain Association/The Catholic University of America Press, 2001.

Geach, Peter. *God and the Soul.* New York: Schocken Books, 1969. Reprint, South Bend, Ind.: St. Augustine's Press, 2001.

———. *Mental Acts.* London: Routledge and Kegan Paul, 1967. Reprint, South Bend, Ind.: St. Augustine's Press, 2001.

———. *Truth and Hope.* Notre Dame, Ind.: University of Notre Dame Press, 2001.

George, Robert P. *Natural Law & Moral Inquiry.* Washington, D.C.: Georgetown University Press, 1998.

———, ed. *Natural Law, Liberalism, and Morality.* Oxford: The Clarendon Press, 1996.

Gilson, Etienne. *The Christian Philosophy of St. Thomas Aquinas.* New York: Random House, 1956.

———. *From Aristotle to Darwin and Back Again.* Translated by John Lyon. Notre Dame, Ind.: University of Notre Dame Press, 1984. Reprinted with a foreword by Christoph Cardinal Schönborn. San Francisco: Ignatius Press, 2009.

———. *The Unity of Philosophical Experience.* San Francisco: Ignatius Press, 1999.

Gomez-Lobo, Alphonso. *Morality and the Human Goods: An Introduction to Natural Law Ethics.* Washington, D.C.: Georgetown University Press, 2002.

Goyette, John, Mark S. Latkovic, and Richard S. Myers, eds. *St. Thomas Aquinas and the Natural Law Tradition.* Washington, D.C.: The Catholic University of America Press, 2004.

Grisez, Germain G. *Beyond the New Theism: A Philosophy of Religion.* Notre Dame, Ind.: University of Notre Dame Press, 1975.

———. *The Way of the Lord Jesus.* Vol. 1, *Christian Moral Principles.* Vol. 2, *Living a Christian Life.* Vol. 3, *Difficult Moral Questions.* Quincy, Ill.: Franciscan Press, 1983, 1993, and 1997.

Grisez, Germain G., and Russell Shaw. *Beyond the New Morality: The Responsibilities of Freedom.* 3rd ed. Notre Dame, Ind.: University of Notre Dame Press, 1988.

———. *Fulfillment in Christ: A Summary of Christian Moral Principles.* Notre Dame, Ind.: University of Notre Dame Press, 1991.

Haldane, John. "A Thomist Metaphysics." In *The Blackwell Guide to Metaphysics,* edited by R. Gale. Oxford: Basil Blackwell, 2001.

———, ed. *Mind, Metaphysics, and Value in the Thomistic and Analytical Traditions.* Notre Dame, Ind.: University of Notre Dame Press, 2002.

Hall, Pamela M. *Narrative and the Natural Law: An Interpretation of Thomistic Ethics.* Notre Dame, Ind.: University of Notre Dame Press, 1994.

Hancock, Curtis L., and Anthony O. Simon, eds. *Freedom, Virtue, and the Common Good.* Mishawaka, Ind.: American Maritain Association/University of Notre Dame Press, 1995.

Hanke, W. J. *God in Himself: Aquinas's Doctrine of God as Expounded in the Summa Theologiae.* New York: Oxford University Press, 1987.

Hemming, Laurence Paul, and Susan Frank Parsons, eds. *Redeeming Truth: Considering Faith and Reason.* Notre Dame, Ind.: University of Notre Dame Press, 2007.

Henle, R. J. *Theory of Knowledge.* Chicago: Loyola University Press, 1983.

Hildebrand, Dietrich von. *Graven Images: Substitutes for True Morality.* New York: David McKay Co., 1957.

———. *Ethics.* Chicago: Franciscan Herald Press, 1972.

———. *What Is Philosophy?* New York: Routledge, 1990.

———. *The Heart: An Analysis of Human and Divine Affectivity.* Preface by John Haldane. Introduction by John F. Crosby. South Bend, Ind.: St. Augustine's Press, 2007.

Hittinger, John P. *Liberty, Wisdom, and Grace: Thomism and Democratic Political Theory.* Lanham, Md.: Lexington Books, 2002.

———, ed. *The Vocation of the Catholic Philosopher: From Maritain to John Paul II.* Washington, D.C.: American Maritain Association/The Catholic University of America Press, 2011.

Hittinger, Russell. *The New Natural Law Theory.* Notre Dame, Ind.: University of Notre Dame Press, 1988.

———. *The First Grace: Rediscovering Natural Law in a Post-Christian World.* Wilmington, Del.: ISI Books, 2002.

Houser, R. E., ed. *Laudemus viros gloriosos: Essays in Honor of Armand Maurer, CSB.* Notre Dame, Ind.: University of Notre Dame Press, 2007.

Hudson, Deal, ed. *The Future of Thomism.* Notre Dame, Ind.: University of Notre Dame Press, 1992.

Hughes, Christopher. *On a Complex Theory of a Simple God: An Investigation in Aquinas's Philosophical Theology.* Ithaca, N.Y.: Cornell University Press, 1989.

Hütter, Reinhard, and Matthew Levering, eds. *Ressourcement Thomism: Sacred Doctrine, the Sacraments, and the Moral Life.* Washington, D.C.: The Catholic University of America Press, 2010.

Jaki, Stanley L. *Road of Science and the Ways to God.* Chicago: University of Chicago Press, 1979.

Jaroszynski, Piotr, and Mathew Anderson. *Ethics: The Drama of the Moral Life.* New York: Alba House, 2003.

Jensen, Stephen T. *Good and Evil Actions: A Journey through Saint Thomas Aquinas.* Washington, D.C.: The Catholic University of America Press, 2010.

John of St. Thomas (Jean Poinsot). *Introduction to the Summa Theologiae of St. Thomas Aquinas.* South Bend, Ind.: St. Augustine's Press, 2001.

———. *Poinsot: Tractatus de Signis.* Edited and translated by John Deely. Berkeley: University of California Press, 1985. New edition, *Tractatus de Signis: The Semiotic of Jean Poinsot.* 2nd ed. Edited and translated by John Deely. South Bend, Ind: St. Augustine's Press, forthcoming.

Jordan, Mark. *Ordering Wisdom: The Hierarchy of Philosophical Discourses in Aquinas.* Notre Dame, Ind.: University of Notre Dame Press, 1986.

Kaczor, Christopher Robert. *Proportionalism and the Natural Law Tradition.* Washington, D.C.: The Catholic University of America Press, 2002.

———. *The Edge of Life: Human Dignity and Contemporary Bioethics.* Philosophy and Medicine Series 85. New York: Springer, 2005.

———. *Thomas Aquinas on Faith, Hope, and Love.* San Francisco: Ignatius Press, 2008.

Kainz, Howard P. *Natural Law: An Introduction and Re-examination.* Chicago: Open Court, 2004.

Kavanaugh, John F., S.J. *Who Count as Persons? Human Identity and the Ethics of Killing.* Washington, D.C.: Georgetown University Press, 2001.

Keenan, James, S.J. *Goodness and Rightness in Thomas Aquinas' Summa Theologiae.* Washington, D.C.: Georgetown University Press, 1992.

Kenny, Anthony. *Aquinas on Mind.* London and New York: Routledge, 1994.

———. *Aquinas on Being.* Oxford and New York: Oxford University Press, 2002.

Kerr, Fergus, O.P. *Immortal Longings: Versions of Transcending Humanity.* Notre Dame, Ind.: University of Notre Dame Press, 1997.

———, ed. *Contemplating Aquinas.* Notre Dame, Ind.: University of Notre Dame Press, 2003.

Klauder, Francis J., S. D. B. *A Philosophy Rooted in Love: The Dominant Themes in the Perennial Philosophy of St. Thomas Aquinas.* Lanham, Md.: University Press of America, 1994.

Klubertanz, George P., S.J. *Introduction to the Philosophy of Being.* 2nd ed. Reprint, Eugene, Ore.: Wipf and Stock, 2005.

Knasas, John F. X. *Being and Some Twentieth-Century Thomists.* New York: Fordham University Press, 2003.

———, ed. *Thomistic Papers VI.* Houston, Tex.: The Center for Thomistic Studies, 1994.

Koritansky, Peter Karl. *Thomas Aquinas and the Philosophy of Punishment.* Washington, D.C.: The Catholic University of America Press, 2010.

Koterski, Joseph W., S.J. *An Introduction to Medieval Philosophy: Basic Concepts.* Malden, Mass.: John Wiley & Sons, 2009.

Krapiec, M. A., O.P. *I—Man: An Outline of Philosophical Anthropology.* Translated by Francis J. Lescoe and Roger B. Duncan. New Britain, Conn.: Mariel Publications, 1985.

———. *Metaphysics: An Outline of the History of Being.* Translated by Theresa Sandok. New York: Peter Lang, 1991.

Kretzmann, Norman. *The Metaphysics of Creation: Aquinas's Natural Theology in Summa Contra Gentiles II.* Oxford and New York: Oxford University Press, 2002.

———. *The Metaphysics of Theism: Aquinas's Natural Theology in Summa Contra Gentiles I.* Oxford and New York: Oxford University Press, 2002.

Kretzmann, Norman, and Eleonore Stump, eds. *The Cambridge Companion to Aquinas.* Cambridge and New York: Cambridge University Press, 1993.

Kwasniewski, Peter A., ed. *Wisdom's Apprentice: Thomistic Essays in Honor of Lawrence Dewan, O.P.* Washington, D.C.: The Catholic University of America Press, 2007.

Lännenström, Anna. *Loving the Fine: Virtue and Happiness in Aristotle's Ethics.* Notre Dame, Ind.: University of Notre Dame Press, 2006.

Lee, Patrick, and Robert P. George. *Body-Self Dualism in Contemporary Ethics and Politics.* New York: Cambridge University Press, 2008.

Leinsle, Ulrich G. *Introduction to Scholastic Theology.* Translated by Michael J. Miller. Washington, D.C.: The Catholic University of America Press, 2010.

Levering, Matthew. *Scripture and Metaphysics: Aquinas and the Renewal of Trinitarian Theology.* Oxford: Basil Blackwell, 2004.

Lombardo, Nicholas E., O.P. *The Logic of Desire: Aquinas on Emotion.* Washington, D.C.: The Catholic University of America Press, 2010.

Lonergan, Bernard, S.J. *Insight: A Study of Human Understanding.* Edited by Robert M. Doran. Toronto: University of Toronto Press, 1992.

———. *Verbum: Word and Idea in Aquinas.* Edited by Frederick B. Crowe and Robert M. Doran. Toronto: University of Toronto Press, 1997.

Long, R. James, ed. *Philosophy and the God of Abraham: Essays in Memory of James A. Weisheipl, O.P.* Toronto: Pontifical Institute of Medieval Studies, 1991.

Long, Steven A. *The Teleological Grammar of the Moral Act.* Naples, Fla.: Sapientia Press of Ave Maria University, 2007.

———. *Natura Pura: On the Recovery of Nature in the Doctrine of Grace.* New York: Fordham University Press, 2010.

———. *Analogia Entis: On the Analogy of Being, Metaphysics, and the Act of Faith.* Notre Dame, Ind.: University of Notre Dame Press, 2011.

Lubac, Henri de, S.J. *The Discovery of God.* Translated by Alexander Dru. New York: P. J. Kenedy and Sons, 1960.

———. *The Mystery of the Supernatural.* Translated by Rosemary Sheed. New York: Crossroad Publishing Co., 1998.

Macdonald, Paul A., Jr. *Knowledge and the Transcendent: An Inquiry into the Mind's Relationship to God.* Washington, D.C.: The Catholic University of America Press, 2009.

MacDonald, Scott, and Eleonore Stump, eds. *Aquinas's Moral Theory.* Ithaca, N.Y.: Cornell University Press, 1999.

Machuga, Ric. *In Defense of the Soul.* Grand Rapids, Mich.: Brazos Press, 2002.

MacIntyre, Alasdair. *After Virtue.* 2nd ed. Notre Dame, Ind.: University of Notre Dame Press, 1984.

———. *Whose Justice, Which Rationality?* Notre Dame, Ind.: University of Notre Dame Press, 1988.

———. *Three Rival Versions of Moral Enquiry.* Notre Dame, Ind.: University of Notre Dame Press, 1990.

———. *Dependent Rational Animals.* Chicago: Open Court, 1999.

———. *God, Philosophy, Universities: A Selective History of the Catholic Philosophical Tradition.* Lanham, Md.: Sheed and Ward, Rowman and Littlefield, 2009.

Magee, Joseph M. *Unmixing the Intellect: Aristotle on Cognitive Powers and Bodily Organs.* Westport, Conn.: Greenwood Press, 2003.

Maréchal, Joseph. See the listing for Matteo, Anthony M.

Maritain, Jacques. *Science and Wisdom.* Translated by Bernard Wall. London: Geoffrey Bles, 1940.

———. *A Preface to Metaphysics.* London: Sheed and Ward, 1945.

———. *Existence and the Existent.* Translated by Lewis Galantiere and Gerald B. Phelan. New York: Pantheon, 1948.

———. *The Philosophy of Nature.* Translated by Imelda C. Byrne. New York: Philosophical Library, 1951.

———. *The Person and the Common Good.* Translated by John J. Fitzgerald. Notre Dame, Ind.: University of Notre Dame Press, 1966.

———. *Integral Humanism.* Translated by Joseph Evans. New York: Charles Scribner's Sons, 1968.

———. *The Degrees of Knowledge.* Translated under the supervision of Gerald B. Phelan, presented by Ralph McInerny. Notre Dame, Ind.: University of Notre Dame Press, 1995.

———. *Untrammeled Approaches.* Translated by Bernard Doering. Notre Dame, Ind.: University of Notre Dame Press, 1997.

———. *Man and the State.* Washington, D.C.: The Catholic University of America Press, 1998.

Maritain, Jacques, and William Sweet. *Natural Law: Reflections on Theory and Practice.* South Bend, Ind.: St. Augustine's Press, 2001.

Matteo, Anthony M. *Quest for the Absolute: The Philosophical Vision of Joseph Maréchal.* De Kalb, Ill.: Northern Illinois University Press, 1992.

May, William E. *An Introduction to Moral Theology.* 2nd ed. Huntington, Ind.: Our Sunday Visitor, Inc., 2003.

———. *Catholic Bioethics and the Gift of Human Life.* 2nd ed. Huntington, Ind.: Our Sunday Visitor, Inc., 2008.

McCabe, Herbert, O.P. *God Matters.* Springfield, Ill.: Templegate Publishers, 1991.

———. *God Still Matters.* London and New York: Continuum Books, 2002.

———. *The Good Life: Ethics and the Pursuit of Happiness.* London and New York: Continuum Books, 2005.

———. *Faith within Reason.* Edited and introduced by Brian Davies, O.P. London and New York: Continuum Books, 2007.

———. *God and Evil in the Thought of St. Thomas Aquinas.* Edited and introduced by Brian Davies, O.P. London and New York: Continuum Books, 2010.

McGlynn, James V., S.J., and Sr. Paul Mary Farley, R. S. M. *A Metaphysics of Being and God.* Englewood Cliffs, N.J.: Prentice-Hall, 1966.

McInerny, Daniel. *The Difficult Good: A Thomistic Approach to Moral Conflict and Human Happiness.* New York: Fordham University Press, 2006.

McInerny, D. Q. *A Course in Thomistic Ethics.* Elmhurst, Pa.: The Priestly Fraternity of St. Peter, 1997.

———. *Perennial Wisdom for Daily Life.* Elmhurst, Pa.: The Priestly Fraternity of St. Peter, 2002.

———. *Being Logical.* New York: Random House, 2005.

McInerny, Ralph. *St. Thomas Aquinas.* Notre Dame, Ind.: University of Notre Dame Press, 1982.

———. *Aquinas: Thought and Action.* Washington, D.C.: The Catholic University of America Press, 1992.

———. *The Question of Christian Ethics.* Washington, D.C.: The Catholic University of America Press, 1993.

———. *Aquinas and Analogy.* Washington, D.C.: The Catholic University of America Press, 1996.

———. *Ethica Thomistica.* Rev. ed. Washington, D.C.: The Catholic University of America Press, 1997.

———. *Characters in Search of Their Author.* The Gifford Lectures, Glasgow 1999–2000. Notre Dame, Ind.: University of Notre Dame Press, 2001.

———. *Praeambula Fidei: Thomism and the God of the Philosophers.* Washington, D.C.: The Catholic University of America Press, 2006.

McMullin, Ernan, ed. *The Concept of Matter.* Notre Dame, Ind.: University of Notre Dame Press, 1963.

Milbank, John, and Catherine Pickstock. *Truth in Aquinas.* London: Routledge, 2001.

Miner, Robert. *Thomas Aquinas on the Passions.* Cambridge and New York: Cambridge University Press, 2009.

Murray, John Courtney, S.J. *We Hold These Truths: Catholic Reflections on the American Proposition.* Kansas City, Mo.: Sheed and Ward, 1960.

Newman, Cardinal John Henry. *An Essay in Aid of a Grammar of Assent.* Notre Dame, Ind.: University of Notre Dame Press, 1979.

———. *An Essay on the Development of Christian Doctrine.* 6th ed. Notre Dame, Ind.: University of Notre Dame Press, 1989.

Nichols, Aiden, O.P. *The Shape of Catholic Theology.* Collegeville, Minn.: The Liturgical Press, 1991.

———. *Christendom Awake: On Reenergizing the Church in Culture.* Grand Rapids, Mich.: Eerdmans Publishing Co., 1999.

———. *Discovering Aquinas.* Grand Rapids, Mich.: Eerdmans Publishing Co., 2002.

———. *From Hermes to Benedict XVI: Faith and Reason in Modern Catholic Thought.* Herefordshire, England: Gracewing Ltd., 2009.

Novak, Michael. *Free Persons and the Common Good.* Lanham, Md.: Madison Books, 1989.

O'Callaghan, John. *Thomist Realism and the Linguistic Turn.* Notre Dame, Ind.: University of Notre Dame Press, 2002.

———, ed. *Science, Philosophy, and Theology.* South Bend, Ind: St. Augustine's Press, 2006.

O'Callaghan, John P., and Thomas S. Hibbs, eds. *Recovering Nature: Essays in Natural Philosophy, Ethics, and Metaphysics in Honor of Ralph McInerny.* Notre Dame, Ind.: University of Notre Dame Press, 1999.

O'Meara, Thomas F., O.P. *Thomas Aquinas, Theologian.* Notre Dame, Ind.: University of Notre Dame Press, 1997.

Osborne, Thomas M., Jr. *Love of Self and Love of God in Thirteenth-Century Ethics.* Notre Dame, Ind.: University of Notre Dame Press, 2005.

Owens, Joseph, C. Ss. R. *An Elementary Christian Metaphysics.* Houston, Tex.: Center for Thomistic Studies, 1985.

———. *Human Destiny: Some Problems for Catholic Philosophy.* Washington, D.C.: The Catholic University of America Press, 1985.

———. *Towards a Christian Philosophy.* Washington, D.C.: The Catholic University of America Press, 1990.

Pagan Aguiar, Peter A., and Terese Auer, O.P., eds. *The Human Person and a Culture of Freedom.* Washington, D.C.: American Maritain Association/The Catholic University of America Press, 2009.

Pasnau, Robert. *Thomas Aquinas on Human Nature.* Cambridge and New York: Cambridge University Press, 2002.

Pegis, Anton C. *St. Thomas and the Greeks.* Milwaukee.: Marquette University Press, 1951.

———. *St. Thomas and Philosophy.* Milwaukee: Marquette University Press, 1964.

Peperzak, Adriaan Theodoor. *Philosophy Between Faith and Theology: Addresses to Catholic Intellectuals.* Notre Dame, Ind.: University of Notre Dame Press, 2005.

Phillippe, Marie-Dominique, O.P. *Retracing Reality: A Philosophical Itinerary.* New York: Continuum Books, 2000.

Pieper, Josef. *The Four Cardinal Virtues.* Notre Dame, Ind.: University of Notre Dame Press, 1966.

———. *Reality and the Good.* Translated by Stella Lange. Chicago: Henry Regnery, 1967.

———. *Josef Pieper: An Anthology.* San Francisco: Ignatius Press, 1989.

———. *A Brief Reader on the Virtues of the Human Heart.* Translated by Paul C. Duggan. San Francisco: Ignatius Press, 1991.

———. *Guide to Thomas Aquinas.* Translated by Richard and Clara Winston. San Francisco: Ignatius Press, 1991.

Pinckaers, Servais, O.P. *The Sources of Christian Ethics.* Translated by Mary Thomas Noble, O.P. Washington, D.C.: The Catholic University of America Press, 1995.

———. *Morality: The Catholic View.* Translated by Michael Sherwin, O.P. South Bend, Ind.: St. Augustine's Press, 2001.

———. *The Pinckaers Reader.* Edited by John Berkman and Craig Steven Titus. Washington, D.C.: The Catholic University of America Press, 2005.

Pope, Stephen J., ed. *The Ethics of Aquinas.* Washington, D.C.: Georgetown University Press, 2002.

Porter, Jean. *Natural and Divine Law: Reclaiming the Tradition for Christian Ethics.* Grand Rapids, Mich.: Eerdmans Publishing Co., 1999.

Pouivet, Roger. *After Wittgenstein, St. Thomas.* Translated by Michael S. Sherwin, O.P. South Bend, Ind.: St. Augustine's Press, 2006.

Pugh, Matthew S. *A Simplified Introduction to the Wisdom of St. Thomas.* Lanham, Md.: University Press of America, 1980.

———. *The Moral Wisdom of St. Thomas.* Lanham, Md.: University Press of America, 1983.

Rahner, Karl, S.J. *Hearer of the Word.* Translated by Joseph Donceel. New York: Continuum, 1994.

———. *Spirit in the World.* Translated by Joseph Donceel. New York: Continuum, 1994.

Ramos, Alice, and Marie I. George, eds. *Faith, Scholarship, and Culture in the 21st Century.* Washington, D.C.: American Maritain Association/The Catholic University of America Press, 2002.

Ratzinger, Cardinal Joseph. *God and the World.* Translated by Henry Taylor. San Francisco: Ignatius Press, 2002.

———. *Truth and Tolerance: Christian Belief and World Religions.* Translated by Henry Taylor. San Francisco: Ignatius Press, 2004.

———. *Pilgrim Fellowship of Faith.* Translated by Henry Taylor. San Francisco: Ignatius Press, 2005.

———. (Pope Benedict XVI). *God Is Love* (*Deus caritas est*). San Francisco: Ignatius Press, 2006.

———. (Pope Benedict XVI). *Saved in Hope* (*Spe salvi*). San Francisco: Ignatius Press, 2008.

———. (Pope Benedict XVI). *Charity in Truth* (*Caritas in veritate*). San Francisco: Ignatius Press, 2009.

Redpath, Peter A., ed. *From Twilight to Dawn: The Cultural Vision of Jacques Maritain.* Mishawaka, Ind.: American Maritain Association/University of Notre Dame Press, 1990.

Reichman, James B., S.J. *Philosophy of the Human Person.* Chicago: Loyola University Press, 1985.

Reimers, Adrian J. *The Soul of the Human Person: A Contemporary Philosophical Psychology.* Washington, D.C.: The Catholic University of America Press, 2006.

Reith, Herman, C.S.C. *Introduction to Philosophical Psychology.* Englewood Cliffs, N.J.: Prentice Hall, 1956.

———. *The Metaphysics of St. Thomas Aquinas.* Milwaukee: Bruce Publishing, 1958.

Renard, Henri, S.J. *Wisdom in Depth.* Milwaukee: Bruce Publishing, 1966.

Rhonheimer, Martin. *Natural Law and Practical Reason.* Translated by Gerald Malsbary. New York: Fordham University Press, 2000.

———. *The Perspective of the Acting Person: Essays in the Renewal of Thomistic Moral Philosophy.* Edited by William F. Murphy, Jr. Washington, D.C.: The Catholic University of America Press, 2008.

———. *The Perspective of Morality: Philosophical Foundations of Thomistic Virtue Ethics.* Washington, D.C.: The Catholic University of America Press, 2011.

Rocca, Gregory P. *Speaking the Incomprehensible God: Thomas Aquinas and the Interplay of Positive and Negative Theology.* Washington, D.C.: The Catholic University of America Press, 2004.

Rourke, Thomas R., and Rosita A. Chazaretta Rourke. *A Theory of Personalism.* Lanham, Md.: Rowman and Littlefield, 2004.

Russell, Daniel C. *Practical Intelligence and the Virtues.* New York: Oxford University Press, 2009.

Rziha, John. *Perfecting Human Actions: St. Thomas Aquinas on Human Participation in Eternal Law.* Washington, D.C.: The Catholic University of America Press, 2009.

Sadler, Gregory B. *Reason Fulfilled by Revelation: The 1930s Christian Philosophy Debates in France.* Washington, D.C.: The Catholic University of America Press, 2011.

Schall, James V., S.J. *At the Limits of Political Philosophy.* Washington, D.C.: The Catholic University of America Press, 1996.

———. *The Order of Things.* San Francisco: Ignatius Press, 2007.

———. *The Regensburg Lecture.* South Bend, Ind.: St. Augustine's Press, 2007.

———. *The Mind That Is Catholic: Philosophical and Political Essays.* Washington, D.C.: The Catholic University of America Press, 2008.

Schindler, David L. *Heart of the World, Center of the Church.* Grand Rapids, Mich.: Eerdmans Publishing Co., 1996.

Schmitz, Kenneth L. *Gift: Creation.* Milwaukee.: Marquette University Press, 1982.

———. *At the Center of the Human Drama: The Philosophical Anthropology of Karol Wojtyla/John Paul II.* Washington, D.C.: The Catholic University of America Press, 1993.

Schockenhoff, Eberhard. *Natural Law and Human Dignity.* Translated by Brian McNeil. Washington, D.C.: The Catholic University of America Press, 2003.

Sherwin, Michael S., O.P. *By Knowledge and by Love: Charity and Knowledge in the Moral Theology of St. Thomas Aquinas.* Washington, D.C.: The Catholic University of America Press, 2005.

Silverman, Eric J. *The Prudence of Love.* Lanham, Md.: Lexington Books/Rowman & Littlefield, 2010.

Simon, Yves R. *Freedom of Choice.* Edited by Peter Wolff. New York: Fordham University Press, 1969.

———. *A General Theory of Authority.* Notre Dame, Ind.: University of Notre Dame Press, 1980.

———. *The Definition of Moral Virtue.* Edited by Vukan Kuic. New York: Fordham University Press, 1986.

———. *An Introduction to the Metaphysics of Knowledge.* Translated by Vukan Kuic and Richard J. Thompson. New York: Fordham University Press, 1990.

———. *Practical Knowledge.* Edited by Robert J. Mulvaney. New York: Fordham University Press, 1991.

———. *Philosophy of Democratic Government.* Notre Dame, Ind.: University of Notre Dame Press, 1993.

———. *Foresight and Knowledge.* Edited by Ralph Nelson and Anthony O. Simon. New York: Fordham University Press, 1996.

———. *Philosopher at Work.* Edited by Anthony O. Simon. Lanham, Md.: Rowman and Littlefield, 1999.

———. *Freedom and Community.* Edited by Charles P. O'Donnell. Introduction by Eugene Kennedy. New York: Fordham University Press, 2001.

———. *The Great Dialogue of Nature and Space.* Edited by Gerald J. Dalcourt. South Bend, Ind.: St. Augustine's Press, 2001.

Simon, Yves R., et al., editors and translators. *The Material Logic of John of St. Thomas.* Chicago: University of Chicago Press, 1955.

Smith, Timothy L., ed. *Aquinas's Sources: The Notre Dame Symposium.* South Bend, Ind.: St. Augustine's Press, 2008.

Sokolowski, Robert. *The God of Faith and Reason.* 2nd ed. Washington, D.C.: The Catholic University of America Press, 1995.

———. *Introduction to Phenomenology.* Cambridge and New York: Cambridge University Press, 1999.

———. *Phenomenology of the Human Person.* Cambridge and New York: Cambridge University Press, 2008.

Stein, Edith, St. *On the Problem of Empathy.* Translated by Waltrout Stein. Washington, D.C.: ICS Publications, 1989.

———. *Edith Stein: Essential Writings.* Edited by John Sullivan. New York: Orbis Books, 2002.

———. *Finite and Eternal Being: An Attempt at an Ascent to the Meaning of Being.* Translated by Kurt F. Reinhardt. Washington, D.C.: ICS Publications, 2002.

Stump, Eleonore. *Aquinas.* London and New York: Routledge, 2003.

Swiezawski, Stefan. *St. Thomas Revisited.* Translated by Theresa Sandok, OSM. New York: Peter Lang, 1995.

Tollefsen, Christopher, ed. *John Paul II's Contribution to Catholic Bioethics.* Philosophy and Medicine 84, Catholic Studies in Bioethics. Norwell, MA: Springer, 2004.

Torrell, Jean-Pierre, O.P. *Aquinas's Summa: Background, Structure, and Reception.* Translated by Robert Royal. Washington, D.C.: The Catholic University of America Press, 2005.

———. *Saint Thomas Aquinas.* Vol. 1, *The Person and His Work.* Rev. ed. Translated by Robert Royal. Washington, D.C.: The Catholic University of America Press, 2005.

Trapani, John G., Jr. *Poetry, Beauty, and Contemplation: The Complete Aesthetics of Jacques Maritain.* Washington, D.C.: The Catholic University of America Press, 2011.

———, ed. *Truth Matters: Essays in Honor of Jacques Maritain.* Washington, D.C.: American Maritain Association/The Catholic University of America Press, 2004.

Twomey, D. Vincent, S.V. D. *Moral Theology after Humanae Vitae: Fundamental Issues in Moral Theory and Sexual Ethics.* Dublin, Ireland: Four Courts Press, 2010.

Van Nieuwenhove, Rik, and Joseph Wawrykow, eds. *Theology of Thomas Aquinas.* Notre Dame, Ind.: University of Notre Dame Press, 2005.

Wallace, William A., O.P. *The Elements of Philosophy.* New York: Alba House, 1977.

———. *The Modeling of Nature: The Philosophy of Science and the Philosophy of Nature in Synthesis.* Washington, D.C.: The Catholic University of America Press, 1996.

Weisheipl, James A., O.P. *Friar Thomas d'Aquino: His Life, Thought, and Work.* Washington, D.C.: The Catholic University of America Press, 1983.

White, Thomas Joseph, O.P. *Wisdom in the Face of Modernity: A Study in Thomistic Natural Theology.* Naples, Fla.: Sapientia Press of Ave Maria University, 2009.

Wippel, John F. *Metaphysical Themes in Thomas Aquinas.* Washington, D.C.: The Catholic University of America Press, 1984.

———. *The Metaphysical Thought of Thomas Aquinas.* Washington, D.C.: The Catholic University of America Press, 2000.

———. *Metaphysical Themes in Thomas Aquinas II.* Washington, D.C.: The Catholic University of America Press, 2007.

Wojtyla, Karol. *The Acting Person.* Translated by Andrzej Potocki. Edited by Anna-Teresa Tymieniecka. Dordrecht and Boston: D. Reidel, 1979.

———. *Person and Community.* Selected essays. Translated by Theresa Sandok, O. S. M. New York: Peter Lang, 1993.

———. (Pope John Paul II). *On the Hundredth Anniversary of Rerum Novarum (Centesimus annus).* Boston: Pauline Books and Media, 1991.

———. (Pope John Paul II). *The Splendor of Truth* (*Veritatis splendor*). Boston: Pauline Books and Media, 1993.

———. (Pope John Paul II). *The Gospel of Life* (*Evangelium vitae*). Boston: Pauline Books and Media, 1995.

———. (Pope John Paul II). *Faith and Reason* (*Fides et ratio*). Boston: Pauline Books and Media, 1998.

Wolfe, Christopher. *Natural Law Liberalism.* Cambridge and New York: Cambridge University Press, 2006.

Woodward, P. A., ed. *Doctrine of Double Effect: Philosophers Debate a Controversial Moral Principle.* Notre Dame, Ind.: University of Notre Dame Press, 2001.

Woznicki, Andrew N. *Transcendent Mystery in Man: A Global Approach to Ecumenism.* Bethesda, Md.: Academica Press, 2007.

Zabrowski, Holger, ed. *Natural Law in Contemporary Society.* Washington, D.C.: The Catholic University of America Press, 2010.

III. Works by Other Authors Cited in This Dictionary

Albert the Great. *Questions Concerning Aristotle's On Animals.* Translated by Irvin M. Resnick and Kenneth F. Mitchell, Jr. Washington, D.C.: The Catholic University of America Press, 2008.

Anselm, St. *Anselm of Canterbury: The Major Works.* Edited by Brian Davies and G. R. Evans. New York: Oxford University Press, 1998.

Aristotle. *The Complete Works of Aristotle: The Revised Oxford Translation.* Vol. 1 and Vol. 2. Edited by Jonathan Barnes. Princeton, N.J.: Princeton University Press, 1984.

Atkins, Peter W. *Creation Revisited: The Origin of Space, Time, and the Universe.* New York: Penguin, 1984.

Augustine, St. *The Confessions of St. Augustine.* Edited and translated by Albert Cook Outler. Mineola, N.Y.: Dover Publishing Co., 2002.

———. *City of God.* Kila, Mont.: Kessinger Publishing Co., 2005.

———. *On Christian Doctrine.* Kila, Mont.: Kessinger Publishing Co., 2005.

———. *On the Holy Trinity.* Kila, Mont.: Kessinger Publishing Co., 2005.

Austin, J. L. *How to Do Things with Words.* 2nd ed. Edited by Marina Sbisa and J. O. Urmson. Cambridge, Mass.: Harvard University Press, 2005.

Averroes (Ibn-Rushd). *Faith and Reason in Islam: Averroes' Exposition of Religious Arguments.* Translated by Ibrahim Najjar. Oxford: Oneworld Publications, 2002.

Avicenna (Ibn-Sina). *The Metaphysics of the Healing.* Translated by Michael E. Marmura. Chicago: University of Chicago Press, 2004.

Ayer, A. J. *Language, Truth, and Logic.* Mineola, N.Y.: Dover Publications, 1952.

Barnes, Jonathan. *Early Greek Philosophy.* 2nd rev. ed. Translated by Jonathan Barnes. New York: Penguin, 2001.

Behe, Michael. *Darwin's Black Box: The Biochemical Challenge to Evolution.* New York: Simon & Schuster, 1998.

———. *Edge of Evolution: The Search for the Limits of Darwinism.* New York: Simon & Schuster, 2007.

Belloc, Hilaire. *An Essay on the Restoration of Property.* New introduction by John Sharpe. Norfolk, Va.: IHS Press, 2002.

Bentham, Jeremy. *The Principles of Morals and Legislation.* Edited by Robert M. Baird and Stuart E. Rosenbaum. Amherst, N.Y.: Prometheus Books, 1988.

Berkeley, George. *A Treatise Concerning the Principles of Human Knowledge.* Edited and with a preface by Thomas A. McCormack. Mineola, N.Y.: Dover Publications, 2003.

Blondel, Maurice. *Action (1893): Essay on a Critique of Life and a Science of Practice.* Translated by Oliva Blanchette. Notre Dame, Ind.: University of Notre Dame Press, 2004.

Boethius. *The Consolation of Philosophy.* Translated by H. R. James. Introduction by Michael V. Dougherty. New York: Barnes and Noble, 2005.

———. *Theological Tractates and the Consolation of Philosophy.* Lawrence, Kans.: Digireads, 2007.

Boff, Leonardo, and Clodovis Boff. *Introducing Liberation Theology.* Translated by Paul Burns. Maryknoll, N.Y.: Orbis Books, 1987.

Bonaventure, St. *Itinerary of the Mind to God.* Edited by Stephen F. Brown. Translated by Philotheus Boehner. Indianapolis, Ind.: Hackett Publishing Co., 1993.

Brown, Warren S., Nancey Murphy, and H. Newton Maloney, eds. *Whatever Happened to the Soul?* Minneapolis: Fortress Press, 1998.

Brunner, Emil. *Divine Imperative: A Study of Christian Ethics.* Translated by Olive Wyon. Cambridge, England: The Lutterworth Press, 2002.

Buber, Martin. *I and Thou.* Translated by Walter Kaufman and S. G. Smith. New York: Simon & Schuster, 1971.

Cahill, Lisa Sowle. *Sex, Gender, and Christian Ethics.* Cambridge and New York: Cambridge University Press, 1996.

Carnap, Rudolph. *The Logical Structure of the World and Pseudo-Problems in Philosophy.* Translated by Rolf A. George. Chicago: Open Court Publishing Co., 2003.

Chardin, Teilard de, S.J. *The Phenomenon of Man.* New York: HarperCollins Publishers, 1976.

———. *The Divine Milieu.* New York: HarperCollins Publishers, 2001.

Christie, Dolores L. *Adequately Considered: An American Perspective on Louis Janssens' Personalist Morals.* Grand Rapids, Mich.: Eerdmans Publishing Co., 1992.

Churchland, Paul. *The Engine of Reason, The Seat of the Soul: A Philosophical Journey into the Brain.* Cambridge, Mass.: MIT Press, 1996.

Cicero (Marcus Tullius Cicero). *Academic Questions, Treatise De Finibus, and Tusculan Disputations of M. T. Cicero, with a Sketch of the Greek Philosophers Mentioned by Cicero.* Translated by C. D. Yonge. Kila, Mont.: Kessinger Publishing Co., 2007.

Cobb, John B., Jr. *God and the World.* Eugene, Ore.: Wipf & Stock, 2001.

Cobb, John B., Jr., and David Ray Griffin. *Process Theology: An Introductory Exposition.* Louisville, Ky.: Westminster John Knox Press, 1978.

Collingwood, R. G. *An Essay on Metaphysics.* Oxford: Clarendon Press, 1957.
Comte, August. *Introduction to Positive Philosophy.* Translated by Frederick Ferre. Indianapolis, Ind.: Hackett Publishing Co., 1988.
Curran, Charles E. *Loyal Dissent: Memoir of a Catholic Theologian.* Washington, D.C.: Georgetown University Press, 2006.
Curran, Charles, and Richard A. McCormick, eds. *Readings in Moral Theology No. 1: Moral Norms and Catholic Tradition.* New York: Paulist Press, 1979.
Davidson, Donald. *The Essential Davidson.* Introduction by Kirk Ludwig and Ernie Lepore. New York: Oxford University Press, 2006.
Dawkins, Richard. *The God Delusion.* Boston and New York: Houghton Mifflin Co., 2006.
———. *The Selfish Gene.* 30th Anniversary Edition. New York: Oxford University Press, 2006.
Dennett, Daniel. *Brainstorms: Philosophical Essays on Mind and Psychology.* Boston: MIT Press, 1981.
———. *Consciousness Explained.* Boston: Little, Brown, 1991.
———. *Breaking the Spell: Religion as a Natural Phenomenon.* London: Penguin, 2007.
Derrida, Jacques. *Writing and Difference.* Translated by Alan Bass. Chicago: University of Chicago Press, 1978.
Descartes, Rene. *Discourse on Method and Meditations on First Philosophy.* Translated by John Veritch. Reprint, New Haven, Conn.: Yale University Press, 1996.
Dewey, John. *Human Nature and Conduct.* Mineola, N.Y.: Dover Publications, 2002.
———. *Reconstruction in Philosophy.* Rev. ed. Mineola, N.Y.: Dover Publications, 2004.
Dionysius the Areopagite. *The Mystical Theology and the Divine Names.* Translated by C. E. Rolt. Mineola, N.Y.: Dover Publications, 2004.
Engelhardt, H. Tristram, Jr. *Foundations of Bioethics.* New York: Oxford University Press, 1996.
———. *Foundations of Christian Bioethics.* New York: Taylor & Francis, 2000.
Epictetus. *The Discourses of Epictetus: The Handbook, Fragments.* Edited by Christopher Gill. Translated by Robin Hard. Everyman library. Rutland, Vt.: C. E. Tuttle, 1995.
________. *The Ethics of the Stoic Epictetus: A Translation.* Edited by Adolf Friedrich Bonhoffer. Translated by William O. Stephens. New York: Peter Lang Publishing Group, 1996.
Fletcher, Joseph. *Situation Ethics: The New Morality.* Rev. ed. Introduction by James F. Childress. Louisville, Ky.: Westminster John Knox Press, 1997.
Foucault, Michael. *The Foucault Reader.* Edited by Paul Rabinow. New York: Random House, 1984.

Freud, Sigmund. *Civilization and Its Discontents.* Translated by James Strachey. New York: W.W. Norton & Company, Inc., 1989.

———. *The Basic Writings of Sigmund Freud.* Translated by A. A. Brill. New York: Random House, 1995.

Fuchs, Joseph, S.J. *Personal Responsibility and Christian Morality.* Washington, D.C.: Georgetown University Press, 1981.

Gadamer, Hans-Georg. *Truth and Method.* 2nd ed. Edited and translated by Joel Weinsheimer and Donald G. Marshall. New York: Continuum International Publishing Group, 2004.

Gustaphson, James M. *Ethics from a Theocentric Perspective: Theology and Ethics.* Vol. 1. Chicago: University of Chicago Press, 1983.

———. *Ethics from a Theocentric Perspective: Theology and Ethics.* Vol. 2. Chicago: University of Chicago Press, 1992.

Haight, Roger, S.J. *Jesus: Symbol of God.* Maryknoll, N.Y.: Orbis Books, 2000.

Hallett, Garth. *Greater Good: The Case for Proportionalism.* Washington, D.C.: Georgetown University Press, 1995.

Hare, Richard M. *Language and Morals.* Oxford: Oxford University Press, 1952.

———. *Essays in Ethical Theory.* New York: Oxford University Press, 1993.

Hartshorne, Charles. *The Logic of Perfection.* Chicago: Open Court Publishing Co., 1962.

———. *Divine Relativity: A Social Conception of God.* Reprint, New Haven, Conn.: Yale University Press, 2003.

Hegel, G.W. F. *Hegel's Phenomenology of Spirit.* Translated by A.V. Miller and J. N. Findlay. New York: Oxford University Press, 1979.

Heidegger, Martin. *Being and Time.* Translated by John MacQuarrie and Edward Robinson. New York: HarperCollins Publishers, 1962.

Heraclitus. See listing for Barnes, Jonathan.

Hick, John H. *An Interpretation of Religion: Human Responses to the Transcendent.* New Haven, Conn.: Yale University Press, 1989.

Hick, John H., and Paul Knitter, eds. *The Myth of Christian Uniqueness: Toward a Pluralistic Theology of Religions.* Eugene, Ore.: Wipf & Stock, 2005.

Hobbes, Thomas. *Leviathan.* Edited by J. C. Gaskin. New York: Oxford University Press, 1998.

———. *Elements of Law, Natural and Politic: Human Nature and de Corpore Politico with Three Lives.* Edited and with an introduction by John Charles Gaskin. New York: Oxford University Press, 1999.

Hume, David. *Dialogues Concerning Natural Religion.* Edited and with an introduction by Richard H. Popkin. Indianapolis, Ind.: Hackett Publishing Co., 1998.

———. *Treatise of Human Nature.* Edited by D. F. and M. Morton. Reprint, Oxford: Oxford University Press, 2000.

Husserl, Edmund. *Crisis of the European Sciences and Transcendental Phenomenology.* Translated by David Carr. Evanston, Ill.: Northwestern University Press, 1970.

———. *Cartesian Meditations.* Vol. 1. Translated by Dorian Cairns. New York: Springer-Verlag, 1977.

———. *The Essential Husserl: Basic Writings in Transcendental Phenomenology.* Edited by Donn Welton. Indianapolis: Indiana University Press, 1999.

Huxley, Aldous. *The Perennial Philosophy.* Harper Perennial Series. New York: HarperCollins, 2004.

Ingarden, Roman. *Time and Modes of Being.* Translated by Helen R. Michejda. Springfield, Ill.: Charles C. Thomas Publisher, Ltd., 1964.

———. *Man and Value.* Translated by Arthjur Szylewicz. Washington, D.C.: The Catholic University of America Press, 1984.

James, William. *Pragmatism: A New Name for Some Old Ways of Thinking.* Introduction by Bryan Vescio. New York: Barnes & Noble, 2003.

John of the Cross, St. *The Dark Night of the Soul.* Translated by Gabriela Cunninghame Graham. Introduction by Margaret Kim Peterson. New York: Barnes & Noble, 2005.

Johnson, Elizabeth A., C. S.J. *Quest for the Living God.* New York: Continuum Publishers, 2007.

Jung, Carl. *Man and His Symbols.* Edited by Joseph L. Henderson, Jolande Jacobi, and Anelia Jaffe. New York: Dell, 1968.

———. *The Archetypes and the Collective Unconscious.* 2nd ed. Translated by R. F. Hull. Princeton, N.J.: Princeton University Press, 1981.

Kant, Immanuel. *Religion within the Limits of Reason Alone.* Translated by Theodore M. Greene and Hoyt H. Hudson. New York: HarperCollins, 1960.

———. *Critique of Pure Reason.* Edited by Paul Guyer and Allen W. Wood. New York: Cambridge University Press, 1999.

———. *Groundwork of the Metaphysic of Morals.* Translated by Thomas Kingsmill Abbott. Mineola, N.Y.: Dover Publications, 2005.

Kierkegaard, Søren. *Concluding Unscientific Postscript.* Translated by David F. Swenson and David Lowrie. Princeton, N.J.: Princeton University Press, 1941.

Leibniz, Gottfried. *Philosophical Texts.* Edited by Robert S. Woolhouse. Translated by Robert S. Woolhouse and R. Franks. New York: Oxford University Press, 1998.

Locke, John. *Two Treatises of Government Student Edition.* Edited by Peter Laslett and Raymond Geuss. New York: Cambridge University Press, 1988.

———. *Essay Concerning Human Understanding.* Edited by Kenneth P. Winkler. Indianapolis, Ind.: Hackett Publishing Co., 1996.

Maimonides, Moses. *Guide of the Perplexed.* Translated by S. Pines. Chicago: University of Chicago Press, 1963.

Marcel, Gabriel. *Being and Having: An Existentialist Diary.* Translated by K. Farrer. New York: Harper and Row, 1965.

———. *The Mystery of Being.* Vol. 1, *Reflection and Mystery.* Vol. 2, *Faith and Reality.* Translated by G. S. Fraser. South Bend, Ind.: St. Augustine's Press, 2000.

———. *Creative Fidelity.* Translated by Robert Rosthal. Preface by Merold Westphal. New York: Fordham University Press, 2002.

Marion, Jean-Luc. *God Without Being.* Translated by Thomas A. Carlson. Chicago: University of Chicago Press, 1991.

Marx, Karl. *Capital.* Translated by Ben Fowkes. Introduction by J. M. Cohen. New York: Penguin, 1992.

———. *Selected Writings.* Edited by Lawrence H. Simon. Indianapolis, Ind.: Hackett Publishing Co., 1994.

McCormick, Richard, S.J. *The Critical Calling: Reflections on Moral Dilemmas Since Vatican II.* Reprinted with a foreword by Lisa Sowle Cahill. Washington, D.C.: Georgetown University Press, 2006.

Merleau-Ponty, Maurice. *Phenomenology of Perception.* 2nd ed. Translated by Colin Smith. New York: Taylor & Francis, 2002.

Mill, John Stuart. *Utilitarianism.* 2nd ed. Edited by George Sher. Indianapolis, Ind: Hackett Publishing Co., 2002.

———. *On Liberty.* Edited by Charles W. Elliot. Introduction by Patrick Hayden. New York: Barnes & Noble, 2004.

Moore, G. E. *Principia Ethica.* Edited by Thomas Baldwin. New York: Cambridge University Press, 1993.

Mounier, Emmanuel. *Personalism.* Translated by Phillip Mairet. Notre Dame, Ind.: University of Notre Dame Press, 1989.

Nietzsche, Friedrich. *The Will to Power.* Edited and translated by Walter Kauffman. New York: Knopf Publishing Group, 1968.

———. *Beyond Good and Evil.* Translated by Helen Zimmern. Mineola, N.Y.: Dover Publications, 1997.

Otto, Rudolf. *The Idea of the Holy.* Translated by John W. Harvey. New York: Oxford University Press, 1958.

Parmenides. See listing for Barnes, Jonathan.

Peacocke, Arthur, and Grant Gillett, eds. *Persons and Personality.* New York: Basil Blackwell, 1987.

Peirce, Charles S. *Charles S. Peirce: The Essential Writings.* Edited by Edward C. Moore, Richard Robin, and Robert M. Baird. Amherst, N.Y.: Prometheus Books, 1998.

Plato. *Plato: Complete Works.* Edited by John M. Cooper and D. S. Hutchinson. Indianapolis, Ind.: Hackett Publishing Co., 1997.

Plotinus. *The Enneads.* Edited by John M. Dillon and Stephen Mackenna. New York: Penguin, 1991.

Quine, W.V.O. *Word and Object.* Boston: MIT Press, 1964.

———. *Ontological Relativity and Other Essays.* New York: Columbia University Press, 1977.

Ramsey, Paul. *The Essential Paul Ramsey.* Edited by William Werpehowski and Stephen Crocco. New Haven, Conn.: Yale University Press, 1994.

Rawls, John. *A Theory of Justice.* Rev. ed. Cambridge, Mass.: Harvard University Press, 1999.

———. *Political Liberalism.* Expanded ed. Foreword by Martha Nussbaum. New York: Columbia University Press, 2005.

Ricoeur, Paul. *Time and Narrative.* Vol. 1. Translated by Kathleen Blamey and David Pellhauer. Chicago: University of Chicago Press, 1990.

———. *History and Truth.* Translated by Charles A. Kelbley. Foreword by David Rasmussen. Evanston, Ill.: Northwestern University Press, 2007.

Röpke, Wilhelm. *A Humane Economy.* 3rd ed. Introduction by Dermot Quinn. Wilmington, Del.: ISI Books, 1998.

Rorty, Richard. *The Consequences of Pragmatism.* Minneapolis: University of Minnesota Press, 1982.

Ross, William David. *The Right and the Good.* Reprinted with an introduction by Philip Stratton-Lake. Oxford: Oxford University Press, 2002.

Russell, Bertrand. *The Problems of Philosophy.* Mineola, N.Y.: Dover Publications, 1999.

Salzman, Todd A., and Michael G. Lawler. *The Sexual Person: Toward a Renewed Catholic Anthropology.* Washington, D.C.: Georgetown University Press, 2008.

Sartre, Jean-Paul. *Being and Nothingness.* Translated by Hazel Barnes. New York: Washington Square Press, 1966.

Scheler, Max. *On Feeling, Knowing, and Valuing: Selected Writings.* Edited by Harold Bershady. Chicago: University of Chicago Press, 1993.

———. *The Nature of Sympathy.* Translated by Peter Heath. New introduction by Graham McAleer. Piscataway, N.J.: Transaction Publishers, 2007.

Scotus, John Duns. *On God and Creatures: The Quodlibital Questions.* Translated by Felix Alluntis and Allan B. Wolter. Princeton, N.J.: Princeton University Press, 1975.

———. *Duns Scotus on the Will and Morality.* Edited by William A. Frank. Translated by William A. Frank and Allan B. Wolter. Washington, D.C.: The Catholic University of America Press, 1997.

Sidgwick, Henry. *The Methods of Ethics.* Indianapolis, Ind.: Hackett Publishing Co., 1981.

Singer, Peter. *Rethinking Life and Death: The Collapse of Our Traditional Ethics.* New York: St. Martin's Griffin, 1994.

Stevenson, Charles L. *Facts and Values: Studies in Ethical Analysis.* New Haven, Conn.: Yale University Press, 1964.

Suarez, Francisco, S.J. *On Creation, Conservation, and Concurrence: Metaphysical Disputations 20, 21, and 22.* Translated by Alfred J. Freddoso. South Bend, Ind.: St. Augustine's Press, 2002.

Swinburne, Richard. *The Evolution of the Soul.* New York: Oxford University Press, 1997.

———. *The Existence of God.* 2nd ed. New York: Oxford University Press, 2004.

Taylor, Charles. *The Ethics of Authenticity.* Cambridge, Mass.: Harvard University Press, 1991.

Tillich, Paul. *The Courage to Be.* 2nd ed. Introduction by Peter J. Gomes. New Haven, Conn.: Yale University Press, 2000.

———. *The Dynamics of Faith.* New York: HarperCollins, 2001.

Tooley, Michael. *Abortion and Infanticide.* New York: Oxford University Press, 1984.

Warren, Mary Ann. *Moral Status: Obligations to Persons and Other Living Things.* New York: Oxford University Press, 1998.

Weithman, Paul J., ed. *Religion and Contemporary Liberalism.* Notre Dame, Ind.: University of Notre Dame Press, 1997.

Whitehead, Alfred North. *Process and Reality.* Corrected edition by David Ray Griffin and Donald W. Sherburne. New York: The Free Press, 1978.

William of Ockham. *Philosophical Writings: A Selection.* Edited by Philotheus Boehner. Translated by Philotheus Boehner, with Stephen F. Brown. Indianapolis, Ind.: Hackett Publishing Co., 1990.

Wittgenstein, Ludwig. *Philosophical Investigations.* 50th Anniversary Commemorative Edition. Translated by Elizabeth Anscombe. Hoboken, N.J.: John Wiley & Sons, 2008.

Wolterstorff, Nicholas. "Unqualified Divine Temporality." In *God and Time: Four Views.* Downers Grove, Ill.: InterVarsity Press, 2001.

LIST OF ENTRIES

suicide (n.)
summum bonum (Latin phrase)
superabundance (n.)
superdetermination (n.)
superego (n.)
supereminence (n.)
supererogatory (adj.)
supernatural (adj.)
supernatural gifts
supersensible (adj. or n.)
superstition (n.)
supposit (n.)
supposition (n.)
syllogism (n.)
symbol (n.)
symbolicism (n.)
sympathy (n.)
symphonic (adj.)
synderesis (Latin n.)
synthesis (n.)
synthetic (adj.)
systematic (adj.)

tautology (n.)
techne (Greek n.)
technology (n.)
Teilhardian (adj.)
teleological (adj.)
teleological structure of human goods
teleology (n.)
temperament (n.)
temperance (n.)
temporal (adj.)
Ten Commandments
tendency (n.)
term (n.)
theft (n.)
theism (n.)
theocracy (n.)
theodicy (n.)
theological virtues
theology (n.)
theology of the body
theonomy (n.)
theory (n.)
theory of knowledge
thing (n.)
third way
Thomism (n.)
Thomist (sometimes **Thomistic**) (adj.)
time (n.)
title (n.)
tolerance (n.)
totalism (n.)
totalitarianism (n.)
totality, principle of
tradition (n.)
transcendence (n.)
transcendental (adj.)
transcendental Thomism
transience or **transitivity** (n.)
transitivity (n.)
transubstantiation (n.)
Trinity, the (n.)
truth (n.)
truth-conditions
truthfulness (n.)
truth-value
turpitude, moral
tyranny (n.)

ultimate end or **good**
ultimate practical judgment
uncaused (adj.)
uncertain (adj.)
uncertainty (n.)
unconscious (adj.)
unconscious (n.)
unconsciousness (n.)
undergo or **suffer** (v.)

JOHN W. CARLSON

is professor of philosophy at Creighton University.

He is the author of *Understanding Our Being: Introduction to Speculative Philosophy in the Perennial Tradition.*